UNITED NATIONS ECONOMIC
COMMISSION FOR EUROPE

Sharing the Gains of Globalization in the New Security Environment

The Challenges to Trade Facilitation

UNITED NATIONS
NEW YORK AND GENEVA 2003

Note

The United Nations Economic Commission for Europe (UNECE) serves as the focal point within the United Nations system for the development of norms, standards and policy recommendations regarding the facilitation of international trade. The secretariat of the UNECE organized a Second International Forum on Trade Facilitation "Sharing the Gains of Globalization in the New Security Environment" on 14-15 May 2003 at the Palais des Nations, Geneva, Switzerland, under the auspices of the Committee for Trade, Industry and Enterprise Development (CTIED) and the United Nations Centre for Trade Facilitation and Electronic Business (UN/CEFACT) of the UNECE.

This book is a compilation of background policy papers and presentations, prepared for the Forum. In the same way as the publication issued after the first International Forum on Trade Facilitation in May 2002, it is expected to become a standard reference work on trade facilitation for the years to come.

The designation employed and the presentation of the material in this publication do not imply the expression of any opinion whatsoever on the part of the Secretariat of the United Nations.

The views expressed herein are those of the authors and do not necessarily reflect the views of the United Nations. Mention of company names or commercial products does not imply endorsement by the United Nations.

ECE/TRADE/330

UNITED NATIONS PUBLICATIONS
Sales N° E.04.II.E.3
ISBN 92-1-116889-9

Contents

CONTENTS

v

CONTENTS

vii

List of Figures and Tables

CONTENTS

Preface

Sharing the Gains of Globalization in the New Security Environment is first and foremost about the idea that policy dialogue is important for the establishment of a system of international trade facilitation, which would contribute to equitable development worldwide. Trade facilitation addresses the problems arising from inefficient trade procedures, which incur high transaction costs. These hinder trade and economic growth as well as the adoption of cutting edge technologies worldwide. The United Nations Economic Commission for Europe (UNECE) has developed and promoted trade facilitation standards and measures for more than 40 years, and we try to build on this pioneering experience to foster dialogue for the construction of a fair, predictable and secure international trading system. In 2002 and 2003, we organized two international forums on trade facilitation, at which everyone, representatives of developed and developing countries and small and big enterprises agreed on the potential benefits of trade facilitation for all. I am pleased to present this publication of the papers from the May 2003 Forum as a highly relevant and thought-provoking contribution to a fruitful global dialogue on these issues.

We at the UNECE are actively committed to achieving the key objectives of the United Nations, such as poverty eradication, sustainable development, and promoting peace and security. Our activities contribute to economic growth, and to the equal participation of all countries, especially developing and transition economies, in building the global trading system. Heads of State and government, who gathered at the United Nations in New York in September 2000, solemnly declared in the *United Nations Millennium Declaration*:

> *"We believe that the central challenge we face today is to ensure that globalization becomes a positive force for all the world's people. For while globalization offers great opportunities, at present its benefits are very unevenly shared, while its costs are unevenly distributed. We recognize that developing countries and countries with economies in transition face special difficulties in responding to this central challenge. Thus, only through broad and sustained*

CONTENTS

efforts to create a shared future, based upon our common humanity in all its diversity, can globalization be made fully inclusive and equitable. These efforts must include policies and measures, at the global level, which correspond to the needs of developing countries and economies in transition and are formulated and implemented with their effective participation. [1]

The Millennium Declaration clearly calls for **a shared responsibility** for managing worldwide economic and social development, as well as threats to international peace and security, among the nations of the world. This responsibility should be exercised multilaterally and, "as the most universal and most representative organization in the world, the United Nations must play the central role". This publication demonstrates just one aspect of how UNECE is contributing towards the Millennium Development Goals, especially Goal 8, Target 12: "Develop an open, equitable, rule-based, predictable and non-discriminatory multilateral trading system." [2]

Brigita Schmögnerová
Executive Secretary

---

[1] United Nations Document A/Res/55/2.
[2] United Nations Document A/56/326, Annex.

Acknowledgements

Sharing the Gains of Globalization in the New Security Environment: The Challenges to Trade Facilitation was prepared by Carol Cosgrove-Sacks (Director of the UNECE Trade Development and Timber Division) and Mario Apostolov (Coordinator of the International Forum on Trade Facilitation), working with Jordanka Tomkova (intern at the UNECE Trade Development and Timber Division).

The following persons contributed to the preparation for publication of the papers in this volume: Liliana Annovazzi-Jakab (UNECE), Virginia Cram-Martos (UNECE), Robert Crowhurst (United Kingdom), Michaela Eglin, Loga Gnanasambanthan (DFID, United Kingdom), Hans Hansell (UNECE), Ray McDonagh (WCO), Nora Neufeld (WTO), Julian Oliver (IECC), Maxence Orthlieb (UNCTAD), Alexander Safarik-Pstrosz (Czech Republic), Aleksandar Stojanoski (ICC), Eskil Ullberg (SMG Consulting, Sweden), Robert van Kuik (Netherlands), and François Vuilleumier (Switzerland). Within the secretariat, we would like to thank Eleanor Loukass, Christina O'Shaughnessy, Sandrine Ballongue, Aruna Vivekanantham, Romi Chopra for editing or preparing this volume for publication.

Many Governments, organizations and individuals made contributions to the work on this volume. The UNECE would like to thank the Governments of Saudi Arabia and Switzerland, as well as a long list of private partners, including SGS S.A., Cotecna, ABB, Microsoft, EAN International, OASIS, Pinkerton, BV Solutions Group, Honeywell, Cargill, Transcore, FreightDesk Technologies, CUBRC, Veridian, Lilly, Intertek, and Dickinson Dees, for their generous support, which made the International Forum on Trade Facilitation possible.

List of Abbreviations

24 AMR	24-hour Advance Manifest Rule (US Customs 24-hour Advance Cargo Manifest Declaration Rule)
ACP	Africa-Caribbean-Pacific
ARIPO	African Regional Industrial Property Organization
ASYCUDA	Automated System for Customs Data Processing
AGOA	African Growth and Opportunity Act
APEC	Asia-Pacific Economic Cooperation
AVI	Automatic Vehicle Identification
BCF	Business Collaboration Framework (of UN/CEFACT)
BE	Business entity
BIE	Business information entity
BO	Business object
CACM	Central American Common Market
CAN	Andean Community (Span Communidad Andina, formerly known as the Cartagena Agreement)
CARICOM	Caribbean Community
CC	Core components
CCC	Customs Cooperation Council (the former name of WCO)
CEPS	Customs, Excise and Preventive Service (in Ghana)
CIF	Cost insurance freight
COMESA	Common Market for Eastern and Southern Africa
CSI	Container Security Initiative
C-TPAT	Customs–Trade Partnership Against Terrorism
DFID	Department for International Development
DIS	Destination Inspection Scheme (in Ghana Customs)
eAC	ebXML Asia Committee
EAPO	Eurasian Patent Organization
EBA	Everything but Arms Initiative
ebXML	Electronic Business using eXtensible Markup Language
ECA	United Nations Economic Commission for Africa
ECA	Economic complementation agreement
ECLAC	United Nations Economic Commission for Latin America and the Caribbean

LIST OF ABBREVIATIONS

ECOWAS	Economic Community of West African States
EDI	Electronic Data Interchange
EDIFACT	Electronic Data Interchange for Administration, Commerce & Transport
EIA	Economic integration agreement
EPC	European Patent Convention
EPM	Electronic PostMark
EPO	European Patent Office
EPZ	Export Processing Zones
ESCAP	United Nations Economic and Social Commission for Asia and the Pacific
ESCWA	United Nations Economic and Social Commission for Western Asia
EU	European Union
FCL	Full Container Load
FDI	Foreign direct investment
FIATA	International Federation of Freight Forwarders
FOB	Free on board
FTA	Free trade agreement
FTAA	Free Trade Area of the Americas
G-3	Group of Three (FTA between Colombia, Mexico and Venezuela)
GATT	General Agreement on Tariffs and Trade
GCMS	Ghana Customs Management System
GCNet	Ghana Community Network Limited
GEFEG	Gesellschaft für Elektronischen Geschäftsverkehr mbH
GSL	Gateway Services Limited
GSP	Generalized System of Preferences
HPH	Hutchinson Port Holdings
HS	Harmonized System
ICAO	International Civil Aviation Organization
ICC	International Chamber of Commerce
ICS	International Chamber of Shipping
ICT	Information and communication technology
IDB	Inter-American Development Bank
IMMTA	International Multi-Modal Transport Association
IMO	International Maritime Organization

INFOCENTREX Centre for processing exports, El Salvador
INS   Immigration and Naturalization Services (in the USA)
IP   Intellectual property
IPEA   International Preliminary Examination Authority
IPER   International Preliminary Examination Report
IPR   Intellectual property rights
ISA   International Searching Authority
ISO   International Organization for Standardization
ISPFS   International Ship and Port Facility Security code
IST   Inspection, sensing, and tracking
ITA   Information Technology Agreement
ITN   Innovative Trade Network
LAIA   Latin American Integration Association
LCL   Less than Full Container Load
LDCs   Least developed countries
MERCOSUR   South American Common Market
MFN   Most Favoured Nation
MTN   Multilateral Trade Negotiations
NAFTA   North American Free Trade Agreement
NTB   Non-trade barriers
NTTFC   National Transport and Trade Facilitation Committees
OAPI   Organisation Africaine de la Propriété Intellectuelle
OASIS   Organization for the Advancement of Structured
              Information Standards
OECD   Organisation for Economic Co-operation and
Development
PCT   Patent Cooperation Treaty
PRSP   Poverty Reduction Strategy Paper
PSA   Partial scope agreements (LAIA)
PSI   Pre-shipment inspection
PTA   Preferential trade agreement
RFID   Read only frequency identification (cards used at United
              States border crossings)
RSAs   Regional scope agreements (LAIA)
RTP   Regional tariff preference (LAIA)
SAD   Single Administrative Document (of the European
              Union)

LIST OF ABBREVIATIONS

SADC	South African Development Community
S&D	Special and differential treatment
SCST	Strategic Council on Security Transport
SECI	Southeast European Cooperative Initiative
SECIPRO	An organization of the national trade facilitation bodies of Southeastern Europe (part of SECI)
SECO	Swiss State Secretariat for Economic Affairs
SELA	Latin American Economic System
SGS	Société Générale de Surveillance, S.A.
SITPRO	Simpler Trade Procedures Board (in the United Kingdom)
SMEs	Small and Medium-sized Enterprises
SOFOFA	Sociedad de Fomento Fabril (Chile)
SPS	Sanitary and Phyto-Sanitary Measures (WTO agreement)
SST	Smart and Secure Trade Lanes Initiative
TBT	Technical Barriers to Trade (WTO agreement)
TDED	Trade Data Elements Directory
TEU	Twenty-foot Equivalent Unit (for cargo)
ToRs	Terms of Reference
TRIPS	Trade related aspects of intellectual property rights (WTO)
UBL	OASIS Universal Business Language
UMM	UN/CEFACT Modelling Methodology
UN	United Nations
UN/CEFACT	United Nations Centre for Trade Facilitation and Electronic Business
UNCTAD	United Nations Conference on Trade and Development
UNECE	United Nations Economic Commission for Europe
UNeDocs	United Nations electronic documents project
UNIDO	United Nations Industrial Development Organization
UNISTE	United Nations International Symposium on Trade Efficiency
UNTDED	United Nations Trade Data Elements Directory
UPU	Universal Postal Union
WCO	World Customs Organization
WEF	World Economic Forum

WIPO	World Intellectual Property Organization
WTO	World Trade Organization
XML	eXtensible Markup Language

Second International Forum on Trade Facilitation 14-15 May 2003

The following two documents are: first, the programme of the Second International Forum on Trade Facilitation, which the United Nations Economic Commission for Europe (UNECE) organized in collaboration with the United Nations Conference on Trade and Development (UNCTAD), the United Nations Industrial Development Organization (UNIDO), the World Bank, the United Nations regional commissions for Latin America and the Caribbean (ECLAC), Western Asia (ESCWA), Africa (ECA) and Asia and the Pacific (ESCAP), the European Commission, the Organisation for Economic Cooperation and Development (OECD), the World Trade Organization (WTO), the World Customs Organization (WCO), and the International Chamber of Commerce (ICC) and, second, a synthesis of the presentations and discussions at the Forum, prepared by the secretariat of UNECE. The second document contains references to the various contributions by participants (the name of the author in brackets), which should help readers find their way through the chapters of this volume.

Programme of the second International Forum on Trade Facilitation, 14-15 May 2003

Opening

Amb. Luzius WASESCHA, Delegate of the Swiss Government for Trade Agreements

Mr. Paolo GARONNA, Deputy Executive Secretary, United Nations Economic Commission for Europe (UNECE)

Session I: How to achieve benefits for all from trade facilitation?

Chairperson:
Mr. Mondher ZENAIDI, Minister of Tourism, Trade and Handicrafts, Tunisia

Rapporteur:
Mr. Ray McDONAGH, Senior Adviser, World Customs Organization

Speakers:
Sharing the gains of globalization
Mr. Pascal LAMY, Trade Commissioner, European Commission

Trade facilitation in the multilateral trade negotiations
Mr. Roderick ABBOTT, Deputy Director-General, World Trade Organization (WTO)

Trade facilitation: benefits and capacity building in customs
Mr. Kunio MIKURIYA, Deputy Secretary-General, World Customs Organization (WCO)

The development dimension of trade facilitation
Mr. John BURLEY, Director, Division for Services Infrastructure for Development and Trade Efficiency, UNCTAD

How can developing countries receive a better share of the benefits of trade facilitation
Mr. Hardeep S. PURI, Ambassador, Permanent Representative of India to the Offices of the United Nations in Geneva

Practical measures for future trade facilitation
Mr. Alberto Di LISCIA, Assistant Director-General and Director of the Geneva Office, United Nations Industrial Development Organization (UNIDO)

Costs and benefits of trade facilitation

Mr. Anthony KLEITZ, Head, Trade Liberalization and Review Division, Organization for Economic Cooperation and Development (OECD)

The economic impact of trade facilitation measures

Mr. John WILSON, Lead Economist, Development Research Group, The World Bank

Discussion paper:

Income distribution impact of trade facilitation

Mr. Adrian HEWITT, Senior Research Fellow, Director of the ODI Fellowship Scheme and Research Adviser to the All-Party Parliamentary Group on Overseas Development, United Kingdom

---

"Identifying Opportunities and Roadblocks", Workshop on IPR and trade facilitation co-organized with the European Patent Office and SMG Consulting

Chairperson:
Zoran JOLEVSKI, Chef de Cabinet, President of the fYR Macedonia

Rapporteur:
Eskil ULLBERG, Senior Consultant, SMG Consulting

Panellists:
Mr. Ulrich SCHATZ, European Patent Office
Mr. Christopher HEATH, The Max Planck Institute
Mr. Timothy TRAINER, UNECE Advisory Group on IP
Mr. David MARSH, UN/CEFACT Legal Rapporteur

Session II: **Trade facilitation policy and new security initiatives**

Keynote address:

Trade facilitation in the new security environment

Mr. Douglas BROWNING, Deputy Commissioner, US Customs

Chairperson:

Mr. Leonid A.LOZBENKO, First Deputy Chairman, State Customs Committee of the Russian Federation

Rapporteur:

Mr. Robert van KUIK, Councillor, Customs Policy and Legislation Directorate, Ministry of Finance, the Netherlands

Speakers:

Insights from the Innovative Trade Network Team

Mr. Robert MASSEY, Chief Executive Officer, Cotecna Inspections S.A., speaking for the companies of the "Innovative Trade Network" Team

The new challenges from the point of view of the shipping industry

Mr. Brian PARKINSON, International Chamber of Shipping

Trade and security: the importance of a multilateral approach – the role of WCO and other players (WTO, UN)

Mr. Bob EAGLE, Director Customs, HMCE Customs and Excise, United Kingdom

Security in a global supply chain

Mr. Selig S. MERBER, Chairman, Customs Commission, International Chamber of Commerce (ICC)

Discussion paper:

Proposal for standards development in support of trade facilitation and security: A collaborative approach

Mr. Hans CARL, President, International Multi-Modal Transport Association (IMMTA)

Seminar on United Nations electronic Trade Documents (UNeDocs): Digital Paper for Trade on Your Desktop

Presentations by:

UN Economic Commission for Europe; Simpler Trade Procedures Board (SITPRO), UK; Universal Postal Union (UPU); Microsoft; Adobe

---

Session III: Mechanisms of Cooperation: The Role of the Business Community

Chairperson:

Mr. Selig S. MERBER, Chairman, Customs Commission, International Chamber of Commerce (ICC)

Rapporteur:

Mr. Julian OLIVER, Director-General, International Express Carriers Conference (IECC)

Speakers:
How to achieve maximum trade facilitation in a regulatory environment
Mr. Rolf JEKER, Executive Vice President, Société Générale de Surveillance SA (SGS)
Trade facilitation, security concerns and the postal industry
Mr. Thomas E. LEAVEY, Director General, Universal Postal Union
New solutions for trade facilitation and e-business accessible to all
Mr. Patrick GANNON, President and CEO, OASIS
The business contribution to development and safe trade
Mr. Patrick De SMEDT, Vice President, Microsoft Europe, Middle East and Africa
The development dimension of trade facilitation
Mr. Vitorino HOSSI, Minister of Trade, Angola
TTFSE.org website: a regional partnership to improve information transparency
Mr. Gerald OLLIVIER, Transport Specialist, The World Bank,
Ms. Kremena GOTCHEVA, BulPRO, Bulgaria
How transition economies can leverage existing logistics and transportation solutions
Mr. Anders NORDAHL, Kuehne & Nagel
Leading edge solutions for trade facilitation
Mr. Ray WALKER, Chairman, Steering Group of UN/CEFACT
Discussant:
Mr. Robert CROWHURST, Market Access, Department of Trade and Industry, United Kingdom

Presentation: Study on the perceptions and priorities of selected developing countries on the inclusion of trade facilitation in the WTO multilateral trade negotiations
Mr. Murray SMITH, Crown Agents / DFID

Session IV: Open Regionalism

Chairperson:
Mr. Alexander SAFARIK-PSTROSZ, Chairman, UNECE Committee on Trade Industry and Enterprise development

Rapporteur:
Ms. Michaela EGLIN, Consultant, International Trade

The UNECE experience in trade facilitation
Mr. Tom BUTTERLY, Trade Facilitation, UN Economic Commission for Europe (UNECE)

The role of ESCWA in promoting trade facilitation
Mr. Nabil SAFWAT, Chief, Transport Section, Economic and Social Commission for Western Asia (ESCWA)

Open Regionalism in Latin America: the impact on trade facilitation
Ms. Vivianne VENTURA DIAS, Director, International Trade and Integration Division, Economic Commission for Latin America and the Caribbean (ECLAC)

The role of ECA in promoting trade facilitation
Mr. Cornelius MWALWANDA, Senior Economic Officer, Economic Commission for Africa (ECA)

Cancún – a golden opportunity for trade facilitation
Mr. David WAKEFORD, Chief Executive, Simpler Trade Procedures Board (SITPRO), United Kingdom

Chairman's Conclusions
Amb. Luzius WASESCHA
Delegate of the Swiss Government for Trade Agreements

Workshop: **LEADING EDGE IN TRADE FACILITATION**
(organized in cooperation with Resonance Communication)

Panel I: Implementing trade facilitation tools to the benefit of all

Chairperson:

Mr. Ray WALKER, Chairman, UN/CEFACT Steering Group

Technology in the context of e-business

Mr. Klaus-Dieter NAUJOK, Chairman, Techniques and Methodologies Group, UN/CEFACT

Enhancing trade and transport facilitation

Mrs. Comfort BOOHENE-OSAFO, Deputy Commissioner (Research Monitoring and Planning), Ghana

Self-financing the enhancement of trade and transport facilitation and security

Mrs. Siti Aminah ABDULLAH, Deputy Director of Customs, Malaysia

Panel II: Trade facilitation in the new security environment

Chairperson:

Ms. Bonni TISCHLER, Vice President, Global Transportation and Supply Chain Security, Pinkerton

Development of the Global Trade Utility

Mr. Dean L. KOTHMANN, Executive Officer, BV Solutions Group

Mitigating supply chain security threats and facilitating global trade

Mr. Bruce JACQUEMARD, Savi Technology

Secure trade is good business

Mr. Richard PEARSON, Managing Director, Rotterdam for Hutchison Ports Holdings

Real world technology: solutions for in-transit freight border security

Mr. Scott BROSI, Area Vice President Secure Solutions, Transcore

? Mr. Rob QUARTEL, Chairman and CEO, FreightDesk Technologies

? Mr. Christopher P. HICKEY, VP Homeland Security, Honeywell

Summary of the Debate at the Forum
Mario Apostolov and Eleanor Loukass, UN Economic Commission for Europe (UNECE)

The 2003 International Forum on Trade Facilitation had two main objectives:
- To clarify the ways in which weaker members of the international trading community (developing and transition economies, small and medium-sized enterprises) could get a better share of the benefits of trade facilitation;
- To examine how the international community could make trade facilitation and the enhanced security measures in international trade work together.

This chapter summarizes the main themes covered in the Forum: sharing the gains of trade facilitation, reconciling trade facilitation with enhanced security, the development of new technologies and tools for trade facilitation, and the means by which developing and transition economies can implement those tools.

In the past, representatives of some developing countries expressed concerns that trade facilitation would impose additional costs to their economies without creating adequate benefits. Yet at the 2003 Forum everyone agreed that there are benefits to be gained for all. Developing country representatives pointed to their achievements in improving the efficiency of their customs services and border crossings. They also indicated the need for more work on implementing trade facilitation through projects on national and bilateral levels, and through the international organizations. Stressing the development dimension of trade facilitation, it is essential for developing countries that the issue be "positioned within a broader framework", responding to the need to reduce transaction costs, but also a broader perspective "of engineering economic growth" (Mwalwanda). The Forum provided a real opportunity to stimulate considerations and to procure concrete proposals, making it possible for developing countries to have more active and effective participation in the international trading system (Hossi). It was also suggested during the discussions that trade facilitation would be an excellent subject to be pursued by further such United Nations forums (Puri).

Several developing countries, however, voiced their scepticism concerning the need for multilateral binding rules in the World Trade Organization (WTO) in order to implement successfully trade facilitation measures. In their view, such rules could create more problems than they would solve. Although the debate on WTO's role in trade facilitation was not a priority in the Forum's agenda, this issue understandably came to the centre of the discussions, just three months before the Fifth WTO Ministerial Conference in Cancún.

The main conclusion of the Forum was that trade facilitation and security can be achieved together, in a coordinated manner, and this is primarily a technical rather than a trade-policy issue. A collaborative approach of all governments, international organizations, and the business community is necessary in order to create efficient security mechanisms, which would protect the global economy from the destructive use of organized violence, and which would not wipe out the achievements of trade facilitation.

Sharing the benefits

Despite effective removal of barriers to trade in goods and services in the past decades, not all countries have benefited equally from the opportunities offered by global markets. This prompted the Forum to focus, above all, on how to achieve better ways of sharing the benefits of trade facilitation among stronger and weaker players in the international trading system.

The development dimension
The benefits of trade facilitation include savings in overall trade transaction costs, valued by the United Nations Conference on Trade and Development (UNCTAD) at 7-10% of the volume of world trade. Although a large part of these costs are fixed, trade facilitation could reduce them by 1-3% of world trade value through eliminating inefficiencies (Kleitz). In spite of the recent uncertainty of the global economy, it is widely recognized that trade

liberalization is a key factor in promoting economic recovery and sustainable development (Garonna). Trade facilitation can contribute to development, as it can improve public capacity to monitor and promote foreign trade, as well as support existing and potential national exports (Burley). Trade facilitation is considered to help "identify solutions in the interest of all parties, thus setting the basis for sustainable development of trade"; it also improves the climate for foreign investment and enables a developing country to better integrate into the global economy (Hossi). Nevertheless, developing countries fail to benefit from the current level of trade liberalization because they lack (a) the industrial production capacity to ensure product diversification and (b) the ability to comply with international standards to secure greater market access (di Liscia).

In the past, concerns have been raised about the real income distribution effect of trade facilitation: concerns such as that multinational companies from developed countries would get the cream of the benefits from trade facilitation, leaving developing countries with a high implementation cost and the destruction of part of their businesses by new competition. Scenarios of customs officers and technical personnel made redundant due to simpler and automated procedures were added to warnings of decreasing government revenue. As development is a more complex phenomenon than measuring total economic growth figures, concerns about the income distribution effect of trade facilitation should be taken seriously.

The UNECE secretariat therefore requested the Overseas Development Institute (ODI) to prepare an assessment study of the impact of trade facilitation on income distribution in a developing country (Hewitt and Gillson). The findings indicate that trade facilitation will generally boost international trade, improve the climate for inwards investment and exports, and will thus foster economic growth. Consequently, income in the developing countries will rise, and the income share of the poor may rise as well. Higher economic growth will eventually result in more resources for governments to use for poverty alleviation and for development. It will generate more employment, thus helping many people to move out of poverty. Small and medium-sized enterprises (SMEs) in developing countries are the primary beneficiaries of trade facilitation as the transaction costs they bear are significantly higher than those of large companies (Hewitt and Gillson, Lamy). Improvements in infrastructure will allow companies and people with limited resources to trade more easily. Last but not least, trade facilitation limits the possibility for corruption, which takes a high toll on developing and transition economies by unjustly redistributing national income and diverting resources from development tasks. Even if a quantitative assessment of the pros and cons of the impact of trade facilitation on income distribution still has to be made, the ODI study makes a case for the positive effect of facilitating measures. A major conclusion, then, is that trade facilitation can be beneficial for all members of the trading community in a developing country, yet this necessitates deliberate action in the sphere of income distribution, so that the additional resources brought about by economic growth are shared fairly among the people.

The Forum identified technical assistance and capacity building for developing and transition economies as a priority. Governments must lead the process, and should involve the private sector to help supply the know-how. The international organizations can provide a multilateral infrastructure for the transfer of knowledge and other resources. A number of positive examples were cited. The five regional commissions of the United Nations have put together a project for technical assistance in trade facilitation, to be funded by the UN Development Account. In 2002-2003, the relevant United Nations agencies, under the auspices of the High Level Committee on Programmes, and on the initiative of UNCTAD, created a mechanism for cooperation in offering developing countries enhanced technical assistance and capacity building (Burley). The European Union has pledged 500 million euros for capacity building in trade facilitation in the next four years. The WCO has developed a Customs Capacity Building Strategy for targeted projects of assistance to improve the effectiveness of customs services (Mikuriya). The WTO has set up a programme to explain in various countries what the issues are and to build their negotiation capacity (Abbott).

Capacity building needs to go beyond a series of narrowly focused activities to embrace a more comprehensive and long-term approach designed, for example, to address all areas of customs administrations, as well as the entire management of trade flows across borders (Mikuriya). At the same time it should emphasize change management and process re-engineering, as making system-wide changes to complex processes is not an easy task (Merber). Capacity building should be targeted (and tailored for each individual case), so that the concrete trade facilitation projects would foster overall economic growth, reinforce integrity in the management and controls of international trade, help implement e-business tools, build a sustainable IT infrastructure, contribute to the protection of society from a range of security threats, and generally promote development.

Regional efforts among developing countries and on a North-South basis, reinforced by capacity building, both bilateral and through international organizations, would be the best way to proceed (Puri). Sub-regional cooperation efforts should be reinforced as a prerequisite for successful trade facilitation (Osafo). The experience of advanced developing countries, such as Malaysia, shows that automation of customs clearance, using modern information and communication technology (ICT) standards is feasible, and saves resources for development (Abdullah).

Greater uniformity and simplification of preferential rules of origin is required to increase transparency and reduce transaction costs for producers and traders (Ventura Dias). Different criteria and administrative procedures on rules of origin from country to country significantly increase transaction costs. The inclusion of *de minimis* clauses in preferential rules of origin may facilitate the access of SMEs to markets opened by free trade agreements.

Trade facilitation and the WTO debate.
Trade facilitation could offer important benefits to all members of the trading community. "We are all for it and therefore all of us want to take the measures necessary to facilitate, to enhance and reinforce trade facilitation" (Puri). However, views differ as to the best way to ensure that these benefits are shared fairly. The various views could be grouped in two clusters (Abbott):
- Developed countries and the business community, who favour a higher level of commitment in the WTO and advancing the current efforts through the establishment of binding rules. The major

argument advanced at the Forum was that trade facilitation would improve the overall efficiency of the international trade process through a WTO agreement, which would help create, implement, and manage fair trade facilitation rules and a sense of discipline (Wakeford).

- Developing countries, which opposed a multilateral settlement based on binding WTO rules out of concern about their limited capacities to implement the rules and about being exposed to rigorous dispute-settlement procedures. These countries would prefer to pursue trade facilitation independently.

Several developing country speakers (including Puri and Mwalwanda) laid out the major objections of developing countries to including trade facilitation in the WTO system of agreements. Other speakers (including Smith and Wakeford) analysed the position taken by certain developing countries, and suggested how these countries could obtain a better share of the benefits of trade facilitation. The following is a list of developing countries' concerns, which are a major challenge in the ongoing debate on the role of the WTO in the international trade facilitation system (Smith and others):

- They link trade facilitation to developments in negotiations on other issues in the WTO framework, such as rules of origin, investment, and agricultural subsidies.
- Their negotiators are not always familiar with the technical issues and the existing trade facilitation instruments.
- They are unhappy with having made a number of commitments in the final stages of the Uruguay Round of trade negotiations, which they now have difficulties in implementing. They worry that they may accept standards on trade facilitation, which exceed their capacity to implement them. Consequently, if they accept mandatory obligations on trade facilitation, which they cannot realize, they will be subject to the WTO dispute settlement mechanism.
- They are concerned that an eventual new WTO agreement on trade facilitation will be developed without any input from them, as they lack the means of providing experts for the drafting process.

- Another concern is the uncertainty over the scope of new obligations. They raise the issue of the difficulty of defining minimum standards for trade facilitation that would enter into an eventual WTO agreement.
- They are sceptical about commitments by donor countries and organizations to provide technical assistance and capacity building.

Developing countries could independently follow a staged path to establish a sustainable trade management infrastructure A global trade facilitation regime that would increase developing country benefits should be progressive, voluntary and not linked to WTO's enforceability provisions and dispute settlement mechanism(Puri). A number of developing country representatives noted that regional arrangements among developing countries and/or bilateral North-South agreements would help the developing countries gradually adjust to a common regime. Reinforcement of capacity building and technical assistance on a bilateral level and cooperation in the international organizations, such as the United Nations, regional and sub-regional development organizations, would catalyse the process. The international financial institutions and the donor community should provide financial resources to developing countries to meet the institutional and other adjustment costs, and to upgrade their infrastructure. Implementing other key aspects of trade facilitation already agreed to in the WTO, such as rules of origin, Technical Barriers to Trade/Sanitary and Phyto-Sanitary Measures (WTO-TBT/SPS) should be a priority for developed-country compliance and positive action. The position of Least Developed Countries (LDCs) was formulated as follows, "To implement laws and procedures [which would be required by an eventual multilateral agreement on trade facilitation] will be very costly for LDCs, which they cannot afford at this stage. Hence, it is too early for the development of an agreement within the WTO in this area" (Mwalwanda).

Developed countries, the international business community and some international organizations, however, strongly supported the idea of negotiating an effective WTO agreement on trade facilitation. They described the development of WTO trade facilitation rules as the centrepiece in building a predictable, transparent and stable global regime of trade facilitation that would benefit developing countries and SMEs.

Improvements to trade processes could save business about $300 billion—a quarter of the total economic benefits flowing from the Doha "Development Round" of WTO negotiations – which would be widely shared among all countries (Lamy). Unlike a tax or duty fees, the lost resources do not go to any productive use but are merely wasted as a result of inefficiency and bureaucracy (Eagle). SMEs in developing and transition economies could be the primary beneficiaries if the process is made more efficient as a result of an agreed system of trade facilitation. If mandatory trade facilitation rules were to become part of a multilateral regime, implementation of these rules would require considerable technical and financial efforts from those countries where trade facilitation still lags behind. Countries often downgrade trade facilitation in their list of priorities, owing to lack of money, but this would change if countries were to become aware of the costs of not implementing trade facilitation (Burley). WTO commitments would, as argued by some business representatives, ensure that all countries could move in the same direction, establish global rules, and avoid the development of discriminatory situations. These commitments would require domestic customs reforms, which might otherwise be blocked by short-term political considerations (Lamy). They can lock in and make the reforms irreversible, as well as creating the basic framework for trade facilitation work of partner organizations – either in developing standards or in delivering aid to developing countries. During the discussions at the Forum, a United States Trade Representative's officer pointed out that the success of the WTO had, essentially, been in bringing about domestic reforms in the country members of the organization. Consequently, it was expected that bringing trade facilitation into the WTO system would produce internal reforms and raise efficiency in many countries.

In the WTO, trade facilitation has been gaining new recognition as an important issue for its members and for the very purpose of this organization's mandate (Abbott) . Governments increasingly see it as a core element of external trade and development rather than a merely mechanical "plumbing" of trade policy. In addition, the WTO could create a basic framework within which other organizations can work as partners, e.g through initiatives such as the "Single Window" concept and standardization and simplification of customs procedures (Mikuriya). In the customs area, an agreement would be vital in bringing about security, as well as providing harmonization and predictability necessary for moving goods quickly and affordably. A multilateral agreement may help ensure political commitment to implementing minimum standards, and this may offer improved service to traders and encourage traders to be more compliant (Eagle) . The consequent increase in trade will mean more economic growth and increased revenue from customs.

A WTO agreement on trade facilitation could offer developing countries the benefits of trade facilitation, while allowing them to reach a voluntarily defined target level of facilitation progressively, step-by-step, measuring progress according to internationally agreed benchmarks (Wakeford). A commitment to assess facilitation through the measurement and reduction of release time (the time between the arrival of goods in port and their release to the importer) could become part of an eventual WTO agreement (Merber). This would allow countries to improve their existing processes and legal systems in a flexible manner, using their current level of performance as a starting point.

Mr. Abbott listed several suggestions on how the WTO could deal with trade facilitation, focusing on transparency, predictability, and non-discrimination. Other proposals envisaged providing countries with reasonable periods of adaptation between a measure's adoption, the legislative process, and the measure's entry into force. This step-by-step approach would cover standardizing; reducing data and documentation requirements; and simplifying procedures. In addition, there was a call for strengthening due process, in particular by creating a right of appeal against customs and other government agency rulings and decisions. Along the lines of this argument, several proposals were made aiming to bring the two clusters of views together. Some involved the possibility of building a two-track mechanism This would mean, first, preparations and negotiations alongside and independently of the WTO, and would imply more flexible "soft rules" or guidelines drawn out of good practice, benchmarking and exchange of national experience. Second, it would involve a rules-based component, integrated in the WTO (on which decisions have not been reached yet).

The proponents of new rules want upfront commitments on technical assistance, capacity building and some other issues, to be an integral part of the negotiations.

A recurrent theme at the Forum was the need for a common regime for the production and fair distribution of the benefits of trade facilitation. But the question was, would the WTO process provide the best framework for such a regime? An additional challenge, as the Ministerial Conference in Cancún showed later, was the linkage with other issues in the WTO negotiating process, such as agricultural subsidies or investment.

The following recommendations were formulated at the Forum:

1. The Forum recognized that trade facilitation was no longer only a technical issue aimed at tactical developments in the international trade transaction. It encouraged governments to adopt trade facilitation as a strategic policy for economic growth and development.

2. Trade liberalization alone may have no or limited effect without a supporting institution building.

3. Governments should contribute to building the political will necessary for imp lementing trade facilitation among various groups of countries, and strengthen the global network for trade facilitation within the United Nations as a place for open policy debate on the issue.

4. The sustainable development aspect of trade facilitation should be reinforced. Trade facilitation strategies have to be conceived and implemented within a global cost-benefit framework: facilitating trade while at the same time conserving the earth's scarce resources.

5. Governments must rationalize the demand for data across all ministries, departments and other agencies using such concepts as the "Single Window" for the submission of a single, simple set of data covering all the regulatory requirements involved in international trade.

6. Existing trade standards combined with latest technology concepts can be instrumental to respond to the new challenges that international supply chains face today. The United Nations system should work together with the private sector to make these technologies accessible

for the implementation of policy driven agendas and ensure accessibility for SMEs and developing countries.

7. Benchmarking of achievements in trade facilitation should be used as a strategic tool for preparing the next steps in capacity development in both the private and the public sectors.

8. Most developing and transition economies require extensive technical assistance, which should build on the existing individual and collective experience of these countries (e.g. within sub-regional economic communities).

9. Sharing of information and experiences on trade facilitation initiatives should be developed as a form of capacity building.

10. In order to guarantee benefits for all from trade facilitation, funds and technical assistance should be provided to those developing countries that need them. In this respect it is crucial to guarantee a coordinated approach among donors. The way to ensure long term sustainable benefit is to measure the degree of facilitation both before and after the support has been given .Targeted trade facilitation measures should be assessed against the broader development goals of each country.

11. In order to make trade facilitation work for development, particular attention should be given to specific measures in the following areas:
   • In order to reduce income inequalities in developing countries, trade facilitation measures should be targeted at lowering trade transaction costs in those sectors where employment of the poor is concentrated.
   • The provision of effective safety nets may be necessary if alternative forms of employment are not rapidly available for any displaced workers.
   • Any increase in government resources brought about by trade facilitation should be used to support pro-poor or social expenditures.

12. SMEs, the dominant actors in developing countries, need to be able to access capital, trade information systems and capacity building to comply with international standards under trade facilitation programmes, if they are to trade efficiently.

13. Irrespective of the difficulties, governments, international organizations and the business community should work together towards a common regime of producing and fair sharing of the benefits of trade facilitation for all members of the international community.

New security measures in international trade

Security concerns have grown as a result of the terrorist attacks on 11 September 2001 against the United States. Mr. Lozhbenko, First Deputy Chairman of Russian Customs, pointed out that the link between trade facilitation and security is a brand new issue for the international community. Partly for this reason the debate revolves around customs issues, yet there are many different players in the international trade security chain who should be incorporated in the broader debate. He commended UNECE on initiating this debate, which would take stock of the different points of view.

International trading has undergone fundamental changes since the security emphasis shifted from threats *to* trade, to threats *from* trade. While some actors in international trade focus on the minimization of security risks stemming from the international flow of goods, especially in container trade, others are concerned with the new security requirements, which will impose an additional burden on fragile economies.

Most participants in the Forum stressed the need for a multilateral, rather than unilateral, approach to security in international trade flows. Mr. Browning, Deputy US Customs Commissioner, said: "What is important is that we move forward together, that our political leaders remain engaged, and that we continue working toward a harmonious balance between real security and real facilitation". The major observation at the Forum was that security and trade facilitation should be regarded as two sides of the same coin, and the effort of the international community should focus on achieving a unity of objectives between the two. Security and facilitation, unless they are mutually reinforcing, may create barriers for smaller players (Eagle).

SUMMARY OF THE DEBATE

If attention is diverted from trade facilitation in the name of security, neither will be increased.

The United States is developing its security initiatives with an eye towards increasing facilitation: "being able to assign lower levels of risk to a given shipment is the key to being able to provide faster processing at the time of arrival" (Browning). Efficient customs procedures, which address security concerns, would also facilitate legitimate trade (Mikuriya).

The current security initiatives address the obvious requirement to respond to an external threat – the threat from terrorism, which strongly influences the way international trade functions today – and they have not been designed as a protectionist trade policy (Browning). However, the implications of increased security are worrying, especially in the following areas:

- Technological and financial requirements: The screening of containers in ports implies the availability and use of costly equipment. The new security initiatives, such as the Container Security Initiative of the United States, and the use of "safe ports", may lead to the rerouting of major trade flows.
- Supply chain management capability: The C-TPAT (Customs-Trade Partnership Against Terrorism) initiative, for example, requires trading partners to work with service providers throughout the supply chain to enhance security processes and procedures. These procedures can only be requested for US-bound supply chains, but may prove detrimental to ill-equipped, though trustworthy, suppliers in developing countries.
- Legal consequences: Changes to current practices and procedures arising from security concerns may have significant legal implications, such as increased liabilities.

Many speakers noted that the new initiatives should not set up either discriminatory elements, where some countries or traders would be treated differently from others (Cosgrove-Sacks and Butterly, Parkinson) or extra costs or other new obstacles to trade. With the increasing risks in international trade flows, security checks are made as early as possible, and risk management carried out on the basis of information provided at earlier stages, necessitating new and expensive technology. Ports are reported to be raising charges, and shipping companies will soon follow suit. If any "gains of globalization in the new security environment" are possible, they will not be easy to achieve. The measures developed to combat terrorism, in addition to terrorism itself, may threaten trade, which is an engine of growth and offers the best chance of steady progress for both developed and developing economies (Parkinson). Trade facilitation opportunities may be overlooked, although they are badly needed and feasible. And ill-designed security measures could have a detrimental impact on trade. Trust between the parties concerned in international trade (governmental and commercial) has already been eroded and must be rebuilt.

Regarding the technical problems in the response to the terrorist threat: whereas, for instance, attention is focused on introducing sophisticated methods for sealing containers, the technical standards for the containers themselves do not meet expectations (Carl, Parkinson). One can open the roof of a "sealed" container in transit, while it is waiting to be picked up from an area which is not secure, and introduce hazardous objects in it. Standard-setting organizations, such as ISO, WCO, IMO, and FIATA, together with UNECE, should include this and similar issues in their work.

It was generally agreed that inter-agency cooperation in trade security was urgently needed. UNIDO proposed a cohesive supply-side approach, ensuring that integrated cooperation would benefit developing countries and also respond to security concerns (di Liscia). UNECE and WCO invited all relevant organizations to hold a coordination meeting in the second half of 2003, with the objective of finding ways to keep the balance in advancing trade facilitation and security (Carl).

Supply Chain security
The focus should be on the supply chain as a whole (Browning). The US security initiatives are designed to examine goods earlier in the supply chain; harden ports of entry with increased technology and staffing; and ensure that sufficient information is available to allow the relevant authorities to intervene effectively when necessary. All of this should be combined with securing fast movement of legitimate trade flows along

supply chains across borders. The international community should concentrate on creating a supply-chain security infrastructure with a truly global reach; for which much work will need to be done (Browning, Mikuriya). Supply-chain security can be achieved through close collaboration and commitment of all parties in the trade transaction chain, combining this with an effective application of technology (Pearson, Cosgrove-Sacks and Butterly).

There is a vital inter-relationship between security, compliance with customs regulations and trade facilitation. Higher compliance with customs and other regulations is of key importance, so compliant trade should be rewarded with more trade facilitation on a selective basis (Eagle, Osafo). Trade facilitation enhanced security, while corruption and various barriers to trade undermined it. No system can be secure if untrustworthy agents run it. Global supply chain logistics is a complex system comprising many actors, and the approach that may best achieve lasting improvements in both facilitation and security is a holistic one (Merber).

The following major recommendations came out of the statements at the Forum:

1. In a situation of increasing security measures in international trade, non-discriminatory technical solutions and standards should guarantee that less developed countries and SMEs could continue to access the global marketplace despite enhanced security of the supply chain.

2. A holistic approach to trade facilitation and security along the whole supply chain, which advances both trade facilitation and security, should be adopted. Programmes for trade facilitation and security should enlist the support and cooperation of the private sector. The relationship between high tariffs, integrity and security should be recognized.

3. Governments and international organizations should not focus wholly on technological solutions to securing the supply chain. Instead, they should ensure that more practical and operational tools and policies are designed and delivered, so that they are inclusive of all countries at whatever stage of economic development they are.

4. In the quest for greater information to secure the supply chain, governments must first demonstrate the need for any new data demands. Then they must rationalize the demand for data across all ministries, departments and other agencies using such concepts as the "Single Window".

5. Trust between the parties involved in international trade (governmental and commercial) must be rebuilt. Security measures introduced must be appropriate to the perceived threat, and should be practical and not political, using appropriately risk assessment techniques and favouring the potentially innocent.

6. The objective of enhanced security measures should be to redefine the point of control; improve information sharing; seek more timely and better information; develop better intelligence; push facilitation issues already much debated (single window, paperless trading, electronic signatures, etc.); seek international standards which are consistent, clear and uniform; and develop co-operation between all the parties involved.

7. The possibility of developing an international standard for security in trade procedures, which would apply equally to all, should be investigated. An expert group might be established to identify and explore the global standards that are necessary.

8. A concerted effort from all the relevant organizations involved in international trade facilitation and standards will be required in order to ensure that the developed standards are effective and that they achieve the dual aim of enhancing both security and trade facilitation for all countries. Strong collaboration and coordination amongst the relevant standards-setting organizations is the way to attain this objective.

9. A meeting of all organizations involved in trade facilitation and security should be arranged to determine who is doing what, and agree on priority areas for new standards development. Models developed for the advancement of trade facilitation such as the International Trade Transaction Global Framework and the Business Supply Chain Model should be used to identify overlaps and gaps in the work on the new security requirements, in order to inform the debate and influence decisions on these issues.

10. Leaders should be encouraged to impress upon their respective governments the importance of action in the area of trade security and facilitation, especially in customs, in a balanced way. Customs services should be encouraged to approach new security issues and trade facilitation in an equal fashion in the World Customs Organization (WCO) and in other organizations. Different agencies within governments should improve their interaction with a view to develop measures and strategies nationally, so that no entity becomes a vulnerable link in the supply chain. Where work is already under way, ensure that it advances with the participation of all relevant government agencies, as well as the private sector.

11. Political will is critical. The engagement of top leadership is essential to how security issues in international trade are managed, and to drive the investment in making the necessary changes. Capacity and resource questions must be considered, and the UN provides appropriate forums where some of the solutions might be found.

Tools enhancing trade facilitation and security in developing and transition economies

During the second day, the Forum focused on the practical tools to help achieve the objectives set out during the first day's discussions, and on how governments and the business community could enable developing and transition economies to implement these tools.

The tools include UNCTAD's development and implementation of computerized systems, such as the Automated System for Customs Data (ASYCUDA) and the Advance Cargo Information System (ACIS); UNECE's standard for Electronic Data Interchange (UN/EDIFACT), and new tools, such as UNeDocs, which provide the basis for internationally recognized electronic trade documents.

Private-sector service providers can help by offering a variety of services and tools including: certification services; risk profiling systems; communications and management systems; and validation, verification and information services. These tools would help traders and supply chain participants comply with security and import/export requirements, exchange information, and simplify and align their systems and procedures (Balchin). Companies can develop risk management systems for customs administrations, cargo scanning, and other innovative techniques and technologies. Companies can implement these tools in developing countries on economically justified terms, provided the tools are tailored to meet needs on a case-by-case basis (Osafo).

Transit trade will improve if haulage transport were readily available (Osafo). Transit countries should seek help for equipment and training to manage transit cargo, so that they can raise their revenue from transit trade.

Industry can help bridge the skills gap in using information and communication technologies for trade and development. It has been working through various projects in the developing countries for many years. Support for open standards in electronic commerce is the key to enabling many poorer countries to find solutions for modern international trade as well as tools for development (de Smedt). The private sector can help markets develop and thus bring the benefits of the global economy to those countries and regions that need them most (de Smedt). While online customs clearance systems, are not prohibitively expensive for developing countries, for instance, acquiring the skills to run them can be.

The participants in the Forum were pleased that the UNECE continues to develop tools for electronic trade documents, which comply with existing paper document procedures, to support national administrations and the trading community worldwide. Working with governmental agencies, international institutions, and the business community, the UNECE will ensure that these tools are made accessible to transition economies, developing countries and SMEs, The UNeDocs project received the support of the representatives of the World Bank, the Universal Postal Union, SITPRO, and a number of private companies, such as Microsoft and Adobe. With its capacity to speed up the information flow, UNeDocs could make a contribution to the security of global supply chains (Pikart, Jiricek, Salzmann, Grey, and Barker).

Concerning the work on electronic business standards, it was noted that the relevant groups of the United Nations Centre for Trade Facilitation and Electronic Business (UN/CEFACT) should establish a close working relationship with the Web Service standardization communities to work towards the same e-Business vision, in order to ensure that both users and providers are benefiting from their currently separate efforts through a common and aligned goal and vision.

Industry, too, has enormous potential to contribute to a safe trading environment, for example, by creating secure technologies, increasing system security, promoting harmonized supply chain security measures, and working with government regulators on law enforcement (de Smedt).

A team of companies (Cotecna, Black and Veach Solutions Group, Honeywell, Cargill, Transcore, FreightDesk Technologies, CUBRC, and Veridian), which have formed the *Innovative Trade Network*, presented their initiative for a coordinated inter-business approach to building an infrastructure that would improve risk management of a shipment and the security of a nation as a whole. They propose it as part of the work towards global and common solutions to facilitate international trade. There exist many examples of commitments made at the national level to comprehensive global solutions for international trade. "Moving back the borders", as defined in the US security initiatives, will be done in compliance with worldwide standards, by employing practical uses of technology and automating customs procedures, by applying commercially viable customs policies and in dynamic teaming by solution providers. The private sector is advancing technology-driven solutions for both facilitating international trade and for trade security, and the way forward is through evolution that would encompass both developed and developing countries (Brosi). Among other solutions proposed was the Smart & Secure Tradelanes (SST) as a global trade security network and a solution responding to the new security concerns (Jacquemard).

The Workshop on Intellectual Property Rights (IPR) and Trade Facilitation addressed the roadblocks for trade stemming from intellectual property related procedures and the whole international system of managing IPR and patents. In an age of globalization, it becomes obvious that there will exist such problems as the territorial limitation of patents (within separate states), the disadvantageous cost/benefit ratio for developing countries, and access to knowledge, finance, and trade infrastructure, related to IP in general. Another issue, which has to be addressed, is the link between the private provision and general use of international standards in trade facilitation and electronic business. This issue has aspects related to IPR ownership, which need to be addressed in the same way as the provision, management and ownership of other global public goods are addressed. The question of setting up a centrally managed agency (or database) and a more coherent global patenting regime, in order to facilitate trade, came up in the discussion. Participants identified a number of issues which need be addressed, such as advantages and burdens of IPR systems for developing countries; improving the understanding of IPR experts of the functioning of the global market; and a coordinated approach of capacity building and technical assistance on IPR issues.

Suggested solutions and tools that can also be implemented in developing and transition economies:

1. Developing countries' private and public sectors should make greater use of ICT in their trade and transport procedures and operations. Experience shows that a collaborative approach between governments, the private sector and international organizations can provide affordable and efficient solutions, which foster further development (Abdullah, Osafo).

2. The infrastructure supporting both trade facilitation and security should be technology neutral, but should also allow new technologies to be applied independent of people and processes. A global trading system should not favour one technology provider, one port, or one state. The inspection, sensing and tracking system of tomorrow should be able to use today's infrastructure (Kothmann).

3. A set of auditable standards for inspection, sensing, and tracking, would help importing countries to gain confidence in the imported goods and in the international trading system, and exporting countries to have a clear set of standards to aim at (Kothmann).

4. Profiling infrastructure, which accommodates data from many locations, should allow for law enforcement and customs agencies, but also ports, freight forwarders, insurers, in developing countries to accede to and use trade data for a fast treatment of trade flows and risk management.

5. In order to facilitate trade, the procedures to determine the origins of goods should be streamlined and standardized, including the use of electronic means.

6. Open standards and cooperative mechanisms (standard-setting organizations) are central to the construction of a global framework for e-business that can be implemented in the developing world (Gannon).

7. Trade facilitation should make use of the Internet and of Web Services, as advanced and practical tools for e-business (Gotcheva and Ollivier, Naujok).

Open regionalism– a key to implementing trade facilitation

A major challenge for trade facilitation is finding the appropriate balance between multilateral, regional and bilateral mechanisms for implementation. Experience shows that regional groupings remain the most successful context for engaging in trade facilitation at the international level (Burley). There are a number of reasons why the implementation of trade facilitation at the regional level is of key importance (Cosgrove-Sacks and Butterly). First, regional and sub-regional trade development and cooperation have been expanding in recent years. Second, international standards and norms are best implemented if regional specifics are taken into account. Third, greater efficiency and harmonization of international trade procedures can be achieved if they are based on a sense of regionalism, which supplements the physical proximity of neighbouring countries. Trade facilitation is increasingly becoming part of the concept of regionalism. Conversely, from an economic point of view, trade facilitation can greatly enhance the strength and integration of a region. Multilateral and bilateral mechanisms can constructively co-exist and be mutually supportive; and the United Nations might be the most appropriate framework for ensuring such consistence and positive energy (Garonna). The five regional, social and economic commissions of the United Nations, together with other regional development organizations, are well suited to carrying out projects promoting trade facilitation, and implementing global standards and norms.

One size does not fit all, and trade facilitation solutions must be adapted to each country's situation and requirements (Kleitz). Any attempt at a multilateral agreement on trade facilitation in the WTO should take account of these differing needs. Improvement is possible and beneficial for almost every country, hence the importance of scalable implementation of standards and a diversity of approaches (Cosgrove-Sacks and Butterly). Standardization should occur at both national and regional levels but taking into account established global standards and reflecting best practices from the business and government experience. For example, UNECE encourages policy debate and develops international standards and best practices for trade facilitation at the global level, primarily through its Centre for Trade Facilitation and Electronic Business (UN/CEFACT). At the regional level UNECE's implementation activities focus exclusively on its member states. There is, however, a contradiction in the term "open regionalism", as regionalism contains an element of closing up a region to the broader community of countries in the world (Ventura Dias). In Latin America, for instance, open regionalism means a collection of sub-regional integration schemes, bilateral and plurilateral preferential trade agreements (PTAs), with no mechanism to make the agreed preferences multilateral.

ESCWA's transport facilitation programmes were regarded as very important for the region. The implementation of trade facilitation measures, standards, and recommendations must be done at the regional and sub-regional levels (Safwat). Hence, meaningful plans at the international and national levels must include a regional dimension. Regional development organizations, banks and NGOs should be proactive in the implementation of instruments and standards, which are developed globally, yet using local expertise.

1

SUMMARY OF THE DEBATE

Sub-regional cooperation is a key to harmonizing customs barriers and removing customs barriers in Africa, Latin America, Asia, and even in Eastern Europe, hence the great importance of sub-regional groupings in the achievement of trade facilitation (Osafo). COMESA, ECOWAS, and SADC, in Africa, and CARICOM, Mercosur, and CACM, in the Americas are notable examples, which have a great potential for advancing trade facilitation. Sub-regional economic communities in Africa, for example, are crucial to the realization of self-sustainable projects and programmes for trade facilitation (Mwalwanda).

A key issue for Latin American economies, to take another example, is to strike the right balance between sub-regional trade liberalization and facilitation and the rights and obligations stemming from PTAs with developed economies in North America and Europe.

Practical tools developed within programmes for technical assistance, capacity building and cooperation at multiple levels should be complementary and represent composite parts of a "trade facilitation system". The regional commissions will continue to cooperate with all organizations that play a major role in setting standards and promoting the exchange of experience and technical assistance in the field of trade facilitation.

The following recommendations were made at the Forum:

1. The five United Nations regional commissions, the United Nations Centre for Trade Facilitation and Electronic Business (UN/CEFACT) and all governments and organizations participating in the Forum should work together on making more resources available for capacity building in trade facilitation in developing countries and transition economies through regional and sub-regional organizations and mechanisms for cooperation.
2. Regional development organizations, banks and NGOs should be proactive in the implementation of existing trade facilitation instruments and standards.

3. Full use should be made of the potential of regional and sub-regional development organizations in the area of trade facilitation, and of initiatives such as the interregional project for capacity building in trade facilitation, developed by the United Nations regional economic commissions following the First International Forum on Trade Facilitation in May 2002, in Geneva.

4. The United Nations should be considered as an appropriate framework for ensuring consistency of efforts for trade facilitation and security on national, bilateral, and multilateral levels.

General conclusion

The Second International Forum on Trade Facilitation achieved its major objective - truly interactive discussions:

- among representatives of developed and developing countries and the major international organizations on how to enable developing and transition economies, and small and medium-sized enterprises, to receive a better share of the benefits of trade facilitation;
- between those who believe that enhanced security measures in international trade can go hand-in-hand with progressing trade facilitation and those who argue that there will be a too high cost burden (especially for the weaker participants in international trade) from the new security initiatives;
- among governments, international organizations, and the business community, on the ways to implement new solutions and tools that would help achieve the double goal of fair sharing the benefits of trade facilitation and imp roving security.

The Forum made a substantive contribution to clarifying the priorities of the major stakeholders in developing a global system of trade facilitation through developing capacity-building projects, tools, and standards in the various international organizations, on global, regional and bilateral bases. The Forum also made a contribution to the preparations for the discussion of trade facilitation in the WTO. Tools provided by the private sector, in cooperation with national and inter-governmental projects and programmes, can help traders and supply chain parties comply with security and import/export requirements, exchange information, and simplify and align their systems and procedures, and make overall movements of goods faster. A collaborative approach is needed for both trade facilitation and security in the international supply chains, and the United Nations can play a major role here. Further, trade facilitation solutions must be adapted to the each country's specific situation and requirements.

The UNECE reiterated in this Forum its understanding of the link between regional and global action in trade facilitation. The UNECE strives to develop standards and encourages policy debate on trade facilitation at the global level, reflecting best practices from the business and government experience. However, integrated implementation of standards, from a regional perspective, is critical. A series of practical tools for technical assistance, capacity building, and cooperation, based on voluntary mechanisms or "open coordination tools" applied within a multi-level approach, including multiple stakeholders, should form complementary and composite parts of a "trade facilitation system". Despite the disappointment of the results of the WTO Ministerial Meeting in Cancún, in September 2003, it is necessary to continue the construction of an international regime that would provide the products of trade facilitation: such as efficient, simple and secure trade procedures, elimination of corrupt practices, and development of global standards that can be used for free by everyone. The major features of such a regime may be traced in the statements of various actors, gathered together in this volume. One of the lessons from Cancún might be that the tight linkages among various issues in the multilateral trade negotiations might not be healthy for the establishment of a stable and fair trade facilitation regime. In cooperation with other agencies, the UNECE has had, and will continue to have a major role in setting standards and promoting the exchange of experience and technical assistance in this field (Garonna).

Increasing compliance with international standards in a transition economy or a developing country, through the improvement of quality management infrastructures, for example, also increases the country's access to foreign markets. If developing countries are to succeed in increasing their share in global manufacturing value-added[3], their products must meet both market demand and product standards. Yet these countries need technology diffusion and capacity building, which can be provided by an international trade facilitation regime.

The introduction of quality management systems based on standardization, certification and accreditation heightens the security of the trade system. Yet it is important to take targeted action so that strengthened security measures do not become yet another technical barrier to trade. The new security initiatives in international trade should be used to develop risk management tools that will foster trade facilitation, in the final resort.

Technical assistance and capacity building would help the developing countries cope with some of the problems of transition to more advanced methods of handling international trade flows. Again, some countries see capacity building and technical assistance as linked to the WTO process, while others prefer to keep it in the area of bilateral relations and cooperation with the relevant bodies of the United Nations, the World Customs Organization, and other organizations dealing with trade facilitation. Trade facilitation should be regarded as a strong development tool, and the work of the regional economic organizations was important here for its implementation. Developing countries' private and public sectors need to make greater use of information and communication technology but, before computerizing, existing administrative and commercial practices need to be overhauled. Interagency cooperation, the effective exchange of information and adequate financial resources are essential for long-term commitments to be made and honoured.

---

[3] According to the most recent estimates, the developing countries (including China) account for a 24.5% share in world total MVA (at current prices) in 2000. *International Yearbook of Industrial Statistics 2003*, UNIDO, p. 32, Figure 1.1.

Introductory Remarks

The three following chapters are the introductory remarks of the editors of this volume, of Mr. Mondher Zenaidi, Minister of Tourism, Trade and Handicrafts of Tunisia and of Mr. Paolo Garonna, Deputy Executive Secretary of UNECE.

Towards a Sustainable and Secure Trade Facilitation System

Carol Cosgrove-Sacks, Director, Trade Development and Timber Division, UNECE
Mario Apostolov, Forum Coordinator, UNECE

In 2002 and 2003 the United Nations Economic Commission for Europe (UNECE) organized, together with its partner organizations[4], two International Forums on Trade Facilitation. The first concluded that benefits from trade facilitation far exceed costs for both developed and developing countries.[5] The second emphasized the need for fairer sharing of the gains of globalization and trade facilitation in particular. Not all countries, companies or groups of people have so far profited from liberalization. The participants in the Forums shared their views on why this had happened, and on the remedies that should be put into practice. Globalization has raised many expectations. On the whole, it is a positive trend in human economic development, yet the problem lies in the way it has been managed. As a major critic, Joseph Stiglitz, former Chief Economist at the World Bank, put it:

> *"I believe that globalization – the removal of barriers to free trade and the closer integration of national economies – can be a force for good and that it has the potential to enrich everyone in the world, particularly the poor. But I also believe that if this is to be the case, the way globalization has been managed, including*

---

[4] The United Nations Conference for Trade and Development, the United Nations regional commissions, the United Nations Industrial Development Organization, the World Bank, the World Trade Organization, the World Customs Organization, the Organisation for Economic Co-operation and Development, the European Commission, and the International Chamber of Commerce.

[5] *Trade Facilitation: The Challenges for Growth and Development* (United Nations publication, Sales No.E.03.II.E.10). This publication containing the papers produced for the 2002 Forum.

the international trade agreements that have played such a large role in removing those barriers and the policies that have been imposed on developing countries in the process of globalization, need to be radically rethought.[6]

It is important to try to find, in a collaborative manner, the proper means of sharing fairly the benefits of global trade facilitation.

In addition, the urgent need to reconcile the goals of trade facilitation with the massively intensified security measures introduced in international trade after 11 September 2001. A study of the trade effects of the terrorist attacks now known as "9/11" estimated that world welfare declined by $75 billion per year for each 1 percent increase in costs to trade from programmes to tighten border security; and that developing countries were particularly vulnerable to cost increases related to security threats.[7]

With these two objectives in mind (fairer sharing of the gains of trade facilitation and balancing facilitation and security in international trade) we organized the second International Forum on Trade Facilitation in May 2003. It took place on 14 and 15 May 2003 and gathered around 500 participants: policy makers and experts from governments, international organizations, the business community, and civil society from some 80 countries. The UNECE much appreciated the contributions of all the speakers and participants for the lively discussions, which were the distinguishing characteristic of the Forum.

---

[6] Stiglitz, Joseph E. *Globalization and Its Discontents*, London, Allen Lane: The Penguin Press, 2002, p.ix.
[7] World Bank. *Global Economic Prospects 2004*, Washington 2003, p. 179 (www.worldbank.org/prospects/gep2004/chapter5.pdf)

The basic subjects were as follows:
- how to guarantee a better share of the benefits of trade facilitation for developing and transition economies and small and medium-sized enterprises;
- how to achieve a balance between trade facilitation and the new security initiatives and measures;
- how to develop and implement new instruments and technical standards for trade facilitation.

Through these International Forums on Trade Facilitation, the UNECE provides a neutral and accessible platform for open discussion about issues concerning trade facilitation. The topics range from the necessity to prepare and carry out capacity-building projects for developing and transition economies to setting technical standards, and to solving the outstanding questions in the way of multilateral negotiations for the creation of an equitable regime for the provision of the global public goods of trade facilitation. The participants in this Forum witnessed a dynamic debate on all these issues, including the role of the various United Nations bodies, the World Customs Organization (WCO) and the World Trade Organization (WTO) in trade facilitation. Being only four months away from the Fifth WTO Ministerial Conference in Cancún, it was not surprising that participants raised some of the leading issues in the debate on trade facilitation in the WTO. Many representatives from industrialized countries and the business sector expressed a strong wish to include trade facilitation in the multilateral trade negotiations. At the same time, representatives of the developing countries, as well as the United Nations regional commissions for Africa, Latin America and the Caribbean, and Western Asia, said that developing countries were concerned about the costs and potential consequences of subjecting trade facilitation to WTO rules-based mechanisms and enforcement.

The purpose of this book is to bring into the public domain the debate on the outlook of a global system for delivering the benefits of trade facilitation. This is not a debate that should occur only in the circles of representatives to the WTO, or behind the closed doors of governments or international organizations. Those whose work and lives will be affected should be involved in the establishment of the system, if it is to be democratic and based on consensus for development. The editors placed absolute priority on the need to communicate these important issues rather than on developing methodologies and ready solutions. Traders, customs services, freight forwarders and other agencies and professional players involved in international supply chains should find these papers of interest. We believe we achieved the objectives set out at the beginning of this project: to carry the political debate on trade facilitation into the public domain; bring the policy deliberations closer to the technical issues in trade facilitation; and contribute to the discussion on the construction of an international system for the provision of trade facilitation and its benefits.

The two UNECE Forums took place between the Doha and Cancún ministerial conferences of the WTO. This was a period when crucial decisions on building consensus for a future international regime of trade facilitation were expected. This book, in the same way as *Trade Facilitation: The Challenges for Growth and Development*, which came as a result of the first Forum, provides information on the positions of small and big players, during these two years, on whether WTO's binding rules should be the centrepiece of an international system of trade facilitation. Analysing this debate may help learn some lessons for the future construction of such a regime, if it has to be fair, equitable, and bearing contributions to security and stability in our world, which has recently become so insecure.

Towards an integrated system of trade facilitation

A trade facilitation regime
In the previous publication that followed the first International Forum on Trade Facilitation we wrote about the concept of trade facilitation in terms of producing international public goods. This was a recurrent theme in the debates at the second Forum as well. As was pointed out there, serious problems for the supply of the public goods of trade facilitation exist.[8] First, there is a strong incentive for free riding: why not sit quietly, while other states pay money to reform and automate their trade procedures - an improvement from which everyone will then profit? Various states and

---

[8] *Trade Facilitation: The Challenges...*, op. cit., pp. 17-23.

actors are thus entering a Prisoners' Dilemma game, which makes it difficult to achieve cooperation. To this is added the problem of ensuring the cooperation of "pivotal" states, such as India, Brazil, and some African countries, which can prevent the establishment of a certain form of international regime (based on WTO rules), if it does not correspond to their interests and vision of development.

The statements at the Forum, therefore, give two reasons for optimism. The first is the unanimous agreement that trade facilitation can create benefits for all. The second is the almost universal recognition of the need to construct an international regime to deal with the problems of public and private provision of the benefits of trade facilitation and with the allocation of its products. The debate is on the form of the future regime. Most developed countries and large companies with international supply chains argue that a working system of trade facilitation can only be based on the clear standards and disciplines of WTO's binding rules. Most developing countries do not agree with this, but they do not refuse the principle of an international regime either. Ambassador Hardeep S. Puri, Permanent representative of India to the United Nations in Geneva, repeatedly pointed out that a global trade facilitation regime, which would increase developing country benefits, is a "laudable goal". Yet he argued that the only way to achieve it would be for it to be progressive, voluntary, and not linked to WTO's enforceability provisions and dispute settlement mechanism. Gradualism, rather than establishing binding rules in the WTO, can help the developing countries "adjust to a common regime". This position was subsequently adopted by several large developing countries at the Fifth WTO Ministerial Conference in Cancún, in September 2003, where the countries did not reach a consensus on building an international system of trade facilitation based on WTO's binding rules. It is also regrettable that after the failure of the WTO Ministerial Conference in Cancún some of the leading trading nations gave preference to bilateral relations and agreements to advance trade facilitation, instead of a multilateral regime which would take care of an equitable system of sharing of the benefits among all participants in international trade.

No voting system on the provision of a public good produces the most efficient outcome, as it does not indicate the gradation of preferences of the various actors. There is an objective tendency to misrepresent preferences in the WTO negotiations, in order to manipulate the outcome. It would be wrong to assume that if representatives of various states did not achieve a consensus in the WTO in Cancún a large number of countries were against a multilateral regime for trade facilitation. Given the complex mechanisms of provision and allotment of the public goods of trade facilitation and of setting and implementing trade facilitation standards, which are often technically complicated, the most likely regime for the achievement of international trade facilitation would be a multilevel one. It would involve the public and private sectors: governments, various inter-governmental and non-governmental organizations, the business community and various segments of international civil society. In order to be sustainable, this system should address a series of concerns:

- How to establish a mechanism managing contributions by various actors.
- How to establish a mechanism providing adequate capacity building and technical assistance to developing and transition economies, small and medium sized enterprises, so that they receive a fair share of the benefits.
- How to give individual actors the right incentives in building an international system of trade facilitation.

Security in international trade
A system providing secure international trade should also be considered as a global public good which is non-exclusive and indivisible. Firstly, an actor who enjoys secure trade does not detract it from others. No state or company can provide trade security in isolation. The smallest breach, if it starts from a small place around the world and then lets a nuclear device enter and explode in the Port of New York, for example, would be fatal to the whole system and would bring world trade to a halt. The public sector is necessarily included in the provision of measures for secure trade, but no single government can provide either the resources or the broader political will necessary for effective security.

The statements at the 2003 Forum clearly demonstrated the fundamental importance of organizing a multilateral, collaborative regime for providing trade security. The collaborative approach has definite advantages over a system based on hegemony or power, as made clear by the US Deputy Customs Commissioner Douglas Browning. A hegemonic system can become an invitation for breaches and free riders, and this can render the cost of maintaining it too high. It would be a mistake to assume that the United States would want to become the world police officer in international trade, and pay for it too. The dilemma is whether a single state, be it as large as the United States, can provide "security from trade" for itself through such initiatives as the Container Security Initiative, or whether it should accept a global regime of trade security.

In terms of consistency with the "collective security" provisions of the United Nations Charter, a collaborative approach to security in international trade recognizes its public nature, as any threat to international supply chains becomes a concern for the whole international community. Recognizing the public nature of trade security will avoid the risk of discontent and upheaval against an eventual "hegemonic regime". Involving regional economic and development agencies is important, but the key is to keeping the global focus through such organizations as the United Nations and the World Customs Organization.

Yet a regime assuring maximum feasible protection for all from the threat of terrorism still has to be constructed. This system should be based on the rule of law (both national and international), and should involve civil society, for which destructive violence using the channels of free trade is unacceptable. It will manage the private provision of a global public good by individual states, interested private companies, NGOs, and international organizations. It may be possible for the United Nations to mobilize expertise in working bodies, in order both to set standards and build the political will for collective action. Yet in order to do this, some important questions need answers. How many and what measures would be enough for the system to be secure? How should order be enforced? Who should provide what? Who should pay – the public sector, traders, shippers, consumers, or others? How should financing (e.g. contributions and management) be organized? If the system is supported through the international organizations, should financing come from budgets of international organizations, special accounts, extrabudgetary programmes? A "club-like" method of financing has shown certain deficiencies in the United Nations, so more thought must be given to this issue. One possible measure for further consideration could be a special account for trade security, established in the United Nations to cover activities of experts and observers dealing with standards and their implementation.

One of the crucial problems in the changing security environment today is the lack of sufficient information on the capacities and intents of global terrorism. This is the reason for the massive and costly measures of urgent response. "Advance information" on cargo, traders, transporters, drivers, companies and personalities has become the catchphrase in this response. The world has entered a game of asymmetric information (and power) in the struggle against the terrorist threat. And a new type of dilemma has arisen from enhanced security measures in international trade - limiting imports from "risky" and poor countries may increase poverty and other social problems that nourish terrorism. Consequently, the response requires a global overview of the potential negative externalities, so that fixing one problem would not produce hundreds of others.

The "global public goods" approach to trade facilitation and security helps bridge the gap between "technical" and "policy" specialists in these areas. For example, at the Forum, a group of companies presented a *profiling infrastructure for trade security*, which would accumulate, fuse and verify data from many locations, and would provide access and flow of data for commercial shipments for each stakeholder involved in the shipment. Users would be all stakeholders, including ports, shippers, freight forwarders, insurers, law enforcement, customs, and security agencies. This tool would address the crucial problem of access to and sharing of data among all participants in the supply chain, as a common infrastructure does not exist, not even in developed countries. The idea is to develop a system working for all goods, modes of transport, and countries; to build "a utility that creates utilitarian good for the world", as Mr. Dean Kothmann characterized it in his contribution to this volume.

Identifying the benefits of a public good is never easy, especially when one faces opportunity costs and a choice between two public goods, as the choice in this case between free trade and enhanced security. Most contributors to this volume argue that, if the right approach is adopted, there should be no need for a trade-off between trade facilitation and secure trade, and that the two can be advanced together. One contributor believes that implementation of inspections in countries with porous borders results in reduced customs fees while country revenues rise. Goods arrive faster, with less theft; logistics suppliers use more accurate and easy to obtain data; society has better information on what is exported and what is imported; efficiency and transparency are improved; and corruption goes down. All participants benefit from improved logistics. Moreover, this improvement could pay for the functioning of the system. Allegedly, those who find value in smoother data flows, access to information and data generated on an early stage in the logistics chain will have an incentive for financing the management of the global trade security system.

The relationship between the provision of two global public goods - free and facilitated trade on the one hand and international trade security on the other – has to be considered seriously. Not all actors value them equally. There are negative externalities in strengthening security measures worldwide, and one should be careful not to wipe out the already established achievements of trade facilitation. Finally, we should consider how stronger security measures can increase efficiency and welfare in the world economy, thus contributing to the Millennium Goals of the United Nations: poverty reduction and development. Enhanced security should not be considered only as a mere response to a dangerous externality: the ultimate "public bad" of globalized terrorism. The response may produce further negative externalities. There will have to be a concerted effort made to achieve both trade facilitation and international trade security, so that all countries advance together, on the basis of the best available technology.

Facilitating the Dialogue

Mondher Zenaidi, Minister of Tourism, Trade and Handicrafts, Tunisia

It was an exc ellent initiative to bring together the contributions of distinguished experts and personalities, who fuelled the dialogue on the means to extend the benefits of trade facilitation to all. I see my participation in this debate as a tribute to a modern country, Tunisia. The topic is timely and important: how to ensure the fair distribution of the benefits of globalization and technical progress. Two challenges highlight the interest and importance of the debate among trading nations. Facilitating trade is at the centre of an important debate which started following the WTO ministerial conferences in Singapore and Doha. These conferences made it possible to tackle several issues related to the subject. There are potential ways to achieve consensus, and Tunisia, as a land of dialogue, has always worked for openness and cooperation, and will again work to promote understanding among countries. Many countries have produced concept documents and have shared experience, while showing their attachment to the multilateral trading system. The WTO Member States express sometimes differing views on the conclusions drawn from the exploratory and analytical work carried out in the WTO work programme. Yet the issues at stake are important and we have tried to bring the different views closer together. We have also tried to give answers to a number of questions related to this issue. How can we ensure the balance between the objectives of overall economic growth, which international trade must help to realize, with the need to ensure development in all its components and facets? This issue has to be addressed, taking into account the existing various points of view. And in this context there are two concerns: first of all the actual contours of the issue, which need to be better specified; and second, we need to create conditions for success in the WTO. It is highly desirable to identify practical measures to bring us closer to these objectives. The Forum benefited from the experience, skills and input of distinguished experts and executives, and the relevance of their points of view was a valuable and stimulating source for our future work.

Trade Facilitation as a Tool for Development

Paolo Garonna, Deputy Executive Secretary, UNECE

The main purpose of this Introduction is to express the most sincere gratitude vis-à-vis all those who contributed to the Second International Forum on Trade Facilitation, which the United Nations Economic Commission for Europe had the privilege of organizing and hosting. A Forum, following a centuries-old Roman tradition, is a place to meet, exchange ideas, discuss policies, and learn from one another. Its success depends on the active participation and different contributions of the many players that gather together and commit themselves to make it work. These players belong to different communities: first, the member governments of the UNECE, and the other countries of the world, which I am happy to remark contributed significantly to this Forum; second, the representatives of international organizations active in the field of trade facilitation, including the other UN regional commissions; the experts coming from the private sector, both the business community and civil society organizations; the academic experts and the people involved in research and development; and finally, the secretariat of the UNECE, which is extremely motivated to enable a productive and result-oriented discussion. To all these dedicated professionals, I wish to pay tribute.

I would like to illustrate the importance of the present discussion on trade facilitation by placing it in a context, with particular reference to the economic situation and the Doha development process, and by highlighting some of the main issues and new challenges that have to be addressed.

Overcoming uncertainty and stagnation in world trade

The economic environment in which the present discussion takes place is characterized by uncertainty and preoccupation. The global economy finds itself in a delicate situation, almost on a razor's edge! The main commentators, including the UNECE *Economic Survey of Europe*, point out that the prospects for output growth should improve in the medium term. This forecast is based on several relatively positive signals, including:

the good performance of productivity growth, the apparent bottoming out of the stock market sluggishness, the stimulus that the evolution of exchange rates should give to US exports, and therefore global demand, and the resilience of the recovery in Eastern Europe and the CIS, pulled by domestic demand.

However, the short-term outlook is still dominated by uncertainty and concern. Growth projections have been revised downwards. World trade is expected to grow at rates that rema in considerably below those of the late 1990s, and below what would be required to significantly bridge development gaps, thereby contributing to improve the standard of living and employment in the transition and developing world.

The well-known major imbalances in the world economy still remain to be addressed, and therefore continue to weigh on the short-term outlook. The *Economic Survey of Europe* has clearly identified these factors. These are, in particular: the excessive reliance on the US economy as the locomotive for world growth, and the inability of the EU to take this role; the structural adjustments required to make the EU more competitive and flexible; the growing US trade and balance of payment deficit; the need for bridging the huge capacity gaps and good governance gaps affecting the transition and emerging market economies. It will take a sustained and persistent effort in the medium term to rebalance these structural obstacles to trade development. The international community will have to keep applying pressure and raising awareness in order to stimulate corrective action.

Making progress in the Doha Development Agenda

One major means promoting economic recovery and sustainable development is trade liberalization. It has often been argued that progress in global trade talks would help remove a major obstacle to growth. This is particularly so in relation to the current round of negotiations, known as the "Doha development round", as for the first time it places the development issues at the centre of the trade liberalization strategy. It is well worth repeating that progress in the Doha agenda is absolutely necessary, even though the signals at this stage of the negotiations are not particularly encouraging.

TRADE FACILITATION AS A TOOL FOR DEVELOPMENT

The United Nations is fully committed to contributing in every possible way to the accomplishment of the Doha development objectives. This commitment is clearly enshrined in the Millennium Development Goals of peace, security and prosperity, towards which the UN as a whole is working. It is also implied by the need to follow up on the Monterrey Summit on Financing for Development, and the Johannesburg Summit on Sustainable Development. In sum, the support for the Doha agenda has been mainstreamed in the programme of work of all UN agencies, including the UNECE and its Principal Subsidiary Bodies, and the Committee for Trade, Industry and Enterprise Development, which has promoted the current Forum on Trade Facilitation. This Forum should be seen as a tool for helping the Doha process. Its ability to stimulate ideas, raise awareness, develop initiatives that can be fed into the process will be the litmus test of the success of the Forum, or for that matter of all that we do in the field of trade development.

To those who believe that achieving the objectives of the Doha development round with good results and in time represents a longer term task, and therefore can be considered as being relatively independent of the short-term outlook for the global economy, we have to say that they are wrong. It has been shown that making real progress in the negotiations, sticking to the agreed deadlines, overcoming obstacles, etc., has an immediate and significant impact on expectations, business and consumer confidence, the stock market and commodity markets. It can therefore stimulate the recovery, investment and job creation. On the contrary, lack of progress increases uncertainty, depresses expectations, and thereby undermines the prospects for stability and growth.

Towards a regional trade facilitation system in Europe and the CIS

Let me now turn to trade facilitation, the topic of this Forum. It is well known that trade facilitation figures prominently in the Doha development round. It is one of those issues, called the Singapore issues, for which preparatory work is under way before a decision is taken at Cancún on whether there will be formal negotiations or not, in the future. Moreover, trade facilitation interacts closely with many, or most, of the other issues studied, discussed or negotiated in the Doha process. It is therefore understandable that the topic has become linked and subjected to all the pressures, the tensions and the constraints inherent in the Doha framework. I hope that the present Forum will provide arguments, ideas and suggestions that can stimulate progress in the discussion on trade facilitation under way within the World Trade Organization.

One of the background papers for this Forum, sponsored by the United Kingdom, has provided a comprehensive review of the preparatory work and the issues at stake. The paper shows that some of the legitimate concerns of developing countries can be alleviated by appropriate measures aiming at bridging capacity gaps. It makes reference to a series of practical tools and ideas, such as regional and sub-regional seminars, the participation of developing and transition countries in setting standards and norms, the promotion of national development strategies, the increase in funding for technical assistance, etc. I trust that these ideas, among others, will be taken up and explored carefully, particularly by the Committee for Trade, Industry and Enterprise Development and its working parties.

The focus on building capacity for trade facilitation

The focus on capacity building for trade facilitation is important and should also be highlighted independently of the Doha process and the state of trade facilitation within that process. We can, therefore, foresee a major role played by the UN, and stimulate close collaboration among all the relevant agencies, national regional and global, and other stakeholders. This point is important and of a more general value: international cooperation on trade facilitation should be considered, and pursued vigorously independently of the WTO preparations and negotiations, given the direct and immediate benefits that such initiatives have on development and trade.

The vision of the "trade facilitation system" that is taking shape at the international level (both regionally and globally) could in fact envisage a two-track mechanism: alongside a possible rule-based component, integrated in the WTO, which is now being considered (but on this there are no decisions yet). There will certainly be a more flexible part, based on cooperation, "soft rules" or guidelines drawn out of good practice, benchmarking and exchange of national experience. It is in this context that capacity building, more flexible and voluntary mechanisms of cooperation or "open coordination" tools, as they are called in the EU experience, can play a fundamental role. The "trade facilitation system" will have to be multi-level, multi-stakeholder and flexible: but it will also have to be well integrated, coordinated and synergetic. In other terms, it will have to be a "system".

The UNECE continues to play a major role in setting standards and promoting the exchange of experience and technical assistance in this field, in cooperation with other agencies. It is now important that cooperation extends also to include implementation and capacity building, particularly to the benefit of the most vulnerable economies. Moreover, the UNECE will also have to take in this field a coordination role at the regional level among all the relevant stakeholders. I would strongly welcome the discussion on a "regional trade facilitation system" focused on capacity building in favour of transition and emerging market economies.

Trade facilitation and security

The present debate is strongly affected by new or emerging issues with relevant implications for trade facilitation. Let me start by dealing briefly with the challenges posed by security. Security represents a growing concern in many countries, not only in the industrialized world but also, and increasingly, in the developing world. The dramatic events of terrorist attacks that have hit the news recently provide a politically sensitive and emotionally charged environment in this question.

It is well understood and widely recognized that in the long run there is a strong positive correlation between trade development and peace or security. It is this very belief that was at the basis of the creation of the Common Market in Europe after the Second World War. It inspired the thinking of the founding fathers of the European Union and the pragmatic thrust of the Marshall Fund that supported the first steps of European integration. The same belief has promoted more recently both the EU initiative for the establishment of a free trade area in the Euro-Mediterranean region (the so-called "Barcelona process") and the project announced by President Bush for a free trade zone in the Middle East. Therefore there can be and there is no doubt that trade development and security go hand in hand.

However, what is true in the long run and in general may not necessarily be true always and in the short run. Indeed, in the new environment created by the 11 September attacks and the enhanced security concerns that these generated, the risk has become apparent that increased security measures and controls may have a negative impact on trade. This could feed a vicious circle of lack of confidence, growing obstacles to trade, and less open economies that in the long run becomes a boomerang on security itself.

The issue is not only analytical. It also has practical implications and specific arrangements to consider. It requires the pragmatic and empirical-evidence-driven approach that characterizes much of the international work on trade facilitation. Besides, this is an area of experimentation and innovation in many UNECE member countries from the US to Russia, from the EU to some CIS countries, under the pressure of emerging needs and in response to growing policy demand. Therefore sharing experience and learning from one another at the international level in this field appears very promising. As an introduction to this discussion, I wish to point out that the growing concern for security has already affected many areas of policy dialogue at the UNECE, and has become established in our programme of work. We can see this in transport and security, in energy security, in environmental security. It would also be interesting to share experience across different sectors. The UNECE has launched a series of initiatives on the economic dimensions of security. These initiatives have culminated in a cross-sectoral discussion at the 2003 annual session of UNECE, where support was expressed by member countries for the strengthening of a common framework for this sectoral work. Moreover, UNECE has been asked to contribute to the ongoing discussion at the Organization for Security and Co-operation in Europe on the development of a new strategy for security in the economic and environmental dimension, which was launched by the OSCE Porto Ministerial meeting in 2002. At the OSCE Economic Forum in Prague in May 2003, the UNECE presented a report on the economic dimension of security, drawing also on the work done to link security and trade facilitation. The basic elements of this common cross-sectoral approach to security are the following: (a) an integrated approach capable of delivering comprehensive "national security strategies" where the various elements - from customs to trade to transport, from trade facilitation to education, etc. – can be brought together, and security is mainstreamed in all relevant policy areas; (b) early warning and monitoring mechanisms: capable of giving value to a pro-active conflict-prevention approach based on robust evidence, sound indicators, and an informed or science based policy dialogue; (c) partnership: between the public and private sector, so that we can create a "security culture" in business and civil society, and all relevant players in fields such as research, statistics and policy analysis can effectively contribute. It is important to verify how and to what extent this common UNECE approach to security in the economic dimension applies to, and interacts with, trade facilitation.

New technologies and trade facilitation

A second emerging challenge concerns a relationship that has become established after many years: that is the relationship between trade facilitation and technical progress. If one wants to achieve multiple objectives, and has to deal with complex trade-offs, investing in technology can provide the best and definitive answer. An example can easily be drawn from the previous case of security and trade facilitation. If we want both enhanced security and easier trade, we need to develop new technical tools. Rather than staying on the trade-offs, we need to shift the trade-offs!

In spite of the long and well-established tradition, best exemplified by UN/EDIFACT and ebusiness, there are now new challenges. New technologies in fact mean not only telecommunications and computing, but also, increasingly nano-technology and bioscience. This concerns not only hardware and software, but also middle-ware and the required adjustments in organization, skill markets and the regulatory environment.

Questions linked to the digital divide, as part of the growing development and capacity gaps between the advanced world and the rest, need to be addressed as a priority, and figure prominently in the current debate in preparation of the World Summit on the Information Society taking place in Geneva in December 2003 and in Tunis in 2005. The discussion on trade facilitation should aim at providing inputs to the WSIS process.

Trade facilitation in post-enlargement Europe

Trade facilitation can play an important role in another of the main political questions facing Europe in this exiting, and critical time, following the decision to enlarge the EU by admitting 10 new member countries. The future relationship between the countries acceding to the EU and the non-acceding ones is a question of much controversy and debate. The future of a "wider Europe" has given rise to a series of initiatives and strategic reflections involving many countries, international organizations and first and foremost in the EU institutions, the European Commission, the Open Convention, the Parliament and the Council. The challenge is to make the enlargement a stepping-stone to a broader and deeper economic integration process involving all countries of the UNECE region.

Trade integration is a primary objective and concern: what will be the future of trade integration in the wider Europe following the EU enlargement? What specific forms and arrangements trade integration may take between the post-enlargement EU and the other non-acceding European countries? How can trade diversion and new obstacles to trade be avoided? What role can trade facilitation play in the wider-Europe integration framework? All these are quite relevant and politically sensitive questions, on which the UNECE has started a strategic reflection. It is important that all the stakeholders concerned cooperate, and that the UNECE, UNCTAD, ITC and other international organizations play an active role in cooperating with the European Commission and other EU institutions in developing ideas and suggestions capable of promoting trade integration and trade facilitation in the pan-European context.

Reaching the appropriate balance between multilateral, regional, and bilateral mechanisms

Finally, a challenge that needs to be addressed is to find an appropriate mix and balance amo ng multilateral, regional and bilateral mechanisms of trade facilitation. In the past there has been the tendency to consider multilateral mechanisms as necessarily alternative antagonistic and irreconcilable with bilatera l or even unilateral mechanisms. Now, a more mature stance is gaining strength, that of seeing those mechanisms as, on the contrary, playing a consistent and complementary role. The reality is that under certain conditions, multilateral regional and bilateral mechanisms can coexist, interact positively with one another and become mutually supportive. The United Nations is the appropriate framework for ensuring such consistency and a positive synergy, and thereby consolidating a sense of legitimacy and world order. As David Mitrany, one of the Founding Father of the UN, clearly envisaged more than fifty years ago, we can, and should establish a "working peace system", rather than a purely formal and legal system; a system based on collaboration, mutual aid, or better "an international ethic of mutual aid", and hope for the future.

The vision of a "trade facilitation system" we aim at designing, developing and implementing together in the future should be able to link together multilateral, bilateral, regional and sub-regional mechanisms, and even unilateral initiatives, in a commonly agreed, flexible and pragmatic framework consistent with both effectiveness and legitimacy. I believe the vision of such an order for trade facilitation would provide food for thought and relevant lesson well beyond the sphere of technicalities, and inspire new thinking in this crucial time of post-Iraq war discussion on UN reform and the new world order.

The Geneva trade facilitation forums will provide to such discussion more than simply a venue and a set of tools. They will bring with them the "spirit of Geneva" (ésprit de Genève), which was best captured and expressed by President Woodrow Wilson in the first of its Fourteen Points proclaimed in the famous Mount Vernon speech of 1918:

21

SHARING THE GAINS OF GLOBALIZATION

"Open covenants of peace, openly arrived at, after which there shall be no private international understandings of any kind but diplomacy shall proceed always frankly and in the public view" *(W.Wilson 1918).*

This is the essence of the Geneva Trade Facilitation Forum, and we are fully committed to translating this essence into reality to the benefit of trade and development.

Part One:

How to Achieve Benefits for All from Trade Facilitation?

There is a risk that transition and developing countries will not be able to receive a fair share of the benefits of globalization and global trade facilitation, and that they will be marginalized. And there is a great chance that the implications of this challenge for the weakest participants in the global trading system will be felt even stronger. The chapters in the following part address these problems and the necessity for the United Nations and the other international organizations to provide a neutral platform for their discussion and possible solutions.

Chapter 1.1
Sharing the Gains of Globalisation: The Importance of Trade Facilitation

Pascal Lamy, EU Commissioner for Trade

The fact that the International Forum on Trade Facilitation, organized by UNECE, took place in May 2003 reflected the enormous amount of international attention being rightly focused on trade facilitation. This conference came at a timely moment. We are preparing for the WTO's Cancún Ministerial Conference in September 2003, where we expect to launch formal negotiations on trade facilitation. So it is a good moment to take stock and see what is really at stake, because all of us want to expand our trading opportunities, all of us need to modernize our trade processes, and all of us want to manage our borders more efficiently. In short, all of us need to ensure that today's trade is not governed by yesterday's rules.

What I would like to do therefore is give you my views on the benefits of action on trade facilitation, why it needs to be tackled in the WTO, and why we need joined-up thinking on this question between the WTO, the UN, the World Bank and other key organizations.

Let me start out by recapping what is at stake in dollar and cents (or Euro) terms. The potential benefits of trade facilitation on a world scale are staggering. Independent and conservative studies suggest that improvements to trade processes could save business about $300 billion – a quarter or more of the total economic benefits flowing from the Doha Round. And these benefits would be widely shared between all countries. Small and medium sized enterprises in developing countries are the obvious targets, since they do not have the resources to deal with procedures, red tape, delays, lack of transparency. And let us not forget that these are fixed, deadweight costs with no benefit: leakages from the system, if you will. Equally, big companies, with modern supply chains and multi-country production structures, will also derive considerable gains.

But that is not the only benefit of simple, modern trade procedures. They are also a key element in creating a helpful environment for inward investment. Ease of import and export procedures have been identified by business as a key factor in taking investment decisions.

And the cost of not taking action on the other hand is huge. If we do not adapt trade procedures to today's trading realities we will lose competitiveness. There is a risk of being marginalized and cut out of international trade flows. Instead of gaining new trade opportunities, countries may lose existing ones. Foreign direct investment might seep out instead of flowing in.

Governments also gain from trade facilitation: in terms of increasing their capacity to collect revenue; in terms of building up a good relationship with the trading community; and in terms of more efficient procedures that save administrative costs and improve border security and controls.

I am sure I am already preaching to the converted. We all understand the benefits of trade facilitation. The issue, as we approach Cancún, is a different one: why do we need WTO to take this important subject forward? And how can WTO, the UN and others work together?

On the first point, by adopting WTO commitments on trade facilitation we ensure that all countries move down the path of reform together. It is easier to do something when everyone is doing it and where the gains for our traders around the world can easily be seen. Through WTO we can all go in the same direction, put in place rules that will apply globally, with massive savings to business, and avoid leaving some countries out in the cold. That, in the end, is the comparative advantage of WTO commitments and it is this predictability and transparency that is valued so highly by both local and international business. Commitments in the WTO lock in and make irreversible domestic customs reforms, which could otherwise be reversed, go off track, or be blocked by short-term political considerations or by vested interest groups, domestic or foreign.

Which brings me to the relationship with work in other international organisations. My own view on this is that with WTO on the scene we complete the international architecture, we add the missing piece of the jigsaw puzzle. The reality has been that while various international attempts within the UN, UNCTAD, UNECE, WCO, and other organizations to progress on trade facilitation have been laudable, and have had some results, they have not yet realised the promise of a high and more uniform level of facilitation worldwide. The WTO can provide a common frame, the political mandate, and a legal basis for common action. The WTO can create the basic framework within which other organisations can work as partners – either by setting standards, developing best practices, or delivering aid to developing countries. The work of other international organisations will also start to yield the results they were meant to yield. UNECE has, of course, an important role to play here.

I hope it is pretty clear from my remarks that trade facilitation is in no way a North–South issue, nor a mercantilist issue, with winners and losers, but rather it is one where all WTO members will have to make some effort but where in return all WTO Members will gain. The EU is a prime example. Our own exporters will benefit from easier import procedures in other countries. But, equally, our companies are keen to see procedures for exporting out of the EU made simpler, and both exporters to the EU and our importers are eager to see more modern and simple processes for import into the EU – faster release at the border and so on - particularly when we are dealing with the challenge of ensuring simple, coherent and modern import and export regimes across an enlarged market of 25 EU Members. So, if the example here in Europe is anything to go by, efforts will be needed by developed countries and developing countries alike.

For developing countries and in particular the least developed ones, I wish to stress three points. First, we must design commitments in the WTO that everyone can implement, and allow sufficient time for implementation. I have insisted on this "acid test", and believe that what is on the table meets the test. Secondly, we should not try to harmonise procedures for trade facilitation. I am more interested in rules that set us all in a common direction of reform than ones that impose a prescriptive, single solution. The road we take is as important as the final destination. And third, we must – and will - supply trade-related assistance to implement the results of negotiations. The EU will carry its part of the burden, and in fact we have pledged about 500 million euros for trade facilitation in the next four years. Other developed countries and international organisations must also help and above all we need to coordinate it. Developing country partners must do their part of the job by integrating trade facilitation and customs modernisation in their national development strategies, and we are starting to see this, I am glad to say.

With the right commitments in place in the WTO, and with a big international effort, we can make real improvements to the global trading system. Improvements that will help our market access, of course, but also improvements to a set of existing GATT rules on trade facilitation and transit that have not been looked at for fifty years, that have not kept up with the revolutionary changes in how business is done, and that are in sore need of updating.

The great irony, given the clear importance of trade facilitation, is how little attention has been devoted to it in the current Doha Development Agenda. In fact someone said to me the other day that trade facilitation has been the Cinderella of the Doha Round. Perhaps it is time, with everyone's help and common effort, that its beauty is recognized, and that it gets its ticket to the ball.

Chapter 1.2
How and under what Conditions can Developing Countries be Enabled to Receive a Better Share of the Benefit of Trade Facilitation?

Hardeep Puri, Ambassador of India to the United Nations Office at Geneva

It is with pleasure that I accept the invitation of UNECE to write on a theme that is not only topical but touches the very heart of the trade facilitation issue – establishing a positive relationship between trade and development. However, I would like to rephrase the proposition somewhat, given the ground reality that we face and to pose it as follows: How and under what conditions can developing countries be enabled to receive a better share of the benefit of trade facilitation?

We base ourselves on the fact that the developing countries are at present significantly handicapped in the race towards trade facilitation, mainly due to resource constraints and physical, social and trade infrastructure related inadequacies, given their stage of development. Their own efforts towards modernization and automation of trade procedures, particularly customs procedures and the support of the international community will thus crucially determine the benefits to them, as will the pace and terms of their integration in this area.

Many developing countries so far have been autonomously moving towards an approximation of the four main ideals of rationalization, simplification, harmonization and automation of trade procedures, especially customs procedures, with emphasize on use of modern IT tools like EDI. Taking my country India's example, we have implemented the EDI at 23 customs locations covering major ports, airports, inland container depots and freight stations which cover 75% of India's international trade. An EDI Gateway Project, under implementation, would provide a flexible and highly reliable framework to Customs for exchange of electronic messages with other partners. Fast Track Clearance Scheme,

Self Assessment Scheme and an Accelerated Clearance of Import and Export Scheme [ACS] have been introduced on a pilot basis at a few ports. A Project team on Customs Re-engineering is working on several projects including Post Clearance Audit and Risk Management Strategy. Transparency is assured through real time availability of all rules and notifications on the DGFT/CBEC websites. Tariff structures have themselves been simplified through slab reductions on a number of duties and exemption notifications.

So it is recognized by developing countries that trade facilitation and efficiency is not only the wave of the future but a necessity of the present. Apart from autonomously working towards trade facilitation, a number of them are participating in voluntary schemes for trade facilitation convergence in the regional integration context. Multilaterally, this matter is being dealt with in the World Customs Organization. Efforts, however, are being made by developed countries to bring trade facilitation within the purview of the WTO as part of the "Singapore Issues", presumably to make compliance with trade facilitation standards mandatory for all countries as part of a single undertaking with all that this implies in terms of binding, dispute settlement linked obligations.

The WTO and the mandatory compliance route to bridge the trade facilitation gap between developed and developing countries is not fair, desirable or in the best interests of either the developing countries or the development-oriented trading system promised at Doha. Such an approach would ignore the reality of their resource constraints and crowd out their own welfare and development priorities. Instead, the correct approach would be a development led route which would allow developing countries to adapt and, as appropriate, adopt global best practices according to their own capacities, interest, priorities, resources and time lines.

This is particularly important when we consider that most of the trade facilitation standards that are being evolved and held up as models are those that are devised by the developed countries in the light of their own needs, experiences, capacities and objectives and bring to bear state-of-the-art technology and tools at their command. Their compliance with a global regime will be virtually cost free for them. Thus, not being standard makers, only standard takers, developing countries have a double disadvantage in trying to upgrade their trade infrastructure. They are challenged to adopt something which is not home grown and bear the cost of adjustment too.

Therefore, in order that trade facilitation yields efficiency and welfare benefits to developing countries, the following prerequisites need to be accepted and put in place:

1. Trade facilitation should not be looked at as an end in itself but a means to the goal of increasing trade revenues and thus development dividends for developing countries from international trade and investment. It is a process not a destination.

2. Trade facilitation should not be treated as a mechanical process which if addressed or redressed will at one stroke remove all the transaction related difficulties that the trade of developing countries faces. What is required is a systemic approach to different obstacles posed to an efficient flow of trade of developing countries that looks at both at the forward and backward linkages and the totality of their trade facilitation needs relating to their exports as much as their imports.

3. By backward linkages, I mean the supply chain of trade efficiency – the entire realm of production, transport, services infrastructure and legal framework which feed into the developing countries' international trade effort. This has an impact on the speed, cost and predictability with which trade operations are actually completed. As we all know, in many developing countries, unless deficiencies in the state of road, rail, air and port infrastructure - physical and institutional and their high costs - are addressed, merely tinkering with customs procedures will not bring the promised benefits in terms of reducing barriers to trade, lowering transaction costs, dealing with corruption, raising revenues, making them more competitive from the perspective of global transnational corporations (TNC) and business community, and giving a fillip to their trade and investment opportunities and prospects.

4. By forward linkages I mean the international transport, logistical and financial frameworks and the complex trade restrictive procedures followed by developed countries which are their main markets. The low level of control developing countries have on the external dimension of facilitation related to their export trade is an issue of major concern and no amount of reform at the domestic end to strengthen the backward linkages will be able to compensate for their vulnerability in relation to the forward linkages. Several studies, including those by the UNCTAD, have pointed to the problems faced by developing countries in this area and to the fact that these external processes are largely controlled by the developed countries and their economic operators and have serious implications for developing countries.

5. One only needs to look at the security related initiatives recently taken such as the Customs, Trade Partnership against Terrorism [C-TPAT] and the adoption of measures such as the Container Security Initiative to understand how these could prove major drawbacks for developing countries in international trade and transport systems. It would involve re-routing of trade flows between certain origins and destinations, in particular those in the United States, and call for a very high level of supply chain management capability, technological and financial resource mobilization and significant disruption of developing country trade while adding costs to their already heavy trade facilitation agenda.

6. There are valid and legitimate reasons for developing countries to follow a staged path to establish an autonomous, sustainable trade management infrastructure. As UNCTAD has emphasized, the "objective is to facilitate in order to better control, and better control for better management". Developing countries have their own security concerns and their cultural, social, political contexts within which they have to work out trade facilitation strategies. These concerns of developing countries are as relevant as concerns that may drive measures taken by some developed country partners and which profoundly affect the trade facilitation environment in key markets for developing countries.

7. Developing countries would like to simplify procedures for their own exporters and for foreign operators trading with their country. They would like to raise revenue realization and compliance, and the

efficiency and cost effectiveness of their international trade transaction. For this, they have a right to set their own methodology and time frame within the human and financial resources that they can spare and mobilize, adopting best practices as they think fit.

8. Those pushing for an enforceable multilateral regime on trade facilitation in WTO argue that a voluntary approach is too slow and ineffective and, therefore, there is need to speed up the process of developing countries joining a world class trade facilitation regime. This logic is unacceptable. It is in developing countries' interest to make haste slowly so that they are able to manage the balancing of the cost and benefit of trade facilitation integration according to their ability, technological and institutional preparedness, and control across the supply chain of efficiency on one hand, and the external elements of the trade facilitation framework on the other.

9. The WTO is not a suitable forum for dealing with trade facilitation issues and there seems to be no reason for duplicating work which has been on going in the World Customs Organization – an expert customs body, in the context of the revised Kyoto Convention of WCO. There is no need to bring procedural issues to the WTO, a body focused more on trade rules, rights and obligations.

10. What could be particularly harmful to developing countries is if binding rules on trade facilitation are lodged in the WTO with the possibility of enforcing these rules through the dispute settlement mechanism. Even a developing country like India will find it difficult to meet standards of automation and modernization at all its ports, airports and land customs stations. Questions could be raised not only about whether the right systems are in place but whether a particular developing country is operationally in compliance. Promises of special and differential treatment (S&D) cannot be taken at face value given the lack of progress in this area in the Doha negotiations so far. The "one size fits all" transition time that may be offered will be of scant comfort and utility. Trade facilitation would thus become another onerous obligation on developing countries and provide developed countries with yet another sophisticated instrument for trade harassment against developing countries.

11. The debate so far in the context of the Doha Declaration to undertake exploratory and analytical work has involved a review of several GATT [1994] Articles, especially Articles V, VIII and X. Developed countries have made proposals to reinforce these provisions with a view to negotiating binding rules. Developing countries on the other hand have not responded positively and pointed instead to the lack of implementation of some of the key agreements with trade facilitation dimensions such as Rules of Origin, Technical Barriers to Trade (TBT), Sanitary and Phyto-Sanitary measures (SPS), and Customs Valuation.

12. It would be far better if there is concentration on finalizing work on these existing agreements which have profound implications for trade facilitation and on which developed country partners have not shown any political will to move. Two such issues are Rules of Origin and TBT/SPS which could go a long way in trade facilitation from the point of view of developing countries and give them real benefits. In fact, the developed countries unwillingness and underperformance on speedy harmonization of Rules of Origin illustrates the double standards on the harmonization issue.

13. For developing countries a flexible approach to harmonization of national systems to some international guidelines as opposed to a set of binding obligations would be optimally beneficial. It would allow them the benefit of progressive trade facilitation and integration while avoiding the loss of policy autonomy and additional institutional burden as well as high imp lementation costs.

14. The issue of costs is very important since we are talking about how trade facilitation benefits to developing countries can be increased. The history of the Uruguay Round of Multilateral Trade Negotiations (MTNs) give us a warning against pushing developing countries into agreements that impose heavy costs on them or are resource intensive without upfront and binding financial commitments from the international community. According to World Bank economists the implementation of only three of these resource-intensive agreements – SPS, TRIPS and Customs Valuation would on average cost a typical developing country at least $150 million, not to speak of outgoings in terms of revenue loss or development and welfare foregone.

In conclusion, I would like to reaffirm that the only way to reach the laudable goal of a global trade facilitation regime in a manner that increases developing country benefits from it and from international trade, is for it to be progressive, voluntary and not linked to WTO's enforceability provisions and dispute settlement mechanism. It could be based on some guidelines and proven systems for trade management. Regional efforts among developing countries and on a North-South basis, which help the developing countries gradually adjust to a common regime, could be useful stepping-stones to a global regime. Reinforcement of capacity building and technical assistance, both bilateral and by organizations such as UNCTAD, would go some way in catalyzing the process. Substantial and additional financial resources should be provided by international financial institutions (IFIs) and the donor community to developing countries to meet the institutional and other adjustment costs, and also to upgrade their entire trade and transport infrastructure both in the short and medium term. Implementing other key aspects of trade facilitation already agreed to in the WTO, especially those which have serious market entry implications for developing countries in regard to developed countries markets and which raise the cost of trade transactions and affect their competitiveness, such as Rules of Origin, TBT and SPS, should be a priority for developed country compliance and positive action. No trade constricting and displacing measures should be taken by developed countries, including in the area of trade, transport and facilitation infrastructure, which may have a detrimental effect on developing country exports and on their trade and investment gains.

Chapter 1.3
Trade Facilitation in the Multilateral Trade Negotiations

Roderick Abbott, Deputy Director-General, World Trade Organization (WTO)

I want to start with a message from the WTO as to where we are and what we are doing with reference to trade facilitation before the Fifth Ministerial Meeting in September 2003. Trade facilitation, in a way, is one of the easiest things to talk about, because it is difficult to find someone who is against it, and if you consider that it is attacking obstacles to trade of all kinds, reducing costs of the transactions and simplifying procedures, then it is easy to see why everyone is in favour. But the challenge that it poses, in fact, is: not everyone is ready to do much about it.

In the WTO, we believe that this is close to the heart of our members, the whole purpose of the WTO and the GATT before it is indeed to facilitate trade. So this subject is not in a way a new issue but just a fresh name for an effort, which is as old as the multilateral trade itself. What is perhaps more recent is the strong recognition of its importance. Governments no longer see this as a mechanical rather technical problem - it has been described as the plumbing of trade policy - but as a core element of the external trade and development policies of members.

Against this background, the participants at the Fourth WTO Ministerial Conference at Doha in 2002 gave an extended trade facilitation mandate to the WTO secretariat and members when launching a new round of negotiations. And you will be familiar with the terms of this in paragraph 27 of the text, which refers to the negotiations which "will take place after the fifth session of the Ministerial conference", that is the meeting that is coming up in Cancún in September, and I am quoting, "on the basis of a decision to be taken by explicit consensus on the modalities of the negotiations". Like many international texts, this is subject to different understandings. Some people believe that a decision of principle has been taken and that all we need to do is to agree on a roadmap, the timetable, what it is that we are going to be doing. Other people feel that the decision of principle has still to be taken because the modalities are essential and therefore there is still a serious decision to be taken by consensus.

Now, be that as it may, we have a job to do until the time of Cancún, and we have been tasked with a comprehensive work program with three main elements: the first being to review and, as appropriate, to clarify or try to improve some of the existing provisions in GATT 1994 and particularly Articles 5, 8 and 10, and I will come back to that below. The second task is to identify the needs and the priorities of members in this field of trade facilitation and particularly the needs of developing countries and the least developed. The third element is that Ministers committed themselves to ensuring adequate technical assistance and support for capacity building in this area. For the latter we have quite a large programme ongoing, the chief component being a large number of missions to various countries in order to explain what the issues are, to help them to understand, and to build capacity for negotiation.

The three elements that I mentioned are the main pillars of the work program and what we therefore have to do is to see how to translate this to day-to-day work. The main item which the members and the delegations have spent time on is the first one, the review and clarification of the articles that I mentioned. Consequently, I will focus the remaining part of this paper on what they have been doing. Ambassador Luzius Wasescha of Switzerland, Chairman of the International Forum on Trade Facilitation, mentioned that there had been unconvincing signals about progress in the Doha negotiations. As a general comment, that is a fair point because, as the press has made clear, we have not made progress everywhere as we would have liked. Yet my message, as far as trade facilitation is concerned, is that the signals are very convincing. No one is against it, and we have stirred up people's interest a bit, to try to do something, to advance work in this area.

The Articles that I mentioned deal with three different aspects. Article 5 fundamentally deals with goods in transit and freedom of transit, especially for land-locked countries, but that is not the only situation.

Article 8 deals with fees and formalities and documents at importation, and Article 10 deals with the obligation for publishing regulations and for transparency in the general sense.

Over the months and in preparation for this Cancún Conference we received about 15 written proposals from members on how we should go about the exercise. Let me highlight the most relevant aspects in terms of what it might mean for new rules. The common thread which runs through many of these proposals is to enhance the transparency and predictability, both by making information more freely available, which means strengthening the obligations to publish - or to at least make texts available - and to expand the involvement of all stakeholders engaged in trade, because this is the feedback that we need to find out what needs to be done. A particular point that members would like to focus on is to allow for reasonable and as far as possible standard periods of time between the adoption of measures, the legislative process, and its entry into force, so that traders and people involved in custom clearance have time to adapt.

These considerations of transparency and predictability are also reflected in other suggestions which aim at standardizing data and documentation requirements and indeed reducing them where possible and simplifying procedures. There has been a certain emphasis on strengthening due process leading to a call for a right of appeal, a legal and non-discriminatory right of appeal against customs and other government agency rulings and decisions. The further enhancement of this non-discrimination aspect is certainly a key objective behind proposals which aim to strengthen the freedom of transit of goods by eliminating any remaining instances of discrimination in that area where we find them.

All of these measures would not only strengthen those GATT articles which exist but would enhance underlying and general WTO principles, transparency, predictability and non-discrimination, well known to be the fundamental principles in our work.

They would also reinforce what is increasingly and importantly becoming a rules-based treaty, a rules-based organization, and one of the aspects which would follow from having a new agreement is that there would be some dispute settlement process which would shed light on some legal questions which up to now have not really been examined. That is a brief resume of what we have been doing.

To what extent these various proposals will be realized, is up to the members to decide in Cancún against the above background. But what we can say at the moment is that all members agree on the importance of this and on advancing the work. Whatever differences there might be of interpretation, there has been very good cooperation and participation. We had a period when, after the events of the 11 September 2001, the United States slightly withdrew from the work, while they thought about the security implications that have been mentioned by others. That is now finished; they have come back and are also participating very actively in the discussion.

There are different views and it is only right to say that our membership remains divided on how some of these suggestions might be used. On the one side, several countries would like to see the obligations seen in GATT Articles 5, 8, and 10 turned into binding rules. They think this is essential to ensure that all current efforts to improve the situation do indeed go in the same direction. It ensures necessary high level of commitment, if it is going to be binding, and probably harnesses private sector support. Other countries have raised objections, especially in the developing world, about having a rule-making exercise. They support the goal, but they do express their concerns about their limited capacities to implement the rules, and in particular to being exposed to rigorous dispute settlement procedures. These members would have a preference for new measures in the non-binding form, something like guideline codes of conduct, best endeavour, clauses, or something of that kind.

Those different views will have to be reconciled in Cancún, which is not the end of the story, but it will be the beginning, I think, of a more specific negotiation, as long as we get the famous "modalities" agreed. The concerns of the developing countries have to be taken seriously. The proponents of new rules have made it clear that they want upfront commitments on technical assistance, capacity building and other issues, to be an integral part of the negotiations, and we are trying already to do so. Special differential treatment is an important element, but it needs to be defined what does this actually mean in this particular context.

We have been giving thought and so have members to the dispute settlement concerns with some delegations looking for "creative solutions"; but whether that means that there would be some differentiation in the commitments of members which goes against the principle of a single undertaking with the same rights and obligations for everybody, whether it means a transitional period where some countries would be allowed not to apply the rules fully or some other form of adjustment, this remains to be seen, and perhaps to be negotiated during the next stage. Any more specific assessment would be, frankly, a risky business.

In conclusion, I would like to say two words about the new security initiatives seen from a WTO angle. This is an area where one risks having contradiction between security objectives and the objectives of trade facilitation. To put it more strongly, some of these initiatives have to try to address the obvious requirement to improve security, for example with reference to containers going through ports, but at the same time they should not set up either discriminatory elements where some countries, some traders, would be treated differently from others, or extra obstacles to trade or indeed extra costs. I would like to be an optimist and say that these two objectives can be combined, but I think this is quite difficult to realize. I am not sure what would be the outcome if some of the WTO members decided to challenge some of these initiatives on the basis that they are not in line with WTO rules. Fortunately, we do not have such a challenge yet. We will have to deal with it the day it comes, and if it comes. But I wanted just to give a few indications of my own hesitations about how some of these security initiatives would play in a broader context.

Chapter 1.4
Trade Facilitation: Benefits and Capacity Building for Customs

Kunio Mikuriya, Deputy Secretary General, World Customs Organization (WCO)

I would like to express my appreciation to the UNECE for its efforts to support trade facilitation, as we believe that customs is one of major players in this area. In this article, I would like to say how customs could play a role in achieving benefits for all from trade facilitation. Then, I will point out how recent security concerns should be based on and incorporated in the existing trade facilitation efforts. Finally, I will introduce a customs capacity building strategy that we are currently developing to assist customs administrations in promoting a comprehensive customs reform.

In responding to the Doha Declaration on trade facilitation, the WTO Council for Trade in Goods (CTG) has made a good progress in reviewing relevant Articles of the GATT 1994. While standardization and simplification of customs procedures has been one of the focuses in the WTO discussion, we welcome this undertaking by the WTO, since this is precisely the area that the WCO has been committing resources to and championing for the past 50 years. We expect that the WTO task will bring the political will and commitment, enhanced cooperation from the trade, and the realignment of resources to customs capacity building, all of which are necessary ingredients for reform and modernization of customs that the WCO has advocated for years. Another important benefit of the WTO focus will be the improvement in co-ordinated intervention of border agencies, resulting in a "Single Window" approach. We will join the efforts made by the UNECE in this regard, as customs procedures are only a part of the entire trade procedures.

Moreover, the WTO discussion has resulted in a general understanding among WTO members on the complementary nature of the WTO rules and the WCO instruments in the customs area. The WTO rules set high principles and the WCO instruments, including the revised Kyoto Convention, provide implementation tools for these principles. In fact, the WCO has developed and maintained instruments that provide the key principles for simple, effective and modern procedures that trade also requires in the competitive business environment. All the provisions and the principles in the WCO instruments are compatible with and complementary to the relevant GATT Articles. Especially, the revised Kyoto Convention and its accompanying guidelines provide the basis and practical guidance and information for the implementation of the WTO high principles. These instruments are designed to offer solutions that allow countries to meet their legitimate goals of revenue collection and protection of society, while at the same time delivering practical trade facilitation dividends.

To elaborate, the revised Kyoto Convention provides international standards based on the core principles for modern customs procedures, including:

- Transparency and predictability;
- Standardization and simplification;
- Maximum use of information technology;
- Minimum necessary control to ensure compliance;
- Risk management to facilitate legitimate trade while maintaining effective control;
- "Fast track" procedures for traders with good compliance record ("Authorized traders" concept);
- Co-operation and partnership with all stakeholders including government agencies, the private sector and other customs administrations.

These principles also provide a long-term solution to address the integrity issue, one of the major obstacles to trade facilitation, and to economic and social development.

In addition, we have been working on a number of supporting initiatives, including the WCO Customs Data Model to establish standard data sets and electronic formats for most commercial declarations. Moreover, we have developed the Unique Consignment Reference (UCR) concept that would provide each consignment with a common reference number to enable authorities to trace and control the whole logistical chain, thereby providing end-to-end prime service. Other examples include the Memorandum of Understanding (MoU) programme to enhance partnership with the private industry and the Time Release Study to identify potential bottlenecks in the clearance procedures for benchmarking activities. These initiatives have been developed as measures to facilitate legitimate trade while ensuring effective customs control. They could also be utilized to secure the entire supply chain, an issue that I will take up below.

We expect the WTO work on trade facilitation to draw the attention of the international community to and considerably enhance the revised Kyoto Convention and other WCO instruments. Indeed, with the growing appreciation of trade facilitation, the revised Kyoto Convention has got a momentum for their effective implementation. In addition to the 14 members that have already ratified the revised Kyoto Convention, both the European Council, in March 2003, and the United States President, in May 2003, approved the Convention, upon the completion of their respective administrative procedures. The two biggest trade players are expected to move forward quickly to complete their parliamentary procedures for formal accession. Moreover, many countries have already incorporated the principles of the revised Kyoto Convention in their national legislation, without waiting for its formal entry into force. The WCO, on its part, has continued to review the Kyoto guidelines and, in March 2003, updated the Kyoto Information Technology Guidelines. Now we need effective implementation of these facilitation measures and this is where capacity building plays an important role. The Doha Declaration has also identified this as a matter of priority, as we will see below.

Addressing the security concerns in international trade, the customs community has continued to make solid progress during the last year. How do we see the new security initiatives in relation to the existing trade facilitation measures? As security is a common concern in a highly globalized world economy, a multilateral approach is imperative to address this worldwide issue in consistence with existing bilateral and regional approaches. In June 2002, the WCO Council unanimously adopted its Resolution on Security and Facilitation of the International Trade Supply Chain[9]. We took special care in responding to security concerns without compromising the facilitation efforts that we had been pursuing. Many people made the observation that security and facilitation are two sides of the same coin, because the efficient and effective customs procedures that address security concerns will surely facilitate the legitimate trade as well. While this is a new area of activity for customs and involves a strategic partnership with the private sector, most of the concepts contained in the Resolution - including risk management, advance electronic transmission of standardized customs data, co-operation with the private sector, and exchange of information - have already been well developed and incorporated in the WCO instruments that are designed to promote trade facilitation while enhancing effective control. That is why the Resolution urged the early implementation of the revised Kyoto Convention.

Under the new initiative, customs attention will be expanded from the traditional focus on import to cover the entire supply chain including the point of export. Security is undertaken as early as possible, ideally before the container is stuffed at the exporters premises. Risk management will be performed to identify high-risk goods on the basis of information supplied at this early stage, normally by the exporter. Our security initiative is based on a secure and authorized supply chain, with all key players in that chain contributing towards an increased level of security. The system will also allow for mutual recognition of authorized traders from one country to another. This should lead directly to more predictable, reduced risk, less opportunity for theft and pilferage in the supply chain and increased opportunities for facilitation of businesses that contribute to enhancing security standards. Whereas the risks of terrorist threats are currently a primary concern, WCO Members, and 161 Directors General of Customs around the world, consider that customs should build their security and facilitation capacity to identify and reduce the risks associated with all types of security including economic and revenue security. These must be

---

[9] www.wcoomd.org/ie/En/Recommendations/Resol 2002 E (8).pdf

integrated with customs efforts to intercept prohibited items, such as illegal drugs, counterfeit products and other form of contraband, which will help to restrict the large scale funding opportunities for organized criminal and terrorist groups.

Since June 2002 the WCO Task Force has been working to implement the recommendations contained in the Resolution with the active participation of all stakeholders, including the relevant international organizations, as well as a wide range of trade and transport bodies. The Task Force is expected to deliver the following three of the key issues identified in the Resolution to the WCO Council Sessions next month for its consideration and approval:

- Re-examination of the Customs Data Model to ensure it includes the essential data elements to identify high-risk cargo;
- Development of guidelines for a legal and other procedural basis to enable the advance electronic transmission of customs data;
- Development of guidelines for cooperation between customs and private industry.

The Task Force has already identified the 27 essential data elements to identify high-risk goods to be included in the Customs Data Model. It has also finalized proposed Customs Guidelines on Advanced Cargo Information, based on the revised Kyoto Convention and supported by the UCR concept, to enable the advance electronic transmission of customs data. A legal draft of a multilateral instrument on Mutual Administrative Assistance and draft Guidelines for national legislation have also been developed in this regard.

In addition to the three tasks that the Task Force has so far concentrated on, the Resolution identified the following five longer-term aspects:

- Promotion of the security and facilitation tools;
- Identification of customs needs in establishing a supply chain security regime;

- Identification of donors;
- Development of customs techniques and implementation of procedures; and
- Development of databank on advanced technology which has already been established.

While the WCO has already made good progress in these areas, it will continue to actively pursue its mission in supply chain initiatives with a longer perspective, because these issues, and capacity building in particular, require longer-term and effective efforts in close partnership with the relevant players.

After these comments on the necessity for effective implementation of supply chain initiatives and in response to the Doha call for trade facilitation, I would like to move on to capacity building. Based on the request from last year's WCO Council session, we have developed a Customs Capacity Building Strategy as a business case for well designed and targeted capacity building investments focused on improving the efficiency and effectiveness of customs. While technical assistance and training for each specific area, which many organizations including the WCO have been delivering, are important, capacity building needs to go beyond a series of narrowly focused activities to embrace a more comprehensive and long-term approach designed to address all areas of customs administrations. We believe that such a broad and comprehensive customs reform can deliver significant dividends for governments, donors and the private sector, and allow developing countries to take advantage of the many development opportunities provided by the global trading system. A well performing and ethical customs administration can make a major contribution to effective revenue mobilization and can help governments to facilitate trade and investment and increase confidence in the quality and integrity of government institutions, leading to good governance. It can also contribute to the protection of the community from a range of threats to social and national security. While the capacity building needs for developing countries are huge in scale and scope, the past capacity building initiatives have not always met the initial expectation. By way of example, in some cases the mistake was caused by an inaccurate diagnosis due to the lack of high quality diagnostic tool or experts, as "one size fits all" solutions simply do not work. We need "situational" solutions. In other cases, the lack of post-implementation support for information technology systems resulted in a failure of sustainable IT infrastructure. We have many lessons to learn from experience, including these examples, to improve capacity building.

The Customs Capacity Building Strategy includes:
- The case for comprehensive capacity building in customs;
- What capacity building means in the customs context by identifying the key principles of the revised Kyoto Convention, including the integrity aspect, as providing the basis for all capacity building activities;
- Lessons learned from the previous capacity building initiatives;
- The outcome of the survey of our members on capacity building needs and challenges, including specific needs associated with the implementation of the Resolution on Security and Facilitation of the International Trade Supply Chain;
- Roles and responsibilities of potential stakeholders and partners;
- Proposal for a standardized and comprehensive diagnostic tool for capacity building, which ensures linkage to WCO instruments and best practice approaches, thus allowing customs administrations to base their procedures on internationally accepted standards.

This Strategy document is an attempt to respond to the Doha Declaration where Ministers committed themselves to capacity building in customs-related areas, particularly in relation to trade facilitation, and a contribution to the WTO Ministerial Conference in Cancún, in September 2003. It will also cover the request of the "Resolution". With this document we intend to help customs administrations and all stakeholders mobilize all available resources for capacity building. While, the WCO is ready to assist members in technical assistance and capacity building support, it is up to each customs administration to take a strategic approach and all stakeholders to commit themselves to the practical implementation of capacity building.

Finally, I would like to stress once again the importance of cooperation among all stakeholders in order to achieve benefits for all from trade facilitation, including enhanced partnership with the trade community, joint and well-coordinated intervention with other border agencies, and better co-ordination with other international and regional organizations working in this area. Indeed, one of the lessons that the customs capacity building strategy will articulate is the need for cooperation and coherence. The WCO has already been working in partnership with most of the participants in the International Forum on Trade Facilitation. I hope that this Forum will contribute to further promoting the coherent approach for international efforts of trade facilitation, in particular by avoiding unnecessary duplication.

Chapter 1.5
The Development Dimension of Trade Facilitation

John Burley, Director, Division for Services Infrastructure for Development and Trade Efficiency, UNCTAD

Trade facilitation must be considered and implemented as a development factor and not simply as an administrative tool with an impact limited to border-crossing trade operations. It can foster better public capacity to monitor and promote foreign trade as well as support existing and potential national exporting trading communities.

Needs and priorities

Individual needs and priorities of countries may differ with regard to the structure of trade, the trading partners involved and the available transport infrastructure and services.

International trade transactions are bilateral by definition: for a given trade operation, there are always one origin and one destination. Transactions may become simpler or more cumbersome depending on commonalities among trading partners (in particular, cultural, economic and geographical proximity or the thereof). Being close or far apart entails having more or fewer commonalities. Trade facilitation is all about creating commonalities in standards and practices not only between the trading partners' respective environments but also between different actors within the same country.

Priorities in implementing trade facilitation measures are therefore usually driven by common interests among trading partners. In most cases, major trading partners are also neighbouring countries, and increasingly neighbours are also becoming associated with regional integration groupings.

Regional frameworks for trade facilitation

Trade facilitation is a priority issue in most regional groupings. Examples of advanced multilateral trade facilitation programmes can be found in the European Union and other regional economic groupings in Latin America, Asia and Africa. Experience shows that regional groupings remain the most successful context for engaging in trade facilitation at the international level.

The ultimate goal of any trade facilitation action is to make it possible to complete an international trade transaction as a one-stage operation, a single, uninterrupted door-to-door physical flow, fully monitored but never interfered in by administrative and financial proceedings agreed to by all the actors concerned. Developing countries wishing to establish a trade facilitation programme should therefore take into account the main origins and destinations of their current and planned trade, and define their needs and priorities – when applicable, together with their partners from a given integration grouping.

Local public and private partnerships

At the national level, needs and priorities are best defined in the context of local trading and transport communities. For this purpose, clusters of interested parties should be created. These clusters should include the private and public sectors, including transport and terminal operators, freight forwarders, traders, customs administrations and other relevant governmental institutions. The core function of the trade and transport facilitation clusters should be to review major obstacles and possible improvements and establish requirements for efficient trade and transport operations.

Facilitation clusters would gather interested parties at the seaport end, at border crossing areas and at main inland destinations/origins of trade and transport operations. Clusters would also serve the purpose of sharing knowledge among members and exchanging information and solutions with associated networked clusters in other locations of the corridor.

THE DEVELOPMENT DIMENSION

International cooperative networks

As trade facilitation measures have been adopted at the national, regional and global levels with contributions from interested international organizations, these organizations have adjusted their respective roles over the years in differing and complementary ways. For instance, UNECE, the International Civil Aviation Organization (ICAO), the International Maritime Organization (IMO), the International Organization for Standardization (ISO) and WCO operate as engineering and development centres for most of the existing international facilitation standards. The World Bank Global Facilitation Partnership is now a well-established focal point for the dissemination of trade-facilitation-related information, as well as a global discussion forum. UNCTAD's technical assistance remains a leading source of effective implementation and development strategies.

Developing countries wishing to improve their foreign trade performance now have a large choice of available instruments and institutional structures. Technical cooperation is certainly an area where multilateral efforts should be coordinated to help developing countries take advantage of each agency's role and competence as part of a knowledge-building, action-oriented machinery.

In April 2002, following a request from the United Nations Chief Executives Board High Level Committee on Programmes (HLCP), UNCTAD convened the first interagency meeting to identify trade facilitation issues to be effectively addressed in a coordinated manner.

Although a very preliminary step, the meeting established contact among the main United Nations agencies dealing with trade facilitation. It agreed to establish a mechanism for sharing knowledge and experiences among participating agencies. It also created a basis for cooperation in providing developing countries with enhanced technical assistance and capacity building.

Trade facilitation and information and communication technology (ICT)

ICT in the form of specifically computerized information management systems offers very cost-effective solutions for obstacles to trade and transport. Such obstacles include inefficient formalities, transmission delays, transcription errors, and other routine and repetitive manual tasks undertaken in public administration offices dealing with international trade procedures. Customs departments have been privileged candidates for automation among governmental agencies. Similarly, private-sector operators handling large amounts of data have been using computer systems effectively for more than 20 years now.

The use of transport operations planning and cargo movement monitoring information systems has also spread rapidly in recent decades. Such systems speed the flow of information on cargo and foster the efficient use of limited assets. Developing countries' private and public sectors should make greater use of ICT for trade and transport procedures and operations. UNCTAD's development and implementation of computerized systems, such as the Automated System for Customs Data (ASYCUDA) and the Advance Cargo Information System (ACIS), are a major step in the right direction.

However, computerizing the activities of the various parties involved in the control or monitoring of external trade flows will be beneficial only if existing administrative and commercial practices are overhauled prior to the computerization of procedures.

This highlights the role of trade facilitation as a means to bring actual benefits to both public administrations and private trading sectors: While unnecessary obstacles to simpler, freer and less onerous regional or global trade have to disappear, at the same time, public administrations responsible for monitoring foreign trade should become more effective and efficient. This important issue has recently acquired new urgency in the light of increased security measures being implemented to counter illegal traffics.

THE DEVELOPMENT DIMENSION

Technical assistance and capacity-building programmes resulting from binding arrangements could ensure actual improvement of administrations' performance and lasting solutions serving the public interest.

Trade facilitation and security

The terrorist attacks on September 11, 2001, in the United States, illustrated the critical yet fragile nature of the international transport system. For the global economy to flourish, this system must continue to provide safe, secure, efficient and reliable services to travelers and customers in all parts of the world. At the 2002 G8 Summit in Kananaskis, Canada, heads of state agreed on a set of cooperative actions to promote greater security of land, sea and air transport while facilitating the cost-effective and efficient flow of people, cargo and vehicles for legitimate economic and social purposes.

Such security concerns may have both immediate and long-term implications for several operational aspects of international trade transactions. The Customs–Trade Partnership Against Terrorism (C-TPAT) launched by the United States Customs and Border Protection office, and the adoption of measures such as the Container Security Initiative promoted by the United States, are being considered in multilateral forums. These actions may result in one or more of the following elements' being taken into account as potential major drawbacks for small players in international trade and transport systems:

(a) *Geographical distribution and concentration of flows:* The selection by the U.S. Customs Service of "safe ports" may lead to the rerouting of major flows between certain origins and destinations, in particular those in the United States.

(b) *Supply chain management capability:* The C-TPAT initiative requires trading partners to work with their service providers throughout the supply chain to enhance security processes and procedures. Various aspects of each stage of the supply chain must be monitored, including employees and the origin of goods. Although these procedures can be requested only for U.S.-bound supply chains, they will certainly influence U.S.-based importers, carriers and brokers to choose supply partners that can produce reliable and suitable information to be submitted to U.S. Customs authorities. This might exclude some ill-equipped, though trustworthy, suppliers in developing countries.

(c) *Technological and financial requirements:* The screening of containers implies the availability and use of costly equipment for which ports in many developing countries may not be able to raise or allocate the required resources.

(d)*Legal consequences:* Changes to current practices and procedures arising from security concerns may have significant legal implications, such as increased liabilities.

On the positive side, these security initiatives may well offer the opportunity to establish a new type of risk management tool based on the concept of "Facilitation (FAL) intelligence". This notion is similar to the one applied by numerous customs administrations, but its scope is wider. It aims at gathering sufficient information on trading communities to sort out "good" trade and transport operators from "bad" ones, and to greatly facilitate operations for legitimate trade. More customs and security resources could then be assigned to the repression of illicit traffic.

Ideally, some sort of FAL intelligence could be achieved on a worldwide basis through the extensive use of interconnected ICT systems. The Internet makes this undertaking easier than ever, and the recent trend towards widely accepted clustering and networking schemes would support this development. Thus, security concerns provide an incentive for increased use of ICT.

Would the current security concerns add not only costs but also value to the operational and institutional trading environment of developing countries? The answer depends largely on whether the necessary assistance is provided to them, in terms of technical and financial resources and of lasting capacity to establish an autonomous, sustainable trade management infrastructure.

THE DEVELOPMENT DIMENSION

The challenges of trade facilitation in the post-Doha context

According to paragraph 27 of the Doha Ministerial Declaration,[10] the WTO Council of Trade in Goods will review GATT Articles V, VIII and X and identify the trade facilitation needs and priorities of WTO members. This exercise is aimed at adopting through explicit consensus a decision to start negotiations on a future trade facilitation agreement at the Fifth Ministerial Conference, scheduled to take place in 2003 in Cancún, Mexico.

Apart from the GATT rules, however, trade facilitation activities have remained mostly the fruit of voluntary efforts by governmental or private sectors. Mandatory rules are still the exception. Other than in international transport conventions such as the Convention on the Contract for the International Carriage of Goods by Road (CMR) or the Uniform Rules concerning the Contract for International Carriage of Goods by Rail (CIM), which include simplified documentation requirements, most trade facilitation instruments recommend, rather than impose or require, compulsory measures.

This situation may change radically in the coming years, if and when trade facilitation rules become part of a multilateral compulsory legal environment for the trading system. This would constitute a major development requiring considerable effort from those countries where trade facilitation still lags. As a consequence, the implementation of trade facilitation will require appropriate technical and financial resources. As a voluntary activity, trade facilitation has been systematically downgraded in

---

[10] "Recognizing the case for further expediting the movement, release and clearance of goods, including goods in transit, and the need for enhanced technical assistance and capacity building in this area, we agree that negotiations will take place after the Fifth Session of the Ministerial Conference on the basis of a decision to be taken, by explicit consensus, at that Session on modalities of negotiations. In the period until the Fifth Session, the Council for Trade in Goods shall review and, as appropriate, clarify and improve relevant aspects of Articles V, VIII, and X of the GATT 1994 and identify the trade facilitation needs and priorities of Members, in particular developing and least-developed countries. We commit ourselves to ensuring adequate technical assistance and support for capacity building in this area."

the list of priorities for the use of scarce financial resources. The reverse approach should be used in contexts where non-compliance with a rule ends up being more costly than the implementation of the required measures. In situations where binding obligations exist, government must lead the process of change and can ask the private sector to help provide the necessary know-how in international trade and transport operations.

Chapter 1.6
Compete and Conform: Practical Measures for Future Trade Facilitation
Alberto Di Liscia, Assistant Director-General, UNIDO

In May 2002, UNIDO submitted to the First International Forum on Trade Facilitation a case for promoting a broader concept of trade facilitation to include concerns such as technical barriers to trade and supply-side constraints. I also stressed, at that time, the need to meet the developing countries' technical assistance needs via inter-agency cooperation based on comparative advantage. This year I submit that inter-agency cooperation is needed all the more in a global trade system displaying a greater sense of security. And I put forward a cohesive supply-side approach as a practical means of ensuring that integrated cooperation to the benefit of the developing countries.

Potential benefits lost

Figure 1.6.1: World trade 1970 – 99 (trillion US$ - constant 1995)

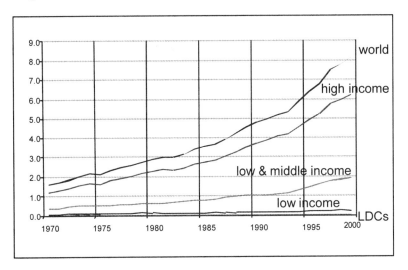

Despite all the significant benefits of globalization, long-established structures of inequality continue to expand and deepen. Appreciable economic gains for few in the world economy have been accompanied by real losses for many. The volume of additional developing country exports to developed country markets and the associated developmental impact has been limited to say the least. The plight of the poorest countries is evident in the graph in Figure 1.6.1. These countries have consistently lagged behind.

Constraints

Over the years, the WTO has been very effective in bringing about the reciprocal removal of barriers to trade in goods and services. It is not for want of reductions in tariffs and quotas that the developing countries have failed to benefit from the opportunities offered by global markets; the reasons clearly lie elsewhere. As the developing countries themselves recognize, they lack:

- Effective industrial productive capacity needed to ensure product diversification;
- Ability to comply with international standards needed to secure greater market access.

In 2001, the United Nations Secretary-General Kofi Annan summarized the problem as follows: the least developed countries had "neither the surplus of exportable products nor the production capacity to take advantage of the new trade opportunities". They would need "substantial investment and technical assistance in order to expand their production".[11] His comments hold equally true today. And if the least developed countries obtained that investment and assistance, the result could be (according to one estimate) an export growth rate of 15-20% or $1.4 billion a year for them.[12]

---

[11] Financial Times, 5 March 2001
[12] Economist, 3 March 2001

PRACTICAL MEASURES FOR TRADE FACILITATION

Technical constraints

The developing countries not only have to improve their supply-side capacities so as to have an adequate volume and range of goods to sell; they also have to compete in a highly demanding rules-driven trading system. Over and above the basic product specifications, exporting countries have to be ready to meet increasingly stringent requirements applied to goods in terms of quality, safety, health and the environment. Their inability to do so entails high actual and potential economic and social costs. Many developing countries lack the capacity to meet such conformity requirements. Their products often fail to comply with innumerable standards and regulations that are primarily intended to ensure safety and security in trade relations - in particular, from the standpoint of the consumer.

In the main, these requirements take the form of Technical Barriers to Trade (TBT) and Sanitary and Phyto-Sanitary Measures (SPS). The post-Uruguay Round TBT and SPS agreements in the WTO have been specifically designed to "ensure that technical regulations and standards do not create unnecessary obstacles to trade". That notwithstanding, those very same regulations and standards still act as non-tariff barriers and obstruct developing country access to markets.

Practical implications

The burden of proof lies with the developing countries. They have to demonstrate compliance with international standards. Moreover, unlike tariff barriers, standards and technical regulations cannot be removed by a simple act of legislation. These are requirements that must be met.

The greater a developing country's compliance with standards the greater its access to foreign markets. Compliance can only be achieved through testing, certification and accreditation. Furthermore, the introduction of quality management systems based on standardization, certification and accreditation, heightens the security of the trade system.

A direct correlation thus exists between trade security and conformity assessment infrastructure. In the new global environment, increased security measures are clearly called for. However, they mu st not become yet another technical barrier to trade – and so impose a further burden on the developing countries.

The challenge for the developing countries becomes one of enhancing the infrastructure. Reforming and upgrading standards-setting regimes, establishing efficient testing, certification and laboratory accreditation mechanisms that conform to SPS and TBTs and enjoy international recognition, as well as asserting themselves in standards-setting bodies, are the objectives that developing countries should meet.

In addition to the strictly technical constraints, developing country access to industrialized country markets is further hampered by shortcomings in such essential trade-related requirements and procedures as registration and documentation, customs valuation, import regulations, licensing and similar issues.

A cohesive supply-side approach

If the developing countries are to succeed in increasing their share in global manufacturing value-added[13], their enterprises need to be able to produce according to client country standards and technical regulations; their products must prevail in highly competitive markets. Supply has to be capable of meeting both market demand and product standards. In other words, the developing countries need technology diffusion and capacity building for market access: two key areas of comparative advantage that are the very essence of UNIDO's corporate strategy.

A strategic approach to market access is called for. The prime objective of the strategy is to secure a palpable increase in the developing countries'

---

[13] According to the most recent estimates, the developing countries (including China) account for a 24.5 per cent share in world total MVA (at current prices) in 2000. International Yearbook of Industrial statistics 2003, UNIDO, p. 32, Figure 1.1

share in global trade. This can be achieved by means of a three-pronged approach or market access chain. Its thrust is encapsulated in the "three Cs": Compete, Conform, Connect.

Figure 1.6.2: Products to market

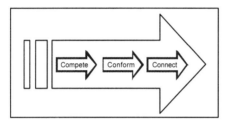

In practical terms, this means:

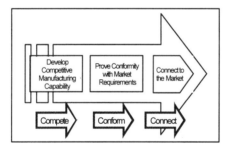

Developing competitive manufacturing capability
Here the focus has to be on the manufacture of products with high-export potential; enterprise upgrading; innovation; technology acquisition; increasing capacity to meet international standards and client requirements; and innovative cross-border and cross-industry partnerships.

Proving conformity with market requirements
Here the focus has to be on upgrading the requisite standards, metrology, testing and quality infrastructure, and securing international recognition of local laboratory analysis - essential elements in any export promotion scheme.

Connecting to the market
Here the focus has to be on integrating with the international trade framework and rules, promoting policies for the settlement of disputes and harmonizing trade agreements. Not to mention simplifying customs procedures, transportation and documentation through the effective application of information and communications technologies.

Practical applications

Meeting known needs in all three components of the market access chain would help to combat the increasing marginalization of the developing countries. By way of illustration, I would like to focus on the second component: conformity.

The recent WTO survey on trade-related technical assistance in the developing countries was most revealing on this point. It stressed the urgent need for building up institutional capacity and infrastructure related to standards, metrology and conformity. UNIDO has already displayed its prowess in this field. Since 2001, it has delivered more than $15 million of trade-related technical assistance, primarily in the fields of upgrading supply capacity and strengthening standards and conformity assessment infrastructure.

For example, with EU funding, UNIDO is assisting the countries of the West African Economic and Monetary Union to set up a system for accreditation, standardization and quality. It is also helping exporters of food products in Egypt to match consumer requirements in Europe. In Sri Lanka UNIDO assisted in developing and securing the international accreditation of five key laboratories, as well as developing national capacity for ISO 14000. In Central America the organization is implementing a major trade facilitation programme, with emphasis on building up national capacities to overcome technical barriers to trade. In all these instances, by ensuring that testing complies with international standards, the projects help to create sorely needed client confidence, heighten consumers' sense of security and nurture a quality culture - ingredients essential to market access and success.

PRACTICAL MEASURES FOR TRADE FACILITATION

In the context of "compete, conform and connect", UNIDO can provide a synergetic set of technical services in two main areas:
- Development of supply-side capacities, including environment-friendly investment and technology;
- Strengthening of standards and conformity assessment infrastructure and services.

These are two essential components or building blocks in the strategy that have to be combined with connectivity. If others could match these inputs, it would generate synergies in the delivery of assistance across a broad spectrum and so lend greater impetus to the common system's efforts to achieve sustainable development.

Conclusion

In conclusion, I would stress that a strategic alliance of all players is called for, with a concomitant shift from trade facilitation in the narrow sense of the term to a broader concept including supply capacity and conformity – and thus ensuring a more secure global trading system. As with all approaches, the key to success is ensuring proper inter-agency cooperation and securing budgetary resources so that long-term commitments can be made - and honoured. An essential input in that process is the effective exchange of information. UNIDO thus welcomes the new United Nations Trade Facilitation Network and the associated website, to which UNIDO will actively contribute.

Ultimately, we trust the strategy will help us to articulate a broad vision and narrow the widening gap in industrial capabilities between countries. Technical progress has integrated the world economy on an unprecedented scale, linking products, markets and people much more closely than ever before. It is an opportunity that should not be missed. For our part, we look forward to meeting the challenges that the future holds for us all.

Chapter 1.7
Costs and Benefits of Trade Facilitation

Anthony Kleitz, Head, Trade Liberalization and Review Division, OECD

In the past year, recognition of the importance of trade facilitation has grown. It has also been recognized that trade facilitation represents a shared interest of all countries at all levels of development though they might perceive their priorities somewhat differently in this field. More specifically, work has continued internationally on the quantification on the costs and benefits of trade facilitation and has explored a wide range of different approaches. The objectives of the following chapter are twofold. Firstly, to understand better the nature and importance of trade facilitation by considering quantitatively what can be said about inefficient trade procedures and the benefits of trade facilitation and, secondly, to focus on a quantitative rather than on a qualitative assessment.

Definitions

Trade facilitation is a rather imprecise term. For the WTO it means simplification and harmonization of trade procedures and this approach has been taken in this presentation. However, it should be recognized that the term is often used in a broader sense to include other procedural or non-tariff barriers to trade (NTBs). Costs and benefits of trade facilitation are not the flip side of each other. The basic concept is that of trade transaction costs that reflect costs arising from supplying documents and information required for border procedures or procedural delays. A different type of costs is related to implementing reform to improve efficiency and reduce trade transaction costs. Finally, the benefits of trade facilitation relate to the benefits of reform, that is, the reduced trade transaction costs.

Quantitative analysis of costs and benefits of trade facilitation

The major challenges linked to such an analysis are: the inconsistent nature of data on trade transaction and implementation costs; the lack of a standard methodology for the analysis of existing data; widely varying results of studies that have been undertaken (according to parameters and assumptions that they are based on); and, finally, the somewhat different costs and benefits faced by the public and private sectors. The public sector is concerned mainly with operating costs, i.e. operating customs and other border procedures that need to be implemented. The private sector is interested in the operation of the economy.

The following example will illustrate the implementation costs for governments through the data for automating customs systems. In Chile, it was estimated to amount to $5 million; in Chinese Taipei, the air-cargo system amounted to $5 million, the sea-cargo system to $6.5 million; in the United States, the Automated Commercial Environment was estimated to have cost an overall sum of $1 billion.

Considerable effort has been made in recent years to model the trade and welfare effects which are mainly concerned with the private sector. The overall trade transaction costs were valued by UNCTAD at 7-10% of world trade. It should be noted, however, that most of these costs could not be saved, as they were the total costs of trade transactions. Typically, trade facilitation is estimated to reduce trade transaction costs by 1-3% of world trade value, which brings about increases in GDP and national income.

Figure 1.7.1: Estimated benefits of trade facilitation (the liberalization assumptions of the cited studies differ)

	ADDITIONAL GDP GROWTH (BILLIONS US $)	SHARE OF TRADE FACILITATION BENEFITS IN OVERALL LIBERALIZATION
Dutch study	72	34 %
OECD study	76	65 %
APEC study	154	56 %

65

The three recent studies in Figure 1.7.1, which are based on various assumptions, give an overview of the range of the results that have been arrived at. Trade facilitation in all cases is a major avenue for achieving trade liberalization benefits. Trade facilitation means in fact eliminating inefficiencies, which are a loss to the economy. By eliminating these inefficiencies the gain should be quite significant.

When analyzing the quantitative cost indications for particular sectors, it should be noted that some goods are more susceptible to border controls than others in that inefficient border procedures may harm these goods by delayed border controls. This is, for example, the case of agricultural produce. In such cases trade transaction costs might be relatively higher and so are, consequently, the potential benefits from trade facilitation. For example, in the Republic of Korea, typically 10-18 days are required for the clearance of new products (cf. less than 3-4 days for most known agricultural products, which is still much higher than the time required for non-agricultural products). In agricultural products this additional factor of border delays can become significant, specifically for those countries which are major exporters of such products.

Observations on perceived quality of the customs environment

SMEs and developing country firms are frequently seen as relatively disadvantaged in meeting trade transaction and implementation costs. In a general sense, there is an advantage for richer countries, as they are more able to meet these costs. However, it should also be stressed that there are many examples of low-income countries with good customs services and examples of countries with good customs can be found in all major regions. This short overview suggests that there are no insurmountable structural factors limiting the possibilities for benefiting from trade facilitation.

Calculations for particular kinds of costs and benefits can include administrative costs. Thus, Japan's MITI estimates feasible reductions of import prices which could amount to 0.5-1.2% for transport machinery and 1.5-2.4% for other machinery and equipment. Other savings will come from paperless trading. Here an estimate from Australia (DFAT) shows

1.5-15% of the landed value, which amounts to 3% on average and could lead to a $60 billion savings across APEC. Another indicator of benefits is the time required for customs release.

Figure 1.7.2. Customs quality by region

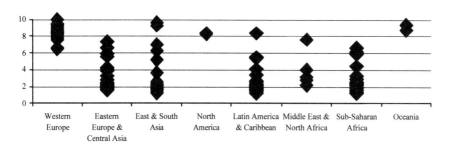

Figure 1.7.3. Average customs clearance time for imports through trade facilitation (hours)

Economy	Before	After
New Zealand	240	0.2
Singapore	48-96	0.25
Greece	5-6	0.5
Republic of Korea	2.8	0.75
Costa Rica	144	0.2-1.9
Peru	360-720	2-24

Source: WTO, OECD, and others

Conclusions

There is no single answer to quantifying costs and benefits. Analytical work is continuing and it helps to understand the different aspects that are important in trade facilitation. It is, however, important to identify key areas where trade facilitation may produce the greatest benefits. Furthermore, one size does not fit all. Country situations and requirements differ considerably. But improvement is almost always possible and very largely beneficial for the country undertaking the measures. Any attempt at multilateral discipline on trade facilitation needs to take account of this diversity of experience, which seems to re-enforce the importance of a coherent approach to streamlining procedures and improving infrastructure.

Chapter 1.8
The Economic Impact of Trade Facilitation Measures

John Wilson, Lead Economist, Development Research Group, The World Bank

I would like to begin my presentation by outlining what the World Bank is actively looking at, in the context of its trade logistics agenda. While preparing for the upcoming fiscal year at the Bank we defined the following three focuses: first, policy relevant research and diagnostics involving new analysis and data; second, World Bank operations; and, third, strengthening partnerships. The Bank is also interested in advancing policy relevant research including new data sets as they relate to trade facilitation. We are actively reviewing Bank operations, as they relate to trade, and that includes trade facilitation and support to our regional operations in trade facilitation. We are also very interested in strengthening our partnerships with other organizations, agencies and the private sector, and I will just list one here, which is the Global Facilitation Partnership for Transportation and Trade, which the World Bank is involved in.

While these three points summarize the basis of this paper, I would like to point out that trade facilitation is more than transport. At the World Bank we understand trade facilitation in a context that is broader than simply transport costs. We are now looking at the issue of security and trade; we believe there is a potential win-win situation in relation to both security and trade facilitation. In this context, it is clear that a framework for capacity building is needed in order to sustain long-term progress.

Mr. Kleitz from the Trade Liberalization and Review Division of the OECD mentioned above the analysis that has been conducted in relation to capacity building in trade facilitation. At the World Bank, we have looked at the relationship between trade facilitation and capacity building in a study centred on the 19 APEC member economies. We identified four indicators for trade facilitation - port efficiency; customs environment; domestic regulatory environment; and e-business usage - as most relevant within this broader context of trade facilitation. The question asked throughout this study was, whether it was possible to say something about the relative impact of the various trade facilitation measures on bilateral trade? What we have been doing up until now, if not groping in the dark, was moving forward with very little empirical evidence, when it comes to the impact of trade facilitation in this broader context. To remedy this deficiency, we created a data set which built upon a number of publications: the World Economic Forum's *Global Competitiveness Report* (GCR); the IMD's *The World Competitiveness Yearbook* (WCY); Micco, Ximena and Dollar (2001) – World Bank Group *Maritime Transport Costs and Port Efficiency* (MXD); and the Transparency International publications.

Figure 1.8.1. Raising capacity half-way to APEC average

		Change in Trade Flows ($ billions)	Change in Trade Flows (%)
Border measure			
Port efficiency	Bring below average members up to the APEC average	116.89	9.7
Customs environment		21.63	1.8
"Inside the border" measures			
E-business	Bring below average members up to the APEC average	27.69	2.3
Regulatory environment	Regulatory harmonization	88.15	7.3
Grand Total		**254.36**	**21.0**

Our previous work showed that there was a significant relationship between the four areas and bilateral trade flows in the Asia-Pacific region, and that the measure of port efficiency and regulatory environment, among others, were important. Subsequently, the question we asked was (assuming that APEC countries jointly agree to raise capacity half-way to the average across all member economies), what would be the impact on trade, would it increase or decrease? We found, as illustrated in Figure 1.8.1, that such an increase in capacity would yield a $254 billion increase in trade.

Moreover, we are not only interested in unilateral, multilateral or regional action, but we are also interested in forming development priorities. Another analysis that we conducted (available on our website) also asked the question what would happen if Morocco or Tunisia or other countries were to raise their capacity unilaterally? How would trade change? Thus the new work that we are carrying out for the Global Economic Prospects Report 2004 of the World Bank, for release in September 2003 prior to the Sixth WTO Ministerial Conference in Cancún, we extended the analysis to 75 countries and established a new data set. This study will ask how global trade would change under different scenarios and what type of capacity-building efforts are needed in order to achieve trade expansion goals.

When it comes to trade and security, and when one looks at the empirical data about the impact of security, and particularly of terrorism, on trade, we can conclude that there is a clear indication that weak security and terrorism have a detrimental impact on growth and trade. If one further looks at the evidence, one comes to two tentative conclusions: firstly, that it is necessary to take into consideration developing country concerns as the new security initiatives unfold, and secondly, that there is potential for a net win-win situation of increased security and trade expansion.

As far as the question of benefits for all is concerned, it also includes the issue of WTO discipline. In the new analysis that I mentioned above, we are going to try to evaluate the idea of raising capacity with reference to the GATT articles under consideration for negotiation and their impact on trade. It is important to suggest at this point that the issues here should be viewed in a development context and that development and capacity building are the primary engines of growth.

In conclusion, I would like to restate that trade facilitation is clearly more than transport, that the development context is critical, and that a policy decision to move forward demands a much better and well informed empirical analysis, which all of us would be interested in contributing to.

Chapter 1.9
Income Distribution Impact of Trade Facilitation in Developing Countries
Adrian Hewitt and Ian Gillson, Overseas Development Institute (ODI)

Executive summary

Openness to trade has long been seen as an important element of sound economic policy and trade facilitation is a necessary step for achieving it. Trading more efficiently tends to increase average incomes, providing more resources with which to tackle poverty. And while it may affect income distribution, it may not do so in a systematically adverse way.

This paper investigates the income distribution impact of trade facilitation in developing countries and makes a number of findings. Among them:

- Trade facilitation has an impact on income distribution and poverty in developing countries through its effects on international trade, economic growth and government revenue.
- Small and medium-sized enterprises (SMEs), the dominant actors in developing countries, are the main beneficiaries of trade facilitation, since trade transactions costs fall disproportionately on small firms.
- While trade facilitation may or may not reduce income inequalities within developing countries, trade facilitation can enhance trade-induced growth, which increases average incomes providing more resources with which to tackle poverty. Trade facilitation measures applied within a closed (or at least less liberal) trade environment can still have a positive impact on exports and foreign investment.
- Trade facilitation may increase employment which may help some move out of poverty.
- Improvements in infrastructure allow the poor to trade more easily and profitably in domestic as well as in international markets.
- Trade facilitation can increase government revenue which can benefit the poor if used to finance social expenditures.

A number of policy recommendations can be made if trade facilitation measures are to benefit the poor. In particular:

- To reduce income inequalities in developing countries trade facilitation measures should be targeted at lowering trade transactions costs in those sectors where employment of the poor is concentrated.
- The provision of effective safety-nets may be necessary if alternative forms of employment are not rapidly available for any displaced workers.
- Increases in government resources brought about by trade facilitation should be used to support pro-poor or social expenditures.
- SMEs need access to capital, trade information systems and capacity building to comply with international standards under trade facilitation programmes if they are to trade efficiently.
- Infrastructure can be particularly beneficial for the poor if they are actively employed in its development.

Introduction

Recently, increasing emphasis has been placed on the importance of non-tariff barriers to export expansion in developing countries. One of such constraint that is gaining in prominence is the role of trade transactions costs or the issue of trade facilitation. Trade facilitation encompasses "a wide range of areas such as government regulations and controls, business efficiency, transportation, information and communication technologies and the financial sector" (UNECE (2002a), p.3). This paper aims to address the income distribution impact of trade facilitation in developing countries. We consider the matter from a general perspective, drawing on economic analysis and practical experience to construct a broad framework to explain the links between trade facilitation, income distribution and poverty.

The report outlines a number of ways through which trade facilitation can have a direct effect on income distribution and poverty in developing countries. Among them are:

- International trade: Trade facilitation changes the prices of traded goods. This paper looks at how these changes are translated into prices faced by different sectors and how they affect the poor.

- Economic growth: The weight of evidence is that increased openness to trade is good for growth and that growth increases the incomes of the poor. For its full benefits to be realized, tariff liberalization needs to be accompanied by trade facilitation measures in areas such as procedures, and transport and communications infrastructure otherwise it will fail to generate the investment and productivity improvements needed for economic development.

- Government revenue and spending: Trade facilitation measures such as customs reform may also affect income distribution and poverty through changes in the government's fiscal position, particularly if trade taxation is an important source of revenue. Trade facilitation can increase revenue, boosting social and anti-poverty programme expenditures.

Trade transaction costs in developing countries

Components and elements
Transaction costs associated with international trade in goods are numerous. OECD (2001) classifies these costs into two forms: direct costs (costs of compliance associated with the collection and processing of information[14] and charges for trade-related services e.g. for freight,

---

[14] There are in an average trade transaction between 27 and 30 different parties involved, handling approximately 40 documents, not only for government authorities but also for related businesses. 200 data elements are required, 30 of which are repeated at least 30 times (APEC (1996)), of which 60-70% are re-entered at least once (ETPAD (1998)). In addition these costs may be multiplied by data-entry errors incurred during the process (SITPRO (1991)). Similarly, Messerlin and Zarrouk (1999) p. 12 find that the average customs clearance transaction in the Middle East and North Africa takes between 25 and 30 stages to

insurance, and handling) and indirect costs (time-sensitive costs brought about by administrative processes and customs procedures[15] which delay goods in the warehouse leading to an increase in transportation fees and inventory charges). Other direct and indirect costs can be brought about by a lack of transparency or of uniformity in the interpretation of regulations and contracts which increase the effective cost of producing the necessary trade and procedural information.

Transport costs
Transport and logistics are one of the more critical trade facilitation problems facing developing countries (see appendix 1 for a summary of studies in this area). A large part of the disadvantage in trade faced by Southern Africa, in particular, has to do with the transport sector, which is a critical variable in determining competitiveness. To remain competitive, exporting firms that face higher shipping costs must pay lower wages to workers, accept lower returns on capital, or be more productive. An example of this in the case of developing countries are the labour-intensive manufacturing industries such as textiles, where high transport costs are likely to translate into lower wages for workers, directly affecting the standard of living of workers and their dependents.

Amjadi and Yeats (1995) find that freight rates for Sub-Saharan African countries are often considerably higher than on similar goods originating from other countries and thus have contributed to the region's poor trade performance over the last decade. This problem is particularly acute for those African countries which are landlocked. Limao and Venables (2000)

---

complete and takes between 1 day to several weeks, with border corruption being evident in the process too.

[15] Customs procedures are only one aspect of improving the overall efficiency of the cargo clearance process. APEC (2000) cites a WCO study of clearance times at Indonesian ports which found that the customs clearance process for certain shipments took an average of 6.4 minutes, compared to 159 hours and 23 minutes for other activities involved in cargo clearance, including problems with incomplete documents, red tape involved in releasing goods from warehouses, and payment hold-ups even after the release of goods by customs officials. Mikuriya (2001) shows that the biggest delay from cargo arrival to release is in the plane-to-warehouse and time-in-warehouse stages of the process.

find that being landlocked raises transport costs by more than 50%, but that this extra cost is not fully explained by the extra overland distance that must be overcome to reach the final destination. They put forward several possible reasons for this, including: border delays, transport coordination problems, uncertainty, higher insurance costs and direct charges that may be incurred (e.g. Kenya charges a road transit goods licence of $200). The rise in cost is due to the fact that almost all consignments from landlocked countries need to transit across neighbouring countries, thus multiplying transportation costs. For Latin America, Guasch and Spiller (1999) report on inter-country differences in inventory levels. They report the very large disadvantage of Latin American economies vis-à-vis the US with respect to inventories: on average these countries hold twice as much raw material and finished products as the US. According to the authors, higher transaction costs explain a relevant part of these inventories discrepancies: Latin American countries faced with uncertain demand, longer delays, and larger costs for small frequent shipments, choose to maintain larger reserves. Considering the cost of capital is normally higher in Latin America than in the US, the authors point out that these high inventory levels translate into considerable costs and ultimately in lower competitiveness and diminished growth.

High transportation costs are also due to anti-competitive policies, such as cargo reservation schemes maintained by a large number of African countries and international shipping cartels and legislated monopoly providers in both industrialized and developing countries (Francois and Wooton (2001); Fink *et al.* (2002)). Fidler (2001) finds that shipping costs and port restrictions of US shipping cartels hinder Latin American and African exports to the US more than tariffs do.

Although being landlocked is a challenge, problems can be overcome. UNECE (2002b) suggests a number of practical solutions – transit corridors, regional integration efforts, legal and regulatory reforms, and institutional / administrative overhauls.

Procedural and compliance costs
Having discussed the types of trade transactions costs faced by developing countries we now turn to discuss the effects of these costs on firms. In developing countries SMEs are the dominant actors. With respect to trade transactions costs related to compliance, there may be asymmetric effects on SMEs and, therefore, on enterprises in developing countries.

A number of factors deter firms in developing countries from seeking to expand in international markets. First, Ernst and Whinney (1987) for the EU suggest that compliance costs have very little relationship with the value of goods traded. They find that compliance costs per consignment are 3% - 45% higher for firms with fewer than 250 employees. By extension to developing countries, this leads to the conclusion that the export of small value consignments, and by small firms, bears disproportionately high cost burdens.

Second, when trade procedures are complicated, demand for labour to complete these activities is high. Two types of trade operators might be particularly adversely affected by such a requirement: small firms who lack human resources, and firms whose productivity in carrying out trade procedures is lower than other competitors. For these two types of firms, trade formalities might require spending significant resources on internal transactions. This could result in disproportionately high compliance costs.

Third, lengthy processing time also affects the capital standing of firms, since capital delayed at the border bears interest. For those operators whose capital reserves are thin, such as SMEs and enterprises in developing countries, lengthy processing might constitute a prohibitive trade barrier.

Finally, lack of predictability also entails significant disadvantages for enterprises in developing countries (IECC (1996)). When the necessary information on applicable regulations is not readily available, trade operators have to spend additional resources in order to obtain information. Enterprises operating in an untransparent environment, as is often the case in developing countries, need to spend more resources to obtain regulatory information. Furthermore they will frequently have to add expenses for bribes, penalties and administrative or judicial appeals. As these additional expenses do not usually vary according to the value of the goods or the volume of the sales, they serve to increase the operational costs per unit and put firms in developing countries in a weaker position than larger enterprises.

Standards

A third category of transaction costs includes those related to standards. As technological advances help developed countries improve their inspection capacities developing countries are beginning to face more stringent standards requirements in industrialized markets. Developing countries have fewer resources to advance as quickly, and the costs for compliance seem to be increasing. Known and agreed standards benefit international trade through ensuring predictability, but overly-restrictive standards can function as technical barriers to trade (either by protectionist design or as an unintended consequence). A difference exists between countries that see standards as an opportunity to gain "market edge" (through meeting the requirements) and others that perceive them as deliberate protectionist measures designed to restrict their exports. The former group is highly represented in Asia and expend resources in upgrading certification bodies and technical training whilst some Sub-Saharan African countries lobby for derogations or special treatment for their exports (Cerrex (2002)). The costs of technical standards and regulations requirements have been estimated in the EU as being equivalent to a tax of 2% of the value of the goods traded. The high dependency of African exports on European markets makes them even more susceptible to European regulatory reforms (Otsuki *et al.* (2001)).

Corruption

In a number of developing countries it is common for there to be significant delays at the border when trying to achieve customs clearance. In addition to complex customs formalities and capacity constraints given limited facilities this can also be due to corruption at the border. Hare (2001) in a recent piece states "it is often asserted that inadequate physical infrastructure...inhibits trade. More often, the real barrier to trade is again institutional, taking the form of unreasonable customs delays at many borders...accompanied by widespread demands for bribes to expedite the movement of goods". In a Mozambican survey of traders Biggs *et al.*

(1999) find that 45% of those surveyed had been solicited to pay or had paid a fee not otherwise required by law or regulation. Most paid between $4 and $40, but 9% paid between $40 and $400. For Thailand, according to results of a survey on 1024 individuals, 74.4% of respondents answered that they had paid bribes in order to facilitate customs clearance (Thai media (2001)). There are, therefore, potential links between corruption and trade facilitation. If developing country producers, domestic or foreign owned, pay costs associated with corrupt practices their competitive position in both domestic and foreign markets is reduced. If they do not pay, the consequent delays or inherent uncertainties also harm their competitiveness (Cudmore and Whalley (2002)).

Some trade facilitation measures are designed to increase transparency and those measures, in particular risk assessment screening and post-clearance audit, have deterrent effects on duty evasion and corruption in customs. For example, in 1996 the strengthening of customs procedures and the implementation of trade facilitation measures by the Mozambique Government selected Crown Agents to manage customs operations, to train customs staff, and to provide other support as needed. One of Crown Agent's tasks had been to reduce corruption and related problems affecting revenue collection and national reputation which has had a continuing effect for example in the first half of 2000, 130 staff members were charged with serious offences (USAID (2002)).

A number of other measures have been taken by countries in an attempt to curb corruption at the border. First, pre-shipment inspection (PSI) refers to the verification of unit prices and to the examination and reporting of the quantity and quality of exports before they are shipped to the importing country. PSI can help to control over- or underinvoicing of imports, misclassification of imports and undercollection of taxes on imports and can assist with monitoring of origin, compliance with national regulations and tariff exemption schemes and consumer protection. The most common reason that governments use PSI is to deal with inefficient or corrupt customs administrations. The effectiveness of PSI in this regard depends on how well it is implemented. Although reported revenue savings generally exceed PSI fees, case studies suggest that the information provided by PSI companies has often been disregarded and customs administrations often do not want the services because they reduce available rents. Furthermore, importers claim that PSI fees are costly to businesses and that the PSI process is time -consuming in the country of origin (Staples (2002)). For example, at the WTO Trade Facilitation Symposium, the Director of the Chilean Customs revealed that the costs of pre-shipment inspection to external trade was equivalent to raising average tariffs by one percentage point (WTO (1998)). In its most recent Recommendation on Pre-shipment Inspection, UNECE (1999) discourages the use of PSI and proposes that it should not be made a regulatory requirement. Where in certain circumstances there is interim recourse to PSI measures it is recommended that these are maintained for less than five years and that procedures should be kept under review (every 12-18 months) to ensure fulfillment of their objectives. In addition, where PSI is being used to carry out customs-related activities, UNECE (1999) recommends that this be combined with a comprehensive programme of customs reform and modernization.

Anti-bribery rules in industrialized countries are also another means to combat corruption in developing countries. The Anti-Bribery Convention (signed in 1998) has resulted in a tightening of rules across the developed world, outlawing widely condemned practices such as allowing companies to count bribes to overseas officials as tax-deductible expenses. However, international inconsistencies in the application of anti-bribery rules could put countries at a competitive disadvantage to those who fail to adopt them. The OECD has recently encouraged its members to comply with their obligations under the Anti-Bribery Convention; pressure that must be maintained if consistency in application of the rules is to be achieved.

The benefits of trade facilitation in developing countries

Since firms in developing countries suffer the heaviest burdens of trade transaction costs the benefits from the removal of these costs are high. A number of studies have suggested that the potential gains from investment in trade facilitation measures are substantial for developing countries. A recent assessment on the impact of trade facilitation, undertaken for the case of APEC, is Wilson *et al.* (2002). Seven indicators of trade facilitation are generated to measure the efficiency of port logistics, customs procedures, regulatory environments, standards harmonization, business mobility, e-business use and administrative professionalism and transparency in each APEC economy. The analysis considers how much trade in the APEC region might increase under various scenarios of "improved" trade facilitation. A practical scenario calculates the increase in trade that would be associated with bringing those APEC members that have trade facilitation measures below the APEC average halfway up to the APEC average. The results show that for APEC as a whole there would be an increase in intra-APEC trade by about $280 billion. Among the study's findings, exports would rise in Indonesia by $2.9 billion (5%), Thailand by $3.9 billion (5%), Malaysia by $6.3 billion (6%), Mexico by $1.9 billion (1%), and China by $32 billion (11%) with investment on trade facilitation in the region. The study also finds that gains from trade facilitation exceed those in tariff cuts on manufactured goods. The greatest gains to developing countries come from improvements in ports and customs efficiency.

There is also evidence to suggest that trade facilitation measures can benefit less liberal economies with higher tariff barriers. USAID (2003) discusses the export successes of Mauritius and Costa Rica, which have experienced dramatic growth in exports over the last three decades, shifting from export of agricultural products to export of manufactures and services. Exports from Mauritius grew from $89 million in 1970 to $2.8 billion in 2000. For Costa Rica, the growth over the same period was equally as impressive – from $276 million to $7.4 billion. Costa Rica and Mauritius clearly achieved what most developing countries want – a dramatic change from production of one or a few primary products to competitive production of manufactures and services in world markets. Costa Rica and Mauritius followed broadly similar macroeconomic polices during the period under study: devaluation of their currencies to improve competitiveness of exports; aligning of labour costs with worker productivity; adoption of tight fiscal and monetary polices. Neither country had a liberal trade policy. In both countries, an import-substitution manufacturing sector protected from world prices co-existed with another manufacturing sector that depended entirely on its capacity to export to world markets at world prices. In addition, however, both countries did implement a number of trade facilitation measures which reduced the cost and risk of exporting.

For Costa Rica, changes in government procedures eased the burden of paperwork for exporters; firms supporting exporters with specialized documentation and packing services were established; contractual arrangements providing clear rules for liability and spoilage en route between producers and shippers were developed; and producers established industry associations in a number of sectors, increasing information flow and making possible cooperative approaches. An illustration of the success of these trade facilitation measures was the establishment of an Intel chip fabrication plant in Costa Rica in 1995. This $300 million plant employs 3500 Costa Ricans and is the country's largest exporter. The decision to locate in Costa Rica was due to the improved capacity of the country to produce in world markets, promote investment and satisfy infrastructure requirements. For example, Intel wanted its high-value chips routed to their destinations as their manufacture was completed, requiring 12 flights daily to the US. Air traffic capacity had been made possible over the previous decade arising from increased shipments of cut flowers, apparel and other new exports, and from the increased tourist flow to Costa Rica.

For Mauritius, the Mauritius Export Development and Investment Authority (MEDIA) was established in 1984 and this organization has become an efficient tool for attracting foreign investment and improving the domestic conditions faced by new businesses. Improvements in procedures for exporters and infrastructure upgrading have also reduced the cost of exporting. With these policy and institutional improvements employment has risen and large numbers of new workers (mainly women) have entered the labour force.

The income distribution impact of trade facilitation

The case of vegetable exports from Zimbabwe (landlocked but with reliable air and land transport, chilled storage and good communications networks) illustrates the enormous possibilities when transport and related services are efficient. In the early 1990s, farmers near the capital supplied fresh vegetables to the London market by picking them, immediately trucking them to the airport and flying them overnight to London where they were put on the shelves ready for sale in the morning. This required cheap and reliable air transport and modern telecommunications because the shipments were delivered to order (Krugman (1998)). Demand increased especially for female labour involved in picking, sorting, selecting and packing of fruits and vegetables (Bennathan (1989)). Equally, for Chile, shipping deregulation eliminated restrictions on foreign shipping companies to supply international transport services. Monopoly rights in cargo loading operations in Chilean seaports were abolished, allowing the entry of new private operators and the development of a competitive market for cargo handling services. In addition, the government tripled port capacity by obtaining labour flexibility. It did this by paying the union for the right to use workers not under union contract which allowed it to move from a union-constrained eight hour day to 24 hour cargo handling. This led to a significant cost reduction and an increase in exports, particularly time-sensitive agricultural exports that were intensive in rural labour.

In theoretical terms trade facilitation has a positive impact on the efficiency of the trading environment which increases average incomes providing more resources to tackle poverty. However, as with most trade reforms, trade facilitation may adversely affect some groups in society even if it increases incomes in total. Trade facilitation potentially affects poverty through the following chain of linkages. Trade facilitation influences: international trade flows which modify the prices of goods and factors of production (capital and labour); government revenue which can be used for pro-poor and social expenditures; and economic growth. These changes alter income distribution and poverty levels.

Figure 1.9.1: Schematic representation of trade facilitation and poverty linkages

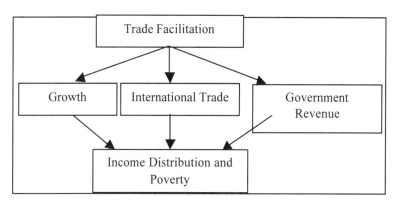

Figure 1.9.1 schematically represents these linkages, ignoring a series of other important issues such as feedback effects of increased poverty and inequality on growth and trade. The following sections describe in detail the influence of trade facilitation on income distribution and poverty via each of these linkages in turn.

Trade facilitation and growth
A large literature emphasizes the important role that openness to trade may have in boosting economic growth (Grossman and Helpman (1991); Romer (1992); Barro and Sala-i-Martin (1995); Obstfeld and Rogoff (1996); Greenaway *et al.* (1998)). Empirical evidence confirms that developing countries applying more open trade regimes have enjoyed higher growth rates than those imp lementing restrictive policies (Dollar (1992); Sachs and Warner (1995); and Edwards (1998)). This conclusion, however, depends crucially on how openness is defined (Harrison (1996); Harrison and Hanson (1999); Rodriguez and Rodrik (1999)). When it is strictly limited to include only measures taken at the border e.g. tariffs, then growth appears to be almost unaffected by greater openness. When openness is measured by a wider range of policies falling under the trade facilitation agenda – including the level and variability of non-tariff barriers, effective infrastructure, level of international competitiveness, degree of state

monopolies etc. – then growth appears to be boosted whenever a country moves towards a more open regime. In sum, although a liberal tariff policy is beneficial because it enlarges the set of opportunities, a long-term effect on growth almost certainly requires such a policy to be combined with trade facilitation measures. For example, investment in public goods, such as transport and communications infrastructure, can greatly enhance the ability of firms and individuals to take advantage of the opportunities that may be created by tariff reduction. Others, however, claim that openness has played a relatively minor role. Indeed, some researchers argue that the high levels of protection and interventionist industrial policies adopted by some East Asian economies promoted an environment conducive to investment and technological learning and that these, rather than openness, may have been the real reasons for growth (see Wade (1990); and Rodrik (1999)).

Assuming trade facilitation contributes to positive growth in developing countries the "trickle down" effect should lift some of the poor above the minimum poverty levels. In addition, Solow's model predicts that poorer countries will grow faster than richer ones or, in other words, that through this process of convergence to the same level of growth, inequalities across countries' income levels will decrease. Therefore, unless growth seriously worsens income distribution, the proportion of the population living in absolute poverty will fall as average incomes increase. The balance of the evidence seems to be that although growth can be associated with growing inequality, the effects on poverty tend to be dominated by the advantageous direct effects of growth (see Demery and Squire (1996) on Africa). The effect also appears to generalize to the very poor, defined as those who live on less than $1 a day (see Chen and Ravallion (1996); Bruno *et al.* (1996)). In recent work, Dollar and Kraay (2001) found that, on average, the incomes of the poorest fifth of the population grew proportionately with GDP per head in a sample of 80 countries over four decades. This was as true of growth induced by openness to trade as that due to other stimuli.

INCOME DISTRIBUTION IMPACT OF TRADE FACILITATION

Trade facilitation and international trade

Transaction costs theory

In contrast with growth economics, international trade economics, with its general equilibrium mutli-sector and multi-factor apparatus, has always been a standard tool to study income distribution and poverty. Trade facilitation can be incorporated into models of international trade through the introduction of trade transaction costs. The key aspect to this is an alteration to the notion of "price". In these types of models there is a buyer's and a (lower) seller's price and the difference yields an income which compensates the real resources used up in the trade transaction (the cost of trade facilitation). When the operation of a market needs intermediaries that provide information or other services to buyers and sellers so that they can realize an exchange, then these intermediaries would receive the income generated by charging a transaction fee (=cost).

Another form of transaction cost has been considered in international trade and explicitly incorporated into models since Samuelson (1954). The basic concept here is that trade involves transaction costs and that these may be simply thought of as a fraction of the traded good itself, as if "only a fraction of the ice exported reaches its destination as un-melted ice." This "iceberg model" shows a reduction in transaction costs saves real resources and makes an economy more efficient.

These models highlight that among the benefits of trade facilitation are:

(1) *More efficient production and allocation of resources:* Trade facilitation increases the degree of competition faced by domestic producers through reducing transactions costs associated with import and export. This may result in closures and consequent unemployment, but can increase welfare in the long term by allowing a country to improve its efficiency of production in three ways:
  - Increasing the efficiency with which existing resources are used;
  - Encouraging specialization and the reallocation of resources towards those activities that reflect the country's comparative advantage;

- Allowing exploitation of economies of scale through exports to the world market.

(2) *Cheaper consumption:* Trade facilitation, by definition, reduces inefficiencies and obstacles to trade. In general, when markets are functioning efficiently, this will result in a reduction in the domestic price of goods, by making either cheaper foreign goods available or reducing the rents that may have previously been captured by domestic producers.

In sum, trade facilitation, through reducing trade transactions costs can lower the price of imports and import substitutes and reduce the cost of exports and exportables. The effects on incomes depends on whether labour is a net consumer or producer of each class of good and whether labour assumed to be mobile within countries. It is to a discussion of these effects that we now turn.

Production effects of trade facilitation: factor markets
In terms of production, trade facilitation will have two likely effects. As the price of imported inputs goes down and exports become more price-competitive, due to the more efficient trading environment, demand for labour to produce exports is likely to grow. At the same time, sectors that compete with imports will be exposed to more intensive competition and demand for these goods will decline. Consequently, demand for labour in import-competing sectors is likely to fall.

Crucial to the effects on income distribution of trade facilitation is the transmission of changes from output prices to wage rates, such as labour and intermediate goods and services. Depending on the situation, this transmission is enhanced, diminished or distorted by the labour market.[16]

---

[16] Two characteristics of developing countries play an important role in this context: the first is the presence in their labour markets of institutional rigidities and the second is the segmentation of these markets. For instance, minimum wages may only operate for specific groups of workers or specific sectors. In the presence of these rigidities and imperfect compliance, it is easy to show that a trade facilitation-induced price shock which adversely affects a labour-intensive sector, may not be felt by those (often more skilled) workers who are protected, but it may exacerbate the negative impact on the non-protected (less skilled) workers.

Labour markets allow the demand for labour to be matched with supply. This is typically done through movements in wage rates, with the result that employment and wages – the two variables of most relevance to poverty – are determined. The movement of labour between sectors plays a crucial role in the poverty effects of trade shocks. There are two opposite assumptions that can be made about the movement of labour: 1) that total employment is fixed but wages are variable and 2) wages are fixed but employment is variable.

Under the first of these assumptions price changes, including those emanating from trade facilitation measures, affect the incentives for firms to produce particular goods. The Stolper-Samuelson theorem proves that under particular conditions[17], an increase in the price of a good that is labour-intensive in production will increase the real wage and decrease the real returns to capital.[18] If poor households depend largely on unskilled wage earners, poverty will be alleviated by the resulting wage increase. Trade facilitation reduces the cost of producing exportable goods (which are likely to use a country's abundant factors intensively) and reduces the price of importable goods (which are likely to use scarce factors intensively). Developing countries as a group are clearly abundant in labour, so that a more efficient trading environment raises their wages in general.

---

[17] Assuming two factors of production, two 'small' (i.e. price-takers on world market) countries, two products, perfect competition and perfect factor mobility within countries.

[18] An increase in the price of any good will increase the incentive to produce it. This will raise the returns of factors of production specific to that good – for example, labour with a specific skill, specialist capital equipment etc. If the production of goods, intensive in the use of unskilled labour, increases, then unskilled wages rise. As these industries expand in response to higher output, they absorb factors of production from other sectors. By definition, an unskilled-labour-intensive sector requires more unskilled labour per unit of other factors than do other sectors, and so trade facilitation increases the net demand for unskilled labour and reduces it for other factors.

This result, however, cannot be generalized to all developing countries.[19] For example, countries in Latin America have abundant natural resources and much less labour than Asian countries and so would probably not be considered abundant in labour. Similarly, within individual developing countries, least-skilled workers may not by the most intensively used factor in the production of tradable goods (see Feenstra and Hanson (1995)).

The approach described above is based on the idea that the supply of labour is fixed. Consequently, an increase in the demand for labour increases its real wage. Another approach by contrast assumes that labour is not fixed in supply, such that any amount of labour can be obtained at the prevailing wage. If this is the case then the wage will be fixed and the adjustment to any change in prices brought about by trade facilitation will take place through changes in employment. If trade facilitation increases employment it may help some to move out of poverty.

---

[19] Outside the 2x2x2 framework, theory does not necessarily yield such clear-cut predictions. If a third factor of product ion – natural resources – is included and if primary products require complementary inputs of natural resources and capital, then their expansion following trade liberalisation may bid up the rewards to both of these factors at the expense of labour. A sim ilar result emerges if a country is assumed to be producing three commodities (export crops, subsistence agriculture and manufactures) using three factors (land, capital and labour) in different combinations. Assume export crops are more land-intensive and less labour intensive than subsistence agriculture and capital does not perfectly move across sectors: trade facilitation by raising export crops' domestic price causes an expansion of the export sector at the expense of subsistence farming. This lowers opportunities for labour and reduces wages. Outside the 2x2x2 framework, theory does not necessarily yield such clear-cut predictions. If a third factor of production – natural resources – is included and if primary products require complementary inputs of natural resources and capital, then their expansion following trade liberalisation may bid up the rewards to both of these factors at the expense of labour. A similar result emerges if a country is assumed to be producing three commodities (export crops, subsistence agriculture and manufactures) using three factors (land, capital and labour) in different combinations. Assume export crops are more land-intensive and less labour intensive than subsistence agriculture and capital does not perfectly move across sectors: trade facilitation by raising export crops' domestic price causes an expansion of the export sector at the expense of subsistence farming. This lowers opportunities for labour and reduces wages.

Neither of the two extremes of perfectly fixed or perfectly flexible labour supply is likely to hold for most developing countries. However, an economy with a highly flexible and mobile labour force will conform more closely to the first extreme than to the second, making wage changes of particular importance. Conversely, an economy with many labour market rigidities and a large pool of unemployed workers may justify a focus on the employment effects of trade facilitation.

In the case of Mozambique, for example, labour regulation is an area of policy where firms often complain. Mozambican regulations require that firms file monthly reports containing large amounts of data on the names of workers they employ, what jobs they hold, and how much they are paid. Far more restrictive are the regulations governing layoffs and hiring foreign workers. While the law allows firms to reduce their workforce, employers are forced to make such high severance payments that firms often keep unproductive workers on the payroll. This policy leads many firms, especially smaller ones, to hire only temporary workers who do not benefit from the same job protection. As a result labour market rigidities in Mozambique add to the already considerable risks of doing business and act to discourage firms from expanding (Biggs et al. (1999)).

A number of other factors, in addition to those discussed above, are critical for poverty-reducing trade facilitation in the international trade framework. First, poor people need to interact with markets to benefit. Yet, they may rely on goods that have no explicit prices (e.g. the environment) or own factors that are not easily marketable. Second, positive trade facilitation effects may eventually relieve the poor, but in the short-term the adjustment process may be more harmful than helpful. The poor may experience increased income risks in the short-term when they switch from producing import-competing goods to producing tradable exports.

Consumption effects of trade facilitation: price transmission
In addition to increasing exports, trade facilitation may also reduce the price of imports depending on the size of the trade transaction costs that are removed. If trade transaction costs have protected inefficient local production – then trade facilitation will result in imports becoming cheaper

which will put pressure on local firms to increase their efficiency or contract their output sufficiently to reduce costs if they are to survive. Bussolo (2001) by attempting to model (and apply empirically to Colombia) the distributional effects due to a reduction in trade transaction costs finds that a reduction in transaction costs can have strong positive effects on private consumption and therefore on households' welfare and their absolute poverty.

However, it is also necessary to consider the extent to which competition and product differentiation exists within world markets. Competition in the world market may affect the price reductions caused by trade facilitation. For example, if production of a good is dominated by a small number of firms, then these firms may be in a position to "price to market"; that is, to set prices above marginal costs according to what the market will accept. This situation is most likely to arise for goods that are strongly differentiated so that only one or two firms make a particular variety. Any trade facilitation measures taken in these markets are likely to be partly captured by increased company profits rather than being passed onto consumers. The same is true for goods whose world markets are truly monopolized, though in reality, there are relatively few of these.

These results only paint a partial picture of the consumption benefits of trade facilitation. One effect of a more efficient trading environment is that goods may shift from being not available to available. The welfare gains associated with the ability to obtain goods that were simply unobtainable before tend to be much larger than the gains associated with changes in the relative prices of existing goods (see Romer (1994)). This applies equally to the poor as Booth et al. (1993) document for consumers in Tanzania and Gisselquist and Harun-ar-Rashid (1998) show for agricultural inputs in Bangladesh.

It is also important to consider how price changes induced by trade facilitation are transmitted to the poor. This occurs directly through the distribution sector, but price changes may also be amplified or reduced due to the "domain" of trade (McCulloch et al. (2002). In determining the effects of a price change brought about by trade facilitation measures on the poor, it is vital to have a clear picture of these transmission channels and the behaviour of the agents and institutions they comprise. For example, sole buyers of export crops (that is, those to whom sellers have no alternative but to sell) will respond differently to price changes than will producers' marketing cooperatives. Domestic regulations that fix market prices by stockpiling can completely block the transmission of price reductions to the level of the poor.

Exactly the same applies for export goods and the price the poor will receive for their produce. This is well illustrated by the contrasting experience of markets in Zambia and Zimbabwe during the 1990s (see Oxfam-IDS (1999)). In Zambia, the government abolished the official purchasing monopsony for maize and the activity became dominated by two private firms, which colluded to keep prices low and abandoned purchasing altogether in remote areas leaving remote farmers with a huge problem. In Zimbabwe, by contrast, when the cotton industry was privatized, three private buyers for cotton emerged, including one owned by the farmers. Here, the abolition of the government sole purchasing requirement resulted in increased competition and prices, and farm incomes rose appreciably.

Second-round effects of trade facilitation
The overall effect of a trade facilitation-induced price change will depend on the poors' ability to adjust, switching consumption away from and production towards goods whose price has risen. But the act of substituting one good or activity for another necessarily transmits the shock to other markets that may not have been directly affected by trade facilitation. Thus, it sets off a whole series of "second-round" effects, which may be an important part of the overall impact. For example, increases in farmers' incomes are often believed to have big "spillovers" to employment-intensive local activities such as construction, personal servants and simple manufactures (see Timmer (1997); Delgado *et al.* (1998) and Mellor and Gavian (1999)). These are precisely the activities in which the poor have a large stake.

Government revenue

The third major link between trade facilitation and poverty is via taxes and government spending. In addition to the benefits derived from better market access, trade facilitation may also benefit the national economy by increasing collection of import duties through improving the efficiency of and reducing corruption in tax administration. Such an adjustment to the fiscal structure of an economy can provide resources to increase social and anti-poverty programme expenditures which tend to protect the poor. Trade facilitation systems such as ASYCUDA are aimed at reforming the customs clearance process through the introduction of streamlined processes and computerization. The objective is to increase revenue by ensuring that all goods are declared, duty/tax collections are correct and uniform throughout the country and exemptions are properly managed (UNCTAD (1996)). WTO (1998) reports ASYCUDA's success stories: following its introduction in the Philippines customs revenue increased by more than $215 million, Sri Lanka by more than $100 million and Panama by 3% in spite of a recent 50% cut in tariff rates. Similarly, Wafa (2001) reports that a mandatory evaluation of the implementation of ASYCUDA in Jordan found that revenue had stayed constant despite significant reductions in duty rates and that the system allowed trade statistics to be compiled more accurately and quickly.

Trade facilitation measures might also save on the costs borne by governments to pursue customs administration and enforcement. An increase in public sector efficiency through trade facilitation measures might enable governments to cut redundant resources or move such resources from resource-sufficient activities (such as document format verification) to more labour-intensive activities (such as physical inspection). Customs reform may, however, entail job losses for customs officials in developing countries. WTO (2001) report that in Costa Rica, which launched a customs modernization project involving the development of a computer information system in the early 1990s, administrative restructuring resulted in a fall in the number of employees from 1268 in 1994 to 555 in 1997 and 612 in 2000.

Other factors influencing poverty

Beyond the linkages between trade facilitation and international trade, growth and government revenue discussed so far, trade facilitation measures can also have an impact on income distribution and the poor in a number of other ways.

Trade facilitation activities such as increased provision of transport services and access to communications and finance can be vital determinants of the ability of the poor to market their production in domestic as well as in international markets. The incomes of the rural poor are strongly dependent on marketing and transportation costs and on the efficiency of transportation networks. High transport, marketing or communications costs lower the prices received by poor farmers and raise the prices of food to poor consumers. Larson (2000) finds, based on household surveys, that farmers' access to a public telephone is positively related to the price they receive in district markets for their output. Decreasing the distance to a telephone by 10% leads to a 1.6% increase in local prices. Even though rural villagers cannot afford a phone individually, they can afford one collectively (Lawson and Meyenn (2000)). Competition in these sectors is very important to poverty reduction, as are resources devoted to improve the efficiency of service networks. According to World Bank (2001a), "improving the road network...can accelerate the short- and long-run growth of agriculture and the economy" (p. 56). Stryker (1997) concludes that "increasing rural infrastructure, especially in the form of roads, is one of the most effective ways of reaching the poor." For Madagascar World Bank (2001b) is clearer still: "...build infrastructure". By way of example, Mozambique has a classified road network of approximately 17400 miles, of which only 22%, is surfaced and 65% is in good or reasonable condition. Many of Mozambique's poor live and work far from any road; they must have access to roads in order to sell their products to local or foreign markets. With the support of donor agencies, Mozambique has improved its road network since the end of the civil war in 1992, rehabilitating more than 1800 miles and keeping approximately 9500 miles under routine maintenance. This expansion has focused on improving the north-south route and access to rural farming and coastal communities which should improve trade opportunities for many of Mozambique's poor, most of whom live in rural communities that thrive on agriculture and fishing, the products of which must be transported to market or port quickly (USAID (2002)). In addition to these benefits, the process of developing infrastructure, and labour-intensive road construction in particular, presents an ideal opportunity to employ the rural poor productively in trade facilitation programs.

Liberalization of services (e.g. transport, communications) under the trade facilitation agenda and the resultant competition is likely to lead to lower prices, greater availability and improved quality of services. In so far as the poor are consumers of these services, they are also likely to benefit. But, there is a twist. Frequently, pre-liberalization prices are not determined by the market but set administratively, and are kept artificially low for low-income users. Thus, prices of public transport may be kept lower than the cost of provision. The structure of prices is often sustained through cross-subsidization within public monopolies or through government financial support. New entrants may focus on the most profitable market segments ("cream-skimming"), such as urban areas, where the cost or service provision may be lower and incomes higher. Privatization could mean the end of government support. The result is that even though the sector becomes more efficient and average prices decline, the prices for low-income households may actually increase and/or availability decline. In the case of agricultural exportables, increased domestic transport efficiency to the port will typically raise inland farm gate prices. This could worsen the welfare of low-income consumers of that product in inland areas. It is also important to ensure that privatization does not simply replace public monopolies with private monopolies, which would most likely be anti-poor and income-concentrating.

Universal service or access goals are not contradictory with liberalization of service markets. The handicap of providing services to low income households can in principle also be imposed on new entrants in a non-discriminatory way. Thus, universal service obligations can be part of the license conditions for new entrants into fixed network telephony and transport. But recourse to fiscal instruments has proved more successful than direct regulation – for examp le, through universal service funds or subsidies for providing services in rural areas.

Another effective mechanism is to fund the consumer rather than the provider through vouchers, as has been the case for education and energy services in a number of countries.

Conclusions and recommendations

Openness to trade has long been seen as an important element of sound economic policy and trade facilitation is a necessary step for achieving it. In general trade facilitation is an ally in the fight against poverty: trading more efficiently tends to increase average incomes, providing more resources with which to tackle poverty. And while it may affect income distribution, it may not do so in a systematically adverse way. Nevertheless, it is important to recognise that, as with most trade reforms, some groups may be adversely affected, pushing them into, or deeper into, poverty, even while other groups may benefit as it boosts incomes in total.

The country evidence presented in this report makes a compelling case for the positive impact trade facilitation can have on increasing exports, incomes and employment of the poor in developing countries. There is also evidence to suggest that trade facilitation measures can benefit less liberal economies with higher tariff barriers, since they reduce the cost and risk of exporting and may attract foreign investment. Since small firms bear disproportionate trade transactions costs, trade facilitation is especially important for SMEs, the dominant actors in developing countries.

Trade facilitation potentially affects income distribution and poverty through its effects on growth, international trade and government revenue.

Growth theory does not unambiguously suggest that tariff liberalization has a positive impact on growth in developing countries. However, those countries that have liberalized tariffs *and* adopted wide-ranging trade facilitation measures, have enjoyed higher growth rates than those implementing restrictive policies.

SHARING THE GAINS OF GLOBALIZATION

An open and simple trade environment can foster external discipline, helping to reduce distortions on domestic markets, and to narrow the scope for wrong or unbalanced policies in other areas, as well as rent-seeking and corruption which do not normally favour the poor. Moreover, improvements in infrastructure allow the poor to trade more easily and profitably domestically as well as internationally.

In terms of trade theory, trade facilitation reduces the cost of competitiveness of exports and reduces the price of imports. In small economies that are abundant in unskilled labour, and capital is scarce, unskilled labour gains at the expense of capital owners. This changes income distribution in favour of the poor. However, if trade facilitation measures benefit some sectors more than others, an unskilled labour abundant country pushing policies to reduce its trade transaction costs can indeed experience increased income inequality whenever cost savings are *lower* for those sectors that use intensively the more abundant, labour, factor.

For government revenue, trade facilitation may benefit the national economy by increasing collection of import duties through improving the efficiency of and reducing corruption in tax administration. An increase in government resources can benefit the poor if they are used to support pro-poor or social expenditures.

Although trade facilitation measures through the channels discussed above can be expected to benefit the poor *as a whole*, in formulating trade facilitation programs developing countries should consider their impact on their poorest citizens and develop measures that will ease the transition for any who are adversely affected and least able to cope. Many of the poor in developing countries may not be affected by trade facilitation. This is especially true for subsistence households who do not produce crops that can be exchanged for goods and who do not sell their labour outside the family farm. Because their subsistence households are "outside the market economy" they are not as affected by external economic circumstances. But most of the poor in developing countries are affected by the general economy. They sell products, cash crops, handicrafts and labour. Most stand to benefit from trade facilitation as a result of increased exports and lower priced imports of inputs and consumables. For some, however, trade facilitation could be disruptive. The poor do not have an asset base to cushion their consumption needs as they adjust their production or labour skills to a new economic environment. Even the near-poor can be thrown into poverty as formerly protected industries are forced to compete or close in a more efficient trading regime.

However, it is important to point out that failure to implement trade facilitation measures should not be justified as a direct pro-poor measure. To be effective policy instruments should be directly linked to their objective. Inefficient trading environments may benefit poor people only though protecting labour-intensive sectors from competitive imports, but they may also create a host of additional distortions (e.g. higher prices, barriers to export) that harm them.

A number of policy recommendations can be drawn from this report. In particular:

- To reduce income inequalities in developing countries trade facilitation measures should be targeted at lowering trade transactions costs in those sectors where employment of the poor is concentrated.
- The provision of effective safety-nets may be necessary if alternative forms of employment are not rapidly available for any displaced workers.
- Any increase in government resources brought about by trade facilitation should be used to support pro-poor or social expenditures.
- SMEs, the dominant actors in developing countries, need t o be able to access capital, trade information systems and capacity building to comply with international standards under trade facilitation programmes if they are to trade efficiently.
- Infrastructure can be particularly beneficial for the poor if they are actively employed in its development.

Reference list:

Amjadi, A. and Yeats, A. (1995), 'Have Transport Costs Contributed to the Relative Decline of Sub-Saharan African Exports?', *World Bank Working Paper Series No.1559.*
APEC, (1996), *1996 Report to Economic Leaders*, APEC Business Advisory Council.
APEC, (2000), *Cutting Through Red Tape: New Directions for APEC's Trade Facilitation Agenda,*
APEC, (2001), *Paperless Trading: Benefits to APEC.*
Barro, R. and Sala-i-Martin, X., (1995), *Economic Growth*, McGraw-Hill.
Bennathan, E. (1989), 'Deregulation of Shipping: What is to be Learned from Chile?', *World Bank Discussion Paper No.67.*
Biggs, T., Nasir, J. and Fisman, R. (1999), 'Structure and Performance of Manufacturing in Mozambique', *RPED Paper No.107.*
Booth, D., Lugngira, F., Masanja, P., Mvungi, A., Mwaipopo, R., Mwami, J. and Redmayne, A., (1993), *Social, Economic and Cultural Change in Contemporary Tanzania: A People Orientated Focus*, Swedish International Development Authority.
Bruno, M., Ravallion, M. and Squire, L. (1996), 'Equity and Growth in Developing Countries: Old and New Perspectives on the Policy Issues', *World Bank Policy Research Working Paper No.1563.*
Bussolo, M., (2001), *How Many Forms Do I Have to Fill To Export My Coffee? The Role of Transaction Costs in Explaining Economic Performance in Latin America?*, OECD Development Centre, Paris.
Cerrex, (2002), *Non-Tariff Barriers to Exports From Southern Africa*, DFID Regional Trade Support Programme - Scoping and Design Study No. 4.
Chen, S. and Ravallion, M. (1996), 'Data in Transition: Assessing Rural Living Standards in Southern China', *China Economic Review 7*, pp. 23-56.
Cudmore, E. and Whalley, J. (2002), 'Border Delays and Trade Liberalisation', *Economic Policy Research Institute Working Paper No.2002-6.*
Delgado, C., Hopkins, J., Kelly, V., Hazell, P, McKenna, A., Gruhn, P., Hojjati, B., Sil, J. and Courbois, C., (1998), *Agricultural Growth Linkages in Sub-Saharan Africa*, IFPRI Research Report 107, Washington.
Demery, L. and Squire, L. (1996), 'Macroeconomic Adjustment and Poverty in Africa', *The World Bank Economic Review 11*, pp. 39-59.
Dollar, D. (1992), 'Outward-Orientated Developing Economies Really Do Grow More Rapidly: Evidence from 95 LDCs, 1976-1985', *Economic Development and Cultural Change*, pp. 523-544.
Dollar, D. and Kraay, A. (2001), 'Growth is Good for the Poor', *World Bank Policy Research Working Paper No.2587.*

Edwards, S. (1998), 'Openness, Productivity and Growth: What Do We Really Know?' *Economic Journal 108*, pp. 383-98.

Ernst and Whinney (1987), 'The Cost of 'Non-Europe': Border related controls and administrative formalities', *Research on the Cost of 'Non-Europe' - Basic Findings, Vol.1,* Commission of the European Communities, pp. 7-40.

ETPAD, (1998), *Trade Facilitation Measures in Processed Food Trade*, Economic and Trade Policy Analysis Directorate - Policy Branch.

Feenstra, R. and Hanson, G. (1995), 'Foreign Investment Outsourcing and Relative Wages', in Feenstra, R., Grossman, G. and Irwin, D. (eds.), *Economy of Trade Policy: Essays in Honour of Jagdish Bhagwati,* MIT Press.

Fidler, S. (2001), 'Shipping Cartels more Damaging than Tariffs', *Business Day 2 March 2001.*

Financial Times. (2003), 'High Ideals and Murky Realities', *Financial Times, Monday, 27 January 2003.*

Fink, C., Mattoo, A. and Neagu, I. (2002), 'Trade in International Maritime Services: How Much Does Policy Matter?' *World Bank Policy Research Paper No.2522.*

Francois, J. and Wooton, I. (2001), 'Trade in International Transport Services: The Role of Competition', *Review of International Economics, 9(2), pp. 249-61.*

Gisselquist, D. and Harun-ar-Rashid, (1998), *Agricultural Inputs Trade in Bangladesh: Regulations, Reforms and Impacts*, World Bank.

Greenaway, D., Morgan, W. and Wright, P. (1998), 'Trade Reform, Adjustment and Growth: What Does the Evidence Tell Us?', *Economic Journal 108*, pp. 1547-61.

Grossman, G. and Helpman, E., (1991), *Innovation and Growth in the Global Economy,* MIT Press.

Guasch, L. and Spiller, P. (1999), 'Managing the Regulatory Process: Design, Concepts, Issues and the Latin America and the Caribbean Story', *Latin American and Caribbean Studies (The World Bank).*

Hare, P. (2001), 'Trade Policy During the Transition: Lessons from the 1990s', *The World Economy 24(4).*

Harrison, A. (1996), 'Openness and Growth: A Time-Series, Cross-Country Analysis for Developing Countries', *Journal of Development Economics 48*, pp. 419-447.

Harrison, A. and Hanson, G., (1999), *Who Gains From Trade Reform? Some Remaining Puzzles*, National Bureau of Economic Research.

Henderson, V., Shalizi, Z. and Venables, A. (2001), 'Geography and Development', *Journal of Economic Geography, 1,* pp. 81-106.

IECC, (1996), *Implementation of ECE/FAL Recommendations [063] - Methodology for Estimating Costs and Benefits of Trade Facilitation*, International Express

Carriers' Conference, (TRADE/WP.4/R.1260), contribution to the UNECE meeting (17 June 1996).

Krugman, P., (1998), *The Accidental Theorist*, Norton: New York.

Lamont, J. (2002), 'African Trade Clogs up Dockside', *Business Day 21 January 2002*.

Larson, D. (2000), 'Crop Markets and Household Participation', *World Bank*.

Lawson, C. and Meyenn, N. (2000), 'Bringing Cellular Phone Services to Rural Areas', *Viewpoint, Note 204, The World Bank*.

Limao, N. and Venables, A., (2000), *Infrastructure, Geographical Disadvantage and Transport Costs*, World Bank Research Paper.

McCulloch, N., Winters, A. and Cirera, X., (2002), *Trade Libralisation and Poverty: A Handbook*, Centre for Economic Policy and Research.

Mellor, J. and Gavian, S., (1999), *The Determinants of Employment Growth in Egypt - The Dominant Role of Agriculture and the Rural Small Scale Sector*, Abt Associates.

Messerlin, P. and Zarrouk, J., (1999), *Trade Facilitation: Technical Regulations and Customs Procedures*, September 1999 for the WTO/World Bank Conference on Developing Countries in a Millennium Round.

Mikuriya, K., (2001), *Overview of Technical Assistance Activities by Japan's Customs*, presentation note for the WTO Workshop on Technical Assistance and Capacity Building in Trade Facilitation (Geneva, 10-11 May 2001).

Obstfeld, M. and Rogoff, K., (1996), *Foundations of International Macroeconomics*, MIT Press.

OECD, (2001), *Business Benefits of Trade Facilitation*, Working Party of the Trade Committee, TD/TC/WP(2001)21/FINAL.

Otsuki, T., Wilson, J. and Sewadeh, M. (2001), 'A Race to the Top? A Case Study of Food Safety Standards and African Exports', *World Bank Working Paper 2563*.

Oxfam-IDS, (1999), *Liberalisation and Poverty*, Report to DFID, August 1999.

Rodriguez, F. and Rodrik, D. (1999), 'Trade Policy and Economic Growth: A Skeptic's Guide to the Cross-Country Evidence', *Centre for Economic Policy Research, Discussion Paper Series, No.2143*.

Rodrik, D. (1999), 'Investment Strategies', in Rodrik, D. (eds.), *The New Global Economy and Developing Countries: Making Openness Work*, Overseas Development Council.

Romer, P. (1992), 'Two Strategies for Economic Development: Using Ideas and Producing Ideas', *World Bank Annual Conference on Economic Development*, World Bank.

Romer, P. (1994), 'New Goods, Old Theory and the Welfare Cost of Trade Restrictions', *Journal of Development Economics 43*, pp. 5-38.

Sachs, J. and Warner, A. (1995), 'Economic Reform and the Process of Global Integration', *Brookings Papers on Economic Activity 1*, pp. 1-95.

Samuelson, P. (1954), 'The Transfer Problem and Transport Costs, II: Analysis of Effects of Trade Impediments', *Economic Journal*, No. 64, (June), pp. 264-289.

SITPRO, (1991), *Exporters' Problems with Commercial Letters of Credit*, UK Simpler Trade Procedures Board.

Staples, B. (2002), 'Trade Facilitation: Improving the Invisible Infrastructure', in Hoekman, B., Mattoo, A. and English, P. (eds.), *Development, Trade and the WTO: A Handbook,* World Bank.

Stryker, J. (1997), 'Impact of Outward-Looking Market-Orientated Policy Reform on Economic Growth and Poverty', *Consulting Assistance on Economic Reform II, Discussion Paper No.6,* June 1997.

Thai media (2001), *Thai no Jimoto Shinbun wo Yomu,* (in Japanese: Reading Thai Newspaper) 7 March 2001, http://member.nifty.ne.jp/jean/Papers/Old/210301-10.html.

Timmer, P. (1997), *How Well Do the Poor Connect to the Growth Process?* CAER Discussion Paper 17, Harvard Institute for International Development.

UNCTAD, (1996), *UNCTAD TD/B/COM.3/3, 22*, November 1996.

UNCTAD, (2001), *Review of Maritime Transport, 2001*, United Nations Conference on Trade and Development: Geneva http://www.unctad.org/en/docs/rmt01sum.en.pdf

UNECE, (1999), *Recommendation on Preshipment Inspection*, Recommendation No. 27 adopted by the United Nations Centre for the Facilitation of Procedures and Practices for Administration, Commerce and Transport, Geneva [now known as the United Nations Centre for Trade Facilitation and Electronic Business (UN/CEFACT)].

UNECE, (2002a), *Trade Facilitation in a Global Environment*, United Nations Economic Commission for Europe (TRADE/2002/21).

UNECE, (2002b), *Landlocked Countries: Opportunities, Challenges, Recommendations, Committee for Trade, Industry and Enterprise Development (UNECE)*, Background Paper for the International Forum on Trade Facilitation, 29-30 May 2002. (TRADE/2002/23 and TRADE/2002/23/Corr.1).

USAID, (2002), *Mainstreaming Trade: A Poverty Reduction Strategy for Mozambique*, Nathan Associates.

USAID, (2003), *Export Success in Costa Rica and Mauritius*, Report for USAID, Washington: Nathan Associates.

Wade, R., (1990), *Governing the Market: Economic Theory and the Role of Government in East Asian Liberalisation*, Princeton University Press.

Wafa, M., (2001), *Implementation of the ASYCUDA System in Jordan as a Means of Facilitating Trade*, presentation at the WTO workshop on technical assistance and capacity building in trade facilitation, WTO Secretariat, 10-11 May 2001.

SHARING THE GAINS OF GLOBALIZATION

Wilson, J., Mann, C., Woo, Y., Assanie, N. and Chio, I., (2002), *Trade Facilitation: A Development Perspective in the Asia Pacific Region*, Asia Pacific Economic Forum, October 2002.

World Bank, (1995), *Improving African Transport Corridors*, in Precis number 84, World Bank Operations Evaluation Department.

World Bank, (2001a), *Mozambique: Country Economic Memorandum*, 7 February 2001.

World Bank, (2001b), *Madagascar: Increasing Integration into World Markets as a Poverty Reduction Strategy*, 16 November 2001.

WTO, (1998), *WTO Trade Facilitation Symposium - Report by the Secretariat*, March 1998.

WTO, (2001), *Trade Facilitation Experiences Paper by Costa Rica*, G/C/W/265, 17 May 2001.

Appendix: Summary of Transport Cost Studies for Developing Countries

Study	Countries/Region	Results
World Bank (1995)	African landlocked	Final prices of imported products are from 30%-80% higher than the f.o.b. value of goods
WTO (1998)	India	Compliance costs for export procedures are 10% of the value of traded goods
Guasch and Spiller (1999)	Latin America	Monopoly port service providers and inefficient regulation of port operations give rise to implicit tariffs of 5%-25% on exports
Henderson *et al.* (2001)	African landlocked	Transport costs are 30%-40% of the value of trade
UNCTAD (2001)	Developing African	Freight costs as a proportion of total import value are 12% compared to 8.21% for all developing countries and 4.5% for industrialized countries
APEC (2001)	APEC	Moving to electronic documentation would yield a cost saving of 1.5%-15% of the landed cost of an imported item
Lamont (2002)	Africa	Freight costs as a proportion of total import value are 5 percentage points higher than the 8% average for all developing countries

* * * * * * * *

Chapter 1.10
Enhancing Trade and Transport Facilitation in Africa

Comfort Bohene-Osafo, Deputy Customs Commissioner of Ghana

As part of the government of Ghana's Economic Recovery Programme, strategic policies were formulated to help revive the country's ailing economy. The Gateway Project is one of such strategies adopted under the Ghana Trade and Investment Programme, which formulate programmes and policies and aim to implement them. The Gateway Programme seeks in the main to turn Ghana into a middle income earning country by the year 2020. One of the strategies adopted to achieve this is to formulate policies that will provide an enabling environment to attract foreign direct investment to Ghana, thus making it the preferred investment destination in the West Africa sub-region. The government therefore tasked various ministries and agencies to design policies to help achieve these objectives. In the following section, I will introduce some of the main initiatives of the Ministry of Roads and Transport and the Ministry of Trade of Ghana in some more detail.

Ministry of Roads and Transport

The Ghana Shippers Council under the auspices of the Ministry of Roads and Transport liaised with the shippers' councils in some of the landlocked countries in the sub-region to negotiate agreements that would facilitate the establishment of a transit corridor through Ghana to these countries.

As a result, the Ministry embarked on the improvement of the road network in the country, particularly the development of a two-route transit corridor from Terna to Burkina Faso through Paga along the western portion of the northern frontier and Bawku-Kulungugu on the eastern frontier with Burkina Faso.

In addition, the Ghana Ports and Harbours Authority, under the direction of the Ministry of Transport was equipped with modern cargo handling equipment while the ports were dredged to enable bigger vessels to berth there. There is also a drive towards privatization of some activities at the ports of Ghana to provide better facilities and services.

Ministry of Trade

The Ministry of Trade, under its Trade and Investment Programme, instituted the Gateway Project to oversee the development of *Export Processing Zones (EPZ)* as enclaves for processing goods for export while liaising with the Ministry of Finance to work out tax exemptions and other financial incentives to attract investments into the EPZ.

Having ratified the protocol on ECOWAS Trade Liberalization Scheme, Ghana is committed to moving towards harmonization of customs tariffs and removing customs barriers in sub-regional trade to foster un-impeded flow of goods within the sub-region. Measurable indicators were identified in consultation with the World Bank and the International Monetary Fund for seven frontline government agencies of the Gateway Project in order to improve these agencies' capacity to facilitate trade, transport and other investment activities. These are:

- Customs, Excise and Preventive Service (CEPS)
- Ghana Immigration Service
- Ghana Ports and Harbours Authority
- Ghana Civil Aviation Authority
- Environmental Protection Council
- Ghana Free Zone Board
- Ghana Investment Promotion Council

As one of the front line organizations in the Gateway Project, CEPS was required to modernize its cargo clearance procedures at ports with regard to importation, re-exportation and transit regimes. Some of the measurable indicators to be put in place by CEPS included:

a) Establishing and using of World Trade Organization (WTO) evaluation systems by the year 2000
b) Simplifying customs clearance procedures
c) Developing human resources and the training of officers
d) Fully automating the entire CEPS operations and networking with stakeholders
e) Reviewing relevant law codes of instruction
f) Developing and bringing into operation appropriate customs regulations to allow delivery of cargo into and out of the Free Zones.
g) Operationalizing the Customs Unit of the Export Processing Zone (EPZ) in line with EPZ regulations
h) Preparing and getting CEPS procedures and processes, ISO 9000 certified

In order to help achieve the objectives listed above, the Destination Inspection Scheme (DIS) replaced the Pre-shipment Inspection Scheme. The DIS, which inspects imports at the port of clearance, is intended to achieve the following objectives:

a) Facilitate trade
b) Provide an efficient price verification of imports
c) Check revenue loss by providing an impartial assessment of duties and taxes to be collected
d) Limit the opportunities for fraud, fiscal evasion and price discrimination
e) Support and enhance professional and technical capacity building for CEPS officers

The government of Ghana therefore contracted the Gateway Services Limited (GSL) aided by Cotecna and GSBV as strategic partners to assist Ghana Customs implement its strategies in line with WCO conventions for trade facilitation.

As part of its strategies, CEPS and DIS companies introduced a computer based *Risk Management System* to select imported goods for examination. In this direction, benchmarks for reduction from 100% examination of cargo to 20% for dutiable and 10% for statutorily free goods by 2003 were established. Based on risk assessment, shipments are separated into three examination categories, namely, *high risk (red channel)*; *medium risk (yellow channel)*; and *low risk (green channel)*. These are further subjected to five different levels of intervention:

Green: These are determined by the Computer Risk Management Systems (CRMS) as low risk. Goods in this category are allowed to leave the port without examination or inspection. However, CEPS is to conduct up to 5% random examination on this channel.

Yellow: (CEPS): These are medium risk, Less than Full Container Load (LCL) consignment dispatched to CEPS, which can exercise its discretion on whether to examine the goods, release them without examination, or subject them to documentary check.

Yellow: (scanning): Full Container Load, (FCLs) dispatched to scanning. These are subject to physical recheck only when the analysis of the scanned image detects a possible discrepancy. This re-check is done to ascertain the type and value of the discrepancy.

Red: *(CEPS):* These are high-risk, sensitive goods determined by the CRMS or intelligence information. They are goods to be physically examined by CEPS.

Red: *(GSBV):* These are high-risk, sensitive goods designated by the Ministry of Trade and Industry (MOTI) for mandatory-physical inspection by GSBV. This list comprises in the main foods, drugs, chemicals, and used clothing.

Scanner

Under the DIS, Scanco Ghana Limited, a subsidiary of Gateway Services Limited (GSL) installed a fixed X-Ray scanning machine for scanning full container loads of homogeneous goods. The scan has done so well that it has attracted customs officials from 22 different countries including the United Kingdom and Israel to observe its operations. 75% of these visits were from other African countries some of whose delegations have visited more than once.

As a result of these visits, Britain has installed seven scanners at its freight stations, and Nigeria has installed 14. There is another scanning facility at the Kotoka International Airport provided by the GSBV to facilitate clearance and at the same time check the types of goods passing through the port. CEPS has, in addition to these measures, reduced customs road checks on the transit corridor to facilitate the movement of goods along the corridor.

GCNet

The Ghana Community Network Limited, GCNet, in collaboration with CEPS has developed an online customs clearing system, Ghana Customs Management System, GCSM, to further facilitate the clearing of goods from ports. This system has enabled the clearing of goods in three hours from documentation to the release of cargo at the Kotoka International Airport freight terminal, where the system currently operates.

Currently, the GCMS is operating at the Tema port as well, and by June of 2003, it should be fully installed there. It is estimated that the cargo clearing time, when the online clearing is fully operational, will be reduced to just one day. By the close of 2003 the GCMS should be also introduced at the Takoradi port. Moreover, it is envisaged that the year 2004 will see the implementation of the GCMS at Aflao and Elubo, the major eastern and western frontiers. In the long run, online clearing will be eventually extended to the northern collection points at Tamale and Bolgatanga to facilitate clearance and at the same time provide audit trail for post-clearance verification.

Improvements in trade transactions

Transit trade
As a result of these strategies, trade statistics since 2000 have shown that there has been a tremendous improvement in the volume of trade through the ports of Ghana to Burkina Faso, Mali, Niger and even Togo and Cote d'Ivoire. In the year 2000 the volume of goods that transited through Ghana was 251, 663 metric tons. This grew by 142.83% to 611,119 metric tons in 2002. Figure 1.10.1 illustrates both re-export and transit for the period.

Figure 1.10.1. Re-export & transit trade

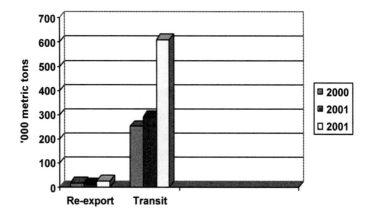

The year 2003 has a lot of promise for transit trade through Ghana. For the first quarter alone, total transit volume has topped 205,050 metric tons, amounting to about 33.55% of 2002 annual performance.

Re-export and transit trade

Figure 1.10.2. Re-export and transit trade analysis 2002-2003

	2000		2001		2002	
	Weight (tons)	CIF ¢	weight (tons)	CIF ¢	weight (tons)	CIF ¢
Re-export	19,694	44,459,739,902	13,613	91,427,805,463	25,417	175,757,004,819
Transit	251,663	761,744,478,076	291,748	1,790,963,167,503	611,119	2,113,567,901,712

It was observed during this period that most of the land-locked countries in the Western Africa sub-region, which until the creation of the Transit corridor through Ghana had used the ports of Côte d'Ivoire, have recently increased using Ghana's ports. All these countries belong to francophone West Africa and the use of a single currency and one official language with Côte d'Ivoire had made it preferable for them in previous times to use the Ivorian ports. Mali, Niger and Burkina Faso have also shown increases in their cargo volumes transiting through Ghana from 1,173 metric tons, 69,170 metric tons and 35,835 metric tons respectively in 2000, to 96,025 metric tons, 99,937 metric tons and 146,942 metric tons in 2002, as shown in Figure 1.10.3 below.

Figure 1.10.3. Transit by country (metric tons)

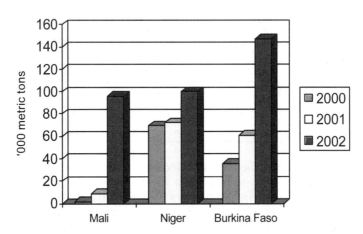

It is recommended that Burkina Faso take steps to establish inland port(s). The Ghana Ports and Harbours Authority has however opened offices there to facilitate transit trade by providing door-to-door cargo delivery services.

Figure 1.10.4. Transit trade, first quarter 2003

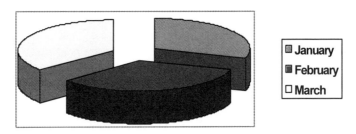

Re-export

Wile transit trade has improved in the last two years, re-exportation of goods previous imported into the country has also been on the ascendancy, showing a 29.05% increase since 2000.

Some merchants have taken advantage of the introduction of the Free Zone enclaves to import and repackage their goods for re-export to other countries in the sub-region. Others who do not qualify to operate in the Free Zones keep their goods in bonded warehouses while they look for market in the sub-region, thus taking advantage of the improved customs warehouse regime.

The improvement in the volume of trade, particularly transit trade, has been attributed, among other things, to the short route through Ghana to those countries that use the corridor, the improved documentation at the ports and the reduction of cargo clearance time from our ports.

Computer Risk Management System

New clearance procedures introduced at the ports as a result of the computer based Risk Management System and the scanning machine has reduced the hitherto cumbersome 100% physical examination of goods.

The new system provides fast clearance of cargo from the ports by concentrating on non-compliant traders thus reducing the cost of doing business for customs itself and the compliant trading public.

X- ray scanner

The scanning cargo in machine has revolutionized examination of container Ghana. It has enabled fast clearance of container cargo, from customs documentation to scanning and release in a matter of 15 minutes. Its effect is an encouragement to other African countries to start the Destination Inspection Scheme and the automation of customs procedure on their own.

Recommendations have been made for homogeneous transit container cargo to undergo x-ray scan and a hard copy of the results attached to the accompanying transaction documents to the country of destination. This will reduce clearing time in the destination country by eliminating the cargo examination time.

Privatization at the Port of Tema

The recent dredging of the Tema Port, the largest port in Ghana, has allowed more big vessels to berth at the same time instead of waiting at the breakwater for days for their return to berth. The Ghana Port and Harbours Authority has encouraged private companies to provide cargo handling equipment in the port to improve the authority's facilities. This has reduced ship turnaround time and had made our ports attractive to shipping lines.

The creation of container freight facilities outside the port area as well as the building of the inland port at Kumasi will further facilitate trade and transit in Ghana. When the new clearing system, GCMS, comes into full operation at the Tema Port, which handled about 75 percent of the country's import trade in June 2003, Ghana's trade facilitation efforts will be boosted.

Recommendations

While the transit trade has improved, it could have done better if haulage transport were readily available. It is recommended that the Ministry of Roads and Transport take steps to encourage investment in long distance haulage transport facilities to further facilitate transit trade.

CEPS has problems with tracking transited non-containerized cargo, thus losing revenue to transit cargo diverted for consumption within Ghana. Help must therefore be sought for equipment and training to manage transit cargo as it passes through Ghana.

Chapter 1.11
The Development Dimension of Trade Facilitation – the Perspective of Angola

Vitorino Hossi, Minister of Trade, Angola

I would like to start by commending UNECE on the excellent organization of the Second International Forum on Trade Facilitation, as it provides a real opportunity to stimulate considerations and concrete p roposals, making it possible for such countries as Angola to have more active and effective participation in the international trading system.

What is normally meant by trade facilitation is an operation of simplification, standardization and rationaliza tion of trade procedures, and in particular, the roles and formalities of imports, exports, and transit applied by customs and other bodies. Less frequently, trade facilitation is considered to be an activity consisting of creating a good environment and of assistance to participants in trade and transport operations, and in identifying solutions in the interest of all parties, thus setting the basis for sustainable development of trade.

Without categorically rejecting the first definition, we consider the second more suitable for the state of development in Angola and the economic situation in which we currently find ourselves. With regard to the specific situation of Angola, which is at the end of a war of more than 30 years, many efforts are being carried out in the global framework of reconstruction and development in the country. Indeed, with its accession to the international specialized agencies and regional agencies, including the World Bank, the International Monetary Fund (IMF), the World Customs Organization (WCO), the World Trade Organization (WTO), and the Trade Protocol of the South African Development Communit y (SADC), several measures have been taken to facilitate the trade of goods and services. Some of these have been the creation of a single window for the constitution of companies; the establishment of a nomenclature based on a harmonized system and the co ding of goods; a proposal for a new law on private investments; liberalization of the bank system making it possible to create private commercial banks; and the approval of the law on the licensing of trade activities relating to formalities linked to imports and exports.

In spite of these efforts, in a spirit of a greater openness of our market and trade facilitation, we are also aware of the existence of problems of a structural nature resulting to a large extent from the war situation, which has led to our being among the 48 least developed countries. These problems exist in sectors which are closely linked to sustainable development such as customs, transport, land and rail, telecommunications, insurance, sanitary measures and new information technologies.

The vital aspect of trade facilitation consists of close linkages that have to prevail between the private and the public sector. Indeed, trade facilitation permits the public sector to better follow the developments in external trade, as well as to provide support to national private commercial enterprises working in exports or who may do so. Thus, microeconomic measures such as a platform for permanent dialogue between the private and public sectors, the modernization of administrative apparatus, the elimination of certain bureaucratic barriers, the modernization and informatization of customs procedures and services, the establishment of transport infrastructure, land and rail, are important aspects to be taken account of in dialogue with our international partners. These are also measures that should be taken as quickly as possible, but with the support of bodies dealing with technical assistance. We thus consider that all of these measures can only take place with the multi-faceted support of the international community, and particularly of the European Union, UNCTAD, WTO, and the International Trade Centre (ITC), so to enable Angola to be better integrated in the global economy.

Chapter 1.12
Using ICT Standards to Advance Trade Facilitation: the Royal Malaysian Customs Experience

Siti Aminah Abdullah, Deputy Director of Customs, Malaysia

The role of customs in trade facilitation is manifold and includes the collection of duties, protection of society, promotion of industries, acting as the only non-discretionary factor in the international trade cycle, simplification, harmonization, automation and use of ICT standards.

UNECE Recommendation 25 on the use of UN/EDIFACT (Customs Information System & EDI Interface), which was adopted in 1994, is an example of such an ICT standard. It addresses data interchange between both public-public and public-private parties. Several examples of EDIFACT messages are CUSREP, CUSCAR, CUSDEC, CUSRES, CREADV, PAYORD, PAYMUL, CREMUL, and SANCRT. Between 75 and 100 per cent of transactions at major ports, airports and customs stations are currently following this Recommendation. In Malaysia, nationwide integration will be accomplished by the end of 2003. The Asia Region Customs Data Exchange Project is also based on this Recommendation, in which regional EDIFACT message specifications have been developed. The project addresses data exchange between Malaysia, the Republic of Korea, and Indonesia (Import & Export CUSDEC). It deals with trade in selected products but also serves for enforcement purposes. Some areas where EDIFACT is used include: payment of duties via Electronic Funds Transfer; the Gate Control System with port and terminal operators; out-bound CUSDEC with other government agencies (for example the Malaysian Statistics Department); "Paperless" Environment initiatives; and web-based Control Files.

Another example of the use of UNECE's trade facilitation standards is the implementation of Recommendation 26 on the commercial use of Interchange Agreements for EDI. Such agreements have been signed between traders and customs, and they mostly comply with the Model Interchange Agreement. Malaysian traders and customs have started using EDI even before Model Interchange Agreement was in place.

Malaysia has launched its TIGeR E-Logistics Project, which is based on international ICT standards. Phase One of the project has already been implemented. It bolstered the competitiveness of the Malaysian E & E Sector, where Intel and Dell are very active. It covers forwarders, air cargo, and selected customs stations by providing web-based software (e-Declare) using XML format over the Internet. The project allows processing steps in the trade procedure to be reduced from 10 to 4. The second phase of the Malaysian TIGeR E-Logistics Project is still under trial use. At this stage, we are testing whether the project is RosettaNet compliant (3B18 PIP), and the trials involve shippers, Dell, Intel, forwarders, and customs. 80% of declaration information comes via RosettaNet PIP. Forwarders make 20% of the data entries. The project thus proves that minimum human intervention is required.

Another example of using UNECE trade facilitation standards in Malaysia is the ebXML Pilot Project. We participate in the ebXML Asia Committee (eAC). We have tested ebXML with respect to invoices from consignors, forwarders, and exporters. We are now evaluating ebXML solution providers. The objective is to provide a fully paperless environment (electronic declarations and electronic invoices).

Malaysian Customs participate in the work of WCO on ICT standards, such as the development of the Customs Data Model, the Unique Consignment Identifier, and the various security initiatives. Agreements between the authorities of the United States and two ports in Malaysia (Port Klang & Tanjung Pelepas) within the Container Security Initiative (CSI) are pending. Discussions are under way with US Customs concerning the implementation of the 24-hour rule by October 2003.

In conclusion, I would like to state that the experience of Malaysian Customs shows that we are committed to trade facilitation: speeding up the flow of goods through the simplification and rationalization of procedures, their harmonization and automation, as well as the use of ICT standards.

Chapter 1.13
Possible Approach for a Trade Facilitation Agreement in the World Trade Organization
David Wakeford, CEO, Simpler Trade Procedures Board (SITPRO), United Kingdom

This discussion paper aims to give guidance related to a potential agreement on trade facilitation within the World Trade Organization (WTO). It is supportive of opening negotiations on an agreement in Cancún, in September 2003. It outlines a possible approach that matches the commitments to such an agreement, with the capacity of WTO members to implement it. The main aim is to improve the overall efficiency of the international trade process through a WTO agreement, and over time increase the wealth of all trading countries. A trade facilitation agreement will complement other WTO agreements, ensuring that international trade is conducted on a fair, efficient and predictable basis.

Trade facilitation and its WTO context

Trade facilitation is about more than just establishing customs procedures; it covers the broad aspects of the border management process associated with the movement of goods across international borders. It is crucial that at the outset there is a common understanding of the potential scope of a trade facilitation agreement. To ensure that the concept of trade facilitation encourages a focused approach to border management we suggest that it be confined to:

- the sustained improvement in the efficiency of moving goods across national borders, in full compliance with appropriate legislation, including security arrangements, and with proper regard to the collection of revenue and commercial payments;
- fully facilitating the border management process by basing an agreement on internationally accepted standards and practices.

The benefits of a WTO trade facilitation agreement

A successful trade facilitation agreement would further stimulate trade and increase the ability of the world's trading system to deliver improved prosperity to all participants. For such an agreement to work, it would have to reduce trade bottlenecks, be capable of objective assessment, and deliver measurable benefits to all concerned, particularly to developing countries.

Trade facilitation is vital to enable the regulatory process to keep up with the growth in trade and with modern trade practices. Trade facilitation does not mean a lowering of control standards or a threat to revenue collection. On the contrary, trade facilitation enables the maintenance and improvement of regulatory compliance, standards and revenue collection whilst allowing trade to flow more efficiently. In particular, by encouraging greater discrimination in the collection and use of data about trade flows, and by promoting modern control techniques (risk assessment, intelligent profiling, etc) it can enhance countries' ability to protect themselves against growing risks of fraud, criminality and the threat of international terrorism.

Trade facilitation will enable developing countries (and SMEs) to benefit disproportionately in a number of ways, including:
- greater efficiency of the border process making the task of revenue collection and detection of illicit traffic more effective;
- eliminating duplication and unnecessary activities, thereby reducing delays, and lowering the overall cost of international trade transactions, giving major benefits to government, business and ultimately the consumer;
- more efficient official controls improving predictability and helping reduce the incidence of theft and spoilage;
- easier access to developed country markets, and to those of other developing countries ("south-south" trade);
- at a time of ever increasing regulation covering security, clear and robust rules that improve the process of border management will improve the security of and confidence in the trading process;

- creation of a more open, transparent and predictable trading environment that will encourage foreign direct investment and improve economic perfo rmance.

Why is trade facilitation best managed within a WTO agreement?

Whilst there appears to be a broad consensus about the necessity to improve the efficiency of the trading process, there is some debate about whether trade facilitation commitments should be negotiated in the WTO. So why do we believe that there should be an agreement within the WTO?

- it will underpin other, existing agreements that are focused on the conduct of international trade;
- trade facilitation already exists in WTO but the provisions on it are not fully operational;
- the establishment of core standards for the border management of trade will ensure a level playing field for all WTO members. Small traders, developing countries, and particularly land-locked countries, have the biggest need of transparency, predictability and non-discrimination. They stand to gain most from a common approach. The WTO is uniquely placed to ensure that an agreement is effectively implemented and managed. It has a proven track record of setting fair rules and reliable mechanisms;
- the establishment of core standards for international trade within the WTO will stop the growth of barriers caused by unacceptably onerous, costly and slow procedures, and put all countries on the same path of improvement. If these core standards are adopted internationally, it will simplify the overall trading process: traders can import and export against globally accepted standards and processes instead of a proliferation of differing national ones;
- without a set of core standards covering trade facilitation, trade will always be subject to unpredictable national preoccupations and interventions. Trade growth in the modern, global economy cannot be sustained if the process is not predictable. A WTO agreement would improve the predictability of individual transactions and minimize national interventions in the trade process. International commitments

in the WTO, in other words, will ensure that the simplified and modern procedures put in place are not reversed;

- countries that are landlocked depend on their neighbours' goodwill for the transit of their goods to third country markets. Unless they have an enforceable international agreement to protect their trading rights, their commercial well-being could be undermined by unjustified border control and transit issues;

- there is currently a justifiable preoccupation with the potential use of international trade for terrorism. If countries operate a robust regulatory regime, guaranteed through the WTO, this should provide assurance to the importing country that security issues are being adequately addressed;

- it is important to ensure that standards of border management are progressively improved and to do this the border procedures need to be enforced. This is more likely to benefit developing countries trading with other developing countries, or developing countries exporting to developed countries, as they will be more able to predict the legitimate costs and procedures that their goods will encounter in export markets.

A possible structure for a trade facilitation agreement

Our suggestion for a WTO trade facilitation agreement is based on the following key principles:

- the agreement must have sufficient substance to create a measurable improvement to trade facilitation;

- the agreement must put all WTO members on the same road towards simplification of trade procedures;

- the agreement must measure and stimulate progressive improvement in the facilitation of trade and the adoption of higher standards;

- the agreement must offer developing countries the economic benefits of trade facilitation, without necessarily requiring them immediately to achieve the same degree of trade facilitation in all its aspects as the developed economies;

- application of the agreement must be subject to objective assessment, enforcement and policy review;
- GATT Articles V, VIII and X provide the appropriate platform for a trade facilitation agreement, whose purpose would be to expand on these articles and make them more comprehensive and operational.

We believe that an agreement should feature special and differential treatment, to allow developing countries to implement progressively a comprehensive package of trade facilitation measures, at a pace that they can accommodate. A "trade facilitation ladder" would define levels of facilitation to which countries would commit themselves. The larger developing countries or those most involved in international trade would commit to a higher level of facilitation than the poorest developing countries, who would take on rather a more basic or minimum set of WTO commitments.

WTO members would self-assess their position on the facilitation ladder, by considering the degree of facilitation that their regime offers related to the facilitation levels in the agreement and their resources capacities and constraints. However, all members would be required to meet the conditions of at least "level one". The core commitments implicit in acceptance of "level one" would deliver an immediate improvement in trade facilitation worldwide, and assessment and review mechanisms would encourage WTO members to move progressively up the facilitation ladder.

Measurement of trade facilitation

Our view is that an initial measurement of facilitation could be achieved using release times for imported goods. What does this mean in practice? As we see it, a trade facilitation agreement should not require WTO members to adopt uniform, harmonized release times for goods – this would not be feasible. Instead, each WTO member would establish for itself its own, domestic average release times, make those publicly known, and commit progressively to try to reduce them. A process of regular assessment either by each WTO member or multilaterally would enable the WTO to track progress in delivering trade facilitation.

The WTO commitment, in other words, would be to ensure that all WTO members engage in a process of simplification and move in a common direction, rather than to fix a completely uniform end result. This process aims to achieve improvement on a national basis to ensure that all member countries are moving in the same direction. It would not be used to compare performance between countries. In the longer term, members would be encouraged to develop more comprehensive measures of facilitation, which could ultimately be considered as an international standard approach. Objective measurement of the impact of trade facilitation would be a key ingredient in establishing its practical value and encouraging members to stick to, and indeed increase, their level of commitment.

Dispute settlement

An agreement in the WTO should be supported by appraisal systems, like country reviews, that are designed to ensure maximum transparency in the operation of the new arrangements, and they should be backed by an appropriate disputes settlement procedure. However, the rules developed should ensure that enforcement of commitments takes in account developing country capacity constraints.

Capacity building

The Doha development agenda firmly linked progress in new agreements to substantial support being given to those countries that do not have the capability or infrastructure to implement such an agreement. It is crucial for the implementation of a trade facilitation agreement that funds and technical assistance are readily available to those developing countries in need of support. The support of funds and technical assistance should be used to achieve an appropriate step-up the "facilitation ladder" referred to earlier.

Up until now the sponsorship given to countries to improve their capability to manage international transactions by a whole range of well meaning donors has been unsatisfactory. A wide range of donor organizations and countries have given significant funds and technical assistance, but because of the lack of coordination between the donors, there has been no consistent approach. The beneficiaries to this random approach to capacity building are not necessarily the recipient countries but the consultants. In future, the support must form part of a consistent and coordinated approach that will ensure sustainable improvement. The only way to ensure long term sustainable benefit is to measure the degree of facilitation both before and after the support has been given. While the primary donors must be the international governmental organizations and governments themselves, business could also be involved in capacity building through the supply of technical knowledge and infrastructural support. Substantial business support for capacity building is unlikely to happen until the funds for capacity building are managed far more efficiently. Greater levels of foreign direct investment in infrastructure at ports, airports, transit systems, etc., are also more likely to materialize if WTO Members can offer investors the predictability and transparency guaranteed by WTO commitments.

Conclusion

WTO agreements covering trade issues improve the overall efficiency and fairness of the international trading process. An agreement on trade facilitation is a natural extension of this approach, and would be a basic building block for the efficient movement of goods. Cancún offers a golden opportunity to improve the efficiency of the international trade process for the benefit of all WTO members and their traders. A WTO agreement would bring synergistic benefit to the process of trading internationally. It would be manageable and would attract funding and technical assistance. Without a WTO agreement, the benefits of facilitation of international trade would be very limited, especially for developing countries and SMEs, and perpetuate the current inconsistency and unpredictability for exporters and importers worldwide.

Chapter 1.14
Study on Trade Facilitation: Concerns, Options and the Way Forward[20]
Murray Smith, Crown Agents

This paper has been prepared by Crown Agents and DMI Associates, at the request of the United Kingdom's Department for International Development (DFID). It draws upon Crown Agents' and DMI's combined experiences in the trade field, and uses these experiences to analyse the concerns of developing countries relating to the possible design and implementation of trade facilitation initiatives.

In drafting this paper, the author has interviewed a number of Geneva-based delegates to the World Trade Organization (WTO), and consulted with a range of officials from developing and developed countries. The author has also sought the advice and input of a selection of officials from within the United Nations Economic Commission for Europe (UNECE), the United Nations Conference on Trade and Development (UNCTAD), the WTO, and the World Customs Organization (WCO).

The author is very grateful for the comments and advice received from all the above-mentioned parties, but any errors or omissions are the responsibility of the author. The views expressed in the paper are personal and should not be attributed to the Department for International Development (DFID). An electronic copy of this paper can obtained from

---

[20] The UK Department for International Development (DFID) supports policies, programmes and projects to promote international development. DFID provided funds for this study as part of that objective but the views and opinions expressed are those of the author(s) alone. This report is submitted to DFID but remains the copyright of Crown Agents and should not be used for any other purpose than for evaluation. It should not be reproduced in whole or part without the express written permission of Crown Agents. For more details: Crown Agents, St Nicolas House, St Nicolas Road, Sutton, Surrey SM1 1EL, United Kingdom, tel. +44 20 8643 3311, Email: pcsenquiries@crownagents.co.uk

DFID, through Jamell Zuberi, e-mail: j-zubeiri@dfid.gov.uk. Please send comments or queries to: Murray Smith, DMI Associates, e-mail: murraysmith@compuserve.com.

Executive summary

Recent years have seen a steadily growing interest in the subject of trade facilitation – amongst developed and developing countries alike. A number of factors have stimulated this. Over the last few decades, the expansion of international trade relative to national economies has brought into sharp focus the economic consequences of complex customs and trade-related procedures. This longer term trend is now being re-inforced by shorter term factors – the rapid spread of information technology, e-commerce and the renewed increase in trade procedures and security following the World Trade Centre disaster of September 2001.

As a consequence, the challenges to developing countries posed by the need to facilitate trade are becoming ever more pressing. Developing countries face challenges to participate in international negotiations on trade facilitation in the World Trade Organization (WTO) – and in other fora that are developing new standards for trade facilitation. At the same time, and more fundamentally, the implementation of trade facilitation measures is a developmental challenge, at both the national and regional level.

Key concerns
The research conducted during the course of this study indicates that developing countries have a number of key concerns about negotiations related to trade facilitation in the WTO. These are that:

- The forthcoming negotiations on trade facilitation in the WTO should be delayed, or their scope narrowed, in order to preserve negotiating room in the overall negotiations.
- The negotiations on trade facilitation will lead to obligations that are expensive and difficult for developing country administrations to implement.

- The scope for new obligations on trade facilitation under the WTO is uncertain.
- Developing countries are reluctant to be subject to new obligations which are subject to dispute settlement in the WTO.
- Commitments to capacity building and trade facilitation by WTO members will prove to be insufficient.

Challenges and opportunities
There are both competitive challenges to be addressed and potential opportunities to be realized which taken together should prompt developing countries to examine and implement trade facilitation initiatives.

The competitive challenges stem from the fact that trade facilitation initiatives will continue to be implemented on a voluntary basis amongst developed countries and those developing countries that are more dynamic traders – regardless of the stance which the majority of developing countries choose to take. This will result in competitive pressures on producers in economies that do not participate in trade facilitation initiatives.

Potential opportunities for developing countries stem from trade facilitation initiatives and related reforms of customs administration that will contribute to their economic development through the expansion of trade, through improvements in customs integrity and reduced incentives for corruption, through more effective and selective border controls, and through more efficient revenue collection.

Key conclusions
Trade facilitation needs to be recognized as a priority for development, since trade facilitation initiatives can be an important means to foster economic growth, creating an enabling policy and regulatory environment that both supports the expansion of trade and encourages investment.

An effort is therefore required from both recipient countries as well as donors (bilateral or multilateral) for clearly identifying trade facilitation as a priority – to ensure that it receives the attention it is due in development co-operation and the promotion of good governance. At the same time, developing countries need to be more active in articulating their vision of what would constitute an appropriate clarification of the rules for trade facilitation.

Introduction and background

Trade facilitation is a cross-cutting issue which impacts upon every country across the world. It involves many aspects of government policy, legislation and administration at the national level – and encompasses various initiatives and organizations at the international level.

Many developing countries have expressed concerns about their capacity to implement trade facilitation measures, and are reluctant to consider international initiatives which promote trade facilitation – either through negotiations in the World Trade Organization (WTO) or through the development of new instruments and standards for trade facilitation. Yet trade facilitation can, despite this, play a crucial role in helping developing countries to gain from trade and to promote their economic growth.

What is trade facilitation?
Trade facilitation refers, in general terms, to the capacity for goods to be moved expeditiously across national borders. However, the scope of the precise definition varies.
Trade facilitation is sometimes defined narrowly in relation to the various customs formalities and procedures which must be passed through to ensure the clearance of goods across national borders. According to this definition, trade facilitation refers to the simplification, harmonization and automation of trade procedures – in particular, the import, export and transit procedures applied by customs and other agencies to control the cross-border movement of goods.

Often, however, trade facilitation is defined more broadly, to encompass all the formalities and procedures related to international trade and the transportation of goods and services across borders – including contractual, transactional and payments issues. The wide scope of potential elements that relate to trade facilitation is suggested by the list of factors included in the diagnostics tool proposed by the World Bank in the context of the Global Facilitation Partnership for Transportation and Trade.[21] These factors include:

- The operational efficiency and integrity of customs services;
- The management of ports through which imports and exports are processed;
- Commercial integrity, and the compliance of the private sector with trade-related procedures;
- The national and international trade-related regulatory framework;
- Multi-modal transport operations and legislation;
- Payment systems for traded goods and services;
- The automation of trade-related systems and procedures;
- Agents' functions and attitudes;
- Institutional resources, and
- The flows of information and consultation between various parties involved in international trade.

Of course, any such list is a matter for discussion. Some observers would suggest that this list, although relatively broad in that it includes trade and transport issues together, still remains very focused on the movement of goods without considering the legal and transactional issues associated with e-commerce and supply chains in a cross-border context.

Scope of this paper
For the purposes of this paper, it is not necessary to choose definitively between a narrow or broad definition of what constitutes trade facilitation, but it is important to recognise that discussions of trade facilitation often shift between the narrower and broader definitions outlined above. Unless elsewhere specified, this paper uses the narrow definition of trade facilitation, since this is the definition that is used in WTO negotiating fora.

---

[21] Raven, J. (2001) *Trade and Transport Facilitation: A Toolkit for Audit, Analysis and Remedial Action.* The World Bank.

Although discussions in the WTO, the UN or in regional bodies can play an important role in promoting common approaches to trade facilitation, it is important to recognize that trade facilitation is also an issue for individual countries in their development strategies, independent of such international negotiations. Efforts to facilitate trade can inform various other development initiatives, such as the preparation of Poverty Reduction Strategy Papers (Preps) – themselves intended to promote greater co-ordination of donor assistance in line with national development priorities.

In response to the Terms of Reference (ToRs) provided by DFID, this paper examines the following questions:[22]

- Why is trade facilitation an issue for developing countries now?
- What are the concerns of, and challenges for, developing countries in the trade facilitation field?
- How can developing countries benefit from measures that facilitate trade?
- What are the related costs for developing countries of such measures? And,
- What steps could now be taken to broaden developing countries' involvement in the design and implementation of trade facilitation initiatives?

Why is trade facilitation an issue now?

<u>Key factors</u>
A number of factors – both longer-term trends and more recent developments – are stimulating current interest in developing and implementing better approaches to the facilitation of trade at the global and the regional level. As the volume of international trade has expanded relative to national economies, so the economic consequences of customs formalities and procedures or other legal and regulatory factors that delay or block the movement of goods across borders have become more

---

[22] In addition to the main body of the report, Appendix A examines a range of initiatives in the field of trade facilitation and Appendix B examines trade facilitation work within the World Trade Organisation.

significant in their economic implications. The response to this trend has been an increased focus on trade facilitation initiatives amongst the most developed countries – as well as some developing countries.

Longer-term factors which have spurred a growing interest in the field of trade facilitation include the overall trend to expanded international trade over the last half century, during a period of relative peace and security at the global level. Specific elements within this include:

- Reductions in transport costs due to new technologies and substantial investments in global transport infrastructure;
- Reductions in tariffs and trade barriers through global and regional agreements, and
- Reductions in international communications costs.

Shorter-term factors include the following:

- Reductions in tariffs and other trade barriers resulting from the Uruguay Round of 1995;
- The rapid spread of information technology, the Internet and e-commerce;
- The agreement under the Doha Declaration to prepare for negotiations on trade facilitation, and
- Renewed concerns about the need to maintain the integrity and security of goods moving across borders, in light of the World Trade Centre disaster and the United States Government's subsequent war on terrorism.

Obstacles to trade facilitation

Significant economic benefits can be realized through the implementation of trade facilitation measures. Even when customs services function relatively well, the costs of documentation and delays in the clearance of goods impose a significant burden on business – especially Small and Medium-sized Enterprises (SMEs). Yet in many countries customs services do not function well. The economic effects of the combination of high transport costs, lengthy delays in border clearance and relatively high trade barriers have compounding effects on the growth potential of many developing countries.

Landlocked Countries and Transport Costs

The combination of high transport costs, poor infrastructure, and the high costs of border clearance can be a substantial obstacle to development – especially in the case of land-locked countries. For example, the cost of shipping a standard container from Rotterdam to Dar es Salaam in Tanzania – a distance of 7,300km by air – costs $1,400, but shipping the same container to Kigali in Rwanda by road over a distance of 1,280km costs about double this amount.[23] So in economic terms Dar es Salaam is "closer" to Rotterdam than to Kigali. Studies by the World Bank confirm that the links between transport costs, poor infrastructure and poor trade performance are mutually reinforcing, particularly for land-locked African countries. These studies suggest that such different factors taken together explain to a considerable extent the poor trade performance of many landlocked countries.[24] The development challenge is to find ways to break out of the vicious circle of high transport costs, poor infrastructure and poor trade performance which besets many landlocked countries.

In considering the distribution of poverty and wealth in a globalising world economy, contemporary economists such as Rodrik and Sachs have brought back into discussion the role of geography and the concerns of the classical economists about patterns of economic development and growth. Tackling the challenges of uneven economic development and improving the development prospects of the poorer nations (and poorer regions of large nations such as China and India) requires a willingness to examine the obstacles to economic growth from the widest possible perspective – considering geography, transport costs, and infrastructure deficiencies. It also requires that policymakers recognize the ways in which inappropriate policies can raise transport costs and impede development.

---

[23] Gallup, J., Mellinger, A. and Sachs, J.D. (1998) *The Geography of Poverty and Wealth* – paper prepared for the World Bank. Centre for International Development, Harvard University.

[24] Limao, N. and Venables, A. (2000) *Infrastructure, Geographical Disadvantage and Transport Costs* – paper prepared for the World Bank.

Obstacles to trade facilitation can act in the same way as geographic barriers and poor infrastructure – reducing the potential for trade and contributing to underdevelopment and poverty. Measures that facilitate trade are comparable to reductions in transport costs. It is readily understood that building a new port or a railway tunnel through a mountain range can open up new trading opportunities, bringing economic benefits and helping impoverished peoples – but it is not always recognized that trade facilitation initiatives can offer similar benefits by expanding trade opportunities and thereby increasing opportunities for poverty reduction. Yet the investment required to introduce trade facilitation measures is frequently less costly and can yield greater returns over the longer term.

For landlocked states, the combination of high transport, transit and customs clearance costs adds significantly to cross-border transactions. The consequent low trade volumes reduce the quality and quantity of investment in transport infrastructure, in turn resulting in increased transport costs – creating a vicious circle. For these states, economic development requires investment in the "hardware" of transport infrastructure as well as the "software" of trade facilitation – but this presupposes co-operation with their neighbours. Costly investment in transport infrastructure will yield substantially more benefits, and would be more likely to be self-financing, if in parallel trade facilitation measures were introduced in order to permit goods to move more expeditiously across borders.

The poorer landlocked countries tend to have very limited capacity to participate in voluntary trade facilitation initiatives, and they are very dependent upon the co-operation of their neighbours if trade facilitation initiatives are to be successful. These landlocked countries are often not represented in Geneva for negotiations in the WTO, and their capacity to participate in the WTO is therefore extremely limited.[25]

---

[25] One notable exception to this is Paraguay, which maintains a Permanent Representative in Geneva at the WTO. The Government of Paraguay has made particular efforts to involve itself in international discussions through its Permanent Representative, drawing attention to and analysing the particular problems which poorer landlocked countries face.

In preparing this report, a special effort was made to contact officials in the capitals of landlocked low-income countries. Many of these countries do not have well-developed positions on the trade facilitation negotiations which take place in the WTO, and they participate only to a limited extent in voluntary trade facilitation initiatives. Yet these poor landlocked countries might benefit significantly from the clearer and more predictable rules for transit trade that could emerge from negotiations in the WTO. At the same time, the countries they import and export through could also benefit through broader economic development.

Challenges and opportunities

There are both competitive challenges to be addressed and potential opportunities to be realized which, when taken together, should prompt developing countries to examine and to implement trade facilitation initiatives. The competitive challenges stem from the fact that trade facilitation initiatives will continue to occur at least on a voluntary basis amongst developed countries – along with those transition and developing countries that are the more dynamic traders. They are therefore increasingly likely to expand their share of world trade, leaving those countries which do not engage in trade facilitation initiatives with correspondingly diminishing shares, leading eventually to further marginalisation and poverty.

Recent trends – such as the development of e-commerce and of inter-connected global supply chains – will continue and may even accelerate in the foreseeable future, despite the collapse of the Internet stock bubble. Even renewed concerns about terrorism and the security of the international shipment of goods, will not stop initiatives for trade facilitation amongst developed countries. Indeed, such concerns will probably serve to increase demand for such initiatives, as the new security measures emphasize the profiling of shippers and cargoes and pre-arrival electronic notification.

See Boettner, L. M. R. (2000) *Trade Facilitation – A Presentation by the Permanent Representative of Paraguay in Geneva.* WTO Paper G/C/W/237. This paper is referred to and discussed briefly in section four of this report.

There is also likely to be an additional stimulus on customs administrations towards the utilization of technology-based applications, to which developing country exporters may lack access.

Taken together, these new trade facilitation initiatives amongst developed countries and the concerns for intensified security surveillance, will lead to competitive pressures on producers in those countries which do not participate in the design and introduction of trade facilitation initiatives.

At the same time, trade facilitation initiatives and the related reforms of customs procedures in developing countries could contribute to their own economic development – through the expansion of trade, improvements in the environment for Foreign Direct Investment (FDI), improvements in customs integrity, more effective and selective border controls, and more efficient revenue collection. Achieving these potential benefits will however require substantial investment – to modernize customs and other border-related services. The ability of developing countries to maximize these benefits will also depend on the existence of complementary policies – such as education policy, and macroeconomic policy.

Trade facilitation initiatives will continue amongst the developed countries and those developing countries that are active in international trade – regardless of whether or not other countries participate in these developments. For developing countries it is important to understand any new proposals, as well as existing trade facilitation measures, and to consider how such instruments can be adapted to benefit them and to contribute to their development. Otherwise there is a clear risk of further marginalisation, especially of the very poorest countries.

Developing country concerns and challenges

General perceptions
In analyzing developing country perceptions about negotiations on trade facilitation in the WTO, a range of issues can be identified. These include:

- Issue linkage concerns
- The lack of familiarity with existing trade facilitation instruments

- Implementation concerns relating to existing Uruguay Round commitments
- Concerns that the mandatory obligations will be subject to dispute settlement
- Concerns that the new agreement will include standards that exceed developing countries' capacity to implement them
- Concerns that the new agreement will be developed without regard to developing countries' input
- Uncertainty over the scope of new obligations, and
- Scepticism about whether commitments to provide technical assistance and support through capacity building are meaningful and realistic.

The following sections discuss each of these issues in more detail.

Issue Linkage

The reluctance of some developing countries to involve themselves in the formal launch of negotiations on trade facilitation seems in part to be motivated by broader negotiating strategies and what can be described as "*issue linkage*". There is much greater reluctance on the part of some developing countries to initiate negotiations on the "Singapore issues"[26] – and thus there is reluctance to launch negotiations on trade facilitation in particular, because this could be perceived as creating a precedent for negotiations on the other issues. Although this concern seems to have been overcome in the agreement reached under the Doha Ministerial Declaration, the reservations expressed by a number of developing countries in the preparations for Doha mean that the issue could re-emerge in the context of the debate about the "modalities of negotiation" at the Mexico Ministerial Conference.

---

[26] The 1996 Singapore Ministerial Declaration mandated the establishment of working groups to analyse issues related to investment, competition policy and transparency in government procurement. It also directed the Council for Trade in Goods to undertake analytical work on the simplification of trade-related procedures, in order to assess the scope for WTO rules in this area. Since that time, these four areas (investment, competition policy, government procurement and trade facilitation) have come to be known collectively as the *Singapore Issues*.

Many developing countries also have concerns surrounding the number of issues being negotiated, and their ability to follow and participate in so many negotiations concurrently.

The potential for issue linkage to block negotiations on trade facilitation will inevitably remain an open question, because the overall balance of interests of various groups of countries is always a factor in the success or failure of a multilateral multi-issue negotiation. Although both developed and developing countries are members of the so-called "Colorado Group"[27] which supports trade facilitation negotiations in the WTO, many developing countries view developed countries as the "demanders" on this issue.

Undoubtedly the prospects for negotiations in the WTO on trade facilitation after the Ministerial Conference in Mexico will be influenced by overall developments in WTO negotiations. Issue linkage could re-emerge as a significant factor if negotiators do not sufficiently recognise the constraints or priorities of other members on more contentious issues in the Doha Development Agenda.

Challenges of implementing existing trade facilitation standards
Most developing countries do not participate in the full range of existing instruments under the United Nations Economic Commission for Europe (UNECE) and the World Customs Organization (WCO). Meantime, virtually all developed countries do participate in the full range of these trade facilitation instruments and conventions.[28] Of the various instruments surveyed, the participation of developing countries is greatest – but not universal – in the WCO International Convention on the Harmonized

---

[27] The Colorado Group was formed in 1998 to promote work on trade facilitation within the WTO, and consists of the United States, the European Union, Japan, Canada, Chile, Costa Rica, Australia, New Zealand, Hong Kong, Singapore, Korea, Hungary, Norway, Switzerland and Morocco. This marked the first time that a group of nations within the WTO assembled in a united front to promote the simplification and harmonisation of trade-related procedures.
[28] See annex entitled 'List of countries or territories having accepted or acceded to trade facilitation instruments' in UNECE (2002) *Compendium of Trade Facilitation Recommendations*. New York and Geneva, pp. 65-9.

Commodity Description and Coding System (1983), the UNCTAD ASYCUDA electronic customs programme, the UN Layout Key and EDIFACT standards for Electronic Data Interchange (EDI).

Furthermore, since these practices tend to be voluntary or best efforts, the issue is not simply a matter of ratification of international protocols, it is instead a matter of effective implementation within national administrations. Thus, there is a substantial challenge to encourage and support the participation of developing countries in these conventions and more importantly to assist them to implement these various instruments and conventions for trade facilitation.

Implementation issues in the WTO
The concerns of many developing countries about negotiations on trade facilitation in the WTO are linked to concerns about the resources necessary to implement existing WTO agreements. Particular examples of such concerns include:

- Requirements relating to the reform of customs valuation legislation and methods;
- The removal of performance requirements on investment;
- Prohibitions on import-substitution and export-linked subsidies, and
- Requirements for the protection of intellectual property rights.

Principally, these concerns have been driven by the belated realization of domestic policy needs and the economic impact of change, and also in part by realization of the domestic political will needed to secure sustainable reform.

An extensive review of the implementation issues facing developing countries in the WTO was undertaken during the period between 2000 and 2002, and agreement on the Doha Ministerial Declaration for future negotiations was only reached in conjunction with a parallel lengthy and detailed Ministerial decision on Implementation Issues. The WTO debate about "implementation", especially in respect to customs valuation, has directly influenced the debate about trade facilitation. Many developing countries have just experienced, or are still facing, challenges in the implementation of obligations such as the reform of customs valuation legislation and administrative procedures. These remain expensive and difficult for them to implement because of the limited capacities of their customs services, and as a consequence they are very reluctant to take on new obligations which impose related but additional challenges.

For example, since many developing countries lack sophisticated tools and operating procedures for comparing prices on invoices for imports or exports of similar products, they remain worried about the shift to the transaction value standard for customs [29], which they perceive as increasing the potential for a greater incidence of price manipulation and customs fraud, which in turn undercuts both tariff and tax revenues. Several developing countries are concerned that WTO negotiations may bind them to new standards that will exceed their capacity to implement.

Mandatory obligations and dispute settlement
Many developing countries state that they support the goal of trade facilitation, but emphasize that they believe co-operation on trade facilitation should be voluntary. Trade facilitation should not, in their opinion, be incorporated in mandatory WTO obligations that are subject to dispute settlement in the WTO. In truth, even voluntary approaches such as the Asia-Pacific Economic Co-operation (APEC) initiatives on trade facilitation have not been without controversy, but many developing countries do seem to prefer a voluntary approach that allows them to be flexible in the implementation of common standards and approaches to trade facilitation.

---

[29] The WTO Agreement on the Implementation of Article VII of the GATT stipulates that customs valuation shall, except in specified circumstances, be based on the actual price of the goods to be valued. This is more generally known as the transaction value, defined by the WTO in the following manner: '...the price actually paid or payable is the total payment made to the buyer to or for the benefit of the seller for the imported goods, and includes all payments made as a condition of sale of the imported goods...'. For further discussion of customs valuation methods and the issues related to their implementation in developing countries see Rege, V. (2002) *Customs Valuation and Customs Reform*, chapter 15 in English, P., Hoekman, B. and Mattoo, A. *Development, Trade and the WTO – A Handbook*. World Bank.

At the same time, it must be noted that many developing countries have not participated in the various existing trade facilitation instruments which they have signed up to– or have fully implemented the agreements which they have ratified. It might be argued that the voluntary approach has significantly failed in unlocking the full benefits of trade facilitation, from which developing countries and small traders stand proportionately to gain the most. The United Nations Conference on Trade & Development's (UNCTAD's) Columbus Declaration[30] – poorly implemented in practice – demonstrates the drawback of "soft law" recommendations where political will to change is absent. The benefit of a WTO agreement on trade facilitation would be the more robust and coherent implementation of trade facilitation concepts and principles.

Negotiating resource constraints
Since many developing countries do not participate in the existing range of trade facilitation instruments and conventions, it is not surprising that they are wary of the development of new standards for trade facilitation. Even voluntary standards have implications for competitive conditions in the marketplace. There is considerable concern amongst developing countries that these new standards (either voluntary or mandatory WTO obligations) will not reflect their needs or concerns, but will nevertheless become accepted as the norm by the wider international community. If developing countries do not actively participate in the design and formulation of these trade facilitation initiatives and ensure that these new standards reflect their needs and priorities, they will risk further marginalisation in world trade and economic activity.

---

[30] The Columbus Ministerial Declaration was adopted in October 1994 during the United Nations International Symposium on Trade Efficiency (UNISTE). The Declaration was prepared in recognition of advances on the field of information technology and states the need to promote electronic trade world-wide, based on the principle of equality of access for all countries to systems compatible with international standards recommended by the UN.

Since many developing countries have limited delegations to the WTO, WCO and other UN agencies (and a significant number of the smaller and poorer nations are not even represented in the Geneva by missions), the capacity of developing countries to follow, let alone participate, in the development of new standards and instruments for trade facilitation in the WTO, the UNECE, the WCO or other forums is extremely limited. Although a number of initiatives are beginning to enhance the capacity of developing countries to engage in international trade negotiations, this is a long-term process that encompasses a great deal more than just trade facilitation.

Uncertainty about the scope of new obligations
A number of developing countries have expressed concerns about the scope of the potential obligations that might be negotiated in the trade facilitation field in the WTO. An example that was cited by one particular developing country during the course of this study was that it feared mandatory deadlines would be imposed on the clearance of goods through customs, something which developing countries would be unable to implement – or could at best only implement at great expense. Although this has never been by proposed by a WTO Member, it serves to demonstrate developing countries' fears that WTO negotiations will lead to unreasonable obligations being imposed upon them.

Of course, it is possible that proposals for obligations on trade facilitation could impose mandatory requirements that would be costly and onerous to implement, but it is less likely that this would be the agreed outcome of broad-based multilateral negotiations. However, because the nature and scope of the precise obligations are uncertain, this does create a significant degree of uncertainty in developing countries. This uncertainty, combined with their limited capacity to participate in the negotiations in the WTO, makes developing countries hesitant to accept new obligations.

Meaningful capacity building
Commitments under the Doha Declaration that WTO members will provide technical assistance and capacity building with respect to trade facilitation (and other WTO negotiations) are viewed with considerable scepticism and doubt by many developing countries. There is a widespread concern that

such technical assistance will be slowly delivered and will be insufficient to address the challenges faced by developing countries seeking to upgrade their customs services and to develop the administrative structures and operational computer networks necessary to speed the movement of goods. Even the European Commission – which supports WTO negotiations on trade facilitation – has recommended that a reliable mechanism for meeting developing country capacity-building needs must be properly integrated into the rules-making process, stating that:

> "...Our experience in implementing the Uruguay Round agreements shows the practical difficulties if one undertakes WTO commitments, however desirable in themselves, if the means are lacking to implement them. The same experience also shows that it is not always enough to establish commitments but then to confine assistance only to training officials to understand what they mean. Assistance should not be afterthought but be designed before the end of the negotiation process and delivered once an agreement is in place... "[31]

Developing countries seem to welcome the position of the EC on capacity building even if they have concerns about negotiations on trade facilitation, but they express strongly the perspective that technical assistance and capacity building needs to precede agreement and be undertaken in parallel with the negotiations on trade facilitation. Otherwise they are concerned that the support for capacity building will be too little and too late. While the absence of agreed standards will make it difficult to target technical assistance accurately (since the aims of the technical assistance will not be clearly identifiable), capacity building in trade facilitation policy will be crucial if developing countries are to fully participate in negotiations – and to ensure that a balanced and workable agreement is reached.

---

[31] European Commission (2000). *Technical Assistance and Capacity Building in Relation to Trade Facilitation,* a Communication to the WTO Council for Trade in Goods (ref G/C/W/235).

These concerns have an objective basis, because the scale of technical assistance required implementing comprehensive reform and upgrading of customs services would b e significant – even if countries such as Chile and others have shown that there can be early and long-term gains from such measures. It can be countered that some aspects of trade facilitation, such as adopting customs documents to standard formats, would be less costly. However, several developing countries and consulting organisations take the view, based on their experience to date with the implementation of customs -related reforms, that it is not possible to address one aspect of the customs system without undertaking more substantial, broad-based investments in the modernisation of the entire customs administration[32]. The various linkages and inter-relationships between different aspects of customs operations tend to favour a more holistic approach to capacity building.

Nevertheless, this need not always be the case – particularly in situations where reforms are designed in close partnership with developing country governments, and have their full support and buy-in. Under such circumstances, incremental, sequential changes can in time be effective. In addition, several proposals for rules (for instance, relating to transparency and non-discrimination, the use of international standards, and the rationalization of border controls) are cost-neutral or will save resources.

It must also be recognized that the while the agreement on customs valuation came into effect on January 1st, 2000 (with an option for developing countries to request an extension until January 1st, 2003 for some selected provisions), many developing countries have not fully implemented their commitments. Some of those who have adapted their legislation are experiencing difficulties with administrative implementation.

---

[32] For a broader discussion of customs reforms initiatives see: Crown Agents (2003). *Review of Crown Agents' Experiences in the Field of Customs Reform* – a paper prepared for the Organisation for Economic Co-operation and Development.

Whilst increasingly customs services have audit capabilities and computerized databases to compare and to track the declarations of traders, along with post-entry audit capabilities to mitigate the potential for fraud by different techniques and means, numerous developing countries still lack these capabilities because of the cost, lack of training and other factors.

How can developing countries benefit?

Benefits from global trade
Regardless of international negotiations or initiatives in the WTO, the UN or the WCO, the capacity of developing countries to facilitate trade is crucial to their economic development and poverty alleviation prospects. The poorest countries face the greatest challenges in implementing trade facilitation proposals, but they could obtain significant economic benefits and enhance their development opportunities as a result.

Trade facilitation is necessary to achieve greater benefits from the Generalized System of Preferences (GSP) tariff programme, or other arrangements – including the Cotonou Arrangement between the group of African, Caribbean and Pacific (ACP) countries and the EU, and US arrangements for Africa and the Caribbean. Preferential market access to high-income markets is of little benefit to developing country exporters and will not serve the objective of promoting economic development if these exporters cannot complete the documentation needed to satisfy rules of origin requirements under the preferential tariffs – or if they cannot satisfy documentation requirements for technical standards and sanitary and phytosanitary measures.

Trade facilitation measures – either to simplify developing country export procedures or to assist developing country exports in meeting the documentation requirements of high-income markets – are critical to enable developing countries to reap the potential gains from trade.

Similarly, expeditious and predictable access to imported products and components is a key element in an "enabling" legal and policy framework that will facilitate the growth and development of SMEs and the private sector. Simplifying import and export procedures in developing countries will also facilitate trade between developing countries.

Trade facilitation is essential if countries are to secure the benefits from trade liberalization strategies. One illustration of this was cited during the preparation of this paper. The case in question was that of a transition economy in Central and Eastern Europe, which had joined the Information Technology Agreement (ITA) and had subsequently removed all tariffs on computers and components when it acceded to the WTO. The country sought to develop export-oriented computer assembly activities – using imported components – through the removal of all computer-related tariffs. However, such activities were blocked by cumbersome customs procedures that delayed imported components in customs for lengthy and unpredictable periods.

Conversely in China, the customs authorities have implemented a trial program for the simplification of customs procedures, based on international standards, in Guangzhou province – and have found that customs clearances can be reduced from an average of 7 days to 24 hours. The Chinese authorities believe that this will bring significant benefits to the electronics and computer assembly industry in the Guangzhou province.

Benefits from regional trade
Many developing countries participate in regional trade initiatives intended to promote expanded trade, investment and economic development. The effective functioning of these regional trading arrangements depends o n the development and effective implementation of common customs forms and procedures. Expansion of trade among regional partners requires that rules of origin and other documentation requirements can be satisfied without undue costs, and that traded goods can move in a timely and cost-effective manner across national borders within the regional arrangement.

Many of the regional trading arrangements among developing countries are not as effective in practice as they could be, because of a failure to implement trade facilitation standards.

Trade facilitation initiatives and practices based on global standards promoted possibly via the WTO, could serve to stimulate trade and investment within regional trading groups in developing countries. This may be a particularly important factor, given that 40% of developing country exports of manufactured goods are to other developing countries (WTO Secretariat, 1999).

Development opportunities for landlocked countries
The special concerns of landlocked countries warrant particular attention. Landlocked states comprise a significant proportion of the world's poorest nations, and improving their economic development prospects will require a co-ordinated strategy. Such a strategy must address the need to increase regional economic co-operation between landlocked states and their neighbours, to invest in the "hardware" of transportation infrastructure, and to invest in the "software" of trade and transport facilitation. And in the case of land-locked countries this also means the borders of their neighbours.

Improving the economic development prospects of landlocked countries is an economic challenge at the global level, and trade facilitation, although only one part of the solution, could make a significant contribution to this goal. Yet the capacities of the poorest landlocked economies to participate in international initiatives for trade facilitation and to implement the necessary reforms in their domestic administration are extremely limited.

However, in a few instances, landlocked countries have made progress – both in articulating their own concerns and opinions with regard to trade facilitation, and also in taking concrete steps to overcome the barriers that they face. The Government of Paraguay, for instance, has participated actively in a number of regional initiatives[33] – as a signature to the

---

[33] Boettner, L. M. R. (2000) *Trade Facilitation – A Presentation by the Permanent Representative of Paraguay in Geneva.* WTO Paper G/C/W/237.

Paraguay-Paraná Waterway Treaty of 1992, and more recently through free port agreements with both Argentina and Uruguay. As a result of its efforts, Paraguay is now playing a more active role within the Mercosur regional economic integration project which covers Argentina, Brazil, Paraguay and Uruguay – with Bolivia and Chile as associate members. By pressing for free ports in both Chile and Peru, and arguing that the main integration corridor from the Atlantic to the Pacific should pass through its territory, the Paraguayan Government has taken a strategic position – aiming to turn its apparent geographical handicap into a longer term asset.

Paraguay's experience suggests that positive steps can be taken to lessen or overcome landlocked countries' handicaps. However, its Government has argued that insufficient attention is paid to landlocked countries. To address this, it may be necessary for the international community to recognize landlocked countries as a separate country category within the WTO, and promote case studies such as Paraguay's to established if similar paths can be followed by other Governments in similar positions.

Benefits from trade and governance reforms

Trade facilitation is conceptually distinct at a policy level from other elements of trade reform, including trade liberalization or improvements in economic governance (such as the prevention of corruption and enhancement of the efficiency of revenue collection). Nevertheless, these areas are inter-linked. Reforms in customs administration and procedures that lead to improved transparency, predictability and efficiency will bring broader benefits in limiting the scope of, and incentives for, corruption, contraband and fraud. Such reforms can also enhance the efficiency of revenue collection activities.

Trade liberalization measures intended to promote economic development– such as tariff reductions – will not be effective if legitimate and reputable traders cannot move their goods expeditiously through customs. Trade facilitation measures can also be designed to reward compliant and honest traders with faster procedures (e.g., systems of "authorized traders"), thus breaking the vicious circle of corrupt officials and dishonest traders.

Benefits from customs reform
Some developing countries see the reform and modernization of customs as being both expensive and technically difficult. But the experience of Chile, Singapore and other countries seems to suggest that the costs are manageable and investments in trade facilitation have the potential for rapid pay back[34]. There is scope for cost-recovery from some trade facilitation measures and practices in relatively short time-frames. In addition, the reform and modernization of customs should severely curtail the need for use of pre-shipment inspection services, which are expensive for many developing countries, and do not serve to enhance customs authorities' institutional capacity.

The costs of trade facilitation

Capacity constraints
It is essential to acknowledge that there are sometimes significant constraints to the capacities of developing countries to implement trade facilitation initiatives, and that significant short-term costs can be incurred in implementing trade facilitation instruments and measures.

In many developing countries, the customs authorities or other agencies involved in aspects of trade regulation are poorly paid, poorly trained and operate without adequate tools and operating procedures or administrative support. Electronic filing and paperless clearance are major challenges for most developing countries, although most simplification measures do not require an electronic environment. It is important to recognize that trade facilitation starts with very simple and paper based instruments, such as common formats for declarations.

---

[34] Illustrations of the potential benefits which can be generated by customs reform initiatives are quoted in Crown Agents (2003). *Review of Crown Agents' Experiences in the Field of Customs Reform* – a paper prepared for the Organisation for Economic Co-operation and Development. This outlines the case of Mozambique, where under a broad-based programme to modernise customs, revenues almost doubled over the 4-year period between 1997 and 2000. Revenue increases were such, that the Mozambican Government recouped much of its initial investment in the reforms within the first 14 months.

The challenges for developing countries have two major elements. One element is to build their capacity to participate in negotiations in the WTO and in international standards-setting fora, under the auspices of the UN and the WCO. The other element is to develop the capacity within their countries to implement trade facilitation instruments and practices. It is evident that the transformation and upgrading of the skills, operating procedures, and infrastructure of customs services and other agencies requires appropriate investment in training, in improved salaries for public officials, and operating infrastructure.

Costs of participating in international fora

For many developing countries, the cost of participating in any international fora, including the trade facilitation negotiations in the WTO, is high. This is true not only because of their small or non-existent delegations, but also because of the support they need from their authorities in the national capital and in the implementing agencies. Participating effectively in international fora costs much more than maintaining small missions in Geneva or sending a few officials from capitals to international conferences and meetings. Effective participation requires that there is adequate capacity in national capitals to track international initiatives and to assess their implications for national interests, policies and administration, on an on-going basis. The relevant international organizations – the WTO, WCO, UN, UNCTAD, WB and regional development banks – can all play a constructive part to ensure an adequate flow of information to developing countries. Yet despite this, developing countries still need the capacity to assess their own interests.

Costs of modernizing customs services

A key component of effective trade facilitation is the integrity and efficiency of customs services and other border agencies. While reform of customs authorities will be crucial for trade facilitation initiatives to be successful, reform is often expensive and resource intensive for many developing countries. Given the large numbers of personnel employed in customs authorities, the costs related to improving pay and training of personnel can be significant. The development of effective and operational open-architecture computer systems and the application of analytical tools for price comparisons and the tracking of shippers and importers, can offer significant benefits, including cost-savings. Yet they can also be expensive and resource intensive.

An important concept within the field of trade facilitation is "being able to do more with less". Once reform measures are in place, there should be a smaller, better paid and more effectively targetted customs workforce, focused on the known areas of greatest risk to trade. This reorientation of customs' resources should in turn lead to increased revenue collection levels and the detection of illicit traffic – eventually offsetting any initial investment costs.

The modernization of customs services is a necessary element of trade facilitation – but is not sufficient in itself. Border controls and inspections are imposed for other reasons and by other agencies – for the protection of animal, plant or human health, for instance. Such controls can have a significant impact on the ease and efficiency with which goods can be traded internationally. Thus, other border-related agencies, such as the inspection and quarantine services, need to be upgraded in parallel with customs modernization, or at least co-ordinated in time and place.

A number of developing countries are concerned that if trade facilitation measures are not implemented properly it will lead to a greater incidence of customs fraud and revenue loss. Therefore, for developing countries to ensure that considerable benefits of trade facilitation are realized they will need significant help in implementing any agreement.

Next steps

Possible action points

Securing commitment for capacity building
It is clear that if the negotiations on trade facilitation in the WTO are to proceed, then commitment to ensuring adequate technical assistance and support for capacity building in this area must be obtained. The research conducted during the course of this study indicates that such commitment can only be secured through a combination of specific initiatives which will directly support negotiations in the WTO, and a much broader set of

initiatives which encourage co-operation on trade facilitation on a regional and global basis.

The case for developing initiatives to promote co-operation on trade facilitation is independent of the negotiations in the WTO, given the potential economic benefits which such initiatives can generate. However, progress in the implementation of trade facilitation instruments and practices in developing countries – either individually or in groups – will influence their perspective on the negotiations.

Proposals to support capacity building in the trade facilitation field have two major components. One component is to assist developing countries to participate in the negotiations in the WTO and in the standards-setting activities under the auspices of the UN and the WCO. The second component is to support the actual implementation of trade facilitation measures by developing countries. Whilst both components are important, it is clear that the second component involves a substantially greater commitment of resources – because it is linked to the administrative reform of customs services and other regulatory authorities. Whilst the first component focuses on the training of developing country officials to understand what negotiations mean, the second component encompasses a much broader and more demanding range of activities, including:

- The training of officials in modern trade management and customs techniques
- The automation of trade-related systems
- Participation in international standards setting, and
- Measures to improve port management and cargo handling.[35]

All such activities will require substantial longer-term maintenance and follow up, to ensure that they become firmly rooted.

---

[35] See European Commission (2000). *Technical Assistance and Capacity Building in Relation to Trade Facilitation,* a Communication to the WTO Council for Trade in Goods (ref G/C/W/235).

A number of proposals have been made that could be useful in supporting both policy dialogue and capacity building in various aspects of trade facilitation. However, there have been no specific proposals as to what might be the best modalities or institutions for supporting and implementing such initiatives. Obviously different donors and different organizations could be involved and in differing ways on different aspects, but it is very important that assistance is given in a co-ordinated and thoughtful manner to reduce the burden and improve the absorption of capacity building initiatives.

Participation in international fora on trade facilitation
At present the capacities of developing countries for effective participation in both the forthcoming negotiations in the WTO on trade facilitation and the various fora under the auspices of the UN and the WCO that are involved in the development of new standards for trade facilitation are limited.

Negotiations in the WTO
No one, including the participants, can or should seek to prejudge the outcome of negotiations within WTO – including those that relate to trade facilitation. The negotiations will only reach a successful conclusion if there is a broad consensus of developed and developing countries on the overall package of commitments.

The WTO negotiations on trade facilitation are more likely to be successful if the proposed clarifications or amendments to existing rules and obligations under the WTO address issues of concern to both developed and developing countries alike. At this time, the real work of identifying specific issues and concerns that might be appropriate for elaboration or clarification of existing WTO obligations under Articles V, VIII and X of the GATT 1994 is now well underway. WTO members, especially those which are promoting the negotiations on trade facilitation, must identify issues and priorities in the WTO Council for Trade in Goods meetings devoted to trade facilitation – and respond properly to developing country concerns.

By the same token, countries that are reluctant to commit themselves to negotiations need to articulate their specific problems, rather than resort to generalities or non-directly related concerns. All participants need to talk frankly if progress is to be made and a genuine resolution reached.

A number of specific initiatives can be put forward to support negotiations and to help developing countries to articulate their perspectives and practical concerns about trade facilitation. These could include country-specific studies and action-plans involving the customs authorities and other border-related agencies. Such initiatives would also help countries to understand the practical costs and benefits of trade facilitation.

Given their limited representation in Geneva, initiatives that analyze and report on the proposals and discussion on post-Cancún trade facilitation negotiations would be useful to developing countries. Regional seminars could help developing countries to exchange their perspectives on trade facilitation and to develop co-ordinated positions. These seminars could examine specific issues and proposals – such as the challenges faced by landlocked countries and the possible elements of a WTO agreement on trade facilitation. The WTO's 2003 Work Programme for trade-related technical assistance includes a substantial component on trade facilitation, as this will greatly help WTO members to understand the issues properly.

Participation in trade facilitation organisations and fora
The participation of developing countries in efforts to develop new standards for trade facilitation under the existing UN and WCO conventions and instruments is limited and uneven.

In parallel with regional seminars to build capacity on the negotiations on trade facilitation in the WTO, these regional seminars could examine in detail the issues involved in trade facilitation instruments developed in the UN system and in the WCO, as well as other organizations. In addition, the participation of developing countries in the design of new standards for trade facilitation should be actively supported. Greater effort needs to be made to disseminate information about proposals for trade facilitation to developing countries.

Promoting cooperation on trade facilitation
Regardless of the negotiating dynamics in the WTO, it is evident that trade facilitation is an important tool in promoting trade with, and investment in, developing countries and that measures to support capacity building and effective implementation of trade facilitation measures will contribute to economic development and help developing countries to gain from trade.

Promotion of trade facilitation in regional integration agreements
Trade facilitation measures can contribute significantly to the effective functioning of regional agreements. Although issues such as the certification of compliance with preferential rules of origin are not addressed in multilateral rules in the WTO, the trade facilitation instruments developed in the WCO and UNECE can facilitate the operation of regional trade agreements.[36]

Trade facilitation should be an important component of the regional integration initiatives of developing countries and this should be a priority for technical assistance and capacity building to support such regional integration arrangements. The UN regional commissions and institutions such as the World Bank may have a particularly useful role to play here, but time is clearly important.

Promotion of trade facilitation in national development strategies
Trade facilitation is much more likely to be actively implemented in developing countries if it is incorporated within national trade, investment and economic development strategies. Since implementation of trade facilitation requires the political will to adjust legislation and to change administrative practice through different parts of the government and the economy, it is necessary for high-level policy makers to be aware of the benefits of trade facilitation and to attach priority to the implementation of trade facilitation measures and practices. One of the consequences of addressing the issue in the WTO is to create and harness the necessary political will and attention to reform.

---

[36] The significance of trade facilitation for regional integration is not happenstance, since the development of the European Community and more recently NAFTA have been a stimulus to the development of trade facilitation approaches.

A specific initiative that could promote the incorporation of trade facilitation in national trade, investment, and economic development strategies could involve sharing of experience in individual countries drawn from different regions and different levels of development – helping to identify success stories and to learn lessons for the implementation of trade facilitation.

The potential for this concept is borne out in those papers which have already been tabled by various WTO members as "national experience" papers.

Making trade facilitation a development priority

Linking trade facilitation to a wider development agenda
Various bilateral and multilateral donors and international financial organizations support technical assistance in developing countries. Specialized technical assistance is available from various international organizations including the UN agencies, the WTO and the WCO. There is much competition for differing priorities for these technical assistance funds – for laudable goals such as development of civil society, social development and promoting sustainable development. Trade facilitation can contribute to economic and social development, but if there is not a significant and substantial investment in customs modernization and reform there are risks that trade facilitation initiatives will not succeed.

Trade facilitation needs to be recognized as a priority for development assistance policies, since trade facilitation can support the expansion of trade and investment and promote a private sector enabling policy framework that will support economic development. An effort is therefore need from both recipient countries as well as donors for clearly identifying trade facilitation as a priority is an important factor in ensuring that trade facilitation receives the attention it is due in development co-operation and good governance.

Strengthening and enhancing the provision of technical assistance
Technical assistance for capacity building in the field of trade facilitation should be linked to, or co-ordinated with, broader initiatives to support the modernization of customs – and should proceed in parallel with the actual negotiation and implementation of new rules for trade facilitation. By starting to address capacity building needs during the negotiation process, there is a greater likelihood that assistance can be made quickly operational once agreements are in place.

At the same time, it is essential that steps be taken to ensure greater co-ordination between the various donor organizations currently funding initiatives in the trade facilitation field. Existing programmes are often narrowly focused – and do not take a sufficiently holistic perspective, addressing all the different stages involved in the trade transaction. There is limited sharing of information and co-ordination between different initiatives – and in the absence of globally recognized criteria or benchmarks against which to simplify trade procedures, there is a very real danger that current reform measures will be counterproductive, maintaining or re-inforcing differences between countries rather than removing them.

Developing countries need to be more active in articulating their vision of what should be encompassed within any new rules for trade facilitation. There is at present reluctance across many developing countries to make proposals, because they fear that in doing so they will undermine their negotiating position – tainting themselves as reluctant partners that must be cajoled into participation. However, if developing countries were to make specific, focused proposals, then this could have a significant positive influence on negotiations.

Bibliography:

Boettner, L. M. R. (2000) *Trade Facilitation – A Presentation by the Permanent Representative of Paraguay in Geneva.* WTO Paper G/C/W/237.

Crown Agents (2003). *Review of Crown Agents' Experiences in the Field of Customs Reform* – a paper prepared for the Organisation for Economic Co-operation and Development.

European Commission (2000). *Technical Assistance and Capacity Building in Relation to Trade Facilitation,* a Communication to the WTO Council for Trade in Goods (ref G/C/W/235).

Gallup, J., Mellinger, A. and Sachs, J.D. (1998) *The Geography of Poverty and Wealth – paper prepared for the World Bank.* Centre for International Development, Harvard University.

Limao, N. and Venables, A. (2000) *Infrastructure, Geographical Disadvantage and Transport Costs* – paper prepared for the World Bank.

Raven, J. (2001) *Trade and Transport Facilitation: A Toolkit for Audit, Analysis and Remedial Action.* The World Bank.

Rege, V. (2002) *Customs Valuation and Customs Reform*, chapter 15 in English, P., Hoekman, B. and Mattoo, A. *Development, Trade and the WTO – A Handbook.* World Bank.

UNECE (2002). *Compendium of Trade Facilitation Recommendations*, New York & Geneva.

UNECE (March 2002). *Trade Facilitation in a Global Trade Environment* – note by the Secretariat.

Wilson, J. & Woo, Y.P. (2000). *Cutting Through Red Tape: New Directions for APEC's Trade Facilitation Agenda.* Asia Pacific Foundation of Canada.

WTO (November 2001). *Declaration of the Doha WTO Ministerial Conference.* World Trade Organization, www.wto.org.

WTO/OECD (November 2002). *First Joint WTO/OECD Report on Trade-Related Technical Assistance and Capacity Building: Management of Trade Capacity Building.* World Trade Organization, www.wto.org.

Appendix A: Current Trade Facilitation Initiatives

The United Nations system, including the United Nations Economic Commission for Europe (UNECE), as well as other UN agencies and business organizations such as the International Chamber of Commerce (ICC) have played a key role in the development of standards for trade facilitation and the development of instruments for all aspects of trade and transport transactions. A *Compendium of Trade Facilitation Recommendations* published by the United Nations Centre for Trade Facilitation and Electronic Business (UN/CEFACT) identifies more than 200 instruments related to facilitation of trade transactions, transportation and payments under the WTO, WCO, UNECE, ICC, the International Civil Aviation Organization (ICAO) and the International Maritime Organization (IMO).[37]

The World Customs Organisation (WCO) is an intergovernmental organisation, which works with the national customs services in member countries. As an organisation devoted to co-operation among customs services, the WCO emphasises objectives such as customs enforcement, security of borders and efficiency of revenue collection as well as trade facilitation. The WCO administers the Kyoto Convention which was updated in 1999 in order to promote trade facilitation, but ratification is still pending until forty member states of the Kyoto Convention (1974) ratify the revised version of the convention. To date ten countries – Algeria, Australia, Canada, China, Czech Republic, Japan, Latvia, Lesotho, Morocco, and New Zealand – have ratified the Protocol and six – Democratic Republic of the Congo, Slovakia, Sri Lanka, Switzerland, Zambia, and Zimbabwe – have signed the Protocol subject to ratification.

The revised Kyoto Convention has as its core governing principle the commitment by Customs administrations to provide transparency and predictability for all those involved in various aspects of international trade. In addition, Customs administrations commit to adopt the use of risk

---

[37] UN/CEFACT, UNECE & UNCTAD (2002) *Compendium of Trade Facilitation Recommendations.* United Nations, New York and Geneva.

management techniques, to co-operate with other relevant authorities and trade communities and to implement appropriate international standards.

The activities of UNECE and other UN agencies and the WCO are complementary with existing obligations in the WTO related to trade facilitation. The activities of UNECE and WCO involve voluntary co-operation between business and customs authorities in the development of standards in a variety of areas ranging from standard formats for customs, trade, and payments documents to the development of standards for Electronic Data Interchange (EDI) and paperless clearance.

The current initiatives in trade facilitation in the UNECE and WCO involve two tracks.[38] One track involves harmonising and implementing existing standards and the other track involves "...developing the next generation of rules and standards to facilitate the emerging new economy, characterised by e-commerce and global supply chains...".[39]

The current level of participation of developing countries in these trade facilitation instruments is low, thus the first track of involving developing countries in the harmonisation and implementation of existing standards is of considerable importance. However, the capacity of developing countries to participate in either track is extremely limited.

Most importantly, with negotiations on trade facilitation in the WTO planned after the Mexico Ministerial, there are now three tracks for addressing trade facilitation, implementation of existing standards, development of new standards, and negotiations in the WTO.

Appendix B: Trade Facilitation in the World Trade Organization

Issues related to trade facilitation are covered by a number of the provisions and obligations under the WTO, there has been a working group on trade facilitation, and under the Doha Ministerial Declaration,

---

[38] UNECE (2002) *Trade Facilitation in a Global Trade Environment* – note by the Secretariat, 21st March.
[39] Ibid, p. 3.

preparatory work is underway in the Committee on Trade in Goods for future negotiations on trade facilitation.

Existing provisions in the WTO

Trade-facilitation-related issues are already addressed by various obligations and provisions under the WTO including:

- GATT 1994, notably Articles I, V, VII, VIII and X
- Agreement on Interpretation of Article VII (Customs Valuation) of the GATT 1994
- Agreement on Import Licensing
- Agreement on Pre-Shipment Inspection
- Agreement on Technical Barriers to Trade
- Agreement on Application of Sanitary and Phytosanitary Measures
- Agreement on Rules of Origin, and
- Agreement on Trade-Related Aspects of Intellectual Property Rights.

This list reflects a narrow definition of trade facilitation as formalities and procedures related to the clearance and movement of goods across borders since the General Agreement on Trade in Services has provisions relevant to the broader definitions of trade facilitation including payment issues.

Current provisions and implementation issues
As Figure 1.14.2 indicates, many aspects of the WTO are related to trade facilitation.

It is important when considering the WTO obligations to examine the core obligations under the GATT 1994. These can be summarised as follows:

- Article I contains the key obligation of *Most-Favoured-Nation (MFN) treatment* which means that imports from, or exports to, any WTO member must receive non-discriminatory treatment in the application of customs duties and all aspects of customs formalities i.e. countries cannot discriminate between countries.

- Article III provides another basic obligation to guard against discrimination by guaranteeing National Treatment – i.e., ensuring imports are not treated less favourably than similar goods, which are domestically produced, countries cannot discriminate between foreign and domestic companies.
- Article V contains obligations related to Freedom of Transit including transportation routes, customs duties and customs formalities.
- Article VII contains key obligations on Valuation for Customs Purposes, which are elaborated on in the WTO Agreement on Interpretation of Article VII.
- Article VIII contains obligations on Fees and Formalities connected with Importation and Exportation, which specifies that all fees – other than customs duties or non-discriminatory domestic commodity, excise and sales taxes – must be limited to the costs of services; that customs penalties should not be punitive, and that countries should seek to simplify import and export formalities.
- Article X is a transparency obligation that requires Publications and Administration of Trade Regulations, which covers all issues related to trade facilitation including, "Laws, regulations, judicial decisions and administrative rulings of general application, made effective by any contracting party, pertaining to the classification or valuation of products for customs purposes, or to rates of duty, taxes or other charges, or to requirements, restrictions or prohibitions on imports or exports or on the transfer of payments, or affecting their sale, distribution, transportation, insurance, warehousing inspection, exhibition, processing, mixing or other use, shall be published promptly in such a manner as to enable governments and traders to become acquainted with them."[40]

Other obligations under the GATT 1994 such as under Article II and Article XI are also relevant, yet the above are the key obligations most pertinent to trade facilitation measures and proposals for negotiation of trade facilitation.

---

[40] Article X(1), GATT 1994, Annex 1A, Marrakech Agreement establishing the WTO.

Logically Article V is of great relevance to land-locked countries since it deals with transit trade, but there have been no formal disputes in the GATT/WTO about obligations under Article V. However under the GATT the practice was to avoid bringing disputes between developing countries to dispute settlement and the overall participation of developing countries in the GATT was limited. Now some developing countries have brought issues to dispute settlement in the WTO, but so far none of the disputes have involved the application of Article V. Of course, since, land-locked countries are often dependent on their neighbours to transport goods etc, they are understandably reluctant to bring dispute settlement cases. However, clarification of the obligations under Article V, which has not been revised significantly since 1947, could be very useful to land-locked countries and could facilitate their "co-operation discussions" with their neighbours without recourse to formal dispute settlement.

It is interesting to note that Article VIII is a broad commitment to ensure trade facilitation. Again, it has not been common practice to bring disputes under this provision. A notable exceptions is that the European Communities brought a complaint against the United States' customs user fees that relate to Articles II and VIII of the GATT 1947. However, until now much less negotiating attention was focused on Article VIII (Fees and Formalities) as compared with Article VII (Customs Valuation), which was the subject of a special supplementary agreement going back to the Tokyo Round but is now a covered agreement under the WTO.

Although the range of existing obligations under the WTO related to trade facilitation is extensive, and the key obligations under Articles V, VIII and X of the GATT 1994 have been elements of the GATT/WTO system since 1947, some of the specific obligations under the instruments now brought fully the WTO were subject to transition periods that delayed their implementation for developing countries. Thus, for example, obligations such as implementation of the Agreement on Interpretation of Article VII of the GATT 1994 Customs Valuation were delayed until January 1, 2000 for developing countries not already party to the Tokyo Round Customs Valuation Agreement, with the option to extend the implementation of selected obligations until January 1, 2003.

The various transition provisions for developing countries that were agreed in the Uruguay Round and incorporated in the WTO have similar characteristics of delays in the implementation of obligations for developing countries. In addition to the obligations on customs procedures just noted, obligations on export-linked and import-substitution subsidies, performance requirements on investment and trade-related intellectual property rights were subject to implementation delays after 1995 for periods ranging from five to ten years depending on the particular provision and the level of development of the country.

Now the obligations on customs valuation, which were subject to transition provisions, are the most relevant to trade facilitation, the fact that many developing countries are now struggling with the implementation of the various obligations under the WTO has created major challenges for their governments. Also the challenges of implementation of these various provisions have affected the climate for negotiations in the WTO since several developing countries have requested extensions of the transition periods for adapting their legislation, policy and administrative procedures and undoubtedly some developing countries have not yet addressed the challenges of implementation.

The Doha Declaration and future negotiations
The November 2001 Doha Declaration commits WTO members to negotiations on trade facilitation after the Cancún Ministerial in 2003, subject to the requirement that there is an explicit consensus decision on modalities of negotiations and mandates a work program under the Council for Trade in Goods to "review and as appropriate, clarify and improve relevant aspects of Articles V, VIII and X of the GATT 1994 and identify the trade facilitation needs and priorities of members, in particular developing and least-developed countries. We commit ourselves to ensuring adequate technical assistance and support for capacity building in this area."[41]

. [41] Declaration of the Doha WTO Minsterial Conference, paragraph 27 (www.wto.org).

The preparatory work for the negotiations is now underway in the Committee for Trade in Goods and a work program has been established to examine the issues related to Articles V, VIII and X of the GATT 1994 from the perspective of WTO members. The work has benefited from a significant number of submissions to the WTO prior to and following Doha. Clearly the results of this work and the extent to which a consensus of WTO members emerges on specific issues related to trade facilitation will determine the results of the next WTO Ministerial session scheduled for Mexico with respect to the decision about the modalities for negotiation on trade facilitation.

Quite different perspectives are expressed on the preparatory work program and the forthcoming negotiations. Negotiations on trade facilitation are actively supported by the Colorado group of twenty (thirty-four) developed and developing countries. The groups is comprised of the large developed countries – European Communities, United States, Japan, and Canada – and several other developed countries, including Australia, New Zealand, Norway, and Switzerland. The group is also comprised of Hong Kong, Korea and Singapore, which historically were developing countries, several developing countries, including, Chile, Columbia, Costa Rica, Morocco, Paraguay, and Turkey as well as transition economies Czech Republic, Hungary and Poland. In contrast some developing countries in South Asia and Africa are deeply sceptical about the forthcoming negotiations on trade facilitation, while other developing countries in South East Asia and Latin America tend to have more moderate positions expressing some concerns about the negotiations, but also recognising that there are benefits to be gained from concluding them.

Part Two:

Trade Facilitation Policy and New Security Initiatives

The chapters in this part address the need for a balance between the enhanced measures of security in international trade and the achievements of trade facilitation. The conduct of international trade has undergone fundamental changes, as the security emphasis has shifted from threats to trade to threats from trade. While some major actors in international trade focus on the identification and minimization of risks to the security of international flows of goods (especially in container trade), others are concerned with the new security requirements, which will impose an additional burden on their fragile economies.

Chapter 2.1
Trade Facilitation Policy and New Security Initiatives[42]

Douglas Browning, Deputy Commissioner, US Customs

For obvious reasons, the issue of increased security in trade has been an important one for U.S. Customs and Border Protection. The changed global environment created by the attacks of September 11, 2001, in the United States, has forced changes in the way my agency, and indeed the U.S. government as a whole, functions. This is clearly reflected in the creation of the new Cabinet-level department in which I now serve, the Department of Homeland Security, and in the expanded purview of my bureau. What had been the U.S. Customs Service, responsible for revenue collection and enforcement of trade-related laws and regulations at the ports of entry, is now a new bureau with added responsibility for managing immigration inspection and enforcement functions at the border and between ports. All of this has been done to improve coordination and create seamless management of the border as a whole. All of this has been done in the name of increasing security in the context of today's environment.

Prior to these sweeping changes, U.S. Customs had been focusing its efforts on how to better facilitate the movement of merchandise into and out of the United States. We were instructed by statute, specifically the Customs Modernization Act, to continually look at ways to improve commercial processing. This is an obligation we have taken seriously since 1994, when the law came into effect, and is one that continues to today – even with the more recent emphasis on security.

---

[42] This paper contains the keynote address of Mr. Douglas Browning, Deputy US Customs Commissioner, at the specialized session on the balance between trade facilitation and enhanced security in international trade, at the Second International Forum on Trade Facilitation.

When we in the United States first started to examine how we would react to the challenges of global terrorism, one of the first conclusions we reached was that international trade was vulnerable to exploitation. Just as commercial air conveyances were used on September 11 for unexpected and destructive purposes, commercial container traffic represented a similar means through which terrorists might wreak havoc. Given the role of customs in managing the flow of commercial traffic, it became clear to us that we would need to become actively engaged in ensuring that legitimate trade was not compromised by those who might seek to undermine the global trade network.

The fact is that international trade is an engine of economic growth and development worldwide. This fact remains unchanged despite recent events. In a global society that depends on efficiency of travel and trade to provide the goods and services that all of our people require, the ability of customs administrations to effectively facilitate such movement while stopping dangerous or economically prejudicial shipments is of paramount importance. For U.S. Customs and Border Protection, and the majority of customs agencies around the world, the focus is now on balancing facilitation with security: facilitation because economic reality demands it; security because nothing – legitimate or not – will be permitted to move without assurances that it is safe.

I would like to summarize for you the approach that U.S. Customs and Border Protection has taken to achieve this goal of balanced security and facilitation. In doing so, I hope to give you a better understanding of thinking behind our focus on the supply chain *in toto*, and show you how our efforts are compatible with greater facilitation. I also hope to leave you with some ideas about the potential role of the United Nations and the international community in this process.

First, let me focus on our strategy in the United States. We have invested heavily in a layered approach to preventing the entry of terrorists and their weapons, believing that we are safest when there is suppression of this activity at every possible point at which a legitimate shipment might be exploited for nefarious purposes. Traditionally, customs' concerns have been limited to what takes place at the port of entry. Now, with the potential threat of terrorists or weapons of mass destruction, such a view is no longer sufficient. The gravity of an event in which terrorists are successfully able to use legitimate trade for destructive ends is such that we felt compelled to take a broader approach – one that would take into account the whole of the logistics and supply chain.

To determine how best to accomplish the goal of a more secure supply chain, we undertook a careful analysis of the global commercial environment. Only by understanding the landscape could we construct effective barriers.

The United States' approach can be understood to consist of elements designed to:
1. engage with our foreign counterparts to undertake examinations earlier in the movement of goods;
2. harden our ports of entry with increased technology and additional staffing;
3. ensure that we have access to sufficient information in advance of the transaction so that we can intervene effectively when there is an indication of risk.

The principal effort designed to push the screening process farther back in the supply chain is the Container Security Initiative (CSI). The objective of CSI is to position ourselves outside the U.S. ports of entry so that we can intercept security threats at the first possible opportunity. The program involves the placement of U.S. Customs and Border Protection officers at seaports around the world to work with host country authorities to target and screen high-risk containers prior to their being shipped to the United States. It works reciprocally as well, with our partners able to place their officers in the U.S. to do similar screening of goods being exported to their countries. Both Canada and Japan have teams stationed in the U.S. to do this type of work.

No less important in this process is the Customs -Trade Partnership Against Terrorism, or C-TPAT. The fact remains that most of the supply chain we hope to secure is managed by private-sector concerns so, while CSI allows us to work with other governments to look for potential security risks, C-

TPAT opens the dialogue with the trade community so that it can mobilize its resources to enhance security in parts of the logistics chain where the ability of customs administrations to intervene is limited. C-TPAT members include importers, carriers, customs brokers, freight forwarders, and others – covering virtually every part of the logistics chain from manufacture to final distribution.

In just over one year's time, the response to both programs has been overwhelmingly positive. Eighteen of the top 20 ports shipping to the United States are engaged in CSI. Over 3,000 companies are participating in GTPAT. And the good news for both programs is that they are expanding. C-TPAT will soon be opened to foreign manufacturers. The CSI effort will move to include strategic ports in other parts of the world as part of the program's second phase.

Still on the subject of CSI expansion, I would like to pause to discuss the importance of European engagement in this program. The transatlantic relationship has been an important one in the context of our rollout of CSI. In our view, CSI is a program that goes to the core of national security interests. The trading relationship between the U.S. and Europe is such that we have to ensure appropriate security measures in transatlantic commerce. Europe sends over $200 billion in goods to the US, nearly 20% of our total import value. This substantial volume cannot be underestimated, nor can the importance of ensuring the engagement of the ports in the region.

We have been in dialogue with a number of states in Europe, based on the locations of the mega-ports, and are expanding these discussions as a result of the locations selected for the programme's second phase. We have also engaged in a dialogue with the European Commission to look at ways to allay concerns that have been raised at the Community level, and have committed to expanding the program to all seaports in the EU that meet certain minimum standards. The objective here – as well as anywhere we are having such discussions– is to develop operational solutions that make sense for the particular locations.

Turning to measures we are undertaking at the ports of entry, U.S. Customs and Border Protection has launched an aggressive strategy for deploying technology and human resources to the field. More specifically, we are augmenting the amount of non-intrusive inspection technology and the number of inspectors present on the front line. If there is a shipment requiring our scrutiny, we are working to ensure that there are people and technology present to examine it quickly, efficiently and effectively.

The last element of our strategy consists of information-based initiatives. We have implemented and are starting the process of requiring more detailed advance information on shipments to better direct our inspections. The key to good decision-making is <u>always</u> good information. For customs purposes, data on shipments is critical to enabling us to focus on those that present the greatest threat, particularly since physical examination of everyone and everything crossing our borders would be impossible. For maritime container trade, we implemented a rule requiring advance manifest information 24 hours before lading at the foreign port prior to coming to the U.S., as well as greater specificity of this information.

This rule represented a major leap forward in our ability to make informed security and facilitation decisions. It has been in effect for several months and the response overall has been good. Nightmare visions had been proffered by some, but none have been realized. There has not been a complete slowdown of trade; no pictures of overloaded terminals around the world; no stalled maritime traffic. The number of denials of lading has been very small relative to the universe of transmitted bills of lading. Compliance has been reported to be well into the 90% range.

Perhaps more importantly, we are expanding the quest for advance information into other modes, as mandated by legislation passed in 2002. Our Trade Act of 2002 requires that we promulgate rules for submitting electronic information for all modes – air, land, and sea – inbound and outbound. The consultative process to begin developing these rules started a few months ago, and the resulting dialogue is helping us to craft programs that will ultimately meet both our needs and those of the trade. We will continue working on this over the next several months to finalize regulations.

We have, therefore, undertaken a wide-reaching effort to address various aspects of security. But in doing this, it is with an eye toward increasing facilitation. Being able to assign lower levels of risk to a given shipment is the key to our being able to provide faster processing at the time of arrival. In nearly every instance, the delays implicit in our conducting security screenings in the U.S. cease to become a factor for those containers that have been pre-screened through CSI or handled by reliable private sector C-TPAT partners who have committed to improving their security measures.

The security-facilitation agenda is a relatively new one for customs administrations, but its concepts are not completely unfamiliar. There are similarities between the fight against smuggling, in which we have been involved for many years, and the relatively new fight against terrorism. Exploitation of trade by terrorists can be thought of as a particular type of smuggling, but one with much more grave consequences. We have the benefit of a good understanding of what types of things can be done to prevent the introduction of drugs and other contraband into the legal logistics chain; however, we are learning more about the specific methods and risk factors associated with terrorism. Our margin for error is much smaller, and the expectations of our people are much higher. For this reason, we have made a serious investment in this process, and are being joined by a number of colleagues in the international customs community.

Even though the developments in the security and facilitation area are somewhat recent, we are already beginning to see how securing the supply chain is having a positive impact on our ability process more efficiently at the border, without compromising effectiveness. In addition to initiatives like CSI and C-TPAT, I would like to share a few other examples that demonstrate this, with the understanding that these are just a beginning. I anticipate that continuing along this path will ultimately lead us to even greater levels of facilitation than we had prior to September 11, 2001.

Many of the examples are drawn from our experience with Canada and Mexico. The greatest impact on our customs processing was felt on the northern and southern borders of the United States, and these are extremely active economic zones. Because of the economic damage incurred during the first days following the terrorist attacks on the U.S., the highest political leadership in the United States, Canada, and Mexico started a dialogue about how we could better manage our respective borders, and provide improved levels of security in the trade between our countries. With Canada, we signed a Smart Border Accord containing 30 action items related to improving border infrastructure, ensuring the secure flow of people, and the secure flow of goods. With Mexico, we signed a similar agreement, a Border Partnership plan consisting of 22 tasks similarly related to providing facilitation of trade and travel through enhanced security.

These discussions, which continue to enjoy substantial political support, have started to bear fruit in the form of programs that dramatically improve the speed of border clearance. On the U.S./Canada border, we have instituted the Free and Secure Trade program, known as FAST.

FAST is a paperless clearance process that uses advance electronic data transmissions and transponder technology to make processing at time of arrival nearly instantaneous. FAST was launched as a way for customs to offer expedited clearance to those carriers and importers that have enrolled in C-TPAT. To be eligible for the program, a shipment must not only be imported by a C-TPAT importer, but also transported by a C-TPAT approved carrier utilizing a FAST approved driver. In sum, the advanced security measures undertaken by the private sector is resulting in a high level of facilitation at the time their shipments arrive.

On our border with Mexico, we are harmonizing the hours and types of service provided by port offices, so that we can reduce bottlenecks in trans-border traffic. We are working on a demonstration project in one of our key border locations to implement a cargo clearance program similar to FAST. And our administrations are exchanging information on how to improve control over, and expedite the processing of, in-transit shipments. When initiatives like this work together, and we can construct a clear picture of the risk that a given shipment poses, we are able to make decisions about whether facilitation is warranted. For the majority of importations, such treatment is appropriate.

Taking a slightly broader view of trade facilitation, I should mention that the United States/Mexico border has an extremely successful program for facilitating the movement of pre-cleared travelers, the Secure Electronic Network for Travelers Rapid Inspection, known as SENTRI. While this might not appear to fit neatly within what would normally be considered part of trade facilitation, it is when one considers the importance of cross-border movement to manufacturing and service industries in this region.

The ability of workers to move more quickly across the border is vital to sustaining the local economy in many locations, given the historically high levels of interdependence and interchange between U.S. and Mexican border towns. In the absence of a free flow of labour, a significant portion of our trade with Mexico could suffer. Following September 11, participation in SENTRI skyrocketed. Over 42,000 motorists now take part. Of course, only individuals who pose no criminal or security risk are allowed to participate, so the emphasis is on pre-clearing participants. With the assurance we have that these individuals do not represent a risk, we again are able to tie together higher security and better facilitation. In facilitating the people, we help to sustain a critical trade-driven sector.

There is one more example which also relates to the movement of people but is no less illustrative of the connection between better security and better facilitation. It is an issue on which the U.S. has been particularly engaged with Europe - the Passenger Name Record, or PNR, data. For months, we have been in dialogue with the European Commission regarding the issue of obtaining PNR data from airlines. For us, it is an issue of knowing more about the traveling public bound for the United States; it is about being able to assess security risks these travelers might pose prior to the aircraft's arrival, so that we can intervene in a targeted manner when the passengers arrive. For us, it is about allowing the vast majority of people, who present no risk, to enter the country unimpeded. Again, we draw the connection between better security and, in this case, continued facilitation of legitimate travelers. While this last example is purely about people, it shows that the entire orientation of our organization is directed to finding a balance, with security as a precondition and facilitation as the goal.

TRADE FACILITATION AND NEW SECURITY INITIATIVES

After this overview of the United States experience and our thinking about the importance of security and trade efficiency, I would like to conclude with some thoughts about the role of other players in advancing this process. Again, U.S. Customs and Border Protection is not alone in emphasizing these themes in terms of managing trade in today's environment. The World Customs Organization is developing standards in this area, and a number of individual customs administrations are instituting measures conceptually similar to those I have described in the U.S. The fact remains, however, that a great deal of work needs to be done in creating a supply chain security infrastructure with truly global reach.

That type of comprehensive regime is what we would hope to achieve in the not too distant future, one which hardens every link of the worldwide supply chain so that no one country,... no one region,... no one commodity, ...no one sector, ... no one trader ... is targeted by those who seek to impair the system.

In November 2002 I had the opportunity to speak at a meeting of UNCTAD in Geneva. I noted several ways in which representatives of various states and organizations, and of UNCTAD in general, could assist customs services in this endeavor. The recommendations I made then, I make again. Many of the issues we confront remain the same, as do the potential contributions government officials can make.

I encourage all of you to impress upon your respective governments the importance of action in the area of trade and security, and the pivotal role that customs plays. I implore you to ensure the engagement of your customs services in the deliberations within the WCO and other groups examining this issue. I also encourage you to facilitate the launch of discussions within your governments to address the question of how measures might be taken nationally, so that none of us becomes the weakest link in the global supply chain. Where these deliberations are already under way, I ask that you ensure that they advance and that they involve all of the relevant government agencies, as well as the private sector.

As is the case many times, political will is critical. The engagement of top leadership is essential to driving the investment necessary to make changes in how we manage security. I think we would all agree that such investments make sense, and these types of preventive measures are something that every government can support. Of course, there are capacity and resource questions that must be considered, and it is perhaps in a UN forum, such as the International Forum on Trade Facilitation, that some of the solutions might be found. Apart from this, the issue for us is moving forward in a coordinated fashion, learning from one another's best practices, and ensuring that we remain focused on maintaining the balance.

The conditions in today's world are not something any of us could have foreseen two years ago, nor are they something for which we would have ever asked. Nonetheless, we find ourselves faced with these difficult challenges. We find ourselves still connected by an intricate web of trade, travel, and services that truly makes us interdependent. Negative events in one part of the world have visible ripple effects elsewhere, and the nature of our world is such that this will always be the case.

As customs administrations - the authorities that manage the borders for our respective countries - we are obliged to look for processes that protect both our people and the trade on which our people depend. In the United States, we have taken a number of steps forward. In this, we are not alone. What is important is that we move forward together, that our political leaders remain engaged, and that we continue working toward a harmonious balance between real security and real facilitation.

Chapter 2.2

The New Challenges from the Point of View of the Shipping Industry

Brian Parkinson, International Chamber of Shipping

They say that every problem is an opportunity. If so, security, in the maritime area, is not a new "opportunity". Shipping has been addressing the "opportunity" of security since man first put to sea in a dug out canoe and someone tried to steal it from him. Not many people outside the industry have been that interested. It has usually been "out of sight, out of mind", "not my problem". Recent threats to shipping have included wars; being used by drug smugglers; as a target for pirates and petty thieves; or stowaways and even terrorists. Over four hundred criminal attacks on ships are reported to the International Maritime Organization (IMO) each year. Last year there were attacks in 46 different countries with over three hundred seafarers killed or injured.

However, these incidents do not make the headline news, except for the case of the *Limberg* in Yemen, and 17 years before that, another attack on a ship, the *Achille Lauro*, hit the headlines, So, attacks on ships are not newsworthy except when committed by terrorists. It makes little difference to the ship and its crew whether it is under threat for political or mercenary motives, because the political consequences to the crew and the ship are more or less the same. Then why, given the history of maritime security, is the industry faced with demands for additional assurances, additional measures and additional safeguards today? Why are there new challenges to the shipping industry?

The reason, I suggest, is that there now proceeds to be not only a threat to ships, but also a threat *from* ships. The protection of ships and crews has never been a big issue, except when they are needed during wartime. But the perceived, and statistically small, risk of ships being used as a tool of terrorists, threatening property and voters, is.

Administrations have demanded action, and this in itself presents another threat. Trade, the engine of economic growth, as we hear it to be called, offers the best chance of steady progress for both developed and developing economies. It may now be under threat, not just from terrorism itself but also from the measures which might be taken to combat it.

"[New security measures] are not a problem", the industry has been told; "they are an opportunity to safeguard crews, ships and cargoes." "They are an opportunity to speed up legitimate trade; better security equals more facilitation." Of course, anything can be given a positive spin. Tax increases are sold as "more money for hospitals, old people and children"; a polluted industrial environment is termed "an industrial growth area", a lack of integrity is called "greasing the wheels" and the opportunity generated by the increased focus on security is called "facilitation".

Let us look at the measures introduced to address security so far. At IMO, a series of measures were adopted in December 2002, establishing legal requirements to paint the ship's official number on the hull; to fit a security alert system (with no guarantees that anyone will respond to that alert); to carry out ship security assessments; to produce a ship security plan approved by flag states; to appoint company and ship security officers and more legal responsibilities for the master; to require to carry a security certificate, declarations of security, a continuous synopsis record - administrative formalities, more pieces of paper and other items of information that are related to ownership. It is difficult to see any gains there.

The World Customs Organization (WCO) is looking at the security in the supply chain and at the security of the goods between origin and destination. To their credit, these issues are being addressed by a Task Force on Security and Facilitation, and we hope that both sides are given equal weight.

Although nothing is finalized yet, suggestions that what might be required as the international norm include: a declaration from the carrier respective of the cargo on board - before it is loaded on board (tricky!); access to commercial records by government officials; an introduction of the concept of authorized traders and secure carriers - which suggests there will be "unauthorized traders" and "insecure carriers". On the subject of increased requirements and increased controls, at the International Labour Office (ILO), new security provisions are being also discussed. These include: new identity documents (ID) for seafarers containing biometric information, fingerprints or retina scans; all port workers being required to carry a photo ID; while government officials who will require access to ships should also carry ID. ILO is also producing guidance on aspects of port security beyond the immediate area of the ship. At the national level also, one state introduced a requirement for armed guards to be employed, not to stop anyone getting on the ship but to prevent the crew getting off. It is also difficult to see the gains of globalization in the new security environment there.

Are these opportunities? Has the impact on trade really been fully evaluated? Let us not beat about the bush, these are not opportunities, they are problems. They are big problems. And why is there a problem? There is a lack of trust.

Some shipping companies have been in existence longer than many countries and their track record speaks for itself. The concept that "Everyone is a crook or a terrorist – we just have not caught them at it yet", must be fought. And it is not just commercial interests that are not trusted. Administrations do not trust each other. Every single import to a country is an export from another. The information collected on an international consignment by both administrations is generally identical. So, why is the majority of the world's trade still encumbered by export and import declarations, export and import cargo declarations; separate import and export declarations in respect of hazardous goods – it is a lack of trust. Even within the same country, different agencies vie to require submissions of more information – customs, excise, agriculture, public health, statistics, and immigration – all requiring separate submissions. Surely in today's world of instant communications we can do better than that.

What are the dangers?

Misdirected energy

The rush towards adopting the quick fix rather than the measured response, the politically expedient rather than the practically effective, the high profile public relations measure rather than the analysis of threat and response, will result in no extra security.

Complacency

How can we ensure that in the absence of another terrorist strike in our particular geographical patch that we do not drop our guard to the point where complacency sets in? If complacency can be resisted, can we be equally immune to security fatigue? Expecting a high level of vigilance to be suddenly achieved and continuously maintained is, in my view, misplaced. Security fatigue will inevitably set in.

The answer must be to find sustainable, supportable measures, measures that become almost routine and which build effective security into daily practices, even if this means changing today's routines.

What are the solutions?

Is it extra forms and certificates of permission or conformity? Is it tighter and more intensive and inconvenient controls – keeping the crew on board of ships all the time? Is it more technology? Is it more experts? Is it more knee-jerk reactions?

Can any merchant ship, employing seamen not armed guards, and where in many places lighting a cigarette is forbidden (let alone carrying weapons), stop a determined terrorist? Could anything have been done to protect the *Limberg*? Is the problem practical or political? What weapons do we have in combating the threat of terrorism?

We have *goodwill*. There is still the goodwill of legitimate trade. All of us realize that the terrorist threat has to be addressed. Those involved in international trade want to contribute, want to be involved, and want to understand.

Carriers have *information* hundreds of data elements on every single consignment; thousands of others connected via commercial data bases to historical data. Together, we must look at the ways in which the information is produced, presented and used. Maritime carriers have well-developed and inter-connected information systems, documented trade patterns, familiarity with regular customers, consignment tracking systems. But information and information systems on their own are not enough. Trade can provide all the information on the cargo that is required, but it takes intelligence to evaluate that information.

Commercial organizations have *experience*. Experience in risk assessment, experience in combating ordinary crime, experience in establishing no risk or at least minimum risk with the vast majority of consignments and ships – profiling not only the suspicious but also the non-suspicious.

Maybe to those coming new to the security problem, there can be no trust. Any ship, any container, any trailer, any truck, can be a threat. Hopefully, those who are involved from day to day, such as customs authorities and carriers, and the traders themselves with knowledge of their customers and their trade partners, know better.

We should be looking at redefining the *point of control*. Current administrative requirements continue to look at border-crossing places, ports of loading and discharge as control points. However, the commercial point-of-control is no longer the port – the place where cargo consignments used to be tallied, checked and individually loaded or unloaded to or from the ship. The administrative point-of-control also has to change and to look to the export-import partnership, rather than the port-carrier-port exchange, as the place where administrative controls need to be exercised. Maybe the importer, who, after all, is usually the party initiating the consignment, needs to be better known and controlled rather than the exporter or the carrier. Moreover, there would seem to be benefits in looking at more or better cooperation between customs services. As I mentioned earlier, one country's exports are another country's imports. Therefore, co-operation between customs authorities in a country and other government agencies in that country would prove beneficial.

Let us also look for ways of providing better or earlier data. While doing so, let us bear in mind that the information required for a security assessment may be different to that required for clearance and may be provided from different sources than today's information providers. For every customs official there are probably a hundred other people involved in any consignment - packers, drivers, warehousemen, stevedores, documentation staff, ships' crews - all ready and able to contribute to security of the supply chain if informed about what to look out for. Can they be encouraged to participate in this? Anomalies, inconsistencies, contradictions, the unusual, the uneconomic, a strange way of paying, an odd address, a strange pattern of behaviour, an unexplainable routing – these are the signs which may alert the observer to a suspicious consignment.

We have had some facilitation measures in the pipeline for some time – most of them developed within the UNECE. The "Single Window" concept has been talked about for years. How about at least implementing "Fewer Windows" before going to a "Single Window" concept? What happened to paperless trading? Have we even achieved a "less paper" environment? What happened to the electronic signature? Well, despite all the work that went on - not a lot. In many parts of the world, people, and I have to say mainly officials, love signatures and the authority that comes with the need for them.

Conclusion and recommendations

The industry remains willing to play its part in the struggle against terrorism. But any measures introduced must have an international dimension; which means, international s tandards. They must be consistent, clear and uniform; be proportionate to the threat; involve cooperation with all parties; be practical - not political; and capable of identifying the possibly suspect and favour the probably innocent.

Experience suggests that trade facilitation opportunities will be overlooked, and yet they are badly needed. The possibilities are there. Ports are reported to be raising charges. For example, one port group indicated $10 per consignment to recover their additional security expenses. Shipping companies, too, will be charging more: $25 per consignment has been one figure mentioned. But any increase in the cost of trade is a blow to trade.

So, are there likely to be any gains in the new security environment? If there are, they will not be easily achieved. However, I firmly believe that if governments and commercial organizations address these issues with the same enthusiasm that new security measures and proposals are being pushed, there is a chance. Governments and trade interests must work together on systems and procedures so that the "probably innocent" can pass more freely through any additional controls. It will not be easy. Any gains will not materialize automatically. It is not facilitation; it is not making things easier, only less difficult for some.

If it is an opportunity and not a problem, my fear is that the issue will prove to be an unsolvable opportunity. Governments and trade interests need to work together – at UNECE, at IMO, at WCO, and at WTO. I believe that we are all on the same side.

Chapter 2.3
Insights from the Innovative Trade Network Team
Robert M. Massey, CEO, Cotecna Inspection SA

In this paper I will present the Innovative Trade Network (ITN), a team of companies that together has developed an international trade facilitation initiative. As the Chief Executive Officer of Cotecna Inspection SA, a very active participant in the ITN, I would like to take this opportunity to brief you on the work-in-progress of this important project. BV Solutions Group, Inc., Calspan UB Research Center, Inc., Cargill, Cotecna, Inc., FreightDesk Technologies, Inc., Honeywell Laboratories, Lockheed Martin, TransCore and Veridian are the nine companies with expertise in transportation, technology and supply chain management that have decided to form the ITN team. (see Annex 1 for a description of each company). Our mission is to invent a global trade network that is both secure and efficient. The team as a whole provides all the elements needed for a comprehensive solution to improving and securing the international trade process using readily available technologies that are accessible to all trading nations.

Cotecna, in particular, brings two relevant capabilities to the ITN team: **Trained Inspectors** and **Scanning and Sealing Technologies**. We specialize in monitoring commercial trade routes in order to ensure their integrity by combining sophisticated scanning and sealing technologies with highly trained inspectors. It is the combination of technologies and skilled inspectors that deliver the required integrity. *Both* components are essential.

Cotecna has an extended, worldwide network. Cotecna employees work on the ground all around the world. Some may be familiar with our work in Iraq, where our inspectors have monitored the United Nations' Oil-for-Food program for the past five years using sophisticated secure satellite communication systems. Others may know of our work in Africa, Latin America and Asia, where we deal with customs officials in several countries, providing services ranging from Risk Management, X-Ray Scanning, Destination Inspection, Customs Valuation Assistance, to name a few.

We have innovative customer relationships. For example, joint ventures with a number of governments have enabled us to introduce the first ship-container X-Ray scanners into several African ports. Today Cotecna fully owns and operates 5 container scanners and was recently awarded a 10-year contract to finance, install and operate 14 X-Ray scanners in seaports, airports and land borders of one West African country.

Nowadays, we are confronted with a shift in focus, where concern for security has become more sensitive than ever, a change which impacts individuals all over the world. Unfortunately, the way we trade today does not adequately address these new apprehensions. We are aware, for example, of the United States' 24-hour manifest rule and its potential impact on international business – the commerce of goods around the globe could suffer from a major slowdown due to the lack of appropriate means and proper coordination between the different stakeholders (international organizations, trade associations, government bodies), should proper action not be taken and implemented. The **antidote** is therefore to produce the required information accurately and swiftly and to securely communicate it to the relevant parties.

In a world where a threat in one single location can disrupt trade everywhere, the only acceptable solution is one that includes and works for all trading nations. For that reason, ITN envisions an infrastructure that is global and which uses readily available technology to all trading nations, anytime, anywhere.

The ITN consortium is the basis for a comprehensive solution that comprises a worldwide network of trusted partners (or agents) with secure communication and software systems, integrating off-the-shelf technology, such as electronic sealing, scanning and tracking.

With this in mind, we foresee 3 major complimentary processes:

- **The first process** entails the inspection and verification of locations, content and people.
- **The second process** consists in implementing data clearinghouses, which distribute appropriate information to the appropriate supply chain trade lane participants *in real time*. This second procedure highlights an important and highly relevant benefit of the proposed ITN solution.
- **The third process** lies in profiling transactions, using historical data to assess the level of risk and prompt appropriate action. This is what the proposed solution will do.

ITN wishes to achieve an ideal scheme with the proposed solution: many of the technologies and processes we require are already operational today, however they must be appropriately and seamlessly integrated. Furthermore, a business model needs to be applied for the solution to become complete and efficient. Figure 3.3.1 offers an illustration of the suggested scheme.

How would such a solution be financed? The basic idea underlying the scheme is for it to be self-sufficient: the enhanced trade process should allow the various stakeholders to bear the financial costs through the benefits generated by the scheme itself.

Figure 2.3.1 The scheme shown in progress

I. A *Buyer*, anywhere in the world, initiates the process by issuing the necessary information and sharing it with the Data Clearinghouse by electronic means.

II. The *Supplier* receives the order and prepares the shipment.

III. An independent third party, a "*trusted agent*", verifies the cargo; seals and time-stamps the containers; releases the collected data to Credentialed Transporters; and forwards them to the Clearinghouse electronically.

IV. The Credentialed *Transporter* takes the shipment to the port of loading and forwards the tracking data to the Clearinghouse.

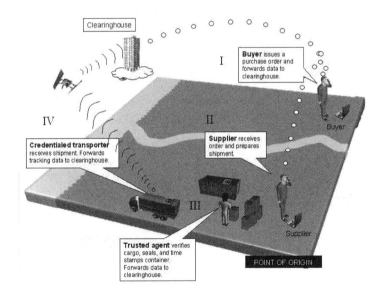

IV. Thanks to the Clearinghouse, the *Carrier* has the information needed to meet reporting requirements and act with confidence to expedite the shipping procedures.

V. The Carrier updates the Clearinghouse when the cargo is loaded on the ship. A manifest is issued from the Carrier to the destination Customs authorities via the Data Clearinghouse.

VI. We understand how the availability of information in real time improves both security and efficiency: with the help of the data originating from the Clearinghouse, the Customs clear the containers.

VII. The final destination Transporters credentials are checked and time-stamped by a trusted agent.

VIII. The Transporter then sends the tracking information to the Clearinghouse and the Transporter delivers goods to the Buyer. The Buyer breaks the seals and receptions the merchandise.

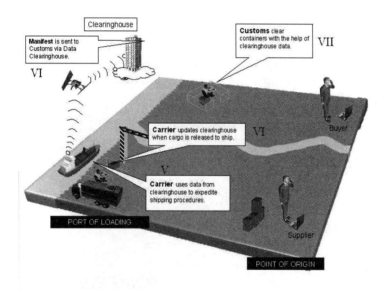

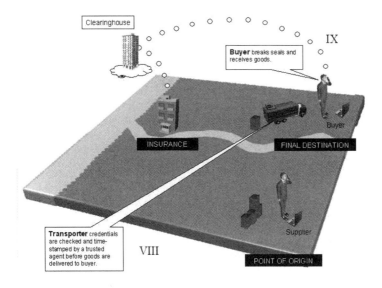

Our experience has shown that investments in improving trade lane efficiency – by removing gaps, by reducing the paperwork, for example – deliver an economic payoff. The level of benefits it brings to its users proves the success of any new technology. In our case, this would be identifiable as: *faster processes, security, real-time accurate information sharing* which will lead to increased economic efficiency and trade facilitation.

This global trade solution is entirely based on the voluntary participation of the stakeholders, whether in the public or private sectors. This solution will facilitate trade, strengthen security and automate mandatory government reporting. A global trade system that improves security and efficiency will expand world trade. By sharing our ideas, concepts, knowledge with different stakeholders (international organizations, trade associations, governments, exporters, and importers) we have conceptualised a solution that addresses the issue of security while improving trade. This is an important point and the very reason why states around the world should invest in a Global Trade Security System.

Annex 1: Innovative Trade Network: Consortium formed to enhance global trade security[43]

Nine companies with expertise in transportation, technology and supply chain industries announced on 13 May 2003 the formation of the Innovative Trade Network (ITN), a team of specialists from: BV Solutions Group, a division of Black & Veatch Corp.; Calspan UB Research Center Inc.; Cargill, Incorporated; Cotecna Inc.; FreightDesk Technologies Inc.; Honeywell; Lockheed Martin; TransCore; and Veridian. The companies joined together to assess techniques for global trade supply chain security enhancements, ensuring that the logistics industry concentrates on best business practices to improve transportation security and economics, rather than focusing on specific technologies. These practices would have global applications, including the oversight of container shipments coming into the United States. Members of the ITN presented their recommendations for facilitating international trade at the United Nations Economic Commission for Europe Forum held in Geneva, Switzerland, on 15 May 2003.

With millions of trade shipments entering the United States each year, government and industry leaders recognize the potential risks in the current environment. Establishing safeguards is clearly essential to hinder the use of the global supply chain as an illegitimate conduit for chemical, biological, nuclear or other weapons of mass destruction. These safeguards must not only secure the flow of goods, they must also enhance the flow through ports and across borders. Together, the companies of ITN will work internationally with governments, agencies and industry partners to create global supply chain systems – from manufacturer, to ports of entry, to consumers – that focus on sound business models which facilitate trade and serve as catalysts for improved security measures.

"The key is to look at the comprehensive business model," said Dean Kothmann, ITN spokesman and BV Solutions Group Chief Development Officer. "ITN's objective is to create the infrastructure and business model to allow all nations, ports, technology providers, and logistics providers to play on a level playing field that improves economics while addressing security issues associated with commercial shipping."

---

[43] For articles and more information on the various companies, see Part Three of this volume.

A memorandum of understanding signed by the nine founding companies outlines the individual roles and responsibilities as the team pursues grants and projects:
BV Solutions Group Inc., a subsidiary of Black & Veatch Corp. ranked 78th on the *Forbes* "500 Largest Private Companies in the U.S." list, is a leading program manager and designer of engineering and operation information systems and processes. BV will provide overall program management, project controls, schedule, cost management, scope management, system architecture design, and data clearinghouse services. Based in Overland Park, Kansas, the company provides IT services to Fortune 1,000 clients. Black & Veatch Corp. is a leading global engineering, construction and consulting company specializing in infrastructure development in the fields of energy, water and information. Visit www.bvsg.com and www.bv.com

Cargill, Incorporated is an international marketer, processor and distributor of agricultural, food, financial and industrial products and services with 97,000 employees in 59 countries. Based in Minneapolis, in the United States, the company provides distinctive customer solutions in supply chain management, food applications, and health and nutrition. Given its recognized expertise in global trading and supply chain logistics management, Cargill will offer project management, food security and tracking, IT systems and support services. Visit www.cargill.com.

Cotecna Inc., based in Washington D.C. and a member of the Cotecna Group of Geneva, Switzerland, is a recognized world reference in the facilitation of a secured flow of goods from market to market (M2M) and has developed a range of innovative trade management tools designed to ensure compliance with national and international standards. Cotecna will serve as a trade lane provider and offer project management, container validation, shipment load overview and audit, sealing of container, tracking up to loading and shipping, satellite tracking, digital photography and x-ray scanning, as well as collecting, treating and formatting all data from empty container inspection up to container loading and shipping. The Cotecna Group has 4,000 personnel in 150 offices in 100 countries worldwide. Visit www.cotecna.com.

Calspan UB Research Center Inc. (CUBRC) is a diverse research, development, engineering and testing company focused on providing defense, intelligence, transportation and homeland security solutions. Based in Buffalo, N.Y., CUBRC is an independent, not-for-profit corporation jointly formed by Veridian and the State University of New York at Buffalo. **Veridian** (NYSE: VNX) provides information-based systems, integrated solutions and services to the U.S. government, focusing on mission-critical national security programs. Veridian operates at more than 50 locations, and employs over 7,300 professionals. The company's annual revenues are approximately $1 billion. Visit www.veridian.com. **CUBRC** and **Veridian,** as strategic partners, will offer data profiling of containers including data warehouse design and development, data mining and knowledge discovery, and decision support tools for analytics and visualization; trade lane threat and vulnerability assessment for weapons of mass destruction and other threats.

FreightDesk Technologies Inc. provides Internet-native software solutions to industry and government for controlling international logistics data and end-to-end processes for cargo moving by parcel, air, road, rail, and sea. FreightDesk will implement the technical architecture and software to manage the flow of information into and from the clearinghouse, and create discreet technical environments to facilitate information access necessary for profiling and reporting by and to appropriate stakeholders. Visit www.freightdesk.com.

Honeywell (NYSE: HON), a Dow Jones Industrial Average company, employs approximately 100,000 people in 95 countries. Based in Morris Township, New Jersay, Honeywell is a diversified technology and manufacturing leader of aerospace products and services; control technologies for buildings, homes, and industry; automotive products; power generation systems; specialty chemicals; fibers; plastics and advanced materials. Honeywell will provide project management, serve as a trade lane provider, offer port management software and services, cyber security and security tools such as cameras and video analysis software. Visit www.honeywell.com.

Lockheed Martin is a world leader in advanced technology systems integration for defense, government IT, and homeland security. Developers of the Global Transportation Network (GTN), the Department of Defense's primary system for logistics and supply chain management, Lockheed Martin brings unparalleled expertise in transportation and logistics systems integration and security. GTN provides in-transit visibility for 6 million shipments per day across the globe with a secure, web-based system that has saved the United States Department of Defense an estimated $2 billion. Headquartered in Bethesda, Maryland, the corporation employs 125,000 people worldwide and reported sales surpassing $26 billion in 2002. Visit www.lockheedmartin.com.

TransCore specializes in intelligent transportation systems with installations in more than 39 countries and a heritage that links to the invention of wireless radio frequency identification (RFID) technology at Los Alamos National Laboratory. TransCore is a privately held transportation services company with 1,700 employees and more than 80 locations throughout the world with research, development and manufacturing facilities located in Albuquerque, New Mexico. TransCore will provide project management and integration for systems to seal and track containers; serve as a trade lane provider; identify technology; install and maintain track and seal infrastructure; identify and provide all data from infrastructure, transfer data, to clearinghouse; and act as a trusted agent transmitting data. Visit www.transcore.com.

Chapter 2.4
Security in a Global Supply Chain – A Holistic Approach

Selig S. Merber, Chairman of the ICC Customs Committee

Global supply chain logistics is a complex system involving many actors. Therefore, measures taken to advance one goal, such as security, must take into account a network of interdependent causes and effects throughout the entire system. A holistic perspective, i.e. one that emphasizes the importance of the whole and the interdependence of its parts, is best designed to achieve lasting improvements in both facilitation and security throughout the global supply chain.

In order to achieve this, the following presentation will put forward seven relevant concepts/ propositions. The emphasis will be on the effects of corruption in the supply chain, the facilitation and security equation and also the relationship between facilitation and security and its effects on revenue generation, a concern of many customs administrations and which many developing countries rely on for large parts of their revenues.

1. Facilitation is a process, not an activity. It involves several actors, several information systems, and many physical facilities. Focusing on any one of these elements can produce incremental improvements but significant lasting results can only be achieved through process improvements.

2. Similar to facilitation, security as well is a process, and not an activity. Security also involves several actors, several information systems, and many physical facilities. And, again, lasting improvement can only result from a process improvement.

3. Facilitation enhances security. In fact, the system improvements necessary to improve facilitation are the same improvements necessary to improve security. They include risk analysis, improved information flows and cooperation with trusted traders. This allows customs and other relevant agencies to focus on high-risk trade where they are most needed and could be most effective.

4. Corruption undermines security, i.e. trade that flows outside of the commercial system will also flow outside of security systems. The best designed system to ensure the integrity of a global supply chain cannot provide security against the terrorist threat if the system is administered corruptly.

5. Tariffs drive corruption, i.e. the higher the tariffs are, the greater the incentive for trade to move outside of legitimate, controlled channels. And if trade moves outside legitimate, controlled channels it moves outside of important security protections. A system that tolerates corruption is incompatible with sound security.

6. Trade liberalization can increase revenue. Trade liberalization and facilitation are not incompatible with revenue collection. If a holistic approach to facilitation and security is perceived to jeopardize revenue generation, it will not take root in the large number of countries for which tariffs are a significant proportion of revenues. But trade liberalization and facilitation are not incompatible with revenue collection. In fact, high revenues cause a revenue gap, a gap between duties owed and duties collected by encouraging cheating and driving large amounts of trade outside the collection system altogether. The example of China shows that by reducing tariff rates over a period of 10 years during the country's accession negotiations to the WTO, duty generation increased. As more trade was brought into legitimate channels, the revenue gap closed and revenue increased.

7. Facilitation works and the holistic approach works. The example of the Peruvian customs reform demonstrates that by taking a holistic approach, facilitation and trade liberalization can result in increased revenue collection.

The two major implications of the aforementioned propositions are that trade liberalization is a security initiative. Existing programmes for trade facilitation and security are important and must be continued, particularly those that enlist the support and cooperation of the private sector in securing the international supply chain. But no system, however well designed, can protect against terrorism if untrustworthy agents administer it. Therefore, the relationship between high tariffs, integrity, and security, should be recognized and it should be stressed that trade liberalization including trade facilitation is a security initiative. If attention is diverted from these important initiatives in the name of security, both goals will be jeopardized. A holistic approach advances both.

The second implication is that capacity building must emphasize change management and process re-engineering. Making system-wide changes in complex processes is not an easy task. It involves skills that are difficult to acquire and even more difficult to apply. Moreover, in order to take advantage of modern risk management techniques, customs administrations must recognize the fundamental truth that most traders want to comply with the law and the majority of failures to do so result not from calculated evasion but from honest error.

In conclusion, it is important to have a culture of security, i.e. not just a security programme in one or another area but a culture of security that runs through the whole supply chain. Similarly, it is important to have a culture of facilitation, i.e. which shifts from enforcement orientation to facilitation orientation. This means that the internal culture of whole organizations has to change and managing change within an organization is the most difficult task. Therefore, when training needs are assessed and capacity-building programmes are designed, prominent attention should be given to training in methods of accomplishing the real organizational and cultural change that is needed to reconcile the goals of facilitation and security.

The preceding chapters have clearly shown that nobody questions the need for and benefits of better trade facilitation but there is some difference over the means to that end and especially the role of WTO in this area. The world business community strongly supports the negotiations of an effective WTO agreement on trade facilitation. One essential goal of trade facilitation stressed by ICC is to reduce the time elapsed between arrival of goods in port and their release to the importer, i.e. the release time. The ICC therefore suggests that as part of a WTO agreement there should be a commitment to assess facilitation through the measurement of release time and to reduce it over a period of time. This would allow improvements within the structure of existing processes and legal systems and leave enough flexibility to countries. This approach accepts each country's current level of performance as a starting point. It also allows for commitments commensurate with that starting point and with the capabilities of the country in question. What is measured improves, and measurement may be an effective means to improve trade facilitation that is sensitive to the needs of developing countries.

Chapter 2.5
Trade Facilitation and Security: The Perspective of HM Customs and Excise, United Kingdom

Bob Eagle, Director Customs, HM Customs and Excise, United Kingdom

I would like to present here a customs perspective to the trade facilitation debate and I will be looking at the increasing security dimension of the issue. Despite the new security dimension, trade facilitation is at least as important as it ever was, and probably even more important now. I will address the vital inter-relationship between security, compliance and trade facilitation and the importance of a multilateral approach to these issues involving the WTO, WCO and other bodies. I will also address the United Kingdom's approach to modernisation, security and trade facilitation.

It has always been in customs' interest to reward compliance by the trade in meeting the necessary customs' rules with trade facilitation, by letting goods flow as easily and as quickly from place of export to place of import, by dealing with any licences that may be required for the goods, and by paying any duties applicable. Security is of course not new. We have always needed to protect ourselves from illegally smuggled weapons, diseases, drugs and other contraband. But there is a new threat to the security of the supply chain – the risk of a weapon of mass destruction, a so-called "dirty bomb" being smuggled in freight, probably a container. That is a new challenge for customs to combat, and I will address it further.

We do have a new paradigm. Whilst more compliance has always been able to feed through into more facilitation for the trade, now more security leads to more facilitation too. When customs is clear that goods are not a risk, their passage will be facilitated and speeded up. There are, of course, justifiable checks which we will have to carry out to protect society, and which takes time. But the new message is, security should go hand in hand with trade facilitation. It is important that they are mutually reinforcing. The right approach will ensure that they are. The wrong approach will set them in conflict, raising barriers and undermining both which for smaller players – whether countries or companies – may prove insurmountable. Many international bodies are involved with security, compliance and facilitation, the United Nations, the World Customs Organization (WCO), the World Trade Organization (WTO), Interpol, to name but a few. I will be focusing today on the WCO and the WTO.

In the customs' area, international agreements are vital in bringing about security, compliance and facilitation. It is only through international agreements that we are all able to agree on minimum steps to modernise and simplify our customs' processes and crucially provide the necessary harmonisation. It is only through harmonisation that we will produce the vital predictability for the movement of goods. This means moving goods quickly, keeping costs low, or at least affordable.

The WCO has clearly an important role in international agreements in the customs' area. The Kyoto Agreement, which soon, we hope, will have Convention status, on simplified, harmonised customs procedures, is one such agreement. The WCO is now doing important work to improve the security of the international trade supply chain, which is focusing on three elements: 1) on new international standards such as harmonised data requirements through the customs' data model; 2) on the development of guidelines for cooperation between customs and private industry to jointly improve the security of the supply chain; and 3) on the importance of using modern technology to provide enhanced security, as Mr. Mikuriya, the Deputy Secretary General of the WCO, mentioned above.

I would also like to say something about the WTO and the need for a WTO agreement on trade facilitation. Trade facilitation, as well as security issues, go much wider than just customs. It impacts substantially on trade and trade policy just as customs duty and other trade barriers do. In our view, clear and robust rules for trade facilitation would benefit all players in the international trade business. According to recent studies, the cost of inefficient trade and customs' procedures are thought to be worth over $300 billion a year, equivalent to the entire GDP of sub–Saharan Africa. No one benefits from this huge sum. Unlike a tax or duty, it does not go to any productive or social output, it just gets lost in inefficiency and bureaucracy.

Therefore, I welcome the work that has been done already looking at Articles V, VIII and X of the GATT treaty to see how they can be developed further to provide for increased trade facilitation. In particular, I think increased transparency is very important with the need for customs' administrations to be clear in their information on trade, particularly about rules and regulations, how the trade can contact customs and how to avoid unnecessary delays in moving goods. It is important for customs administrations to be clear on what services trade can expect and to have appeal mechanisms in place for when problems arise. Traders need clarity, certainty and consistency, regardless of their differing export markets.

So, what specific steps should be taken? I have already mentioned *transparency* - the publication of all border related laws, regulations, procedures and practices, mechanisms to make such information readily available (e.g. gazettes, websites), mechanisms allowing stakeholders to comment.

Simplification is important too. Advance rulings for particular regular transactions, simplified, streamlined procedures for authorised traders and express consignments. Charter standards setting how long traders should expect processes to be carried out, for example, for their goods to be cleared.

Last but not least, *due process*. Accessibility to independent judicial or administrative tribunals and the necessary procedures to review and correct administrative actions ensures protection against arbitrary decisions by customs officers and increases confidence. For customs, authorised traders, based on sound risk management, are the key to squaring the circle between security and trade facilitation.

So, why do we need a multilateral agreement? A multilateral agreement will help ensure political commitment to implementing new, minimum s. It will encourage customs administrations to offer improved service to the trade and will encourage the trade to be more compliant and therefore be rewarded by more trade facilitation.

The UK Blueprint

The United Kingdom's approach to customs modernisation is set out in the *Customs Blueprint for International Trade* a strategy document that we published a year ago, and working with the trade we are now beginning to implement. The *Blueprint* represents modernisation of the UK's Customs Controls for the 21st Century. Its focus is the electronification of all customs processes and documents so that we can eventually eliminate all paper in international trade transactions. The aim is to achieve fully electronic end-to-end processes in the next five years. This will save the trade and customs significant resources. Under the *Blueprint* authorised traders which have compliance plans in place setting out a trader's responsibility to customs and customs' responsibility to the trader, will have access to a range of different service options for handling his customs business. The watchword for us is that compliance will be rewarded by more facilitation. We should not forget that most traders are honest. Their commercial integrity and reputation are important to them. And similarly, most transport operators, international airlines, shipping companies and logistics operators will not knowingly risk carrying dodgy, unsafe and risky goods. So, they provide a powerful back-up check.

The introduction of the *Unique Consignment Reference Number* in the trade transaction will be a vital means of improving security in the day-to-day trading process. I know this is something the WCO is working hard on. But we are taking other measures to tighten security through better use of the latest technology to track down illicit goods, and in particular to protect our citizens from the risk of illegal import of nuclear materials; through implementation of the Container Security Initiative (CSI) at all ports in the United Kingdom, which trade with the United States, through minimum data requirements for imports to meet customs security needs and through a better partnership with the private sector which is focused on security, and with whom we are currently working on a partnership agreement.

However, will not this extra security cost the trade too? Certainly, we must see to keep the costs down to a minimum. Although, there will be extra costs to protect our citizens, but not introducing better security is not an option.

The key to all of this, as we say in the United Kingdom, is a joined-up approach between all the players or economic agents involved in international trade from both the private and public sectors. This means, government departments and agencies cooperating fully on a coordinated, joint agenda. It means, traders working with customs administrations and with the international bodies, for example, with the WCO and the WTO. Without this joint effort, we shall achieve very little.

A new set of commitments to standards will bring with it greater predictability in the movement of goods process. That will speed up processes and encourage confidence in the system and encourage more trade. More trade will mean higher customs duty so customs administrations will not lose out in revenue terms. More trade also means more economic growth. Yes, as you have heard many times before, everybody wins!

Chapter 2.6
Proposal for Standards Development in Support of Trade Facilitation and Security: A Collaborative Approach[44]

Hans Carl, President, International MultiModal Transport Association (IMMTA)

This paper considers possible collaborative approaches to developing required standards for international trade security that facilitate the participation of companies worldwide in international trade and avoid the introduction of undue costs and procedures.

Security has always been a factor in international trade and many mechanisms and procedures already exist to address this issue. However, both the nature of the security threat and, importantly, the perception of the nature of that threat have changed dramatically since the recent terrorist events in the United States. Effectively, the focus has shifted from the relatively minor threat to trade (from theft, hijackings, terrorist interventions, etc.) to the much more alarming threat from trade, where terrorists could use the mechanisms and processes of trade as a weapon against the developed, and indeed the developing world.

Although the nature and extent of this threat is, fortunately, mostly speculative at present, it is essential to understand the seriousness with which many countries approach the issue. Essentially, the major fear is that weapons of mass destruction, or the materials to construct such weapons, could be smuggled into a country through the trade system and could then be detonated by terrorists or other enemies of the state once they have entered the country.

---

[44] This paper was commissioned by the UNECE secretariat to Mr. Hans Carl, President, International MultiModal Transport Association (IMMTA) for presentation at the 2003 International Forum on Trade Facilitation, 14–15 May 2003, and was prepared with input from the UNECE secretariat. It was published as UNECE document TRADE/2003/22 on 28 April 2003.

Several approaches to addressing this issue have been launched by leading trade-related organizations over the past year and much work is currently under way in developing standards and systems to increase the security of the international trade transaction process. The task is enormous; and there is the obvious danger that the immediate responses to this threat (whether real or perceived) may not be consistent with the longer-term development of an efficient trading system.

This paper reviews some current initiatives in the trade security area and considers how the resources and instruments of the many organizations involved in international trade facilitation can best be harnessed to ensure both a more secure and a more efficient trading system that will accommodate the longer-term stability and profitability of global trade. The paper pays particular attention to the work of the World Customs Organization and the International Maritime Organization and considers how other major players in the field, such as the United Nations Economic Commission for Europe and the United Nations Conference on Trade and Development, can complement and add value to these efforts.

The author recognizes that this security shock to the trade system presents an opportunity to re-examine current trade procedures and processes and to speed up implementation of advanced technologies and approaches, such as risk assessment based on advance information. The challenge is to facilitate the majority of legitimate international cargo movements, and as efficiently as possible, while at the same time dealing effectively with the small percentage that could pose a threat to security. To achieve this, all parties in the trade transaction chain need to work closely together.

Trade, trade facilitation, economic development and the role of the United Nations

Trade is an important engine of economic growth and the globalization of trade is a dominant feature of today's economy in many countries. The creation of an open and equitable trade environment is a key United Nations goal, particularly in relation to economic development and poverty reduction. Millennium Development Go al 8 focuses on achieving a global partnership for development. Specifically, the goal is to "develop further an open trading and financial system that is rule-based, predictable and non-discriminatory and includes a commitment to good governance, development and poverty reduction both nationally and internationally".[45] The Monterrey Consensus further states that "globalisation should be fully inclusive and equitable",[46] and the recent report by the UN Secretary-General (Strengthening the United Nations, September 2002) states that developing and implementing a proper framework of rules, norms and standards for international trade is necessary to help the international community respond effectively to the challenges posed by globalization.[47]

Security issues clearly pose a real threat to the stability, further development and equalisation of global trade. However, these security issues must be addressed in such a way as to minimise the potentially negative side effects; otherwise a real, and perhaps intended, reward may be handed to the very groups these measures are intended to defeat. For example, new measures to support security must not add undue procedures and costs to international trade transactions. Further, we must ensure that no specific country or group is excluded from the international trading system through these measures, as exclusion would undermine the basic foundation of security, which is a fair and just society, free from poverty and degradation.

Current initiatives

Not surprisingly, the United States Government was one of the first countries in the world to assess the potential security threat from international trade. Based on an initial review of trade security following the attacks of 11 September 2001, the government identified seaborne

---

[45] UN Millennium Development Goals, www.un.org/millenniumgoals, Oct. 2002.
[46] Monterrey Consensus: Draft Outcome of the International Conference on Financing for Development, 1 March 2002. (A/CONF/198/3).
[47] Strengthening of the United Nations: an agenda for further change, Report of the Secretary General (A/57/387), September 2002, p. 10.

containers[48] as a major security threat and subsequently developed several initiatives to tackle this threat. These initiatives focus mainly on the provision of advance information on cargo entering the United States and on securing the supply chains of major international corporations.

In January 2002, United States Customs launched the Container Security Initiative (CSI) to prevent global containerized cargo from being exploited by terrorists. The initiative is designed to enhance security of the sea cargo container – a vital link in global trade. Effective 2 December 2002, carriers and/or automated NVOCCs (Non-Vessel Operating Common Carriers) must submit a cargo declaration 24 hours before cargo is laden aboard the vessel at a foreign port.

United States Customs held a series of public meetings in accordance with section 343(a) of the Trade Act of 2002 to assist in the development of proposed regulations to provide for the mandatory collection by customs of electronic cargo information prior to importation into or exportation from the United States. The focus is on 343(a) Cargo Information, which will require promulgation of regulations providing for advance electronic submission of information pertaining to cargo heading out and arriving in the United States. This requirement extends to all modes of transportation.

The Aviation & Transportation Security Act was passed by the 107th Congress on 19 November 2001 - Public Law 107-071. This Act established a series of challenging but critically important milestones towards achieving a secure air travel system.

A number of international organizations have also undertaken recent work in trade security and facilitation, often using the United States initiatives as a base for developing new recommendations and instruments. For instance, the World Customs Organization (WCO) Task Force on Security and Facilitation is basing its security initiative on the idea of closer international cooperation, and calls for the mobilization of all the links in

---

[48] Some 200 million sea-cargo containers move annually among the world's top seaports, and nearly 50 per cent of the value of all United States imports arrive via sea containers.

the supply chain and the encouragement of partnerships already existing in the field of international trade. This cooperation depends on an extensive exchange of information between all the players, public and private, involved in the international supply chain. The Task Force will develop sectoral guidelines to formalize and define the terms of this collaboration. These will make it possible to assist WCO Members in concluding cooperative agreements with business partners to increase supply-chain security and facilitate the flow of international trade. A basic concept in this approach is the establishment of an effective risk management system at international level, requiring customs controls from the very beginning of the supply chain.

The International Maritime Organization (IMO) has developed a new comprehensive security regime for international shipping, which is set to enter into force in July 2004. This follows the adoption by the IMO Diplomatic Conference on Maritime Security, held from 9 to 13 December 2002 in London, of a series of measures to strengthen maritime security and prevent and suppress acts of terrorism against shipping. IMO Secretary-General, William O'Neil, has strongly urged all parties concerned "to start putting in place all the necessary legislative, administrative and operational provisions needed to give effect to the decisions of the Conference as soon as possible".

The United Nations Economic Commission for Europe (UNECE) is currently reviewing its relevant instruments in the trade and transport areas. For example, the Inland Transport Committee at its meeting in February 2003 took note of a number of initiatives in the transport and security area, requesting its subsidiary bodies to identify, within their respective fields of competence, the difference between "security" and "safety" concepts and the relevant concrete questions that could be addressed in this respect. In addition, UNECE held a meeting of leading government and trade organizations in early 2003, *Achieving Trade Security Within a Standardized, Efficient and Transparent International Framework*, to consider the evolution of a longer-term approach to trade security and facilitation. It was suggested at this meeting that a useful basis for future work could be the UN/CEFACT Supply Chain Model, and possibly also the International Trade Transaction Model. UNECE is currently updating both of these models. This work is being further reviewed and developed by UNECE, in the light of the above suggestions and complements the framework set out in the Netherlands and WCO papers on advance cargo information[49].

Analysing the needs – the International Supply Chain Model

International trade and security can best be assessed in the context of the international supply chain. This has been the approach of UNECE to trade facilitation and e-business analysis for many years and is also the approach adopted by the WCO Task Force on Security and Facilitation.

The international supply chain involves a potentially large number of activities performed by a considerable number of different parties. An activity may be carried out by different parties depending on the terms of business, type of product, country and market etc. as well as on the methods of operation of the buyer and seller. For a supply chain to operate effectively and efficiently, the relationships and activities have to be clearly identified and managed.

The UN/CEFACT International Supply Chain Model (UN/ISCM) sets out to identify and model the key processes and relationships of the parties involved in international trade. This Model helps in the understanding of how a supply chain operates, and it can be used to highlight opportunities for "best practice" improvements in international trade for all countries, businesses, governments or economies. The Model can also be used to identify procedures that do not add significant value or enhance security or safety, and it can indicate opportunities for facilitation actions.

---

[49] WCO Proposed Customs guidelines on advance cargo information, TF0005E1; Supply chain security, discussion paper prepared for the WCO Trade Security Task Force by the Netherlands

Within the international supply chain some 40 or more actors are potentially involved. These may be categorized according to 4 "actor types", namely:

- **Customer:** A party who acquires, by way of trade, goods or services.
- **Supplier:** A party who provides, by way of trade, goods or services.
- **Authority:** A statutory body existing within a jurisdiction and within a specific area of responsibility that administers legislation to regulate trade and/or monitors compliance with existing legislation.
- **Intermediary:** A commercial party who provides services to customers, suppliers or authorities within the international supply chain.

Each type includes several possible actors or roles, some of which are listed below:

Actor Type	Possible Actors & Roles	Actor Types	Possible Actors & Roles
Customer	Buyer	Intermediary	Bank/Financial Institution
	Consignee		Broker
	Payer		Carrier
	Importer		Credit Checking Company
Supplier	Consignor		Credit insurer
	Payee		Commission Agent
	Seller		Export Agent
	Manufacturer		Freight forwarder
	Exporter		Import Agent
Authority	Chamber of Commerce		Insurer
	Consular		Inspection company
	Customs		Receiving authority
	Health		
	Agriculture		
	Environment		
	Nuclear/Atomic Energy		
	Intervention Board (EU)		
	Licensing		
	Receiving Authority (Port Authority)		
	Standards Institute		

This large number of actors is a key factor in the vulnerability of the Supply Chain to infiltration or interference for security reasons.

There are also many processes that take place in the completion of an international trade transaction. The five main Use Cases (processes) in the Supply Chain Model are:

- **Identify Potential Trading Partner** (Market intelligence gathering).
- **Establish Business Agreement** (Selection/negotiation, Establish framework or contract with selected supplier including agreement on payment terms and delivery terms (Data Alignment).
- **Order** (Including order change, confirmation etc.).
- **Ship** (Including transport and all appropriate administrative and regulatory actions).
- **Pay** (Including invoicing or other means of instigating a payment, disbursements, taxes, and the payment itself).

Although the Model covers the whole trade transaction process, the most relevant component in the security context is the Ship Use Case in which all actors - Customer, Supplier, Intermediary, Authority - are involved. Within the Ship Use Case, the supplier dispatches the products according to the terms of trade specified and the customer receives the product, all transport arrangements are made and executed, and the requirements laid down by the relevant authorities are met.

The Ship Use Case Description is presented below and is elaborated in the annex to the current paper.

Figure 2.6.1. Ship use case description

Name	Ship
Traceability Indicator	D-P&SI-1.U-Ship-2-4
Actors	Customer, Supplier, Intermediary, Authority
Description	The necessary preparations are made to enable goods to be delivered to the customer. Goods are cleared by authorities and delivered t o the agreed customer location.
Pre-condition	Order has been confirmed.
Post-conditions	Cleared goods have been delivered to customer.
Scenario 1.	Starts when Supplier has accepted the order from the Customer Supplier requests Export license from Authority Authority responds Health certificates requested from Health Authority Authority provides certificates (required by Import Country Health Authority) Radiation, isotopic and salubrity certificate Conformity certificate for Import Health Authority Bacteriological certificate Physical Chemical certificate Veterinary and sanitary certificate Analysis certificate Dangerous Goods Note prepared and provided to Carrier Supplier requests and obtains certificate of Origin from Chamber of Commerce Supplier produces and supplies relevant export documentation including:- *For Customer* Packing Weight List/Delivery Note/Invoice *For Export Customs* Relevant Customs Documents (e.g. Customs Product List T1, C88A-LEC,T5 documents, EUR1,Customs Invoice) *For Import Customs* Relevant Customs Documents.(e.g. Certificate of Origin Age certificates and batch codes, Customs Invoice) Intermediary (insurer) provides Supplier with Insurance Certificate (for Customer) Transport booked with Intermediary (carrier or freight forwarder) by Customer and/or Supplier according to agreed delivery terms.

Name	Ship
	Supplier provides Standard Shipping Note and Bill of Lading Instructions to Intermediary (carrier/shipper) Intermediary (carrier or freight forwarder) agrees contract for transport of goods and collects and delivers goods to Customer's agreed location. Supplier (Ship from) issues Despatch Advise to Customer (Ship to) Intermediary (carrier/shipping line) provides supplier with Certificate of Shipment and Bill of Lading (for Customer, shipper/carrier) Pre-shipment inspection arranged, order details provide by Supplier and inspection carried out by Intermediary (inspection company) Goods cleared for export by Authority (customs) after checking documentation and goods Goods cleared for import by Authority (customs) after checking documentation and goods Ends when Customer records receipt of cleared goods at agreed location.

The process of shipping is thus quite complex and any approach to strengthening the security of this process must be well thought out and coordinated.

Papers[50] presented at the 3rd Meeting of the WCO Trade Task Force on Security and Facilitation in February 2003 detailed a high level supply chain approach to the provision of advance cargo information for risk assessment. These papers also outlined a possible model for the overall operation of customs in the new supply chain context, and propose that stringent controls be introduced over the entire supply chain in an attempt to make the movement of goods more secure.

In June 2003, the Task Force will report to the WCO Council on the progress made in the development and implementation of the measures recommended. Officials of the Member administrations will then assess the results and decide how to proceed. The success of the initiative will always depend on the political will to act and the long-term commitment,

---

[50] WCO Proposed Customs guidelines on advance cargo information, TF0005E1; Supply chain security, discussion paper prepared for the WCO Trade Security Task Force by the Netherlands.

alongside customs, of the private sector and all the competent authorities. There is no doubt that the WCO is able to promote modern risk management techniques on a global scale, and that the application of such modern techniques will be extremely helpful in combating terrorism.

However, the task of addressing the security issues in the International Supply Chain at the detailed level, and the need for relevant standards, will be a complex task. This can clearly be seen from the Ship Use Case Description. Possible approaches to this task are considered below. Possible specific areas where trade security standards are required

Given the plethora of actors in the full supply chain, standards should be developed, amended or implemented in a variety of different areas. The following are some examp les from sea transport:

- Documentation
- Submission of documents (manifests and transport documents) to the next link(s) in the transport chain and to Customs authorities
- Handling of goods before they are loaded into ocean containers
- Quality of seals
- Quality of containers
- Handling of the goods inside the containers
- Handling of the containers themselves
- Storage of the loaded container
- Storage of the empty container
- Transport of the containers
- Tracking of the containers
- Control of personnel who may come into contact with the cargo/container
- Reporting between customs authorities
- Procedural reporting
- Training.

A brief explanation of the needs in each of the above areas is presented below:

Documentation:
Poor documentation can lead to incorrect reporting of information and subsequent difficulty in checking the accuracy of information. This clearly creates many possibilities for fraud. ized aligned documentation would help overcome this problem. UN/CEFACT has already drawn up global standards for documentation, the United Nations Layout Key (UNLK), and the task here would seem to be more one of implementing such standards than of developing new ones. In addition, the application of UNeDocs, which provides for standardized "digital paper" documents, could help bring about the early availability of "document" information in electronic form (XML and UN/EDIFACT), especially in developing countries.

Submission of documents (manifests and transport documents) to the next link in the transport chain
For goods/containers bound for the United States, US Customs has already introduced sweeping new measures regarding advance cargo information that will have to be complied with regardless of any UN standards being introduced. WCO is preparing recommendations for the submission of advance cargo information as a global application. As a follow-up, it is suggested that more in-depth analysis be undertaken to develop a more efficient longer-term approach and standard.

The current problem is one of getting the required information to the United States Customs in time. It has already proved impossible to comply with the "24-hours prior to departure" requirement in the air cargo industry. The measure has therefore been modified to "one hour before landing". For ocean transport the measures may be implementable.

Packing of the goods into containers
This is an area of the utmost importance and where implementable standards must be developed. For example, this would require that only authorized personnel may in any way be admitted to the vicinity and into the container itself. Once the container has been filled, it must be sealed

with an approved, tamper-proof seal. The problem here is the lack of control regarding the quality of the workers who engage in the stowage of the goods inside the containers. And it becomes even more complicated in the transport of Less then Container Load (LCL) shipments. When containers may legitimately be opened several times along the transport chain to add or subtract individual consignments, this becomes an extremely sensitive area, as goods already inside the container may need to be restowed when new goods are added.

Although a global policy on restricting access to containers and their nearby environment may be difficult to implement, particularly in some developing countries where security concerns may be less pronounced, it is clearly desirable to have an agreed standard, based on best practice, for the packing of containers to an agreed security level. Containers packed to this standard could be certified as such. It is suggested that the joint IMO/ILO/UNECE *Guidelines for Packing of Cargo Transport Units*[51] be reviewed in the light of current security issues. If necessary, UNECE should also consider establishing a fast-acting working group to consider these aspects with the full participation of WCO, IMO, ILO, the other regional commissions and UNCTAD.

Quality of seals

Originally, container seals were used by customs to verify that the container, once it had been sealed by one customs authority, had not been opened before it had been inspected by a subsequent customs authority. The first seals were rather simple aluminum devices with a seal number stamped on them. They were, however, also very easy to break, or worse, easy to tamper with. It was possible to remove the seal, open the container and then to put the seal back in place. This in due course led to the introduction of stronger seals that could not easily be removed, but miscreants soon learned to manufacture almost identical-looking seals - even with the same seal numbers and markings - and then break the original seal and replace it with a fake once entry into the container had been made. There is obviously a great need for "tamper-proof seals" to be

---

[51] IMO/ILO/UNECE Guidelines for Packing of Cargo Transport Units, IMO, London, 1997, IMO-284E, ISBN 92-801-1443-3

invented and used by all customs authorities. The International Organization for Standardization (ISO), in cooperation with other interested parties, is currently developing standards in this area.

Quality of containers

For the supply chain to be more secure, only tamper-proof containers will be of any security value. By "tamper proof" is meant that it will be impossible to enter a sealed container by any means without this being evident. In other words, new manufacturing standards for standard ISO containers should be developed. Today it may be possible to enter containers without breaking the seals, e.g. by lifting off the doors, or lifting off the entire roof of a container and then putting the container back into "perfect" condition with the seals intact.

Several initiatives are currently under way to address this issue. The IMO is considering possible updating of the International Convention for Safe Containers, (Geneva, 2 December 1972). This Convention contains in its annexes I and II a series of requirements for the containers that fall under this Convention.

The standards included in the Convention are of an operational nature, established to ensure that containers can be lifted and stacked without harming the goods or the containers themselves. Security aspects were by no means top priority when the Convention was negotiated in the early 1970s.

UNECE and the WCO are now considering where and how the Customs Convention on Containers, adopted in Geneva in 1972, can be updated. This Convention contains in chapter III, Approval of containers for transport under customs seal, and its annexes 4 and 5, a series of instructions on how the containers may qualify for the treatment set out in the body of the Convention. There are some instructions regarding security aspects of the construction of containers; however, practical experience over the years has shown these to be inadequate. There is, however, a possibility that increased security concerns may add kilos if not tons to the weight of each container, thus restricting their carrying capacity and increasing the transport costs.

Careful consideration of these aspects must be given before new standards are adopted. It is suggested that a meeting be called by the UNECE to consider the overall issue of container security, with UNECE handling technical issues, WCO covering customs, operational aspects with the IMO (for the CSC), and quality aspects with ISO. The harmonization and/or alignment of the above two conventions should also be considered.

Handling of the containers themselves

ISO sea containers are handled by mechanical devices such as cranes and forklift trucks as well as by the various means of transport such as lorries, river and ocean-going vessels, and trains. Handling of containers thus takes place either in some terminal where the containers are stationary for long periods, or when they are moving onboard some of the transport means listed above. In the air transport industry the use of "containers" is mainly in the form of igloos or small "belly containers". The problem is that loaded, sealed containers are often left unattended for considerable periods. This issue needs to be exa mined and practical standards developed regarding the handling of containers.

Storage of the loaded container

Storage of loaded containers occurs in many places along the supply chain. For instance, in ocean terminals (ports) or inland clearance depots (ICDs), both of which are normally under customs control, the security risk is manageable. However, containers are stored in many other places as well. This may be in unsecured container yards or just at a drop-off point along the route. The parking of a trailer with a container onboard may also be considered as "storage", even if it is of a temporary nature. Such parking often takes place outside proper container yards or terminals. The problem is again one of lack of supervision with the containers. While one could suggest that containers should always be stored inside secure container yards, this again will turn out to be a requirement that will be impractical if not impossible to enforce. This is an issue that needs to be examined and practical standards developed.

Storage of the empty container

Storage of empty containers normally takes place outside restricted areas such as port terminals where space is at a premium. Instead, containers are relegated to convenient empty areas where land prices are low and security non-existent. Containers may "go astray" and end up on top of mountains where they may be discovered months after having found their way to such locations. It would appear impractical to attempt to set standards for the storage of empty containers. However, it may be possible to set standards for the inspection of empty containers before they enter the supply chain.

Transport of the containers

The sealed container moves the goods along the supply chain. At any point during the transit terrorists may be in a position to tamper with the container, even if they do not penetrate its walls, doors, ceiling or floor. While it may be impossible, at all times, to keep containers out of contact with unknown persons, for example, when the containers are located on a train or a truck, major efforts should be made to limit the possibility for unauthorized persons to gain access to the containers in transit. This could, for example, be done by minimizing stops of trains and trucks outside secure areas. It is suggested that individual countries may wish to review the manner in which container trains are scheduled to minimize such stops, and where they are necessary for operational reasons, then ensure that container trains are kept under constant surveillance while immobilized. Similarly, countries may need to establish special secure holding areas for container road vehicles so that stops will only be allowed in secure parking areas where constant surveillance is possible. It is clear that both of these new requirements will add a considerable amount to the cost of transport of goods. When the containers are on board a means of transport the safety aspects differ according to the mode. Those on board aircraft probably have the least security risks. Next on the list come those on board ocean-going vessels; but with regard to containers on river craft, trains and trucks, which all move in close vicinity to humans, the risk to the security of the container is high.

It is suggested that a Recommendation be developed regarding the transport of containers, based on current best practice.

Tracking of the containers at all times

Knowing where the container is at any given time will give considerable assistance in the fight against terrorists, but of course will not in itself make tampering with the container impossible. It would, however, seem to be desirable for some form of guidelines or standards to be set for the concept of container tracking. The problem at present is that only a small minority of containers are fitted with transponders that will allow the container to be tracked 24-hours a day. A solution would be to force the installation of such transponders and then to make sure that not only has someone the necessary tracking equipment, but also that intelligent evaluation of containers that may go astray is undertaken. It is suggested that a Recommendation be developed regarding the tracking of containers, based on current best practice.

Control of personnel who may come into contact with the cargo/container

While it may be possible to tamper with a container without persons physically touching or handling it, the persons who actually handle containers are clearly the best placed to interfere with its safe transit or its contents. It would therefore be desirable to have strict standards regarding who may come in contact with the container and standards for their screening. Unfortunately, realities of life would seem to indicate that this might not be implementable in a number of countries.

Reporting between customs authorities

In order to ensure that all customs authorities in the country of importation can be confident of the quality of the information they receive from the customs authorities located in the country of exportation, it may be desirable for the WCO to establish standards for such reporting. At the moment, very few customs authorities have the capability of undertaking such reporting. WCO is currently addressing this issue of the exchange of information between customs authorities and the use of ICT and EDI standards such as UN/EDIFACT are strongly recommended to enhance the exchange of this information.

Security of information and procedural reporting

The transmission of information concerning goods in the supply chain must be secure and computer records of such information must be kept safe. Standards on ensuring the security (from theft or copying etc) of information provided by trade and exchanged between customs and other government authorities will need to be developed. Further, a set of standard procedure should be developed for reporting cases where incorrect information is provided or tampering with the container or the goods is suspected.

Training

For standards of the type described above to be introduced in an effective and consistent manner, high-quality training would have to be introduced all along the supply chain. Such training mu st start at the very beginning of the chain, often the "weakest point", in some small factory in a developing country. The cost of such training is likely to be high and also to be resisted because its needs would be ill understood at that point of the chain. It would be of the utmost importance to make available the necessary funding to develop such training schemes as a top priority. The following are examples of areas that would seem to be the most critical ones and also those that may be relatively amenable to standard setting:

- Quality of employees (minimum standards)
- Vetting of employees
- Restriction of access to premises
- Quality of documentation
- Licensing of companies

How can trade security standards be verified and by whom?

It is envisaged that once the standards have been endorsed and published, authority would be given to specific accreditation bodies to audit and accredit suitable certification bodies.

The accreditation body could, for example, be the WCO, which could accredit individual customs authorities and/or private sector certification bodies. Alternatively, those customs authorities accredited by WCO could, in turn, audit and accredit private sector certification bodies that would act to complement the work of customs.

Such accredited certification bodies would be permitted to certify the compliance of the various parties in the supply chain with the standards. The certification process would involve periodic audits at the premises, and locations of operation, of the parties in the supply chain. Hence whole supply chains could become certified which would facilitate cooperation between customs authorities in different jurisdictions with a view to granting various trade facilitation measures to such supply chain parties.

Although a major task, with good coordination it could reasonably be achieved. UNECE would be an appropriate forum to host an international conference to discuss the details with representatives from the key parties concerned. Obviously this would have to be well focused to avoid duplication.

Possible areas for a collaborative approach to the development of standards to enhance trade security and facilitation

The task of developing and enhancing standards for trade facilitation and security is vast and this work has been undertaken by many organizations for over 40 years. In recent times, the work has accelerated, with new organizations entering the standards development area and existing organizations taking a broader approach to the topic. Within this environment, greater collaboration and coordination will be required to ensure harmonization and integration of the standards development work. Based on the above examples of where standards development is required, some possible areas of collaboration in the development of trade security and facilitation standards are as follows (the list is meant to be more illustrative than exhaustive):

Documentation
This would seem an obvious area for the UNECE to tackle in cooperation with the IMO, the WCO and ISO.

Submission of documents (manifests and transport documents) to the next link in the transport chain
This would also seem to be an area where the WCO, UNECE, IMO could make a positive contribution in setting global standards.

Quality of containers
The UNECE Inland Transport Committee working closely with the ISO and the WCO may be the right bodies to deal with this issue.

Handling of the goods inside the containers
This would seem to be an area where WCO, IMO, FIATA, UNECE, the regional commissions and UNCTAD might be well placed to develop standards.

Handling of the containers themselves
This would seem to be an area where IMO, the International Road Transport Union (IRU), EAN International, International Chamber of Shipping (ICS), UNECE and UNCTAD might develop standards.

Tracking of the containers at all times
Standards in this area could be developed through collaboration between the UNECE Inland Transport Committee, the regional commissions and UNCTAD's Advance Cargo Information System (ACIS) programme.

Control of personnel who may come into contact with the cargo/container
This area would probably require collaboration between the UNECE Inland Transport Committee, the regional commissions, UNCTAD, IMO, IRU, EAN International and ICS together with the WCO.

Procedural reporting
This would also seem to be an area where UNECE could make a positive contribution in setting global standards.

Conclusions

Setting standards in the area of security and having those standards implemented in the near future will be an enormous task that will require very considerable resources. The sums having already been spent at United States airports and seaports would seem to lend credence to this.

The international community needs to decide whether it wants global standards for the security of goods in transit from country of origin to country of consumption and, if so, whether it is ready to pay the considerable cost associated therewith. Inability to agree on global standards is likely to increase the overall cost of implementation and also reduce the effectiveness.

On the other hand, the implementation of security standards which enable the parties in the supply chain to demonstrate their compliance should provide an excellent opportunity for customs administrations to grant trade facilitation benefits to the parties in such certified supply chains. This could include green channel cargo clearance and implementation of the integrated seamless transaction concept whereby the export declaration data may be used as the import declaration data. The objective should be that the costs associated with the implementation of security measures would be more than compensated for by the trade facilitation benefits.

A concerted effort from all the relevant organizations involved in international trade facilitation and standards will be required in order to ensure that the developed standards are effective and that they achieve the dual aim of enhancing both security and trade facilitation for all countries. Strong collaboration and coordination amongst the relevant standards-setting organizations is the only way to achieve this.

It is recommended that a meeting of all organizations involved in trade facilitation and security be arranged as soon as possible to determine who is doing what and identify and agree on the priority areas for new standards development. It is also recommended that prior to the meeting, the UNECE International Supply Chain Model should be used as an analytical tool to prepare an analysis of the current work and standards on trade facilitation and security within the framework of the international supply chain. This analysis should attempt to identify current overlaps and gaps related to the new security requirements.

Annex: Ship Use Case Elaboration- Prepare for Export

The Ship Use Case described in the text is elaborated below based on the information provided in the International Trade Transaction (ITT) Model. This scenario is based on the ITT model scenario "Preparation for Export" and references the Activities/Roles used in that model description.

Name	Prepare for Export
TRACEABILITY IND.	D-P&SI-1.U-Prepare for Export-3-1
Actors	Customer (consignee), Supplier (exporter), Intermediary (Freight Forwarder, Insurer, Export License Authority, Health Authority, Consul, Carrier, Export Customs, Chamber of Commerce, PFI Agency)
Description	Supplier makes arrangement for export including obtaining / preparing export documentation. Depending on the terms of transport agreed, the Customer or Supplier arrange for the insurance and transport of goods.
Pre-condition	Contract exists and Order has been confirmed.
Post-conditions	Preparations for Export have been completed.
Scenario	Starts when Supplier has accepted the order from the Customer Supplier requests insurance from Intermediary (insurer). (Exprt1).

Name	Prepare for Export
	Intermediary (insurer) draws up contract based on agreed scope of cover, type of cargo and route. (CarIns1).
	Supplier requests transport reservation to Intermediary (freight forwarder or carrier) (Exprt2). Information provided by Supplier includes location for collection and delivery, type and physical details of goods, special handling instructions, etc.
	The Intermediary (Freight Forwarder) makes arrangements with Intermediary (carrier) for completion of shipment and prepares shipping note.
	Freight Forwarder requests booking confirmation from Carrier and provides it to Customer. (FrFwEx1).
	Carrier confirms booking including estimated dates and arrival time and destination. (Carrir1)
	Supplier prepares Invoice for Customer and Customs. Packing List may also be required. (Exptr3)
	Freight Forwarder prepares and agrees delivery instructions with Customer based on Carrier information.
	Freight Forwarder confirms with Carrier when the consignment is to be collected from Suppliers premises, date and time of collection and any special handling requirements. (FrFwEx2)
	Carrier creates delivery contract by confirming the booking with Freight Forwarder. Carrier requests details of where and how the goods are to be delivered and any special arrangements. If necessary carrier prepares request to determine if goods need any special packing. (Carrir2).
	Supplier (exporter) applies for an Export licence from the Export Control Authority. (Exprt r4)

Name	Prepare for Export
	On receipt of appropriate documentation, the National Export Control Authority provides licence to Supplier (exporter) if appropriate conditions are met. (LiAuEx1).
	Supplier (exporter) applies for Health certificate from National Health Authority, if nature of goods require such approval. (i.e. Foodstuffs, livestock etc.). (Exprtr5). Health Authority issues certificate if goods meet qualifying criteria. (HeAuEx1).
	Supplier (exporter) applies for Certificate of Origin from Chamber of Commerce or other competent authority. (Exprtr6). Competent Authority issues Certificate of Origin on receipt of certificate set from Supplier (exporter) and possible legalization by Embassy. (ChmCom1)
	Supplier applies for Consular Invoice from Consul of Importing Country who is based in Supplier's (exporter's) country. Other documents such as sanitary certificates, certificates of origin, may need to be legalized. Supplier pays fee to Consul. (Exprtr7). Consul checks and certifies the invoice and other documents once fees have been paid. (Consul2)
	Supplier prepares Dangerous Goods Note (including packing certificate and Dangerous Goods Declaration) and sends to Carrier (Exprtr8).
	Supplier (exporter) completes preference certificate to claim preferential rates of duty if applicable and provide to customs for certification at the point of departure.

Name	Prepare for Export
	(Exprtr9) Customs certify preference certificate and return to Supplier (exporter). (CustEx1). Supplier (exporter) prepares packing list showing how goods are packed, their weights and measurements, if this information is not contained on the invoice. Packing list provided to Carrier etc. (Exprtr10). If a pre shipment inspection is needed, the Supplier sends a proforma invoice to the Customer (consignee). Customer (consignee) instructs Inspection agency. Inspection Agency sends a request for inspection to Supplier (exporter). This indicates the documents and procedures necessary to meet the PFI requirements. (Exprtr11). The Inspection Agency inspects the goods and documents and issues an opinion on the goods and their price. If satisfied, a Clean report of Findings will be issued to the Customer (consignee) and Supplier (exporter). If not, a non-negotiable failure report will be issued. (PSICom1). Supplier assembles and submits relevant documents to accompany goods. (to receiving authority (Standard Shipping Note, Export Licence etc.) or directly to Intermediaries(freight forwarders, chamber of commerce etc). (Exprtr12). Ends when all documents to meet regulatory requirements have been provided and arrangements made for transport and insurance of goods in accordance with the agreed Terms of Delivery.

Alternative scenarios	There are many different scenarios depending on the Terms of Delivery and other terms agreed in the contract. To be developed further.

Part Three:

Mechanisms of Cooperation: The Role of the Business Community

The following section presents a number of practical solutions offered by the private sector, international organizations and governments to enhance security measures and facilitation in international trade. Most contributors paid special attention to how these tools can become available and affordable for developing and transition economies and for SMEs, in order to cope with the risks of marginalization because of globalization and enhanced security measures.

Chapter 3.1
Maximizing the Trade Facilitation Effect
Nigel Balchin, SGS Société Générale de Surveillance S.A.

Keys to trade facilitation are numerous and include compliance by trade; cooperation between the government and trade sector, as well as between government agencies; tools to facilitate communication, verification and validation; improved infrastructure; and simplified regulations and procedures to name just a few. In addition, there are many opportunities to actually accelerate trade facilitation. UNECE, various other trade facilitation organizations and consultants have been recommending certain trade facilitation measures for years but the extent of implementation is, in many cases, very limited. Recent additional security and compliance measures provide an opportunity to accelerate long-awaited trade facilitation measures to ensure that compliant traders benefit from facilitated trade. There is increasing demand for advance validated information to facilitate early risk profiling and identification of high risk transactions as well as for the exchange of information between the parties in the supply chain for both regulatory and facilitation purposes.

Furthermore, there is an urgent need for greater use of key trade facilitation measures in various areas. For example, authorized traders or authorized supply chains need simplified procedures for parties with good compliance records. Risk profiling is another measure, which will facilitate low risk and target high-risk shipments. The "Single Window" approach, whereby a single authority receives import/export information from trade/transport operators and coordinates exchange of information between relevant government departments is a further very valuable measure. In addition, key information submitted to customs in country of export to be used by customs in country of import will guarantee seamless integrated international trade transactions.

The role of the business community

There are many ways in, which the business community can help define, advance, and implement trade facilitation measures. Private sector s ervice providers can assist by offering a variety of services and tools including certification services, risk profiling systems and information, communications and management systems as well as validation, verification and information services. Thus, traders and supply chain parties could voluntarily demonstrate compliance with security and import/export requirements, cooperate with information exchange or simplify and align their systems and procedures e.g. by taking into account UNECE Recommendations.

International supply chain compliance standard

A further step in this direction would be an International Supply Chain Compliance Standard for the whole supply chain. Such a standard could be based on existing supply chain security standards, including the Business Anti-Smuggling Coalition (BASC), US Trade Partnership Against Terrorism (C-TPAT) and the Technology Asset Protection Association (TAPA). An international standard could have a general section applicable to all parties and specific sections applicable to each individual party (manufacturer, seller, forwarder, transporter, importer, etc.). For trade facilitation purposes, the standard should cover not only security but also other compliance issues relevant for import or export clearance such as health, phyto-sanitary, safety, customs classification, valuation, rules of origin, etc. Compliance with such a standard could be verified by customs and/or accredited certification bodies.

Compliance

Parties in the supply chain should have the opportunity to voluntarily demonstrate their compliance with governmental requirements in exchange for trade facilitation benefits. Such compliance can be demonstrated by requesting accredited certification bodies to conduct periodic audits and certify the party's premises / systems / procedures against a new international supply chain compliance standard. Some accredited certification bodies already have experience in supply chain security audits. Such certifications of supply chain parties would be recognised by customs and other authorities for granting simplified clearance procedures. Certification procedures could be similar to those currently used for ISO 9001, ISO 14001, SA 8000, OHSAS 18001, etc.

Validation of export data and risk management

Other means aim at risk prevention, analysis and validation of export data. The latter was proposed to the WTO by India, with support from some developing countries. The proposals outlined that customs administrations in importing countries should be able to request customs administrations in exporting countries to provide export data, in specific doubtful cases in order to assist in combating valuation fraud. However, there are numerous obstacles to such a proposal. Generally, customs administrations are not concerned with, or staffed for, verification of the accuracy of data declared by the exporter. Furthermore, rather frequently, the level of detail contained in export declarations is inadequate for customs valuation purposes. A possible solution would be to provide customs administration with additional resources to carry out the required investigative work to validate the export data, or have customs outsource the validation to accredited verification companies.

Figure 3.1.1 Risk database

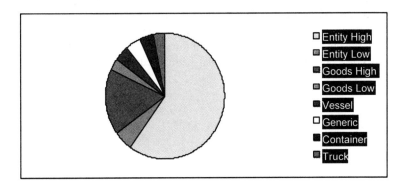

Figure 3.1.2 Risk types

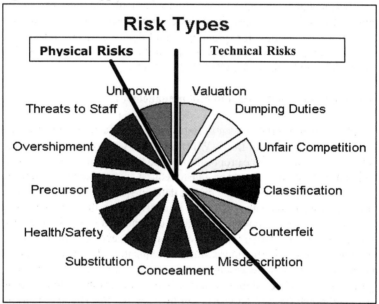

An important tool which can guide risk analysis and thus facilitate trade are specific risk profilers such as e.g. the "SGS Profiler" which is a *knowledge-based* risk management system. It provides government agencies with a transparent, efficient and rapid means to target high-risk shipments for further examination and provide trade facilitation for low risk shipments. It builds up risk databases from global knowledge of trade practices and historical information on detections of smuggling, fraud, wrong declarations, violations, etc. The risk information is of a qualitative nature reflecting actual risk situations that have occurred in historical trade transactions.

Case study

An example for an efficient integrated trade facilitation approach is Ghana and the establishment of the Ghana Community Network Services, a government-private sector joint venture with the mandate to provide an EDI service (Ghana TradeNet) with a customs management system (GCMS). The objectives of the project are to improve the speed of import clearance, to protect Government revenues, improve transparency, reduce customs officer discretion, enhance management information and trade statistics. Its initial focus is on the customs process and, specifically, on the customs clearance process. Since November 2002, the project has been implemented gradually at Accra airport and two major seaports and its major achievement is a reduction of customs clearance from days to hours.

Chapter 3.2

Trade Facilitation, Security Concerns and the Role of the Postal Industry for the Global Economy in the Information Society

Thomas Leavey, Director General, Universal Postal Union

The Information Society 2008

The digital world currently lacks a trusted and neutral third party who can provide evidentiary s ervices aimed at increasing the amount and efficiency of transactions currently being conducted online. Postal organizations have enabled commerce by playing a vital trusted role for centuries and are now preparing to extend this vital role into the Information Society by providing the same evidentiary services in the digital world. As part of this evolution in the traditional postal role, there must be an awareness of what the world will be like in the forthcoming years. Therefore, below are some potential scenarios that the world may experience five years from now.

- In most countries, Internet access will be 100% via the home, office or schools. Broadband Internet access will also be 100% and it will virtually be taken for granted that the Internet is "Always On".

- Electronic documents and e-mails will be verified as legal documents. Digital TVs will be ubiquitous and start to be used as a primary interactive communications channel.

- Addresses are now personal zip codes that link our home, business, telephone, mobile telephone and e-mail (or perhaps an Electronic Postbox) through distributed directories that are globally linked via a common standard.

- Governments provide access to all their services online. Financial Incentives to be online have been implemented when "doing business" with organizations such as banks, utilities, governments, and insurance companies. If you want to do business offline, you must pay an additional service fee.

- Digitals Rights Management systems have been implemented to protect music, software, games, etc. so that piracy is virtually eliminated.
- All computing devices and appliances (e.g. PC, Kiosk, Mobile Phone, PDAs, etc.) have smart card readers or smart card chips.
- Many of us live in "Smart Homes" where the refrigerator, electrical system, heating system and other appliances are all connected to the Internet. We can control these appliances from anywhere using our mobile phone.

Why has this happened? What has driven our society to operate this way? Companies and governments are moving to digital because it reduces cost and delivers faster. For example, in the banking industry, individual transaction processing costs have been reduced from dollars to cents. And taking a much broader view, when companies and governments become more efficient, economies become more efficient, productivity increases and ultimately so does GDP.

What are the risks?

In this society, who will you trust with your personal information? How will you be identified, recognized, authorized for doing business on the Internet? What if you move house – how will you change your address? How will the integrity of your sensitive and private information, business documents, and transactions be protected and kept confidential on the Internet? How will contracts, agreements, patents, copyrights, business documents, business transactions, government to citizen transactions be electronically stored and archived for the required periods by law? What if you need to recall this information in five years for a legal challenge in a court of law?

There are many, many more of these questions to be answered. But how does society deal with or how has it dealt with similar issues today and in the past. The world is always changing and has had to adapt to new methods of communication and doing business many times before.

The traditional role of Posts in economic development

In many countries the Post Office has played an essential and fundamental role in economic and social development by helping develop the transportation and communications sectors. In North America, in the nineteenth and early twentieth centuries the Post Office contributed to economic development by its use of the railways for transportation and inter-city sortation of mail. The airline industry also developed in a similar fashion as a major carrier since its early stages, starting in the early 1900s.

The Post Office encouraged the improvement and expansion of the transportation system and provided a network for distributing retail goods and acted as a medium for mail-order cataloguing. It provided a commercial link with the outside world through money orders, parcel post and cash-on-delivery (COD) services. It assisted the development of the newspaper and periodicals industry via free or inexpensive circulation and free rural delivery.

A World Bank study summarized the significance of the postal sector to all countries as, "one of the infrastructural facilitators of economic growth.... As economic activity grows, so does the number of commercial and financial transactions by mail. An efficient postal operation is important to the success of this growth cycle...".

In larger, geographically dispersed countries, the postal business is also one of the very few public institutions that can have a regionally balanced influence on the economy. This is not surprising, given the universal accessibility of postal services at uniform prices. Through Universal Service Obligations, postal employees are spread across the world with more than six million postal employees working in over 700,000 postal outlets.

Businesses, organizations and private households have, for a long time, relied heavily on the postal service for meeting their daily communications needs. Therefore, postal services form a significant part of the socio-economic environment of any country. The nature of providing affordable, universal postal services is such that all countries (developed and developing) experience nationwide economic benefits from the operation of a well-functioning postal service. Similarly manufacturers and processing industries can only establish a presence in economies in which raw materials, supplies and finished products can be readily transported to and from their facilities. Retailers can only operate in markets that provide stable and consistent support to the supply chain for the goods and merchandise they sell. The Post is a value-added player in each of these economic needs.

The universal postal service, by capturing the well documented economies of scale inherent in the collection, processing and delivery of mail allows consumers and businesses to meet their vital, basic communication and small parcel distribution needs in the most cost effective way. Thus, postal services also promote the expansion of the key domestic trade sector. By facilitating the least expensive means of communications across the whole country they also serve as a strong unifying force in any country.

The inefficiencies of the Internet today

In today's information society, there is already a lot that can be done online with shopping, banking and some government services, but it should be highlighted, that most transactions are quite simple, low value and low-risk. These applications work, but still contain inefficiencies. For example, when buying online, merchants cannot verify the identity of the individual making the purchase. This results in credit card fraud and higher charge-backs for merchants. The inefficiencies of today's information society extend far beyond those of the simple online merchant example. There are many applications that are prevented from going online, because the risk is perceived as being too high. Why are real estate transactions not conducted online? Why cannot, for the most part, contracts be signed electronically? Why are costly paper trails maintained for high value business-to-business transactions? The inefficiencies of today's information society certainly have a significant opportunity cost.

There are three missing elements required to improve the ability to transact online. The first is user-friendly technology. However, technology companies are currently building the platforms required to facilitate more and more digital commerce. The second is government policy and law concerning online commerce. Many governments are moving to address these requirements but more can and no doubt will be done. The third shortcoming is a global network that provides recognized and trusted digital evidentiary services. Some technology companies recognize this void and are partnering with the Posts to address this market need.

The Information Society of 2008 – how will it work?

In the predicted Information Society of 2008, how will it work? Why will the Posts have a significant role in this society? Returning to some of the issues highlighted earlier: Whom will you trust with your personal information? How will you be identified, recognized and authorized for doing business on the Internet? How will contracts, agreements, patents, copyrights, business documents, business transactions, government to citizen transactions be electronically stored and archived for the required periods by law?

The posts currently provide many services related to these issues, such as authentication required to obtain a passport, address management and registered mail services. The "Postmark" in many countries signifies legally binding proof of mailing. Posts are also a "hub" for the world's principal economic flows – information, goods and money. And Posts are global through their partnerships with other postal organizations under the umbrella of the Universal Postal Union (UPU), the second oldest international organization in the world, a specialized agency of the United Nations and the primary forum for cooperation between postal services.

For the Information Society, posts have developed new services. For example, non-repudiation services, such as an electronic postmark that will provide the following for an electronic business transaction:

- What document was signed
- When the document was signed
- Who signed the document
- Why the document was signed (declaration of intent)
- Storage and archival of all non-repudiation evidence data required to support subsequent challenges.

The posts are generally viewed as a neutral, independent provider of Trusted Communication services, regulated by their governments and international organizations such as the UPU. Through this regulation, the provision of universal services is sustained, which is of utmost importance to the developing world. The digital divide presents many challenges, but the UPU's universal service obligation as a UN agency ensures that people's right to communicate is maintained. Communication rights do not change – only the medium used will change. Already posts are addressing many of these issues with physical mail services integrated with electronic services and Internet kiosks in post offices.

New services offered by the posts are further strengthened in that they have legal recognition. Many Posts are mandated to ensure that the same privacy and security provided to physical mail is also provided to the electronic messages that they deliver.

The postal industry has recognized what the Information Society needs and through global initiatives facilitated with the UPU, can ensure global standards, policies and services to meet these needs. Without it, the problems we sometimes hear about, but often ignore, such as identity fraud, credit card theft and the cost of processing paper trails will only get worse.

Conclusion

Businesses, governments, consumers, the World Trade Organization, and others are constantly striving to adopt new services which improve efficiency. Conducting business online has delivered benefits, but there is still much inefficiency. Technology companies are building the platform required to facilitate more and more digital commerce. While governments and organizations are moving to develop the policy and legal framework for digital commerce, a gap still remains.

The postal industry is committed to filling this gap. Posts have centuries of experience in the role of a trusted third party and are moving aggressively to establish the strategic partnerships required to enable the services that will remove the inefficiencies.

If trust and digital evidentiary services are global, the opportunities for organizations to become more efficient suddenly become possible. Ultimately, as organizations become more efficient, whole economies realize improvement. To an audience that is perhaps not familiar with the services, skills and capabilities of the postal industry, the role for the posts in the Information Society may seem surprising.

Therefore, to summarize the important role of the posts in the Information Society:

- Posts facilitate international and domestic trade.
- Posts assist in building economies.
- Posts are the hub for the three principal economic flows in the world: information, goods and money.
- Posts bridge the digital divide.
- Posts provide a universal communication service to the whole world.
- Posts manage addresses.
- Posts are trusted.
- Posts are very busy building the digital evidentiary services required by the Information Society.

Chapter 3.3
New Solutions for Trade Facilitation and e-Business Accessible to All
Patrick J. Gannon, President and CEO, OASIS

The following paper will discuss the latest Information Technology trends and the related business benefits, as well as make a value proposition for open standards and explain the role of cooperative mechanisms such as OASIS in such a framework.

In recent years there have been a lot of new Information and Communication Technology trends, i.e. trends which affect trade facilitation procedures, software and data exchange, and they have overwhelmed the business community. With this "eBusiness tidal wave", the Internet delivers services to consumers and today even governments are delivering services to their citizens. The challenge today is how to build on an architecture that has been in place for many years and has withstood the test of time, keep it from being marginalized, keep it from being washed away in the technology tidal wave and turn it into the centerpiece of a thriving marketplace that people want to use in the digital economy. Today a shift can actually be seen, towards a New Era built on a service-oriented architecture with many business benefits for trade facilitation.

Such a service-oriented architecture for global trade can provide the opportunity of ubiquitous and organically integrated services that operate the way people think and work – globally and locally. They could provide places where both users and providers of information have integrated services interact. In short, it would be a world where technology is implemented within industry frameworks that operate on a global and local scale, enabled by open, interoperable standards, standards for software information exchange.

This, however, requires investments and, today, investors are more critical with regard to taking such decisions. Sustainable business benefits in such a setting can only be achieved through a common web service framework.

In order to achieve these there is a vital role for open standards to help bring about these benefits in a sustained fashion. This can be illustrated best through a traction-sanction curb where the adoption of standards is a function of a degree of sanction and traction in the marketplace. The degree of adoption is measured by the number of software companies that are creating solutions built on standards as well as the number of end-user companies that are implementing the standards. Through such an interactive mechanism, xml has become the broadest and widest adopted market technology.

Similarly, OASIS tried to follow the best possible path and looked at working together in a cooperative way with other organizations including UN/CEFACT for three and a half years already to create a series of specifications that became known as the Electronic Business using Extensible Markup Language (ebXML). Using the combined forces of OASIS as an open consortium and UN/CEFACT it was possible to create this standard in a rather short period of time, i.e. over the last 2-3 years. During the same period, in the web-services arena other specification developments in the marketplace took place as well. The benefits linked to the open standards development are numerous and include compatibility of products, extensibility, predictability, and most importantly the interoperability to achieve the kind of global trade necessary, rapid development and leveraging on existing skills.

Representatives from businesses, governments and regulatory agencies have a vital role to play in this setting. It is important to understand the standards that are appropriate and necessary in the industry. It is equally important to work with the industries and vendors to impress upon them what the needs are and explain why standards are important and when they are needed over time. It is also essential to participate whenever possible in the standards-setting process to be sure that business practices that one needs are understood by the technologies and priority is given to the procurement of solutions that support open standards such as for instance, ebXML.

Vendors will be convinced of the utility of standards once they have examined and understood software standards that are pertinent to industry, understood the respective interoperability needs and what standards one relies upon today and in the future and why such standards are important, as well as through the participation in standards bodies that relate to a company's business practices.

ebXML standards enjoy broad endorsement and utilization already today (including even the EU Commission, which recommended its use for the highly-regulated controlled interchange of information messages between government administrations). Today, ebXML provides the best secure method to do that. Other web-services are probably better for more unregulated interchange of messages. As these new technologies come forward, and as the spectrum of ways to exchange information grows; they are complementary to, for instance, electronic data interchange (EDI), which remain the backbone of data transmission.

An example of how businesses can work together in a cooperative approach to provide an open, neutral framework for people to come together is OASIS. OASIS drives not only convergence but also development and ultimately the adoption of e-business standards. Membership today facilitates the cooperative approach and brings together technology suppliers, the public sector, and end-user organizations. OASIS targets many important issues and also has several technical committees dealing today with the various aspects of secure transmission and authentication of transactions and has many activities in the public sector.

In summary, open standards are required for software used to support global trade. Broadly adopted open standards for new technologies enable lower cost software and drive down the costs for transition and developing countries. Close coordination is needed across standards organizations on a global level. Standards should be relevant, open, and address the issue of implement ability. As St. Francis of Assisi said "Start by doing what's necessary; then do what's possible; and suddenly you are doing the impossible".

Chapter 3.4
The Business Contribution to Development and Safe Trade

Patrick De Smedt, Vice-President, Microsoft Europe, Middle East and Africa

The contribution of business to development and safe trade is a particularly important topic since expanding trade appears to be one of the few possible ways to revitalize the current sluggish global economy. And as Benjamin Franklin once stated: "No nation was ever ruined by trade".

We are all aware that the barriers to expanded trade are not just tariffs. The average post-Uruguay Round tariff on industrial goods is only 3.8%. By contrast, a recent OECD study concluded that poor border procedures cost up to 15% of transaction value. Therefore, anything business can do to develop safe and efficient trade is beneficial. In 2002, the World Bank concluded that improved facilitation would increase trade in the Asia-Pacific region alone by €275 billion.

The contribution of business to development and safe trade is an enormous subject. I will focus on only some of the key contributions that we see for the industry and where the private sector can be of assistance.

Pillar I: Developing markets

Related to developing markets, I would like to highlight four areas where we can help: 1) foreign direct investment; 2) help close the skills gap; 3) supporting open standards; and 4) solution development.

Foreign direct investment
One of the most effective ways in which industry helps develop markets, particularly in developing countries, is through direct investment. This is about more than just cash infusions and jobs. There are substantial spillover effects as well. According to the OECD, these spillover benefits include: transfer of technology and know-how, international trade integration,

business sector competition, and human capital formation. Moreover, these investments help local small and medium-sized enterprises (SME) as they become suppliers and vendors, and enjoy the fruits of a better-trained population and expanded infrastructure. Although it is difficult to quantify these benefits, few people doubt the value of decisions such as that by Renault to invest an additional €230 million in a Russian production line, or Bayer's €3 billion pledge for a new plant in China.

At Microsoft, we have committed €80 million for software research and manufacturing facilities in China. In addition, we recently unveiled the European Microsoft Innovation Center. Located in Germany, the Center will employ people from throughout Europe, and will complement the Microsoft Research Center in Cambridge, a facility in the United Kingdom that employs some 60 researchers from 16 countries.

Our "partner-centric" strategy is meant to stimulate a broad IT ecosystem that expands local skills development and high-tech investments. This promotes a healthy IT environment in which a range of companies are constantly striving to develop ever more exciting technologies.

Addressing the skills gap

Kofi Annan eloquently stated, "the main input is brainpower – the one commodity that is equally distributed throughout the human race." Unfortunately, e-skills training is not equally distributed.

Industry has long been working – often in conjunction with public authorities – to bridge this skills gap. For example, the technology industry and the European Commission have together formed the Career Space initiative to develop guidelines for schools on how to best teach IT skills. Other initiatives include the WEF Digital Divide task force and the New Partnership for Africa's development and many other initiatives for schools, universities and underserved communities.

Supporting open standards

In addition, helping to address the skills gap, industry is also trying to reduce trade burdens by promoting open standards. XML is particularly important because it provides a means of separating actual data from how it is presented to users.

One particular benefit of XML is its ability to enhance trade efficiency and security. Most are familiar with the United Nations *UNeDocs* initiative, a system which maintains the core information on trade documents in a standardized, encoded format using XML. This allows any XML-enabled application to validate trade data against the *UNeDocs* code requirements resulting in greater efficiency and security. Microsoft supports *UNeDocs* in Office by allowing users to easily develop, process and digitally sign XML forms using Web services. Such a platform provides clear opportunities for local smaller companies and developing countries to participate in the global economy in a cost effective way.

Development of solutions

Technology can open markets and expand business opportunities. For example, in Thailand, *Thaigem.com* has grown to become the world's largest online vendor of gemstones and jewellery, while in India *Everythingaboutwater.com* offers the country's first e-marketplace for water and water products.

Also, technology can enable development by facilitating trade and reducing trade burdens. Consider these following two examples. First, in Dubai, we assisted the Department of Ports and Customs in developing the e-Mirsal Customs On-line Service. This web-based service uses the most up-to-date security technologies to deal with the paperwork generated annually by 20,000 importers and exporters, 450 clearance companies and over 70 banks and other financial institutions. The system allows importers to input customs data and calculate tariffs online, and provides guaranteed electronic duty payments.

Second, Czech Customs use digital lines to form a secure private network linking offices. They also added a public website that provides information about tariffs, while traders can monitor the progress of their goods through the customs process on-line thanks to the "Electronic Customs Declaration" project. Due to these changes, 80% of customs declarations are submitted electronically, and the Czech Republic has become the first Eastern European country connected to the EU New Computerized Transit System (NCTS).

Pillar II: Creating a safe trading environment

Let me turn now to the second pillar of industry support, the creation of a safe trading environment. We see a clear role for the industry in reducing piracy, improving system security, promoting harmonised supply chain security measures and evaluating export control regimes.

In terms of software piracy, it is estimated that one in every three copies of software in use worldwide (36%) is an illegal copy representing a market value of over €10 billion. This compares to piracy rates of 34% for the EU and 63% for Eastern Europe. Illegal software sales reduce the economic incentive for companies to innovate, and harm consumer confidence by distributing flawed and poor quality replicas. The industry commits vast resources to fight against piracy through awareness and education programmes and by working with government regulators on law enforcement.

By creating secure technologies industry can promote safer trade and greater development. *"Trustworthy Computing* is computing that is as available, reliable and secure as electricity, water services and telecommunications". At Microsoft, we are focusing on building trust in each of our products by investing in increased reliability, security, privacy, and business integrity. Security is an industry-wide issue and we are committed to work together with many third parties on this key topic. One example is our work with the Universal Postal Union to enable the easy use of digital signatures that comply with local legislation, supported in our Office applications.

Another way in which industry helps ensure a safe trading environment is by creating and promoting *supply chain security measures*. The industry is constantly working to address the numerous technical and legal issues involved in securing the movement of goods through global supply chains. From "smart" shipping containers that transfer remotely content information to port officials, to content tracking software, new technologies can help customs officials gather and process all the data they need in a rapid, efficient and secure manner.

Finally, let me close with a comment about *export control regimes*. In the post-September 11 world, many governments have imposed new obligations on international trade shipments. Industry certainly agrees with the need for a safe trading system. At the same time, we remember the flawed attempts to control encryption technology in the 1990s, and we should be attentive that new rules do not impair companies' ability to invest in other countries.

In conclusion, industry cannot answer all the big picture political and social questions raised by global trade and development. For that, the world turns in large part to our government leaders and policy makers. However, we in the private sector can help markets develop and help create a safer trading environment, and thus play a key role in bringing the benefits of a global economy to those regions that need them most.

Chapter 3.5
TTFSE.ORG: Adding value for business through transparency
Gérald Ollivier, TTFSE Regional Trade Facilitation Coordinator,
Kremena Gotcheva, BULPRO[52]

TTFSE.ORG is a regional website created by national trade facilitation bodies (public-private committees on trade and transport facilitation: the so-called PRO-Committees), under the framework of the Trade and Transport Facilitation in Southeast Europe Program (TTFSE) (for more information, please see www.seerecon.org/ttfse). The site aims at increasing transparency in international road transport of goods across eight countries of Southeast Europe, in line with Article X of the GATT.

The site has been designed as an advanced portal consolidating information from more than 50 governmental bodies involved with international road transport and trade in the region. Several of its present value-added features (automated notification, route planner) show the way toward the long-term sustainability of the site beyond the TTFSE Program, which ends in about a year. The free provision of border agency requirements will be coupled with value added features, enabling a commercialization of part of the site and making it evolve from an information center into a regional service hub.

---

[52] Gérald Ollivier is a Transport Specialist in the World Bank. He is the TTFSE Regional Trade Facilitation Coordinator and Team Leader for the TTFSE projects in Bosnia and Herzegovina, Bulgaria, Croatia, and Serbia and Montenegro. Kremena Gotcheva has studied Microelectronics and Finance. Prior to joining the Bulgarian Chamber of Commerce and Industry, she gathered experience as a computer specialist and foreign trade consultant. Within BULPRO, she is responsible for the co-ordination of the TTFSE website and monitoring of XML-based technology developments in trade facilitation.

In this context, the site managers are seeking new partners to introduce a consolidated administrative interface between border agencies and traders, XML-based, to integrate value added feature (more interactive maps), to extend the tool to other countries in Central Europe and Turkey and to develop training programs under the GFP-DLI[53]. Discussions are on going to integrate UNeDocs into the TTFSE.ORG platform. An estimated sum of $400,000 is required for the second phase of development of TTFSE.ORG. We are soliciting your financial support today to crystallize these grassroots' efforts and support SEE countries in their effort to provide a transparent, predictable environment. BULPRO as the eldest and most active PRO committee in the region is willing to implement the pilot phase and has the necessary networks to promote it both in Bulgaria and the entire region.

Main presentation topics:

During the preparation of the Trade and Transport Facilitation Program in Southeast Europe (TTFSE)[54], surveys of users indicated the difficulty SMEs were facing in complying with rapidly changing laws and regulations, particularly as SEE countries aligned progressively their legal framework to EC requirements. These changes combined with insufficient information channels and an explosion in the number of SMEs in the forwarding and road transport sector, meant significant increased transaction costs at borders and lack of predictability in transit times toward the EC market. Increased transaction costs took the form of delays and frequent "facilitation" payment, sometimes justified, sometimes not.

---

[53] The Global Facilitation Partnership-Distance Learning Initiative aims at developing high quality program for professionals active in trade, transport and logistics. We encourage you to visit its website at www.gfp-dli.org.
[54] For complete information on the TTFSE Program visit www.seerecon.org/ttfse

In order to fight corruption and reduce those transaction costs, six countries[55] of SEE (later joined by two others[56]) requested support from the World Bank and the United States Government to facilitate trade and transport in the region in 1999. The resulting TTFSE Program, a \$123 million facilitation program, offers technical services for Customs modernization, improvement of border facilities and information systems and a trade facilitation component.

This trade facilitation component was designed jointly with SECIPRO and each of the national PRO Committees. PRO Committees are public-private bodies focused on trade and transport facilitation. The trade facilitation component is managed by the American College in Thessaloniki, implemented by the PRO-Committees, funded by the US Government and the Dutch Government and supervised by the World Bank. It contains in particular conventional training for SMEs in road transport and forwarding, distance learning for the same target group (visit www.gfp-dli.org) and the creation of the TTFSE website.

The TTFSE Website aims at reducing transaction costs through increased transparency, and targets the user group identified during project preparation (small and medium-sized enterprises in road transport and forwarding). The site became operational for data input in late 2002. Content is being uploaded by all PRO Committees in the region, under the regional coordination of BULPRO, with a target date of end of September 2003 to have all information entered.

The first feature of the TTFSE website is the consolidation of procedures, laws, documents required by about 50 governmental bodies in South-Eastern Europe in respect to trade and transport. Each TTFSE country committed to provide information on a sustained basis, through their respective loan/credit agreements.

---

[55] Albania, Bosnia and Herzegovina, Bulgaria, Croatia, fYR of Macedonia, and Romania.
[56] Serbia and Montenegro, Moldova.

These countries operationalized this requirement by entering into Memoranda of understanding with each of the Ministries concerned. This is a unique effort in meeting partially the GATT Article X on transparency of procedures and legal requirements.

PRO committee experts of Albania, Bosnia and Herzegovina, Bulgaria, Croatia, the former Yugoslav Republic of Macedonia, Romania, and Serbia and Montenegro defined the information structure, and established the information links with the various ministries concerned. The foundation of a unique information tool has been laid down.

The TTFSE site goes beyond mere information consolidation. It offers in particular three value added services: (i) automated notification when changes take place; (ii) a route planner; and (iii) a user forum. Currently, all these services are free. The site provides tailored alert services to registered users via e-mail. Users select the categories they are interested in such as changes in legislation, required documents and procedures. When new items are entered in the database, they are notified. This saves time for users by removing the need to visit the site simply to check if some new information has been added.

For the convenience of freight forwarders and road transport operators, especially SME who cannot afford specialised software, the TTFSE site includes a route planner enabling users to select an itinerary, and to display roads, distances, border agency locations, and documentary requirements (import/export/transit). Registered users are able to save their usual routes and view rapidly all cargo, person and vehicle documents applicable to the countries through which the route passes. Automated notification when changes take place on a preferred route will be developed shortly.

BULPRO, the regional coordinator in the first year, conducted usability surveys after the site's software was released. Periodic usability tests are conducted in the course of information uploading with potential users from the Bulgarian business to ensure usability of the information templates. Beyond perception testing, the results showed interest on the part of the business and NGO to participate in the effort.

The site is supported by Schenker Bulgaria, which provides valuable inputs on the contents and structure. The Bulgarian Business News section is vastly provided for by the Bulgarian Economic Forum's news service.

The promotion of the site will start during a bilateral meeting BULPRO - ROMPRO (May 28), followed by a promotional phase of beta-testing that will take place until 30 September 2003 to fine-tune the site functionalities. A set of user interfaces is being developed to facilitate information input by different service providers - NGO and businesses – to let them offer their services in the region.

The second phase of development of the TTFSE website includes the development of business to business and business to administration platforms, and the attraction of content providers, software vendors and other companies offering value-added services, along with the classic service providers such as food, lodging and gas sales points. As part of the B2A effort, there are ongoing discussions to integrate UneDocs in the website on a regional basis. If integrated into the TTFSE website, the UNeDocs would provide a government-supported, universal, transparent, multilingual service to business in eight countries, with the option to spread the efforts to other countries.

The initial pilot phase would take place in Bulgaria. The country has favourable conditions: traditions in document alignment (BULPRO was founded in 1990); Digital signature act allowing authentication, and clear efforts towards eGovernment, part of which is giving priority to the implementation of UN/CEFACT recommendations 25 and 26.

The rollout of UneDocs to other countries would build on the existing website team the support of the TTFSE countries' governments, as well as on other partnership and networks in the region. For example, synergies may be achieved with the Association of Balkan Chambers.

Beyond the UNeDocs implementation, the TTFSE Website would need an estimated $400,000 over the next two years to build new partnerships, further develop data integration and integrate new tools (such as XML platform translation for B2B B2A, more interactive maps, consolidated administrative interface between border agencies and traders). The modest cost of this effort can be explained by the extensive reliance on local experts to manage the website and the unique high quality, low price software development possibilities in Bulgaria.

The TTFSE.ORG project is currently seeking $400,000 support and new partnership offers. BULPRO is prepared to use synergies with current and former projects and activities of the Bulgarian Chamber of Commerce and Industry (EAN barcoding, electronic ATA-Carnets and cross-border services, digital signatures, one-stop-shops for administrative services, training and public outreach) all over the country, with focus on over 2000 BCCI members of the transport and freight forwarding branch and in close co-operation with the leading transport and forwarders' associations participating in the committee.

In parallel to the website, training and know-how exchange are playing a major part in the TTFSE effort. Under the TTFSE Program and under the umbrella of the Global Facilitation Partnership for Transportation and Trade, a distance learning initiative has been launched (www.GFP-DLI.org). This initiative builds particularly on the support of the National Centre for Vocational Training within BCCI and other regional projects. Support would be needed to build training curricula, facilitating the introduction of e-business tools in South-eastern Europe. Experience has demonstrated that the TTFSE website approach could be easily and usefully extended to other countries such as Turkey and the Central and Eastern European countries in the framework of regional partnerships. TTFSE.ORG participants will welcome such partnership arrangements.

Chapter 3.6
Mechanisms of Co-operation: The Role of the Business Community

Robert Crowhurst, United Kingdom Department of Trade and Industry

The private sector is making an essential contribution to developing the technological infrastructure to allow trade facilitation. This is not just a question of automating paper, but also of development because technology may provide solutions to conventionally unsolvable problems. Yet we must also focus on the contribution business users - traders and transporters - can make. So I welcome this opportunity to offer some personal thoughts and observations.

Trade facilitation is about removing the economic frictions that get in the way of trading across borders. Stripping away the inefficiencies that add cost but not value. Why should it be *that much more* difficult for an Indian manufacturer to sell his goods in the US, UK, Uganda or Uruguay than in Uttar Pradesh? A primary function of Customs authorities should be to facilitate legitimate trade; at best, inefficient procedures act as a tax on the honest trader. And both Customs and legitimate traders have a common interest in squashing out the dishonest trader.

To reach this goal requires a **partnership** between administrations and traders - well displayed by attendance at the UNECE Forums on Trade Facilitation by so many from both business and governments from so many countries, as well as various key international institutions. Only by working together can we remove the frictions which delay goods getting to their customers, and which cost, according to the European Commission, €300 billion a year to the international trading process. That vast sum - equal to the entire GDP of Sub Saharan Africa – is lost into the black hole of bureaucracy and inefficiency, and none of it benefits anyone.

But all economic constituencies stand to benefit from the savings that can be made:

- customers and consumers, through wider selection of goods with guaranteed and cheaper supply;
- citizens who want efficient and effective public administrations with better value for money;
- businesses – who not only need their goods to reach their customers cheaply, quickly and safely, but also because in many cases, it acts as proxy for these other constituents;
- and also customs administrations, government agencies and taxpayers who stand to benefit substantially from the need to maximize revenue and save public expenditure – which in turn can be returned to the economy either by lowering tax burdens or by increasing resources to other public-sector priorities such as education or health, further boosting the macro-economy and developmentally enabling.

Business worldwide is unanimous in its support for trade facilitation and the need for multilateral rules. It is eager for negotiations to start at the WTO Ministerial Conference in Cancún. A business needs only to be marginally more expensive to lose a sale to its competitors – or marginally held-up in delivery to incur penalty costs or lose the next and future sales. And of course, most businesses are SMEs – invariably, by definition, they operate on the margin.

Businesses are therefore calling for the confidence, clarity, certainty, consistency and commitment that only WTO rules will provide – the voluntary approach followed up till now has failed to deliver that annual €300 billion. So, of course, do many countries – including several developing and transition economies.

They recognise the need to make efficiency savings (and provide better jobs) in their customs services and to enable their business community – their wealth-generators, in expanding macro-economic activity and providing the wherewithal for improving the common weal.

The example of Chile in the early 1990s is well known – in summary, faced with an external trade growth of about 130%, the Chilean customs overhauled their system at a cost of $5 million, two-thirds of which was borne by the private sector. Pay-back (to both customs and the private sector) was less than one year – in all, the reform is estimated to have saved business some $12 million per year – while:

- average time for processing import declarations fell 75% - from 10.8 hours to 2.2;
- data-submission costs to the private sector fell by 80%.

More recently, Ghana has implemented similar initiatives. Other countries have also taken progressive measures, for example, Singapore.

Such changes require a substantial effort, not only in resource terms but also in political will. As business will be the first to recognise, there is no such thing as a free lunch. However, evidence and experience tells us that while there will be costs to making border procedures more trade facilitatory, the payback is quick and there are significant long-term gains.

And the alternative is not cost free: world trade has grown 20-fold since 1950, and will continue to do so. So, at the very least, countries would have to devote more and more resources in their existing systems to cope with that – or, if they do nothing, risk an ever-decreasing share of international trade and consequent marginalisation.

The difference is that trade-facilitation is the sustainable approach. The other two options only offer a vicious spiral of unsustainability. Furthermore, the question arises as to whether either of those would attract the extra money, and more integrated approach, required from donors. Multilateral rules, on the other hand, will provide a context, a framework - and a guarantee of action-commitment.

But while much needs to come from governments and donor-institutions, there is a key role for the private sector. Business support will be instrumental and they must participate and contribute. This will mean companies *investing*, as well as ensuring their systems and procedures meshing in with those required of customs agencies. So, businesses - and especially multinational companies (MNCs) and other globally operating companies – need also:

- to accept the responsibilities that "Authorised Trader" systems will entail, accepting that there needs to be trust which entails ensuring that regulations are adhered to and supported and that their trade movements have integrity. It is worth noting, in passing, that part of the checks and balances on which governments can rely is traders' and transport operators' commercial reputation. Leading companies, whether small or large, are simply not going to risk questionable consignments – and they invariably maintain robust controls against such involvement;

- in some circumstances perhaps be willing to contribute to the development of local "hard infrastructure" requirements, e.g. port-handling equipment; power and communication requirements. In the UK, we would have an analogy of "Planning Gain" – where a building-developer, in order to gain his planning approval, incorporates also provision of other facilities of wider community benefit into the site-project. At the very least, can such businesses, in this context of trade-facilitation, help contribute IT-systems and support to local administrations?

- as stakeholders of the regulatory environment, be prepared to engage constructively with administrations, perhaps through "User Group" forums, to input on the design of procedures. So I commend the concept of "PRO" organisations. Our own – SITPRO – has an impressive record, and we stand ready to share with others the UK experience and way of working;

- banks and insurers must ensure that their systems are trader-friendly, efficient and not unreasonably costly in the way they deal with business – e.g. in process payments and credit transfers. Traders themselves must pay their bills promptly;

- the private sector too may well be able to offer local help in the training and development of customs officials.

Of course, none of these particular suggestions could or should be reflected in WTO rules. But the business-sector – who will be primary beneficiaries– needs to give practical effect of its commitment to its desire for such rules. And those rules should give them the confidence to do so, providing as they will the justification of commercial return.

Both sides – government and business – have their contributions to make. That is what partnership is all about. And partnership relies on **trust,** cooperation and working together. Equally, countries must work in partnership and trust – with (and also like companies) proper and fair legal remedy for when things go wrong. That is why the opening of negotiations on a WTO trade facilitation agreement at the Cancún WTO Ministerial Conference must be a priority for all of us.

Chapter 3.7
Technology in the Context of e-Business
Klaus-Dieter Naujok, Chairman, Techniques and Methodologies Group, UN/CEFACT

Summary

The goal of UN/CEFACT's Business Collaboration Framework (BCF) is to provide businesses with a solution to define their external information interchanges and related business activities (business collaborations) independent of the underlying implementation and infrastructure technology. Because the BCF is not depending on any specific implementation technology, it protects the investment of developing the Business Collaboration Models against future changes in the underlying infrastructure. This paper outlines how the BCF provides the basis for implementing brand-new infrastructures that were not known before the creation of the BCF such as Web Services.

Introduction

Over 25 years ago the idea was born to eliminate the use of paper documents for exchanging business data by linking computer systems together so that the data, normally on paper, could be sent from one system to the other. This concept became known as EDI, Electronic Data Interchange. The advantages are still valid today, no re-entering of data and therefore fewer errors, if any. No dependency on postal services, cost savings per transaction from $75.00 to 50 cents, to mention just a few. However, looking at the statistics of who are currently utilizing EDI, one must wonder why it is not used by every business. Of the top 10,000 companies on the global scale (Fortune 1000 in the top 10 countries), almost everyone is using EDI, 98% to be exact. However, for the rest of the world only 5% are EDI users. In other words, millions of companies are still using faxes and paper documents. Why? The answer is well known: start-up cost. EDI saves a lot of money, over time. However, before that happens, companies must spend resources up front to identify their data requirements in order t o map their in-house data to the EDI messages. This process is required for each new trading partner implementation, and for each EDI message with that partner. Thus, a very costly effort that only the Fortune 1000 companies in each country can afford.

In order to reduce the cost so that the implementation becomes transparent, one would have to agree to a single data requirement for a particular EDI message. This would allow software vendors to create an EDI application that would have a large enough market to reduce the cost for small and medium-sized companies to be able to afford. This will never happen. So what would it take for software companies to build software that is not tailored for each of the different EDI message implementations but will be able to adopt to the different data requirements for a particular customer and their trading partners?

The success of any new way to exchange data among businesses depends not only on the adoption by the Fortune 1000 companies of standard agreements but on their adoption by the rest of business through out the world, the other 25,000,000. In order for business of any size, anywhere, to benefit from the next generation of e-Business standards, those standards must contain all the information to allow software developers to create programs that can be purchased off-the-self (shrink-wrap-solutions). The question that now arises is, will the software industry deliver such "cheap" off-the-shelf, shrink-wrapped solutions?

UN/CEFACT's primary objective in finding the solution to the above problems was to focus on a new e-Business standards that would make e-Business technology widely available, non-obtrusive to the business process, and cost effective for all organizations of any size, anywhere. The requirements to make this objective a reality included:
- Production of well-defined, consistent standards for interoperability, i.e. reduces the number of ways of doing things;
- Utilization of off-the-shelf tools that are available for analysis and implementation;
- Separation of analysis from application design and programming;

- Availability of training and reference sources (i.e. take advantage of a mainstream methodology for new projects in industry);
- Provision for automatic generation of e-Business interactions;
- Separation of data definition and format from the transport layer.

In looking towards the next generation of e-Business standards, it became clear that the best solution would be to separate the "how" from the "what". Or more to the point, that Business Process and Information models would define the "what" independently of the transport mechanism, the "how". This way, the same models can be used to move the information using EDI messages, distributed object technology or whatever new technology may surface, such as today's Web Services (Figure 3.7.1).

Figure 3.7.1. Separating the "what" from the "how"

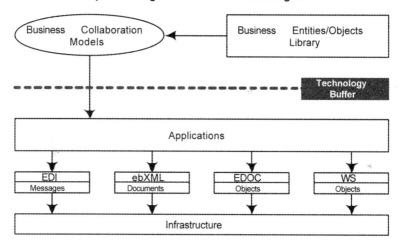

This line of thinking is consistent with the Open-EDI approach (Figure 3.7.2) of looking at the world through two views, the Business Operational View (BOV) and Functional Service View (FSV). Where the BOV would utilize modelling and the FSV would be the technology used for transporting the information. This is often called developing technology-neutral models.

Figure 3.7.2. Open-EDI reference model

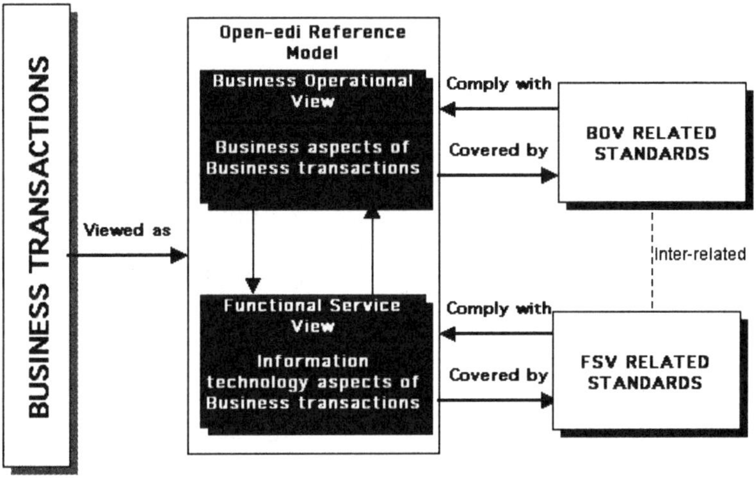

Brief introduction to the Business Collaboration Framework

The primary goal of the BCF is to capture the business knowledge that enables the development of low cost software components to help the small and medium-sized companies, and emerging economies engaged in e-Business practices. By focusing on developing business process and information models in a technology-neutral manner, the BCF provides insurance against obsolescence by allowing recasting of the business scenarios into new technologies.

At the heart of the BCF is the UN/CEFACT Modeling Methodology (UMM). The UMM is an incremental business process and information model construction methodology that provides levels of specification granularity that are suitable for communicating the model to business practitioners, business application integrators and network application solution providers.

A commercial trading agreement is modeled as a business collaboration model according to the UMM Meta Model (the model that defines the UMM modeling language). The UMM Meta Model is defined as an extension of the UML Meta Model by extending the UML stereotype syntax and semantics with the syntax and semantics of the business collaboration domain.

Figure 3.7.3. Overview of the business collaboration framework

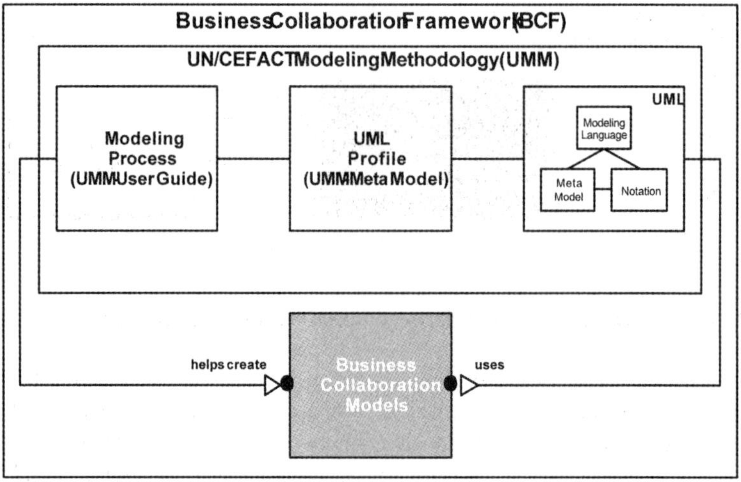

The bottom line – ending up with business information exchanges

Scope of engagement between partners

A business environment may be large and complex. Its understanding starts from information and documentation provided by business experts. Business experts provide a categorization and breakdown of the business environment into business areas, process areas, and business processes. Business processes are further divided into business process activities in order to understand how the stakeholders in this business environment view the discreet units of work done within their organization. Business process activities are either one-partner activities or multi-partner activities. Those which are multi-partner activities are by definition business collaboration activities, and extend outside the organization. Business collaboration activities define the scope for business requirements gathering and specification. Since the business environment includes identification of requirements placed by one-partner activities on multi-partner activities, the interaction of one-partner activities with multi-partner activities needs to be taken into account as well. All of this takes place in the language of the business environment experts and stakeholders.

Business requirements

A business collaboration activity is a predefined set of activities and/or processes of partners that is initiated by a partner to accomplish an explicitly shared business goal and terminated upon recognition of one of the agreed conclusions by all the involved partners. Business information is gathered for the purpose of specifying business collaboration activities in terms of goals, requirements, and constraints. These are then expressed in formal representations that can be understood and confirmed by the business environment experts. Business collaboration activities are specified by a business process analyst as use cases, requirements and business object flow graphs that define the choreography of atomic business processes, referred to as Business Transactions. The selection of a business collaboration pattern that fits the requirements of a business collaboration activity, if one is available, optimizes business process and information model reusability. However, in the absence of a suitable business collaboration pattern, the selection of pre-specified Business

269

Transaction patterns simplifies and prescribes reusable components in a business collaboration activity.

Business requirements are expressed with reference to business information structures that are affected by a business collaboration activity, e.g. order information, customer information. Preconditions and postconditions of the atomic business processes and of the business collaboration itself are best expressed by states of affected business entities, e.g. customer information - pending and customer information - accepted. In support of this, business entities (BEs) must be understood as to the states in which they may exist and the permitted state transitions in one or more life cycles (Figure 3.7.4). Business requirements are also expressed in terms of events that trigger the state transitions of BEs and of the business collaboration, e.g. receipt of a Positive Registration Response triggers the transition of Customer Information from tendered to assigned.

Figure 3.7.4. Business entity life cycle

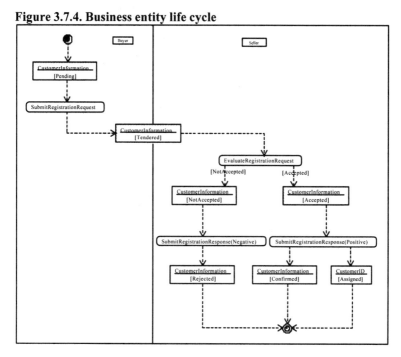

Business information construction

Analysis of the business requirements specifications is required to define the contents of business information to be exchanged in a business collaboration. Business information that is exchanged must contain information needed to identify the BEs affected by a Business Transaction. In addition, business information structures contain information content that satisfies the requirements for exchange of information required to be shared in the business collaboration. Shared information is generally the attributes of affected business objects (BOs) that must be shared in order to align the partners' views of those BOs.

In order to construct business information exchanges with standardized information items, reference is made to (BOs) in a registry as the primary source. If, in the business information modelling workflow, appropriate

271

attributes of BOs cannot be found, new BOs must be defined. A resource for defining new BOs would be core components (CC) and business information entities (BIEs). The selection of BIEs, or the creation of BIEs when they cannot be found in the core component registry, makes use of the core component context categories and rules. (Context categories should already be identified in the requirements gathering step and can be checked off at this point to utilize the core component context rules.) As BIEs are selected or created, they are included as attributes in the newly defined BOs, which are registered for subsequent reuse. However, in the normal business information modelling workflow, BIEs would not be used directly to create Business Information structures but would be used as needed to define BOs, which would then be used to create Business Information structures. These modelled structures would then become payloads by applying messaging technology specific syntax, e.g. XML, according to production rules.

The Business Collaboration Framework constitutes the new e-Business standard. This new standard is independent of the interchange data syntax, transport infrastructure, and server software and therefore satisfy UN/CEFACT e-Business Vision for a "framework" that utilizes Business Process and Information Modelling, UML and UN/CEFACT's Modelling Methodology (UMM) in such a way that any industry group or standards body, including UN/CEFACT, can create models that identify every possible activity to achieve a specific business goal.

Figure 3.7.5. Business information structure

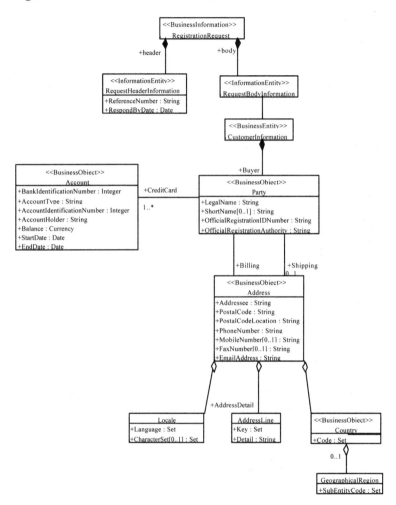

Business Collaboration models will be registered and stored in a global "virtual" repository. Users (trading partners - TP) will register "their" particular path/paths through the model (scenario(s)) so that others who want to engage with that TP can determine if they share at least one scenario. To ensure that the models not only follow the underlying UMM Meta Model but also are interoperable, the models will use reusable and most common objects (Business Objects/Business Entities) that will be used by the modellers as they document a particular business Collaboration. However, the messaging format, packaging and routing and the meta-model for the repository are not defined by UN/CEFACT but by the underlying implementation and infrastructure technology.

Business Collaboration Framework and Web Services

XML's role in e-Business
From a business viewpoint, doing business electronically means having a ubiquitous Internet dial tone; a promise that Web Services can fulfil. Because, from the software vendors viewpoint, doing business electronically means setting up and operating Web Services. All the major IT vendors are rolling out road maps and new product sets that will "enable your business". However, the underlying technologies for today's World Wide Web (WWW) "TCP/IP, HTTP and HTML" are limited in their capacity to support what businesses actually need: to find each other; to buy/sell services from each other; to find potential markets; and to have all this in a seamless, straightforward, predictable e-world. The key is systems interoperability, both between businesses and, more importantly, within a business. This desire is not new, but what is, are the capabilities offered by new technologies based on XML.

Is XML enough for e-Business?
XML and e-Business is synonymous with Web Services. Therefore, one must look at Web Services to determine if they have what it takes to provide the full solution for e-Business. Many feel that Web Services have the potential to transform e-Business into a plug-and-play affair. Not only will Web Services simplify how businesses will interconnect, they will also enable businesses to find each other. One reason for the increased interest

in Web Services is the promise of interoperability, in the same way that Web pages can be accessed from anywhere on the Internet.

However, complex standards are needed to achieve true interoperability, not only at the messaging and transport layer, but also at the business (application) layer. The success of Web Services will depend on how easily businesses will be able to engage interoperability at all levels.

There are many efforts in standardizing Web Services, but none of them provide the required features for e-Business transactions. Web Service standards only address the infrastructure side. There is a need to provide standards for interoperability at the business layer. UN/CEFACT is addressing this aspect of standardization with its the "Business Collaboration Framework".

Web Services and business collaboration
There is a clear relation between the Web Services and the BCF. Most organizations are eager to jump onto the Web Services bandwagon but they also need to maintain standards to ensure interoperability between their applications and their trading partners' applications. Organizations will take Web Services technologies like BPEL, WSDL, UDDI and SOAP and understand their application within the realm of other e-Business standard such as the BCF. Web Services technologies must be applied within the context of standards such as the BCF, or they will end up with simple, stateless Web Services, and not the complex and collaborative business transactions that organizations are longing for.

To achieve transaction integration does not automatically mean wholesale conversion to one specific technology. One needs to put a digital communication system through the whole business irrespective of who the software provider is and what the application are, so that the work flows and processes are available across the business. It does, however, help if organizations stick to one specific infrastructure technology.

It is time to look at available technologies in the total context, so that whether one is talking about development platforms, or about building next-generation natural language based speech interfaces, or using open web services to connect business partners, one must have a common theme in mind - to use the Internet, as a whole.

What is needed to bring this vision to reality is a common vision shared by users (businesses) and software vendors.

Business to business integration

Two distinct trends will help to solve the platform plurality problem. First, there is a consensus that of the different technologies available for eCommerce development, companies should standardize on either J2EE (Java 2 Enterprise Edition) or Microsoft.NET - or even both. Secondly, Web Services, virtually removing the problem altogether since they are based on open standards - irrespective of Microsoft or Java - they will be a uniting theme around the enterprise.

Figure 3.7.6. Web service standards overview

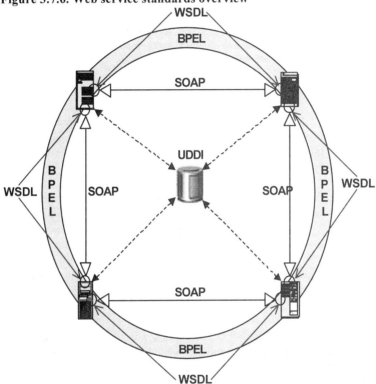

This Web Service trend will also help business-to-business integration; and so will XML. For years, organizations have been able to communicate electronically using e-mail, yet it seems incredible that without an expensive investment in traditional EDI, issuing an invoice usually entails printing and mailing a piece of paper.

This, too, will start to change because of another key standard in the adoption of Web Services – the BCF, which provides an open technology-neutral framework for interoperability at the Business Layer. Undoubtedly, such a fundamental cultural change away from paper to electronic transactions will not stand much chance of success without a champion.

Conclusion

UN/CEFACT's vision for e-Business is to create a single global electronic marketplace where enterprises of any size and in any geographical location can meet and conduct business with each other through the exchange of relevant business information.

For enterprises to conduct electronic business with each other, they must first discover each other and the products and services they have to offer. They then must determine which business processes and documents are necessary to obtain those products and services. After that, they need to determine how the exchange of information will take place and then agree on contractual terms and conditions. Once all of this is accomplished, they can then exchange information and products/services according to these agreements.

To facilitate this, Web Services and the BCF provide an infrastructure for data communication interoperability, a semantic framework for commercial interoperability, and a mechanism that allows enterprises to find, establish a relationship, and conduct business with each other. Data communication interoperability is ensured by a standard message transport mechanism with a well-defined interface, packaging rules, and a predictable delivery model, as well as an interface to handle incoming and outgoing messages at either end.

Commercial interoperability is provided by means of specifications for defining business processes and core components and a context model for defining Business Information Structures. The BCF recommends a methodology and provides a set of worksheets and guidelines for creating those models.

A business library (catalogue) of business process and information models promotes business efficiency by encouraging reuse of business processes or parts of predefined business processes.

For the actual conduct of business to take place, Web Services provides a shared repository where businesses can discover each other's business offering by means of partner profile information, a process for establishing an agreement to do business, and a shared repository for company profiles, business-process specifications, and relevant business information structures.

Recommendation

Web Services and UN/CEFACT's Business Collaboration Framework will enable anyone, anywhere, to do electronic business with anyone else over the Internet. However, compliance with and adoption of the various standards components is expected to be incremental, over time. As a first step, UN/CEFACT through its Techniques and Methodologies Group (TMG) must establish a close working relationship with the Web Service standardization communities to work towards the same e-Business vision to ensure that both communities, the users and providers, are benefiting from their current separate efforts through a common and aligned goal and vision. Without such collaboration neither will achieve what they want and the end result could be that instead of business driving the technology, we end up with technology being forced on business.

Chapter 3.8
Global Trade System: A Public/Private Partnership

Dean L. Kothmann, Executive Officer, BV Solutions Group[57]

The Global Trade System is a unique solution to develop secure global trade and to mitigate the impacts of incidents affecting commercial logistics. The goal is to develop a practical alternative to traditional security measures and government-mandated or government-driven systems that pose a substantial risk of disruption to global commerce. Currently, the necessary infrastructure and processes are being tested so that the tools of technology can be used effectively to improve trade development and security for all nations and all peoples.

The Global Trade System will:

- Improve trade security both to and from all participating nations;
- Use off-the-shelf technologies to physically verify, or refute, the manifest of each cargo that is shipped to and from each participating nation;
- Initiate the necessary processes to solve the people interface problems with commercial shipments;
- Improve the logistics processes for the buyers of the products being shipped.

Trade security: a global problem

Trading partners had been warning the United States of America for many years that in time, the terrorist actions that were occurring globally would reach their shores. These actions were viewed as a low priority, in part because the financial impact could not be felt. Beginning on September 11, 2001, America felt the financial impact and became vulnerable.

---

[57] BV (Black and Veach) Solutions Group, Inc., participates in the Innovative Trade Network. For information: kothmannd@bvsg.com, tel.: +1-913-458-7553.

The immediate reaction was to secure the harbours and then work to force the world to provide the United States with safe commerce.

Trade will not be secure for any country until all modes of commercial transportation are secure not only for themselves but also for all their trading partners. Proof of this fact can be found in the inability to secure the borders from the current flow of contraband and people into most countries. The streets are full of illegal drugs and illegal immigrants. A large portion of this illegal importation occurs using commercial trade. The immediate reaction has been, and continues to be, to add additional locks to the door. The United States has placed fences on its southern border. Other nations have engaged their military. All of these efforts have had an inadequate impact.

The challenge is not solely container security, consolidated shipment security, or bulk shipment security. The challenge is also not solely the creation of safe shipping corridors. The challenge is to engage the world in a global trade system that is good for all nations; a solution that does not favour one nation, one port, one vendor, or one individual over another. The challenge is to prepare the world for the near future--a near future in which a disgruntled high school student from any country in the world will have the ability to create a new biological agent and kill millions of people, and spread terror through entire continents by using commercial shipping as the low cost, guided transport mechanism to spread a weapon of mass destruction.

Risk of disruption

Operation Safe Commerce, a United States of America security programme, has articulated the problem well. In the Operation Safe Commerce - Pacific proposal, they state, "The absence of a robust capacity to filter the illicit from the licit in the face of: (a) a heightened terrorist threat environment, and (b) the growing volume of people and goods moving through international trade corridors, places the United States and global commerce at frequent risk of disruption. Absent alternatives, when confronted with credible intelligence of a terrorist attack or an attack itself, authorities will find themselves compelled to order a shutdown of our transportation systems as one of their first preventative or responsive measures. Executing this order will have the net effect of creating a self-imposed blockade on the U.S. economy. The ripple effect throughout the international trade corridors will be immediate and painful because there is no alternative to a container for moving over 90 percent of general cargo between North America and Europe, Asia, Africa and Australia."

A successful terrorist attack on a trading partner's port of departure by a weapon of mass destruction followed by the threat that this bomb was headed to any other port will likewise result in a self-imposed blockade. The only strategy to secure the world's economies is to secure all trade lanes.

Global Trade System is intended to provide the global infrastructure necessary for all nations to become engaged in solving the global trade security problem--a problem that could disrupt and possibly result in long-term damage to the economies of all nations.

Meeting the challenge

The challenge, a global trade system, demands that more information flows, that it flows faster, and that it becomes more truthful while being shared by most stakeholders. A global trade system must have the following attributes:

- Be available for adoption by all nations
- Apply to all commercial shipments by all modes of transportation
- Be useful for all contrabands
- Obtain global acceptance and use
- Be universal, not unilateral
- Improve commerce versus being a tax on, or delay of, commerce
- Provide a global response in case of any transportation event
- Increase development and security as more countries adopt the system

- Provide truthful data to all shipment stakeholders
- Provide physical verification of manifest
- Provide tracking of contents
- Achieve rapid adoption
- Be successful without 100% adoption

The challenge can be overcome. However, the response has been to focus only on technology to solve the problem. This approach also requires change in people and processes to meet the needs of the technology.

A more productive approach is to produce an infrastructure that is neutral to technology and allows new technologies to be applied independent of people and processes. The interfaces to the infrastructure must be disseminated to all technology providers, so they can develop and advance their technologies in a fair and measured manner.

An infrastructure strategy

Three inter-linking infrastructure components are required to achieve a global trade system. These components are inspection, sensing, and tracking (IST), profiling, and a business model with a data-sharing mechanism. To be successful, no one component can be effective without its other two partners. Each component supports and supplies answers to the other components.

The sensing and tracking infrastructure is the physical infrastructure that provides the knowledge of where a shipment is, what is in a shipment, and who has been involved with the shipment. This infrastructure has three key components. A visibility network allows a shipment's stakeholders to have access to IST information that creates logistical value. A set of auditable inspection standards allows the Customs agency of the importer country to gain confidence in the validity of the initial goods that are loaded. The network helps track all people, cargoes, and stakeholders and their actions. Sensors allow for the physical verification of cargo by the use of technologies such as sniffing, infrared imaging, light sensing, and nano-sensors. These are the sensors that are available now.

By design, tomorrow's sensors will use the same infrastructure.

The profiling infrastructure will accommodate data from many locations. The data must be fused and verified. Profiling is an activity that has three major objectives. First, governments want the data to improve the security of imports arriving in their country. Second, buyers of goods want commercial logistics improvement and response in case of a logistics event. Third, all stakeholders want valid data. Profiling provides a means to compare data fields throughout the shipping cycle to test the validity of each entry.

The infrastructure makes possible the access and flow of data for commercial shipments for each stakeholder involved in the shipment. Data accumulation for a shipment will begin with the buyer of goods to be imported. Data will continue to accumulate as each stakeholder uses and adds to the database for each shipment. Users will be all stakeholders including ports, shippers, freight forwarders, insurers, law enforcement, customs, and security agencies.

The system will provide the ability to:
- Implement ISO 9000 quality assurance rules for the loading of inter-modal containers
- Gather real-time pictures of the loading of sensitive cargoes and ensure the sharing of those pictures
- Implement background check processes and share those data
- Provide tracking information
- Manage theft-resistant mechanical and electronic seal data
- Manage many other functions

A Global Trade System

Observation 1: When one has a single choke point, one is building a fortress. The fortress will be breached. The history of warfare has shown that a fortress can be breached.

Observation 2: The community is the best policeman. The police enforce the rules of the community, while the community does the real policing.

The solution must create a community of all those involved in logistics. All nations must be able to place their technology into the solution and have equal access to the markets generated. The solution must allow participating nations to control their goods, without interfering in the world's commercial business. A nation's independence must not be breached. A global trade solution must not favour one technology provider, one port, or one nation.

The global trade system will be a self-regulating organization. The system may be viewed as a utility because it provides a utilitarian good that is owned and shared across the community. The system will create the rules of operation, and the government agency responsible for logistics security will approve the rules of operation. The global trade system will be an international franchise with local franchises owned and run by local members. These members will recruit importers/buyers from within their country that wish to use the utility. The system receives a transaction fee for data that is entered and reused.

The system is managed at several levels. At the country level, the buyers in the country of importation manage the system. At the security level, the country of the buyer manages the security. The buyer continues to manage its own logistics, and uses the system because it provides a common benefit to all those involved in their supply chain.

The system is only infrastructure. It does not replace the laws on liability and damages or proprietary information for the country of the buyer. The system facilitates trade, development, and security. The system is not a legal system but uses existing laws.

Proprietary information is handled in the same manner as it is today. The information is gathered and shared along the supply chain today by the parties that own the data. Whoever generates the data owns it and controls its usage. The data owner will give access to countries that have a valid need.

Today, data is not easily accessible or shared among all members of the supply chain because a common infrastructure does not exist, not even in the developed countries of the world. Some very large retailers have very good systems. Some customs organizations have very good systems. But these systems are single function or company or country focused. Our approach is to have a system that is good for all goods, all modes of transportation, and all nations. Our approach is to build a utility that creates utilitarian good for the world.

The benefits

Implementation of inspections in countries with porous borders has resulted in reduced customs fees while country revenues have risen. Importers / buyers of goods will find that goods arrive more quickly and predictably with less theft. Logistics suppliers will use data that are more accurate and more easily obtained. Nations need to know what they are exporting. Importing nations need to know what is entering their countries.

All participants will benefit by improved logistics. Improvement in the economics of the logistics process will pay for the system. Payments will be made to the global trade system by those that find value in smoother data flows, new information and knowledge, and the ability to not re-enter data that has already been generated by someone earlier in the logistics chain.

Chapter 3.9
Real World Technology Solutions for In-Transit Freight Border Security

Scott Brosi, Area Vice President, TransCore

In this paper I will discuss the use of intelligent transport systems for border security as an effective technical tool for trade facilitation. I will also list some examples where such security systems were employed most successfully, namely, at the US-Mexico border, and in trade with China.

The types of intelligent transportation systems for border security mentioned below share some particular characteristics. They are designed similarly to Electronic Toll Systems and focus on security rather than financial pre-clearance. Such border security systems aim to alleviate commercial pressure for importers and exporters alike by decreasing congestion and by concentrating administrative and security attention where most necessary.

Figure 3.9.1 The SENTRI system – how it works

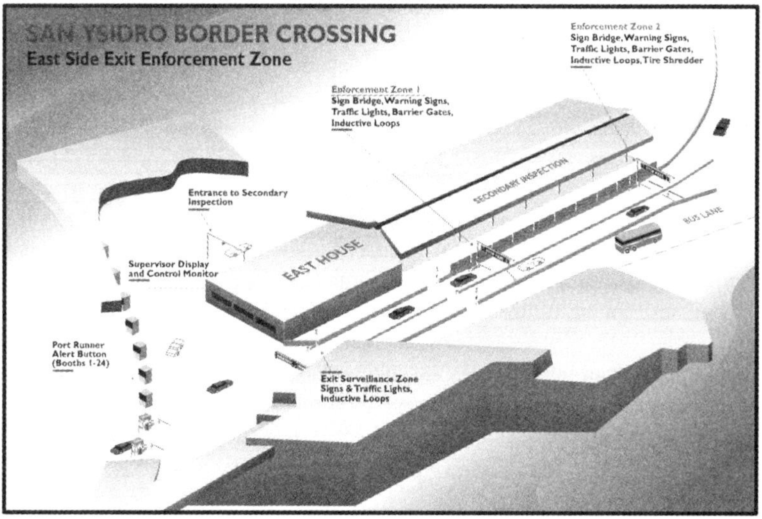

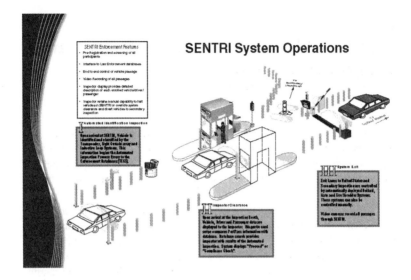

The SENTRI System was introduced at the southern border of the United States, while at the northern border between the United States and Canada a similar intelligent transportation system called *Nexus* was put into effect as part of the INS Program. The *Nexus* system instituted the use of RFID identification cards to detect and identify the driver/passengers only, for pre-processed commuters between the United States and Canada. The SENTRI RFID system involves slow-speed processing of authorized vehicles and driver/passengers of the vehicles are identified and cleared on the basis of *Radio Frequency Identification* (RFID) sensors. The SENTRI system includes an Exit Control System designed to prevent "Port Runners". The clear advantages of the SENTRI system include removal of the old traffic control barriers, preventing border congestion and rapid processing of "trusted travelers". Currently 100,000 users are benefiting from the program while officials hope for these numbers to rise significantly in the future.

In another case at border crossings in China, Chinese Customs introduced an effective anti-smuggling initiative by integrating the RFID for drivers and vehicles into one system.

SOLUTIONS FOR FREIGHT BORDER SECURITY

At border crossings at Shenzhen, Dalian, Qingdao, Chengdu, Tianjin and Ningbo, 125 lanes and 100,000 trucks are using the RFID system. Between Shenzhen and Hong Kong, SAR, the RFID system is most developed. Plans to expand and implement the usage of the system throughout China are under way.

Another important customs security clearance initiative in China is the matching of the driver, the truck and the freight in one tracking system. The idea is to process pre-clearance of goods, truck and driver one working day in advance of movement. The operational side involves simultaneous AVI reading of the truck tag and driver tag as it is correlated to pre-designated weight of goods, which then generates and assigns the truck tag a random customs number. Through the implementation of this system, the Chinese customs have managed to reduce the processing time to 10 seconds per AVI lane versus 3 minutes per manual lane. In addition, the system employs a centralized database and sharing of information for consistency and precision. Tags can be mounted permanently or temporarily, for example, on the front window of commercial vehicles.

Similar to the Chinese example, Free and Secure Trade (FAST) commercial vehicle processing system, the Just-In-Time-Inventory Management process deployed along the North American land border between the United States, Mexico, and Canada, a border clearance system pre-clears the authorized driver, up to three authorized crew, and their truck at a time. The FAST program evolved from National Customs Automation Prototype (NCAP) and is currently used on six sites between USA and Canada. Its expansion to additional sites on the borders with Canada and Mexico is in progress. FAST is also currently testing the use of a tamper-resistant tag.

Figure 3.9.3 FAST's tagging system at Ambassador Bridge site

One of the most progressive projects in the making is the *Northwest International Trade Corridor and Border Crossing System* in the state of Washington and province of British Columbia and the plan is to go beyond checking the driver and the truck. The chief objective of the project is to secure the chain of custody and to move back the border by tracking the vehicle, the driver, and the container/cargo, as well as the status of the container from point of origin to inland designation. The project will place emphasis on the use of electronic seals, which have increasingly become a favoured technical tool in the protection of cargo security. Electronic seals, as pictured in Figure 3.9.4, are effective in that they are disposable, reusable and can work in multiple frequencies. The ambitious *Northwest International Trade Corridor* initiative represents the collaborative efforts of private industry, DOT, Customs, Department of Agriculture, and regional ports - the Ports of Seattle and Tacoma.

Figure 3.9.4 Container electronic seal

In bringing my paper to a close, I would like to stress the importance of the need for us to work towards global and common solutions in order to facilitate international trade. The customs programs and initiatives I listed above are clear examples of commitments made at the national level to contribute to a vision of comprehensive global solutions for international trade. Some of the key areas where we still need to work together to facilitate trade are in moving back the borders by complying with worldwide standards, by employing practical uses of technology and automating customs procedures, by applying commercially viable customs policies and in dynamic teaming by solution providers. We, at Transcore, are committed to technology driven solutions in facilitating international trade and we also firmly believe that the way forward is through evolution and not revolution.

Chapter 3.10
Supply Chain Security: The "Virtual Border"
Donald Robert Quartel, Jr., Chairman and CEO, FreightDesk Technologies, Former Member, US Federal Maritime Commission

I will review some of the things driving the United States approach to the issue of container and shipment security. First and foremost is the notion that every container, every shipment presents a potential danger given the uncertain state of the world. But, the fact of the matter is that neither we in the United States, nor anyone else, can inspect every one of the tens of thousands of containers that move through all of our ports. We **can** create a hierarchical approach combining physical inspection, human trust procedures and a new process of early electronic inspection employing the latest in information technologies. This is the subject of my paper.

Why is this electronic border a necessary approach? The key point is that international trade is a tremendously complex business. A typical trade will have as many as 20-25 involved parties – buyers, sellers, inland transporters on both sides of the ocean, ocean and other water carriers, middlemen, financiers, governments and others – and will generate 30-40 documents. Some 6 million containers, many carrying cargoes for multiple owners and valued on average at $60,000 each, entered the US in the year 2000, on ships carrying from 1000 to 6000 containers each. If we were to add a physical inspection to one of the very large ships carrying these cargoes to the US through the world's hub ports – the Regina Maersk, for example – a single hour's delay per 20-foot container would add from 150 - 250 man-days (roughly 1 ½ to 3 man-years of work shifts) to the time it took to offload the 6000 containers riding that one ship.

Literally millions of people and hundreds of thousands of companies worldwide are engaged in the business of moving cargoes internationally. In the United States alone, there are an estimated 400,000 importing and exporting companies, 5,000 licensed forwarders and customs brokers, perhaps as many as 40,000 consolidators, large and small, and millions engaged in the transportation industry. Worldwide, there are at least in theory some 500 ocean carriers – although probably 10-15 carry 90 per cent of cargoes shipped between continents – an estimated 50-70,000 forwarders and tens of thousands more intermediaries, not to mention several million companies moving goods.

This is a process that literally spews data – data on the contents, on who touched the cargo, who paid for it, where it has been, where it is going. And it is a process into which commercial shippers – the people who own, buy, or sell a cargo – tap into daily, in one form or another, to collaborate on transportation and financial transactions, to exchange documents, to meet regulatory requirements of the various jurisdictions in which they operate, in addition to documenting the basic buy-sell transaction that begins the shipment. Figure 3.10.1 below illustrates the complexity of the trade information flows.

Figure 3.10.1 Complex data flow for international shipments

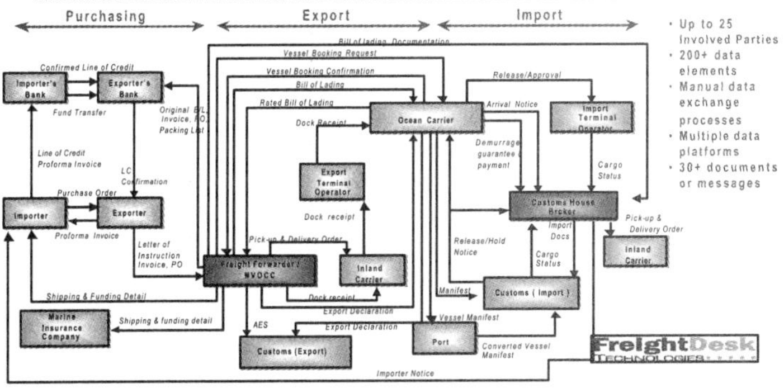

The second key point is that, in order to evaluate this information on a timely basis, we need to push its receipt back to an earlier point in the supply chain. Data capture on the transaction should be pushed back to a point prior to the shipment being placed on its final transport. Because the action starts well before the port, the data starts prior to that. Figure 3.10.1 shows some of the pre-port data forms and processes, and the parties from which the data might be generated and in whose hands it may lie.

Figure 3.10.2: Aggregating commercial data - sample data elements and application data

	Data Elements	Buyer	Seller	Supplier	Export Forwarder	Carrier	Import Forwarder / Broker	Consignee	
Carriers/ Parties Data	Shipper's/ Exporter's Name Address	x							**Carrier/Party Data**
	Supplier		x						
	Agent of Exporter/ Packer		x						
	Inland Carrier (origin)		x						
	Ocean Carrier name				x				
	Customs Broker							x	
	Inland Carrier (destination)					x			
	Delivering Carrier (destination)							x	
	Seller's Bank Name & Address	x							
	Buyer's Bank Name & Address	x							
	Intermediate Consignee's Name & Address				x				
	Ultimate Consignee's Name & Address	x							
Conveyance Data	Country of Origin	x							**Leg Data**
	Point of Origin (City & State)	x							
	Method of Shipment to forwarder		x						
	Inland Carrier Route (origin)		x						
	Ocean Carrier Route				x				
	Voyage Number				x				
	Vessel Flag				x				
	Foreign Port of Export				x				
	Country which Shipped				x				
	Loading Pier					x			
	Trans-shipment Ports					x			
	Port of Unloading				x				
	US Port of Arrival				x				
	Inland Carrier Route (destination)					x			
	Delivering Carrier Route (destination)							x	**Route**
	Country of Ultimate Destination	x							

▓ At time of Purchase Order   ▒ Prior to shipment

☐ En route to port of export   ■ On water/ After arrival

Using standard commercial information, a government, just like a private party, can look back to the beginning of the process, before the port, before the ship, before the port of embarkation, before even sealing the container. They can look to the buy-sell transaction and the purchase order that is generated from it; to the manufacturers or suppliers overseas, their manufacturing and supplier processes, how and where they or a consolidator somewhere load the container, when and how it was sealed, how it was moved, who touched it, who paid for it – and even where it might be going once the cargo reaches its final destination. For the most part, every bit of that data is available – somewhere and in some form, but not necessarily captured in one place by the private sector, and certainly not by a government – but there nonetheless, before the cargo ever gets loaded onto a ship.

The focus of logisticians and companies – particularly United States companies – over the last several decades has been on making cargo flow faster, more cheaply, and with increasing transparency – the visible supply chain. That is a development that gives many companies an enormous competitive advantage and it makes a huge contribution to the reduction in the cost of numerous articles and products crucial to everyday life around the globe.

As far as supply chain data and the government needs of information for security purposes crosscut, information can have dual uses. Businesses need this information – in-transit *visibility* – for contract management, planning, process tracking, risk mitigation, government and commercial documentation, and so forth. Governments can use this information to create *transparency* – to combat corruption, for counter-terrorism purposes, for product and safety regulation, compliance, and trade processing.

So, the question is, what are you looking for in the data surrounding a shipment, and why? Is the cargo likely to be what it was said to be, where did it come from, what is the likelihood of being what it is stated to be, who handled it from packing through transport to a port, who would be handling it afterwards, where it had been and where it was going, who had a financial interest in it?

The reason for these questions is that it is not just about what is in the container, but the circumstances in which the container finds itself in the trade and transportation process.

Figure 3.10.2 represents a scheme for government risk profiling. According to this scheme, commerc ial data would: (a) be captured prior to loading of a container on a ship, train, plane, or truck in international commerce, from the shipper, consignee, intermediary, banks, and all others that had an interest in or touched or processed the shipment; (b) combined with certain relevant law enforcement and national security information; and, (c) be processed through a form of artificial intelligence (including evolutionary computing) to provide a "profile" for every container and shipment within it. The profiling process would generate a "go-no-go" decision driving further actions – loading on a carrier, physical inspection, further profiling, etc.

Figure 3.10.3 Commercial data key to the security schema

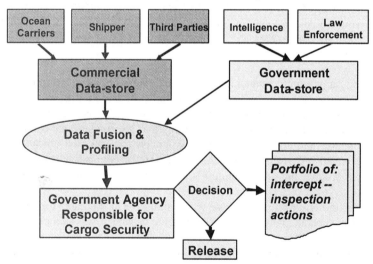

At its simplest level, this is what the new US *24-Hour Rule* is all about, and it is a concept that underlies the new Trade Act of 2003 rules that will be released in September 2003. The algorithm used to analyze it should consider not only fact-based data (e.g. what the product was and who touched it), but situational data – e.g. a container originating in an unstable country and passing by Yankee Stadium in New York City on the day and hour the President of the United States was scheduled to throw out the first ball.

Fundamentally, there is no single best approach, which suggests an array of synergistic techniques data mining for threat and risk assessment. We are familiar with and employ: knowledge based assessments based on rules and known facts; statistical pattern analysis; mathematical models; and the new evolutionary or learning algorithms to detect changes in patterns that humans cannot see. Based on some probability calculus air, ocean, train, or truck carriers could be told that the government either felt the cargo was safe to carry, or, that further investigation, including perhaps a physical inspection, was necessary. Analysis can detect numerous anomalies from the data contained in commercial documents alone: cargos incongruent with stated origin, values inconsistent with the trade pattern or transportation methodology chosen; simple document discrepancies up to complex conflicts; discrepancies in origin, values, and others.

Finally, I would like to close by making the point that this is not an issue for the United States alone. The European Union and US Customs have agreed on major principles for future cooperation here – the most important perhaps being reciprocity and common standards. And now, the International Maritime Organization and the World Customs Organization are making these concerns a mandate of their organizations.

How this plays out at the political and business levels is yet to be finally determined. I will say that one of the most crucial areas for focus needs to be the impact of these new rules and procedures on small importers and exporters, as well as on least developed countries and non-CSI ports. Security can be a cost disadvantage as well as an operation advantage. For the parties I have just named, it can entail longer lead times for moving cargoes, delays in transshipped containers, a general concern about a country's processes and procedures which lead to built-in biases in other country's customs responses, and so forth.

In the end, however, these processes are implemented, they need at the core to be business-centric, meaning that they reflect the way commerce actually operates – although this is not to mean they should not disturb or change the business process; they need to be dynamic and flexible to reflect the realities of trade; and, at the analytical level, these processes need to be able to discern patterns and activities beyond the simple ken of human expertise.

Chapter 3.11
Doing More with Less through Real Time:
Holistic view command and control
Christopher Hickey, Vice President, Homeland Security

Trade security has been redefined since September 11, 2001, and it continues to evolve. As a result, growing concerns exist over the economic impact of security solutions at all levels in the organization of commerce. Owing to newly surfacing security threats, security effectiveness and economic efficiency should be part of all transportation operations and in the planning of design of all relevant systems. To date, approaches focused on supply chain and local facility vulnerability analyses result in solutions to address local issues. There is a growing recognition that security solutions must be global in scope, establishing both security and economic value to all significant stakeholders. Thanks to technology and innovation, advance communications make it possible to share data at the global level providing better accuracy and security while improving costs and operations at the local level. Subsequently, integrating islands of information into holistic command and control solutions with full audit of transaction can improve security, and also improve operational efficiencies. The global chain of custody for freight is very complex. It involves a multiplicity of steps, bringing together oceanic freight, ground freight, freight transaction, transaction processing, and freight delivery.

Some emerging themes growing from the recent events lead us to understand that security is not just for emergencies but is a daily event. Security thus needs to be incorporated accordingly into everyday systematic routines and transactions. In order to do so, clear and transparent procedures must be put in place, while at the same time the chain of command and authority must be explicit and formal. For example, a key component to a successful security strategy for a seaport is a dedicated operations centre. In addition, seaports should also leverage from the strategies in other industries and agencies such as oil refineries, data centers, the government, defence and airports. In this context, security is a

<u>journey</u>, not a destination, and the road to secure environment is <u>always</u> under construction.

Nevertheless, successful monitoring of a highly complex set of transactions such as those involved in trade and supply chain security faces many hurdles and challenges. Ensuring supply chain security requires efficient use of security technology when processing cargo results in safer commerce and improved port operational efficiencies. Although in many cases adequate levels and sophisticated forms of security technology are not available, the following are some important questions to ask when evaluating your cargo security system:

- How do you identify and track handling of important or dangerous cargoes?
- How do you verify container contents if they match shipping manifest?
- How do you verify that shipping container contents have not been compromised?
- How do you verify that shipping container does not contain undocumented hazardous or illegal contents?
- How do you provide a history of where the container has been and who has had access to it?
- How do you provide physical security of seaport, air terminal, or border entry facility?

In order to be able to assure cargo security effectively, we at Honeywell believe that a holistic approach, meeting all possible security threats with adequate and proactive prevention security methods and data systems management, is one way of improving safer commerce and greater port efficiency. Inefficient efforts to address container security significantly increase cost of operations and reduce free flow of goods and services. Figure 3.11.1 shows a holistic view and the numerous on-site security dimensions to be considered.

Figure 3.11.1 Holistic approach to the numerous dimensions of supply chain security

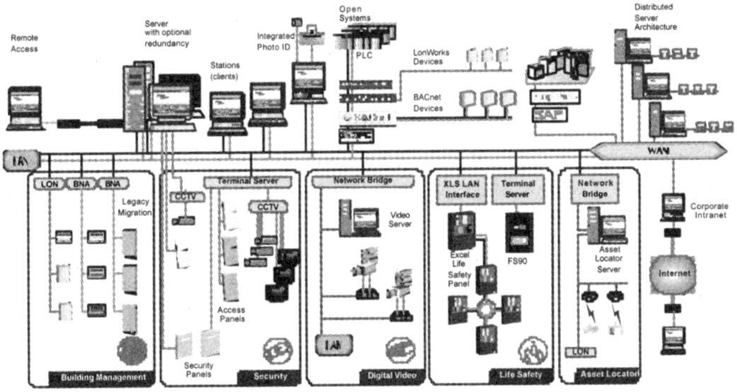

In addition to an efficient and thorough on-site security operations framework, an integrated systems architecture is the key. One of the leading systems in use today to manage infrastructure systems is the Supervisory Control and Data Acquisition protocol, or SCADA. The simplest SCADA systems collect measurements, throw railway switches, close circuit-breakers or adjust valves in the pipes that carry water, oil and gas. More complicated versions sift incoming data, govern multiple devices and cover a broader area. Besides SCADA, other factors play into a well-integrated systems architecture, such as high availability, command and control integration as a key to flexibility, managed risk with real time data, employing common user interface, and using digital tracking.

There is no doubt that security risk management in commerce requires vast amount of legwork and efficient application of technology. As a result, the private sector has been called to action and has an important role to play. Ways in which private companies can contribute are many. We can provide advanced technologies to automatically track, assess shipping contents relative to manifest and verify the integrity of the cargo. Establishing a global view is also important when developing and adopting a distributed, secure World Wide data exchange utility where public and private shareholders are able to obtain highly secure information for any shipment. Integration is a third way in which the private sector can contribute by

301

deploying a standardized, dynamic open information systems architecture for integrating people, process and technology data into cargo management systems with supply chain security in mind. Making security a core part of companies' business process is a fourth approach, which can enhance operational efficiencies daily and provide efficient risk management when required.

In conclusion, given the current security challenges, heightened security effectiveness and responsive security solutions need to be applied to everyday transport transactions. Efficient application of technology and data management systems in tracking and assessing shipping contents is also essential, and this is where private companies can play an important role.

Chapter 3.12
Mitigating Security Threats and Facilitating Trade through the Deployment of a Global Security Network

Bruce Jacquemard, Executive Vice President, Savi Technology

This paper focuses on the Smart & Secure Tradelanes (SST) network, which we are developing at Savi Technology in cooperation with our partners. The SST's global information network and physical infrastructure involve more than 40 SST partners in 12 of the world's largest and busiest trade lanes. SST provides real-time visibility of location and security status tracking infrastructure from point of origin to destination. It also compliments security initiatives of the United States Government, other Govern ments, and major international agencies.

Figure 3.12.1. SST network in 2003

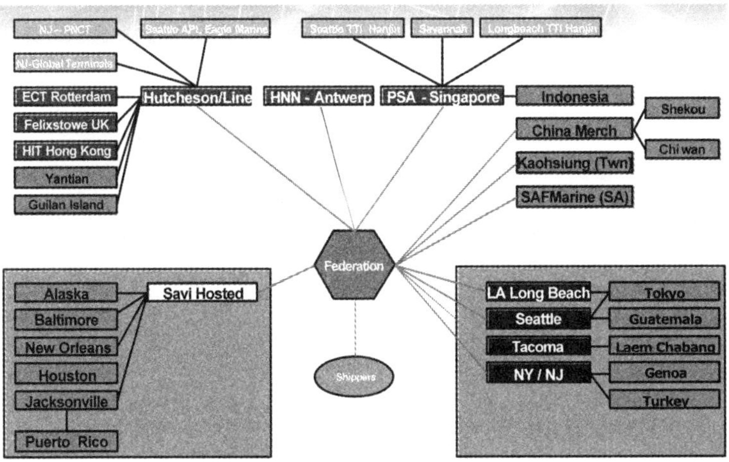

Rather than securing a specific person, place or object as we have done in the past, we are now looking at the security of the trading process as a whole. No single process change or technology device offers a complete solution by itself. Another major feature of the SST is that we are increasingly focusing on containers and not only on vessels. This also calls for integrating new processes or applying new technologies to facilitate efficient distribution of information. Automated methods of collecting and distributing data, further up the supply chain, and linking the information flow to the physical flow through more real time capabilities will be essential parts of the process. Moreover, software systems need to be in place to identify, analyze and respond to real time information.

Key drivers in supply chain security

A key element of greater security and efficiency in international trade is transparency and visibility across the entire supply chain, which increases the capability to track and locate containers at any given time. This will enable people to locate containers using information from within the system (automatic reporting of location, status, routing and content, among others).

Figure 3.12.2. Two representative customer scenarios

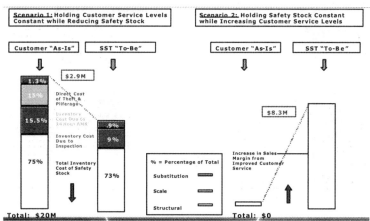

In addition to data layers of defense, physical layers of defense for cargo, containers, ports, supply chain facilities, and people, are necessary. Conveyance should be made smarter, in order to integrate deterrence and provide automated detection capabilities for location, security status, secure history and event log, automated manifest, and sensing.

Complete system intelligence is necessary to meet the new requirements. Decisions and solutions can sub-optimize the entire network, so it is necessary to address global supply chain security as a network problem. Processes must be made smarter: what is measured should be managed. Real time information drives the optimization of the processes that leverage all available information from within or from outside the logistics system.

Another aspect in supply chain security is regulatory compliance. By "making the enforcement smarter", here, we understand automating the checks and information collection; for example, for the implementation of the US Customs and Border Protection initiatives – CSI, C-TPAT, and the US Customs 24-hour Advance Cargo Manifest Declaration Rule (24 AMR) in an integrated approach. This means recording authorized access or linking it to manifest, AMR stored with container at origin, Automated Seal verifications, etc.

Concerning forensics and other activities, we are still learning and adapting. We are analyzing and diagnosing events, with a view to responding appropriately, and have the ability to segment issues and restart. Systems and networks need to be judged not only by how well they perform but also by "how well they fail" and restart.

In order to achieve the key goal, securing the supply chain, the process should start with strong security at the port of packing. Terrorism threats (such as dirty bombs or contamination) should then be limited in the next stages, such as road transport, distribution centre, and at the port of loading. The key choke and transit points - vessels, ports of discharge, and road and railroad transportation systems - should also be monitored. In addition, shrinkage needs to be reduced by identifying pilferage points -

manufacturing and retail distribution centres, ports of discharge, road and railroad transportation, and retail stores.

Figure 3.12.3 SST deployment around the world

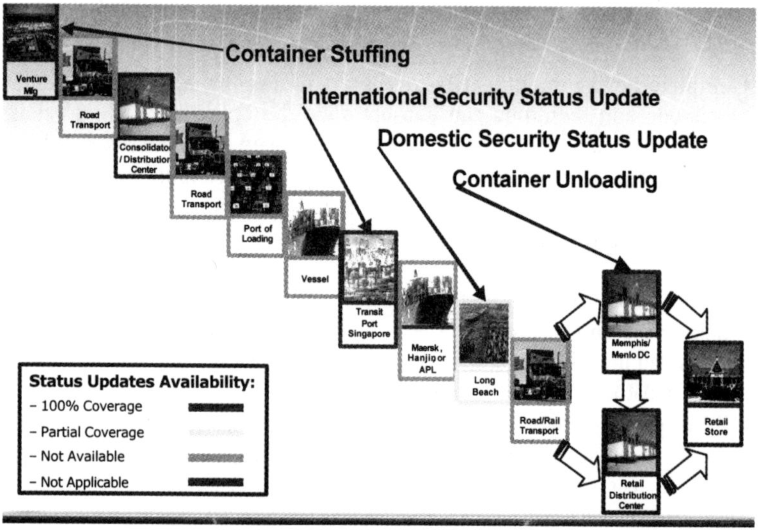

The SST uses a specific software application: the Transportation Security System. This software application maintains audit trails of container security and route histories, manages deviation alerts, including route and schedule and tamper alerts. It also provides sealing and unsealing functions in handheld terminals. It allows work flow configuration to enable management of business processes, provide visibility of current container movements for further supply chain operational benefits and offers a register of authority enabling selected personnel to perform seal and unseal activities.

Figure 3.12.4 Current SST participants

Category	Participants
Supply Chain and Security Domain Expertise	Stanford Global Supply Chain Forum, King's Point Merchant Marine Academy, MIT, Pinkerton Logistics, Georgia Institute of Technology, and Transportation Logistics Institute. *- These institutions are assisting in the security assessment, process analysis, evaluation, and the development of an economic model for efficiency and security*
Shippers (Importers)	Target, Boeing, GE, Unilever, Michelin, Dow Chemical, Semblog Logistics, Transoceanic, LINE Logistics, PSA Logistics, Venture Mfg., and Batmindo *- Total of 15 shippers and service providers across 13 vertical industry sectors.*
Global Port Operators	**Stevedoring Services of America**: largest terminal operator in the Western Hemisphere (16M teus') **Hutchison Port Holdings**: largest port operator in the world, over 30% of world's container trade (30 ports) **PSA Ports**: second largest port operator, 18 ports worldwide, including China **P & O Ports**: 20 ports worldwide, including many regional ports **China Merchant**: operator of 6 ports worldwide
US Port Authorities	Port of Seattle, Port of Tacoma, Port of Los Angeles, Port of Long Beach, Port of New York/New Jersey, Port of Houston, Port of Savannah, and Port of Charleston
US Terminal Operators	Stevedoring Services of America, Eagle Marine Services, Marine Terminals Corporation, Total Terminals Inc., P&O Ports, Georgia Ports, Charleston Port Authority, Port of Houston Authority
Carriers	Mitsui OSK Lines, Evergreen, Hanjin, Yang Ming, K-Line

Service Providers	Sandler Travis Trade Advisory Services, SembLog, Parsons Brinckerhoff, SAIC, Cotecna (3rd party shipment inspection), Pinkerton, and Boeing
Technology Providers	Oracle, Qualcomm, Savi Technology, OneSeal, Symbol, Intermec, Sun Microsystems, Compaq, Microsoft, IBM, EXE, Manugistics, Vigilos (security integration: access control, video surveillance, and perimeter security) *- Total solution approach combining 13 different technologies to enable supply chain security*
Infrastructure	CIMC (world's largest container manufacturer), Transamerica (world's largest container lessor), GE Capital Container Leasing, Savi Technology, and Qualcomm *- Prototyping new types of low cost, smart and secure containers*

Conclusions

The economic benefits of SST networks are many. In terms of substitution cost savings, direct and indirect cost avoidance is attributed to the substitution of existing 24-hour AMR compliance and security processes with automated processes, thus reducing bill of lading surcharges and expedited freight. There is also a reduction of safety stock as a result of improved certainty. Across-the-board direct and indirect savings result from improved trade compliance, reduced United States customs inspections and incidents of cargo thefts. Fundamental or structural savings and margin increases can also be achieved. This is due to the flexibility provided by improved container security, transparency and visibility. This means reduction in safety stock from reductions in transit time variations or inventory optimization, or margin increases from improved transparency and customer service. There are also reductions in human error costs, reductions in insurance premiums and reductions in manual security processes. All of these measures are essential in dramatically reducing, if not altogether eliminating security threats and facilitating trade in the global trade lanes.

Chapter 3.13
Implementing Supply Chain Security in the Global Logistics Network

Richard Pearson, Managing Director, Rotterdam, for Hutchison Ports Holdings

In my paper, I will highlight some of the key benefits, hurdles and challenges that concern logistics companies and subsequently the global trade networks when it comes to supply chain security and trade facilitation, in the light of the experience of Hutchinson Port Holdings (HPH). HPH is one of the world's leading port investors, developers, and operators. We operate 175 berths in 31 ports and 15 different countries in Asia, the Middle East, Africa, Europe and the Americas.

Figure 3.13.1. HPH global logistics network

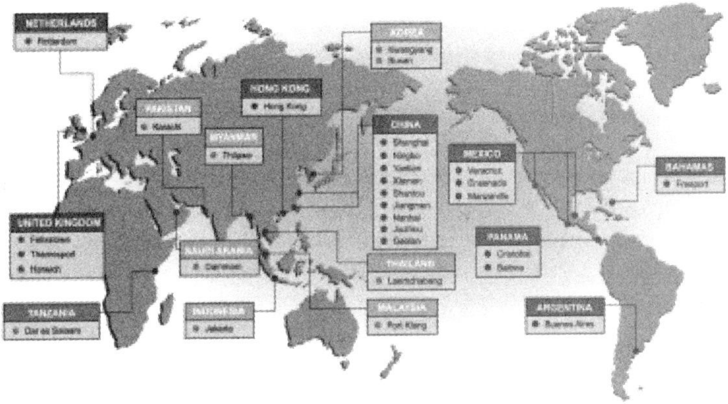

In 2002 HPH handled 35.8 million TEU[58]. In addition to our port services, through Hutchinson Whampoa Limited we expanded our investments in the telecommunications sector, property and hotels, retail and manufacturing, and energy and infrastructure. The scope of the network can be seen in Figure 3.13.1. With over a century in the transport and logistics business, we at HPH firmly believe in the importance of and the benefits that can be drawn from efficient security measures protecting the supply chain. Proper security not only secures the integrity of the supply chain but it also increases the visibility into the status of shipments, drives operational efficiencies and improves businesses' ability to manage all global inventory in real time.

There are a number of ways to achieve supply chain security. Transparency and visibility of different stages in the supply chain, and the development of a single, common-user system for enhanced operational clarity are some of the key requirements. Aspects of physical security such as the provision of an effective barrier to prevent loss and act as a deterrent, and the enhanced ability to detect any breach immediately while automatically informing the appropriate authorities is equally important. Effective forensics and competence in collecting historical data in order to provide an accurate audit trail for each container move is also essential in achieving adequate supply chain security levels.

In addition to the above measures and given our long-standing experience in the business, we consider that there are three essential factors when implementing supply chain security. The first factor to consider is the constant effort to improve practices and procedures which look at the combined input of people, process and technology. Effective communication and thus collaboration between all supply chain participants and regulatory bodies is also critical.

---

[58] TEU is an abbreviation for 'twenty-foot equivalent unit'. One TEU represents the cargo capacity of a standard container 20 feet long, 8 feet wide, and (usually) a little over 8 feet high, or half the capacity of a similar container 40 feet long. One TEU equals about 12 register tons or 34 cubic meters.

Thirdly, we find that selling and sharing the benefits of security enhancements and "best practice" to all supply chain participants reinforces effective trade partnerships and bolsters participants' commitment to the supply chain security.

At the micro-level, one of the most important operational aspects of supply chain security is smart and secure trade lanes (SSTs). These are important in that they clear procedures for loading containers at the point of origin.

Figure 3.13.2. Smart and secure trade lanes participants

	Participants
Supply Chain Domain Expertise (to evaluate supply chain vulnerabilities and solutions)	Stanford Global Supply Chain Forum, Transportation Logistics Institute, King's Point Merchant Marine Academy, MIT, Georgia Institute of Technology *(Note: These organisations are assisting the process analysis, evaluation, and the development of an economic model for efficiency and security)*
Shippers (Importers)	Target, GE, Boeing, Hewlett Packard, Unilever, Michelin, Expeditors Int'l., UPS/Fritz, Kuehne & Nagel, Semblog Logistics, Transoceanic, Maersk Logistics, LINE Logistics, PSA Logistics
Global Port Operators	SSA, Hutchison Port Holdings, PSA, P&O Ports
US Port Authorities	Port of Seattle, Port of Tacoma, Port of Los Angeles, Port of Long Beach, Port of New York/New Jersey, Port of Houston, Port of Savannah, and Port of Charleston
US Terminal Operators	APL, Marine Terminal Corporation, Total terminals Inc., Hanjin, P&O Port Newark Container Terminal, Georgia Ports, Charleston Port Authority, Port of Houston Authority
Carriers	Mitsui OSK Lines, Evergreen, Hanjin, Yang Ming
Service Providers	Parsons Brinckerhoff, SAIC, Sandler Travis Trade Advisory Services, Cotecna, Boeing

Technology Providers	Qualcomm, Savi Technology, OneSeal, Symbol, Intermec, Sun Microsystems, Compaq, Microsoft, IBM, Oracle, EXE, Manugistics, Vigilos
Infrastructure	CIMC, Transamerica

Moreover, they ensure the integrity of upstream security when background screening is carried out on authorized individuals. The operational logic of smart and secure trade lanes is for authorized personnel to affix an electronic seal (*E-seal*) to the container and digitally certify that they have verified the content of the sealed container. The former procedure is further supplemented by data capturing hardware and software infrastructure, which have been installed at ports and other SST participants, such as mobile handheld "readers". Subsequently, through the application of these customized hardware and software security systems, SST participants have the capability to monitor all activity in real-time at strategic checkpoints and in-transit from point of loading until final destination. A list of existing and involved participants in the operation of smart and secure trade lanes can be seen on Figure 3.13.2.

There are a number of additional or extra precautionary measures that can be employed and costs to be incurred to bolster supply chain security. The use of security fencing, access controls, recruitment of more security guards and port security officers, as well as better protected storage and higher insurance coverage, are examples of such measures and costs that can be added on.

Given the latest developments in world affairs and particularly due to the rise of terrorist threats, governments have instituted heightened protective measures and new security initiatives to remedy the rising threats and potential harm to global trade networks and supply chains. With the United States being the hardest hit (by these new developments), it is understandable that some of the most progressive, and in many ways controversial security initiatives have been drafted by the US administration. In spite of their contentious nature and because they significantly affect the global trade networks, in the next section, I would like to talk about some of these initiatives and what they are about.

Among the mentioned security initiatives and new protective measures that directly affect international trade and supply networks was the development of the Smart & Secure Trade Lanes Initiative (SST), the Container Security Initiative (CSI), the International Ship & Port Facility Security code (ISPFS code), the Customs-Trade Partnership Against Terrorism (C-TPAT), Automatic Identification System (AIS), the *Tran*sport *Sec*urity (Transec), Safety of Life at Sea (SOLAS), Strategic Council on Security Transport (SCST). The US Port and Marine Security Act is another example of a US national security initiative which directly impacts port and sea transport.

In response to higher security concerns related to transport of cargo in containers, the US Port and Marine Security Act came into effect in 2002 mandating all ports, facilities and vessels to instigate comprehensive security/incident response plans, and coordinate between all relevant authorities. To achieve the former, the Act mandates a regional Area Maritime Transportation Security Plan, developed by the Coast Guard, as well as it directs the US DOT to develop regulations to create secure areas in ports, and to limit access to sensitive areas (e.g. through the issuance of identity cards, and background checks of employees). In an efforts for greater coordination among different agencies, the Act established local port security committees to act as a focal point for federal, state, local and private law enforcement agencies. The Act aims to boost supply chain security by allowing for secure maritime borders and an efficient cargo transportation system through initiatives such as the implementation of enforceable standards for container seals/locks. It further requires that all cargo be pre-cleared for entry into the US at the port of origin and for commercial vessels to be equipped with and operate an automatic identification system (AIS) when navigating in US waters. Moreover, the Coast Guard is authorised to board and search ships entering US ports while the Secretary of Transportation is directed to assess the anti-terrorism measures maintained by foreign ports, and to deny entry to vessels that call on ports with insufficient security regimes.

The Maritime Security Advisory Committee was also created to make recommendations on national maritime security matters and to be supported by the developments of a maritime intelligence system, which will collect and analyse information on vessels operating in waters under US jurisdiction.

Unilateral in nature, the above security measures introduced by the US administration have significant spill-over effects on different participants in trade logistics and repercussions for the implementation of supply chain security. The former clearly demonstrates the complex and often-vulnerable nature of global trade logistics and the diverse demands placed upon them as trade flows increase and external circumstances change. We at HPH believe that it is only through joint effort, where all stakeholders involved in trade commit to implementing efficient policies and security measures, that goods can securely and in real time reach their destinations. Through close collaboration, commitment and effective application of technology, supply chain security can be achieved.

Part Four:

Open Regionalism

The contributions to this chapter reflect the understanding that standards, best practices, recommendations and other instruments for trade facilitation are developed globally, using local expertise, but are implemented most often on a regional or bilateral level. Ms. Ventura-Dias also points to certain ambiguities in the term, and the link of trade facilitation to other issues in international trade, such as rules of origin.

Chapter 4.1
The UNECE Experience in Trade Facilitation
Carol Cosgrove-Sacks, Director, UNECE Trade Development and Timber Division, Tom Butterly, Team Header, Trade Facilitation UNECE

Trade facilitation as a key tool in economic development

Economic development and poverty reduction are key United Nations goals. Trade, and the facilitation of trade, can play a leading role in achieving these goals. Indeed, following many years of multilateral trade liberalization under the General Agreement on Tariffs and Trade, implementing trade facilitation measures is now generally regarded as being more effective than reducing tariffs for developing international trade.

Trade facilitation is particularly important for the UNECE region, which accounts for two thirds of world trade. Reducing the multibillion-dollar costs of trade transactions is a high priority for our member states, both from a competitiveness and efficiency perspective. A properly facilitated trade infrastructure is also a major asset in attracting and maintaining foreign investment.

The United Nations places great emphasis on sharing the gains of globalization and the full, equitable and open participation of all countries in trade, for the benefit of all, and trade facilitation can contribute to achieving this objective. For example, UN Millennium Development Goal 8 seeks to "develop further an open trading and financial system that is rule-based, predictable and non-discriminatory and includes a commitment to good governance, development and poverty reduction – both nationally and internationally".[59] The recent report by the UN Secretary-General (*Strengthening the United Nations*, September 2002) further states that the

---

[59] UN Millennium Development Goals, www.un.org/millenniumgoals, October 2002

development and implementation of a proper framework of rules, norms and standards for international trade is necessary to help the international community respond effectively to the challenges posed by globalization.[60]

Current trends in trade facilitation

The conceptual thinking around trade and transport facilitation has changed radically in recent years. While once considered a back-room technical issue, trade facilitation has now emerged as a critical element of trade and economic policy. This is reflected in the fact that trade facilitation is a key issue for negotiation in the WTO Doha Development round. Countries should re-examine their current strategies and procedures on this issue in order to take advantage of the latest developments and to better position themselves for any possible strengthened inclusion of trade facilitation into the WTO process.

Another important trend is the shift in emphasis from the development of trade facilitation technical instruments to implementing existing recommendations, tools and techniques, especially in transition and developing countries. A concerted effort will be required in this area and the UNECE secretariat is developing strategies to achieve greater implementation in UNECE Member States.

There is also an increased emphasis on the sustainable development aspect of trade facilitation. It has to be conceived and implemented within a global cost-benefit framework: facilitating trade while at the same time conserving the earth's scarce resources.

The new security focus presents a unique challenge and opportunity to re-examine current trade procedures and processes and to speed up the implementation of advanced technologies and approaches, such as risk assessment based on advance information. The challenge is to facilitate the majority of legitimate international cargo movements, and as efficiently as possible, while at the same time dealing effectively with the small

---

[60] Strengthening of the United Nations: an agenda for further change, Report of the Secretary General (A/57/387), September 2002, page 10

percentage that could pose a threat to security. To achieve this, all parties in the trade transaction chain need to work closely together.

UNECE's regional approach

Regional and sub-regional trade development and cooperation has been deepening and expanding in recent years, and this is likely to continue. Trade facilitation will, therefore, logically be implemented at the regional level. However, it is essential to base such regional approaches to implementation on international standards. These standards provide countries with a scalable approach to trade facilitation – utilizing the same norms and standards as their trade grows both within the region and beyond the region.

Within this environment, the UN regional commissions can play an increasingly important role in developing both a regional and trans-regional approach to trade facilitation. UNECE will actively participate in the regional commissions' joint project for promoting trade as an engine of growth through knowledge management, information and communication technology. This project, which is to be implemented in 2004-2006, aims to strengthen both the international competitiveness and the negotiating capacity of developing countries in trade facilitation and e-business. It will focus on sharing knowledge of problems and best practices in the various countries and regions on trade promotion and diversification; a greater participation of small and medium-sized enterprises (SMEs) in global supply networks; designing and implementing trade facilitation policies at national and regional levels, and a greater use of knowledge management and information and communication technologies in supply chain management.

UNECE approaches trade facilitation from both a global and regional perspective. At the global level, we develop international standards that are freely available to all countries and greatly facilitate the flow of world trade. Our implementation activities, on the other hand, focus exclusively on UNECE member states and we place particular emphasis on assisting implementation activities in transition economies.

In both cases, we adopt a perspective that covers the total trade transaction process from the producer to the final consumer.

We also facilitate the debate on policy development at both the regional and global level. The International Forum on Trade Facilitation is one example. This type of activity has become more important in recent years with the increased emphasis on the policy dimension of trade facilitation.

Our work over the past decades has resulted in over 30 Recommendations being developed under the Centre for Trade Facilitation and Electronic Business (UN/CEFACT). Many of these instruments, such as the United Nations Layout Key for trade documents (Recommendation 1) and the UN/EDIFACT standard for electronic commerce, have been implemented worldwide and have greatly facilitated trade. UNECE's work on agricultural quality standards is also widely used in global trade. We have developed close to 100 standards in fresh fruit and vegetables, dry and dried produce, early and ware potatoes, seed potatoes, eggs, meat and cut flowers. Many of these standards serve as the basis for European Union legislation and Codex Alimentarius standards, which are promoted by all member States of the Organisation for Economic Co-operation and Development (OECD). We also carry out extensive work on technical harmonization and standardization policies, providing a unique intergovernmental forum for debating and addressing issues related to the coordination, harmonization and conformity assessment of standards and associated accreditation issues.

Our *Strategic Plan for Trade Development for 2003-2005* details an ambitious but realizable programme of work aimed at enhancing international trade. It includes:

- **Developing and maintaining** effective international trade-related instruments, norms, standards and recommendations, in response to the needs of the global economy;
- Reducing barriers to trade in goods and services in all countries, and UNECE member States in particular, through greater **implementation** of international and UNECE norms, standards, instruments and recommendations, especially in trade facilitation;

- **Trade facilitation policy development** through the provision of an international platform for the exchange of views, particularly for the benefit of countries with economies in transition. Examples include trade security, European integration and sustainable development;
- **Promoting the** value and effectiveness of trade facilitation instruments and standards in trade and economic development;
- **Integrating** UNECE's trade activities with those of other United Nations (UN) and international trade-related bodies.

The Plan covers work on many projects in the above areas and includes new developments in the trade facilitation area such as:

- Single Window Recommendation, 2003 (Recommendation and implementation guide in 2004)
- Recommendation and guide to Trade Facilitation Benchmarking (Guide will be available later in 2003, Recommendation in 2004)
- Contribution to Trade Facilitation and Security (see background paper by Mr Hans Carl for a proposed collaborative approach)
- Enhancement of the International Supply Chain Reference Model - to focus on trade security and trade facilitation policy development.
- Development of Policy papers on trade facilitation and standards

The implementation guide to the Single Window will include a survey of all existing single windows, outlining what was useful, what worked, what were the lessons learned, etc. The Trade Facilitation Benchmarking Guide and Recommendation will provide countries with tools to measure progress and to see where their achievements are situated with respect to those of other countries. Benchmarking can also help countries measure the progress they are making in implementation. It is also of value in capacity-building projects to measure the impact of the project. We are working closely with SITPRO, the United Kingdom's trade facilitation organization, who are very active in this area.

Trade facilitation and security – a collaborative approach

Security has emerged as a key area of concern for international trade and this has important implications for trade facilitation. We believe that a properly facilitated trade environment will enhance trade security but we must ensure that efforts to improve security do not roll back the gains made in trade facilitation over the past decades. Rather, we have to be very vigilant in both of these areas to ensure the establishment of norms and standards that address the needs of all players in international trade. We must also work to ensure that security initiatives do not result in the exclusion of particular regions or countries from international trade, as this would directly conflict with the overall United Nations goal of an open and inclusive approach to trade.

We support the recent work undertaken by the WCO aimed at maintaining the balance between trade facilitation and security. However, this is a very big task and we believe that strong collaboration between the major relevant organisations will be required in order to ensure a harmonized and least disruptive approach to trade facilitation and security. Suggestions in this regard are outlined in the paper by Mr Hans Carl of IMMTA published in this volume.

Implementation and capacity building

In trade facilitation, the focus has shifted from technical standards development to the policy and economic development implications. It is at the policy level where the decision to implement trade facilitation measures really takes place. Without strong political will, both at the government and business level, implementation will never take place. We strongly support a diverse approach to implementation, with local application within a local context, provided it is based on international standards. UNECE's Recommendations, which are based on best practice, share the experiences of the business community and governments around the world on how they have implemented trade facilitation, what works, and what may not.

UNECE is assisting its Member States in this implementation process. For example, we have a joint project with two of the other regional commissions: the Economic and Social Commission for Western Asia (ESCWA) and the Economic Commission for Africa (ECA) entitled *Capacity Building in Trade Facilitation and Electronic Business in the Mediterranean*. Several capacity building exercises have already taken place under this project (including a workshop in Malta in June 2003) with businesses and government representatives to look at ways to implement trade facilitation.

Other capacity building projects in the trade area undertaken by UNECE include:

- Capacity building to Improve Trade Finance and Investment Prospects for the Sustainable Development of the Russian Timber Sector
- United Nations extensions for aligned electronic trade documents (UNeDocs) – see the articles on this topic in Part Five below
- Development assistance for the implementation of Electronic Data Interchange (UN/EDIFACT) information technologies in selected eastern European countries
- Participation in the Southeast European Cooperative Initiative (SECI)
- Participation in the United Nations Special Programme for the Economies of Central Asia
- Collaboration with World Trade Organization (WTO) in the Doha Development Agenda
- Seminars on quality control for perishable produce
- Implementation of the UNECE recommendation on International Model for Technical Harmonization
- Strengthening of the UNECE Trade Multiplier Point programme
- Development of additional promotional and information material, both electronically and in hard copy.
- Broad range of publications.

We strongly believe in public-private sector partnership in capacity building, because we feel there will never be enough donor money available for this. In our experience, there is often financing available in countries from the private sector, especially if you can develop a strategy where there are revenue gains both for the government and for the private sector.

Conclusion

UNECE cooperates closely with the other United Nations regional commissions, the United Nations Conference on Trade and Development (UNCTAD), the European Union (EU), the WTO, the Food and Agriculture Organization (FAO), ISO and many other national, regional and intergovernmental organizations in the development of an open-end, efficient trade environment. We believe that such a collaborative approach is the only appropriate model for developing trade facilitation development and we strongly encourage both governments and the business community to adopt this approach and to use the work and instruments of UNECE and other relevant organizations in enhancing their trade environment.

Chapter 4.2
The Role of ESCWA in Promoting Trade Facilitation

Nabil Safwat, Chief, Transport and Trade Facilitation Team (TTF), ESCWA

The Economic and Social Commission for Western Asia (ESCWA) is one of the five regional economic commissions of the United Nations. It comprises 13 Arab member States in Western Asia extending from Iraq and the Gulf countries in the east to Egypt in the west, Syria in the north and Oman and Yemen in the south.

One of the most important issues for regional cooperation and integration in Western Asia is the facilitation of trade and transport between ESCWA member countries. Intra-regional trade represents less than 10% of total international trade of ESCWA countries. This weak interaction is mainly due to the complexities of border formalities, administrative procedures, required documentation and unpredictable high costs and delays at border crossing points.

Facilitation of international trade and transport is a multifaceted approach that involves improvements in the infrastructure as well as the operation of the international transport, trade and administration systems.

In May 1999, a statement was issued by ESCWA member countries in which they agreed on the start of the development of the Integrated Transport System in the Arab Mashreq (ITSAM), and the adoption of the regional transport network including the major roads, railways, seaports and airports of international importance in the region. Efforts to develop the ITSAM have proceeded in three major tracks, namely the integrated regional transport network, the associated information system and the methodological framework for policy analysis.

Following extensive efforts since 1998, the ESCWA member countries adopted on 10 May 2001 the Agreement on International Roads in the Arab Mashreq (the "Roads Agreement"). As of today 11 out of 13 ESCWA members have signed the Roads Agreement and four have ratified it. The Roads Agreement is the first United Nations treaty to be negotiated within ESCWA and, therefore, represented according to the UN Secretary-General, Mr. Kofi Anan, a significant landmark in the history of the Commission. The Roads Agreement will enter into force 90 days after the ratification of five ESCWA members. This is expected to happen very soon.

More recently, on 14 April 2003 in Beirut, a similar Railways Agreement (i.e., the Agreement on International Railways in the Arab Mashreq) was adopted by ESCWA member states during the 22nd session of the Commission. As of today 8 out of 13 countries have signed the Railways Agreement.

Efforts have been made by ESCWA to simplify and improve trade and transport procedures, since the late 1970s; however, with limited success. Since 1998 the subject is being tackled again with renewed vigour. During 1998 and 1999 a major study and an expert group meeting on trade efficiency were conducted. These resulted in an action plan including the establishment of national facilitation committees. In 2000, a major field study on the facilitation of international freight transport procedures in the region was completed. The six-volume study contains a detailed review of trade procedures including a comparative analysis in five selected member countries, namely Egypt, Jordan, Lebanon, Syria and the United Arab Emirates. The study also identified obstacles and their causes. Eleven major recommendations were formulated to facilitate trade in the region, i.e., simplification of formalities, procedures and documentation; transparency; abolishing illegal practices; development of human resources; computerization and the application of Information and Communications Technologies (ICT); institutional, legal and administrative reforms; unification of goods valuation methods and tariff classification; adoption of non-stop working hours; the conclusion of new agreements and accession to existing ones; and the implementation of multimodal transport. Moreover, the study recognized the importance of setting up national facilitation committees as a first priority to ensure the effective implementation of these recommendations that were endorsed by the twenty-first session of ESCWA in May 2001.

Along with such recommendations, ESCWA took further proactive steps during 2002 and 2003 to promote the creation of semi-permanent frameworks for government-private sector consultation and cooperation, with the view that this would speed up the implementation of facilitation measures in member countries and ensure that trade efficiency reforms would be client oriented. A guide for the establishment of National Transport and Trade Facilitation Committees (NTTFC) in the ESCWA region was published in Arabic. Pursuant to ESCWA recommendation and utilizing the NTTFC Guide, four members (Jordan, Syria, Yemen, and Palestine) have issued cabinet decrees to establish NTTFCs. Egypt and Saudi Arabia have initiated positive steps in the same direction.

ESCWA is very much aware of the fact that national facilitation committees have been established in several developing countries and transitional economies with various levels of success and that successful trade facilitation reforms require strong political will and long-term commitment; a clear vision; adequate resources, both human and technical; and close cooperation between and among the private and public sectors. Therefore ESCWA is currently deploying considerable efforts for capacity building in the field of Facilitation both within relevant government agencies and important stakeholders in the private sector.

In this respect we are particularly pleased to be an integral part of two joint projects funded by the United Nations Development Account. The first is a $1.25 million five-year (2002-2006) project for capacity building in developing interregional land and land-sea transport linkages and is jointly implemented by the five UN regional commissions with ESCWA being the project coordinator. The second is a $600,000 two-year (2002-2003) project on capacity building in trade facilitation and electronic business in the Mediterranean, jointly implemented in cooperation with the United Nations economic commissions for Europe and Africa (UNECE and ECA). Under the second project, an interregional seminar was conducted on 29-31 January 2003 in Geneva. Parties to the project agreed on the specific set of activities to be conducted and a tentative timetable for implementation. Of particular interest are the national trade and transport facilitation studies that will be conducted in five participating countries in the ESCWA region including Egypt, Jordan, Lebanon, Syria, and Palestine. Except for Egypt, national consultants would conduct studies in the other four countries. In Egypt, because of additional resources expected to be made available by the Dutch Trust Fund through the World Bank, the study team would be composed of one Dutch consultant to be selected by the World Bank, a regional consultant to be selected by ESCWA in consultation with the Government of Egypt and a team of national experts to be designated by the government. All five studies will subsequently be discussed in national workshops respectively and a regional seminar with participation of the consultants as well as key stakeholders in order to learn from their collective experiences. The studies are expected to complement and update those conducted by ESCWA in 2000.

Several countries in the region are making significant efforts to enhance their respective trade, customs and transport systems. Some are already enhancing their computerization and the application of information and communications technologies. A new customs law was adopted in Lebanon and began implementation on 23 April 2001. Another customs law is being prepared in Egypt. Additional ESCWA countries are expected to accede to existing facilitation conventions. Activities to develop the Integrated Transport System in the Arab Mashreq (ITSAM) will be continued and enhanced.

Promoting the implementation of trade facilitation measures, standards, and recommendations must be done at the regional and sub-regional levels. The role of ESCWA and other sister United Nations regional commissions is vital in promoting trade and transport facilitation in their respective regions. Hence, meaningful plans at the international and national levels need to include a regional dimension and involve the regional commissions.

In conclusion, I would like to recommend that UN/CEFACT and the Forum work together on making more resources available for capacity-building activities in developing countries in the field of trade and transport facilitation. The five UN regional commissions could best work together in coordination with other actors to increase the opportunities and effectiveness of the realization of trade facilitation in developing countries and hence in the international trading system worldwide.

Chapter 4.3
Open Regionalism in Latin America: The Impact on Trade Facilitation

Vivianne Ventura Dias, Director, Division of International Trade and Integration, ECLAC

Open regionalism and preferential rules of origin

The expression "open regionalism" was adopted in Latin America to differentiate the regional economic integration movement of the 1990s from the regionalism of the 1960s. There were major reasons for this: (a) from the mid-1980s to the 1990s, all Latin American countries adopted liberal trade regimes after abandoning the import substitution industrialization model; (b) the scope of their trade preferential agreements was expanded to include flows of capital, the protection of property rights of private investors, the protection of intellectual property rights, and broad regulatory convergence; (c) the membership of such preferential trade agreements (PTAs) also changed to include industrial countries as well as developing countries from other regions.[61]

In particular, Chile and Mexico have individually established quite a few PTAs, including a bilateral agreement between themselves. They became indirect hubs of several agreements with other Latin American countries that ultimately aim at the United States as the dominant hub of a vast network of PTAs. Both countries adopted PTAs as a market access strategy both in terms of trade and investments.

---

[61] It is important to contrast Latin American experience with the concept and performance of open regionalism in Asia-Pacific. Open regionalism in APEC was defined as a process of unilateral liberalization agreed between governments and multilateralized by a Most-Favoured Nation (MFN) clause applied unconditionally.

For many economists, the term "open regionalism' is an oxymoron, a contradiction in terms. Regionalism implies discriminatory trade unless there are mechanisms to progressively extend preferential market access to third parties. Latin American open regionalism is a collection of sub-regional integration schemes, bilateral and plurilateral PTAs with no mechanism to multilateralize the agreed preferences. Bhagwati and Panagariya have compared the complex network of PTAs to the disorder of a spaghetti bowl.[62] They were concerned with the consequences of PTA proliferation on the creation of new barriers to market access that could be generated by fairly selective rules of origin. Partial liberalization agreements necessarily require definitions and procedures to separate goods that are entitled to the contracted benefits from those that are not.

ECLAC has decided to concentrate its research on the operational and administrative aspects of rules of origin. In other words, the focus is on trade facilitation, with a view to streamlining and promoting greater standardization of certification procedures and the overall administration of preferential rules of origin.[63] The term "rules of origin" encompasses a set of rigorous criteria to assign geographical origin to imported goods. They are divided into preferential rules (to prevent products processed in one country, which does not belong to the PTA, from benefiting from trade preferences) and non-preferential rules. The determination of origin is always related to the adoption of a discriminatory measure, except when the purpose is trade data collection.[64]

---

[62] See Bhagwati, J. and Panagariya A. (eds.) (1996), *The Economics of Preferential Trade Agreements*, The AEI Press, Washington, D. C.

[63] See Izam, Miguel (2003), *Rules of origin and trade facilitation in preferential trade agreements in Latin America* (LC/L. 1907-P), Serie Comercio Internacional nro. 31, July, ECLAC, Santiago de Chile. See also the full version in Spanish *Normas de origen y procedimientos para su administracion en América Latina*, (LC/L.1907-P), Serie Comercio Internacional nro. 28, May, ECLAC, Santiago de Chile.

[64] UNCTAD (1998), *Globalization and the international trading system - questions related to rules of origin*, (UNCTAD/ITCD/TSB/2), Geneva.

As with any set of rules, certain formalities must be followed which entail public and private costs. The public sector has to enforce the rules of origin and implement proper controls with a view to monitoring external trade in goods, minimizing budgetary expenditures, and transaction costs. Likewise, private agents involved in preferential trade will be required to follow certain procedures, which should be efficient and expeditious. Although there is no single definition of the term "trade facilitation", all working definitions take into account the matter of customs procedures, and many also explicitly refer to rules of origin. In both cases, the idea is to reduce the transaction costs associated with internationally traded goods. The proliferation of PTAs with different families of rules of origin and related procedures may, however, add elements of "complication" to trade.

In Latin America, there are three "families" of rules of origin that were generated by three types of PTAs: (a) the traditional economic complementation agreements signed in the context of the Latin American Integration Association (LAIA); (b) PTAs signed with Canada, Chile, Mexico, and the United States that follow the lines set up by the North American Free Trade Agreement (NAFTA), and (c) PTAs signed with the European Union. The direct and indirect costs to exporters are significant although they are not easy to quantify. This paper provides a brief review of the main problems brought by the operation of these three sets of rules. The purpose is to draw attention to the effects of the lack of standard definitions and procedures for assigning origin to goods on transaction costs associated with internationally traded goods.

Rules of origin: conceptual and economic problems

In the context of highly mobile enterprises and in the presence of global supply chains, rules of origin necessarily become complex. They are increasingly based on content requirements as well as on the identification of processing operations that should be performed in the countries belonging to the PTA. Until the Agreement on Rules of Origin, as one of the results of the Uruguay Round, there were no multilateral disciplines for assigning origin to imported goods. The World Trade Organization (WTO), however, has not yet developed binding multilateral disciplines for preferential rules of origin. Some progress has been made, although only in the field of non-preferential rules of origin in the context of trade policy instruments applied to MFN trade (e.g. antidumping duties, quantitative restrictions, safeguards, trade statistics, and public procurement, others).[65]

In the global economy, goods that are entirely processed in the exporting country are exceptional cases. The majority of goods that are internationally traded incorporate in their production inputs produced in several other countries. Rules of origin define the conditions under which products with inputs processed in third countries should observe in order to ensure that they can be considered as originated in the country member of the PTA. Generally, rules of origin are based on the concept of substantial transformation, which defines the minimum level of processing and the characteristics of inputs originated in third countries that classify the product as originated in the exporting country member. The nature of the substantive rules to attribute origin to a product determines the level of protection that they provide. Narrowly defined rules of origin in one PTA can affect third-country producers of inputs. On the other hand, loose rules of origin will allow third countries to supply inputs to the preferential area through the territory of the country with a more open trade regime (trade deflection). Consequently, preferences will be given to products that are only superficially processed in the preferential area.

It is difficult to estimate the costs derived from the compliance with rules of origin, either in terms of trade deviation of in terms of their administration. There are technical difficulties related to the measurement of *ex-ante* and *ex-post* situations, mostly because suppliers from third countries prefer to operate in countries that are members of the agreement. Some authors have estimated that the administrative costs may account for roughly 1.4% to 5.7% of export value.

---

[65] The harmonization of criteria for determining origin is a complex task even for non-preferential rules. For instance, in the case of fruit juices, governments have to agree on whether origin is ascribed to the country that produces the fruit or to the country that processes the imported fruit (Thorstensen, V., 2002, "Regras de origen, as negociaçoes e implicaçoes para a política de comércio exterior", *Revista Brasileira de Comércio Exterior*, octubre-diciembre, págs. 42-53.

Garay and Cornejo have indicated that net operational costs tend to increase with a higher level of administrative complexity, the lack of transparence in the procedures, the multiplicity in the criteria of certification and the diversity of rules of origin.[66]

A recent study analyzed the network of rules of origin as barriers to intra-area trade, with reference to the case of NAFTA.[67] Using disaggregated trade data between Mexico and the United States at six-digit level, between 1992 and 2000, the authors concluded that there had been reduced modifications in the industry composition of Mexican exports to the United States, particularly in sensitive sectors such as textiles, apparel, shoes, food, and steel products, in which preferences are high but rules of origin are very restrictive. The empirical evidence suggests that rules of origin protect intermediate inputs produced in industrial countries, which end up being the real beneficiaries of preferential trade liberalization.

Rules of origin and trade facilitation in Latin America

In Latin America, several origin regimes coexist with different criteria and administrative procedures. First, there is the regime created by the LAIA that was adopted by the Andean Community and the Caribbean Community (CARICOM). Second, there is the NAFTA regime, which has become the model for all PTAs negotiated with Canada, Chile, Mexico, and the United States. There are also intermediates schemes, such as that found in the Central American Common Market (CACM) and the European Union criteria introduced in the recent PTAs signed with Chile and Mexico.

The rules of origin have moved towards greater product selectivity as opposed to general criteria of LAIA. In NAFTA, rules of origin are also defined at the level of product at six-digit level of the Harmonized System

---

[66] Garay S., L. J. Y R. Cornejo, 2001, Metodología para el análisis de regímenes de origen. Aplicación en el caso de las Américas, *Intal ITD/STA Documento de Trabajo 8*, September, Buenos Aires.

[67] Cadot, O., y J. De Melo, A. Esvadeordal, A. Suwa-Eisenmann, B. Tumurchudur (2002), Assessing the effect of Nafta´s rules of origin (World Bank).

(HS). Likewise, the rules of origin negotiated between LAIA members and the European Union were negotiated product by product, which makes them very selective. The LAIA rules of origin are simp le and general in nature, although product-specific rules are also allowed. The basic criterion for origin qualification in the agreements negotiated is a change in the tariff nomenclature at four-level digit (HS), or a change in the value of regional content equal or superior to 50% of the FOB value of the product. Nonetheless, country members can adopt specific origin requirements for a given set of goods.[68]

For instance, the Mercosur regime establishes the requirement of 60% of aggregated value together with a change in the tariff schedule. When the substantial transformation cannot be measured by means of movements in the tariff classification, the value CIF of inputs originated in third parties cannot exceed 40% of FOB value of the product. There are also specific requirements for sectors such as chemical, steel, and information and communication technology.

And there are direct costs associated with the compliance with rules of origin, since inputs become more expensive. Further, there are operational and administrative costs related to the issuance and verification of certificates of origin, with reference to both customs and exporting enterprises. The rules of origin applied under NAFTA and the PTAs between Latin American countries and the European Union require efficient and detailed procedures and mechanisms to enforce them. In the case of PTAs under LAIA rules of origin, as well as in those between LAIA members and the European Union, issuance of origin certificates involves a governmental agency (public law). LAIA rules allow the public sector to delegate the origin certificates issuance to the private sector. In any case, the origin certificate must be revised and authenticated by a public institution. NAFTA-type agreements allow exporting enterprises to be directly responsible by the emission of origin certificate without the interference of public authority (private law). Moreover, the enterprise can use the same certificate for similar operations for a whole year whereas in LAIA and European Union origin regimes the certificate has to be issued

---

[68] Garay S., L. J. Y R. Cornejo, 2001, op. cit.

for each commercial transaction. In the NAFTA family of rules of origin, when doubts arise on the origin or of fraud, the private parties involved sort out the problem.

Both in the NAFTA and the European Union family of rules of origin, the costs of non-compliance with formal rules of origin fall on importers. In NAFTA rules, if fraud is discovered, the responsibility falls on the exporter, as the certification issuer. In the European Union rules, in case of further doubts, there are consultations between the national public institutions involved. In the LAIA family of rules, there are no clear procedures for the settlement of disputes. If an origin certificate does not fulfil the formal procedures, the authority of importing country will contact the public institution in the exporting country, which should adopt the necessary measures to solve the problem that was created. There are no clear procedures or deadlines. Since LAIA does not have a dispute-settlement tribunal, each agreement has had to define its dispute settlement mechanism.

Oversight in connection with certificates of origin in the three families of rules is a complex and sometimes a slow process. Oversight is undoubtedly more stringent in NAFTA, which uses basically two methods for verifying origin, which are not exclusive. The first involves the use of questionnaires, which are widely used because of their low cost, although they are less efficient than the second method, which entails sending inspectors to the exporting country to verify the documents, and ultimately the plants in which the goods are produced or assembled but is not often used because of the high costs involved. The parties concerned can use their own institutions to resolve this type of conflict, or if previously agreed, have recourse to the specialized body in WTO.

In the PTAs between LAIA members and the European Union, national authorities can enforce the rules of origin and require evidence by inspecting the accounting books of exporting enterprises. They are entitled also to require any kind of document that they may consider relevant to a full investigation and due process. Authorities from the importing country can promote random search when doubts exist with respect to formal procedures of origin certificates.

In case of strong doubts, customs authorities of the importing country will send back the documents to those of exporting country requesting background documents.

The current negotiations on the Free Trade Area of the Americas (FTAA) provide a clear indication of the lack of consensus on certain operational issues relating to preferential rules of origin. The United States has proposed a new procedure that is different from that of NAFTA. Under this proposal, importers, who are most likely to be affected in cases of fraud, would issue certificates of origin. The problem is that importers would have difficulties in obtaining the necessary information from exporters, a situation that can discourage and complicate reciprocal preferential trade in goods. Canada, Chile and Mexico have proposed self-certification, while Mercosur has proposed yet another system, which is also different from that suggested by the Andean Community. As a result, despite the considerable progress that has been made so far, there is still no agreement on rules of origin within FTAA.

Final considerations

In Latin America, the wide diplomatic action of Latin American governments to obtain a contracted liberalization of importing markets is a clear indication that they perceive this as the best way to ensure a predictable access to those markets. In parallel to their participation in multilateral negotiations, they have advanced several initiatives with industrialized countries, which include disciplines more restrictive than those that they had previously agreed at the multilateral level. The current negotiations aiming at the creation of the FTAA is the most ambitious of such initiatives.

In determining how efficient a given set of rules of origin is, it is important to take into account not only the content of the rules, but also the formal procedures associated with them. When there are significant differences in the economic capabilities of countries belonging to a PTA, consideration should be given to adopting a system providing for equitable distribution of costs of inspection visits together with improving the administrative capabilities of less developed countries. Since countries will have to learn to live with different preferential rules of origin efforts should be addressed to streamlining certification procedures, including the adoption of electronic signatures as well as an effective mechanism for settling disputes.

Chapter 4.4
Trade Facilitation in a Multilateral Framework: Challenges for Africa

Cornelius T. Mwalwanda, Senior Economic Affairs Officer, United Nations Economic Commission for Africa (ECA)

Many of the contributions to this volume have tried to show the costs and benefits that may arise from intensified efforts at trade facilitation and at the adoption of multilateral rules that could govern "trade facilitation". Indeed, many acknowledge, including us in Africa, that trade facilitation can contribute significantly to reducing "transactions costs" in both domestic and international trade.

As some of the other contributors have stated, trade facilitation should not only be perceived as a "transportation problem", but rather as a broader issue, which straddles many aspects of the weak capacities that exist in many developing countries which inhibit their ability to effectively participate in international trade. This aspect is nowhere more true than in Africa. Accordingly, the problem of trade facilitation in Africa has to be perceived in a broader context of the weak capacities existing in all aspects of African economies, ranging from weak transportation networks, dilapidated communications systems, poor port facilities, lack of automation systems, lack of transparent regulatory frameworks, cumbersome customs procedures and low-level of human capacity.

Many of our countries and sub-regions in Africa accept this fact and indeed have been trying to implement programmes aimed at facilitating trade in Africa. Some of these programmes have included those implemented by sub-regional organizations, such as the Common Market for Eastern And Southern Africa (COMESA), the South African Development Community (SADC), and the Economic Community of West African States (ECOWAS), among many others. In the COMESA sub-region, significant efforts have been expended on harmonization of customs procedures, facilitation of transport systems and networks, development of transport corridors, and automation of trade and customs data. Promotion of a free trade area and a common tariff structure has been one of the milestones in the efforts by COMESA to facilitate trade in Africa. This sub-regional organization has put much effort into regional harmonization of customs and trade statistics systems, developed a standard COMESA customs form and transparent COMESA rules of origin, created databases for producers/exporters/importers, promoted transit corridors in the sub-region, supported cross-border initiatives in order to facilitate trade and encouraged the creation of an Africa Trade Insurance Agency. COMESA has also been promoting the implementation of the "Automated System for Customs Data and Management (ASYCUDA)" developed by UNCTAD in many of its member countries.

Similar efforts have been under way in other sub-regional organizations, such as SADC and ECOWAS. The process of simplifying, harmonizing and speeding up the flow of goods in and out of African countries is progressing rapidly. Many African countries acknowledge the benefits that arise from improved trade facilitation and the economic gains that could be generated. It is in this context that most African countries have welcomed the efforts of institutions and organizations that tried to assist them to develop the requisite capacity needed for trade facilitation. The Economic Commission for Africa (ECA) has played its role when it has been called upon to do so. Nonetheless, most of the efforts on trade facilitation in Africa have been by the sub-regional organizations.

Trade facilitation in Africa: challenges for the future

Effective participation in modern international trade requires that all actors, be they governments, corporations, or individual firms operate on the cutting-edge of technologies not only in the production processes but also in chain management. Globalization and liberalization of the world economy has led to the contestability of domestic markets to a scale never known before and it is placing demands on firms, small and large, to adjust to the new environment or face liquidation and bankruptcy. Reducing transaction costs is one important factor for a firm (and a country) to remain competitive in international markets.

Such an environment poses even greater challenges for corporations and firms operating in third world countries, due to the various constraints and weak capacities that they face. Many African countries fall in this league.

The experience of many African land-locked countries, where the margin between CIF and FOB can be as much as 50%, is a clear example of the savings that can be made from improvements in transport networks in Africa. However, this aspect is more than the traditional notion of "trade facilitation". It becomes a fundamental problem of "development" in African countries.

The challenge that faces many African countries is the need to develop requisite capacities to implement modern techniques for doing trade. Developing the necessary infrastructure and human skills are two of the most important challenges Africa faces. Progress in these two areas is fundamental for African countries to have the capacity to effectively participate in any trade facilitation programmes that may emerge.

In summary, it is essential for African countries that the issue of trade facilitation is positioned within a broader framework, and is responsive to the need to reduce transactions costs to both domestic and international trade in these economies, within a broader framework of engineering economic growth. A narrow view of trade facilitation runs the danger of focusing more on rationalization of trade procedures and less on dealing with the fundamental constraints, which inhibit the participation of these countries in international trade.

The basis for the new security rules governing international trade, while understood and appreciated, poses serious concerns for many African countries. The cost for African countries of implementation and compliance to these new rules for African countries, especially for LDCs, should not be underestimated. The benefits from preferential schemes, such as the African Growth Opportunity Act (AGOA) and Everything but Arms (EBA), could be seriously undermined by the non-tariff barriers emanating from security concerns.

Trade facilitation in a multilateral framework

Many African countries at the Seattle WTO Ministerial Conference, while appreciating the importance of trade facilitation as an "economic phenomenon", expressed reservations at that stage about the need for a "multilateral framework" on trade facilitation. This view was reflected in the positions of many African countries at the Doha WTO Ministerial Conference.

While acknowledging that African countries were coerced to accept the wording of the Doha Declaration on "trade facilitation", many would have preferred for this issue, like many of the Singapore issues, not to be included on the Doha agenda. The *Abuja Ministerial Declaration on the Fourth Ministerial Conference of the WTO*, adopted by African Ministers of Trade in Abuja, Nigeria in September 2001, stated as follows:

> "We recognize that issues such as trade and investment, competition, transparency in government procurement, trade facilitation, trade and environment and e-commerce are important. However, we agree that these issues are not a priority at this stage and on-going processes should continue in order to prepare for possible future work in this area".

Furthermore, in the *Africa's Negotiating Objectives for the Fourth Ministerial Conference of the WTO* adopted by the same Ministerial Conference, Ministers stated that:

> "The general assessment is that trade facilitation measures are necessary and beneficial to all countries. In this context, on-going work within and outside the WTO (e.g. rules of origin, customs valuation) should continue. Improved facilitation will require increased technical and financial assistance to narrow the technology and human resources gaps that exist between developed and developing countries".

As preparations for the Cancún WTO Ministerial Conference progress, certain positions are emerging on the issue of a multilateral framework on trade facilitation. The position that appears to be emerging among LDCs may be stated as follows:

> "Paragraph 27 of the Doha Declaration instructed the Council for Trade in Goods to review and as appropriate clarify and improve the relevant aspects of Articles V, VII and X of the GATT 1994 and identify the trade facilitation needs and priorities of members, in particular developing and LDCs. Some aspects of trade facilitation are vital for LDCs. For instance, the question of understanding of international standards is vital for the promotion of LDC exports. Our standards institutions should be strengthened immediately, so that they can properly advise our exporters. On the other hand, much current thinking on trade facilitation pre-supposes the establishment of common procedures, rules and regulations on the movement of goods. To implement such laws and procedures will be very costly for LDCs, which they cannot afford at this stage. Hence, it is too early for the development of an agreement within the WTO in this area. Outside of the WTO framework, current efforts to assist the LDCs in this area may continue".

Trade facilitation: the need for technical assistance for Africa

African countries will require extensive technical assistance in order to master the art of doing business in a competitive and highly sophisticated trading environment, with or without a multilateral framework on trade facilitation. There is a need to build on the current efforts by African countries individually and collectively through sub-regional economic communities to reduce transaction costs for both domestic and international trade. The Economic Commission for Africa intends to play its modest role in this respect.

Following the First International Forum on Trade Facilitation in May 2002, the United Nations regional economic commissions proceeded to develop a project on trade facilitation.

The objective of the joint project of the five regional commissions is to strengthen both the international competitiveness and the negotiating capacity of developing countries by sharing knowledge on problems and best practices in the various countries and regions on (1) trade promotion and diversification; (2) a greater participation of small and medium-sized enterprises (SMEs) in global supply networks; (3) designing and implementing trade facilitation policies at national and regional levels, and (4) a greater use of knowledge management and information and communication technologies in supply chain management.

This in our view should be the focus of efforts to enhance capacities for trade facilitation in Africa. A great deal needs to be done to equip African countries with the necessary infrastructure and skills needed in order for them to be able to effectively participate in global trade. The ECA, in collaboration with other regional economic communities and UN agencies, intends to play its role in this respect.

Part Five:

United Nations Electronic Trade Documents Project: Digital Paper for Secure and Efficient Supply Chains

The papers in this section describe the achievements and prospects of the United Nations project for electronic trade documents, UNeDocs. With this project, the UNECE offers a tool for electronic trade documents, based on existing national procedures for paper documents, offering easy migration path between different languages and formats (such as XML stylesheet, EDIFACT message, pdf, and paper) using Web Services and international trade document standards (e.g. the UN Layout Key for Trade Documents and the UN Trade Data Elements Directory).

Chapter 5.1
Digital Paper for Trade

Markus Pikart, UNECE, UNeDocs Project Manager, Jean Kubler,
UNECE, e-Med Project Manager, Mario Apostolov, Forum Coordinator

Every year goods to the value of more than $ 5,500 billion are sold on
international markets. In today's open and global economies the exchange
of these goods is managed through increasingly specialized supply chain
processes, relying on sophisticated logistic and information and
communication technologies. However, when analysing the information
exchange that takes place between the supply chain operators one will find
a rather surprising situation: the core information exchange that steers and
controls the acquisition, transport and payment processes is still relying on
traditional, paper based documents. Most current procedures for
international trade are based on the availability of paper documents. The
collision between the digitalized in-house information processing
technology and a historic, analogous document system introduces
enormous costs in the supply chain: paper based trade documentation
usually is estimated to cost between 5 and 10 per cent of the value of traded
goods. Improving standards and technologies for trade documentation is,
therefore, highly important for integration and development in the global
economy.

Standards and technologies for trade documents

The UNECE recognized already in the early 1960s the crucial role of trade
documents in international trade and set up a working party to develop the
United Nations Layout Key (UNLK), an internationally accepted standard
for trade documents. The UNLK made a significant contribution to trade
efficiency by allowing the design of aligned series of trade documents,
such as the Single Administrative Document (SAD), the IATA airway bills,
the FIATA standard freight forwarders documents, or the ICC standard
documentary credit forms.

The work on standardization of international trade documents was later followed by the development of a standard for Electronic Data Interchange (EDI) reflecting the computerization of international trade and the increased need for electronic data exchange. The United Nations Electronic Data Interchange for Administration, Commerce and Transport (UN/EDIFACT) is today the most widely used international EDI standard. However, owing to the high investments required for UN/EDIFACT implementations the technology did not provide for a universal solution for electronic trade documents. UN/EDIFACT is the basis for developing electronic messages for trade, and not exactly the support for trade documents, as we know them, in electronic format.

In recent years, the creation of affordable, global networks such as the internet and related document description standards, such as XML, has provided new opportunities to transmit and process electronic trade documents. It is assumed that the use of electronic trade documents will lead to stronger integration of supply chain processes, significantly reduce transaction costs and risks and contribute to combat fraud. Furthermore, the UNECE believes that by combining electronic documents with coding technologies such as two-dimensional barcodes, a co-existence between paper and electronic document processing can be established. This would facilitate the adoption of electronic documents for SMEs and developing economies, and would open a migration path into electronic business environments.

United Nations electronic trade documents: objective, phases and outputs

The UNECE has therefore initiated the United Nations electronic Trade Documents project (UNeDocs), in which it studies the feasibility of an international standard for aligned electronic trade documents. The project does not aim to eliminate paper documents but rather to open a migration path from paper to electronic documents by defining electronic document layouts that are equivalent to their paper-based peers. The project consists of a research and development phase that will be conducted in cooperation with research institutes and the private sector. Results will be made available on the Internet in the form of standard layouts and data definitions both for paper and electronic documents. Traders and software vendors can then use them to interface between their proprietary systems.

In developing the electronic forms the United Nations will ensure that the solution is compatible with the Internet and affordable standard software systems typically found in small office environments. UNeDocs is based on international trade standards and best practice. It makes use, for example, of the UN Layout Key, a global standard for the layout of international trade documents, recommendations on the use of code lists in international trade and the UN Trade Data Element Directory (ISO 3535), a global definition for trade data elements. The adoption of UN electronic trade documents will thus promote and enforce the application of existing trade facilitation standards and increase the capacity of the country to participate in international trade. As UNeDocs is linking paper and electronic documents, traders can choose the technology they can support best. The transition from paper to electronic documents is an important step towards electronic business and a knowledge-based economy. To provide access to electronic trade documents in transition economies and developing countries the UNECE plans to develop a simple software solution that can be used on the Internet.

The United Nations electronic Trade Documents Project (www.UNeDocs.org) currently prepares a set of international trade documents which can be easily transferred between paper and electronic formats (e.g. UN/EDIFACT and XML) using standard technologies. In a world where trade procedures are still based on paper documents (and both paper and electronic documents have their pros and cons – see Figure 5.1.1), UNeDocs provides an easy path of transfer between paper and electronic modes. The document set will be made available for free to governments and traders worldwide for implementation. UNeDocs electronic documents can provide access to UNECE trade facilitation standards based on latest Internet technology.

Figure 5.1.1. Pros and cons of paper and electronic documents in international trade

Documents:	paper and	electronic
Instantly accessible	+ + + +	+
Global acceptance	+ + +	+
Archiving	+ + +	+ + +
Reproduction	+ +	+ + +
Transmission	+	+ + + +
Standardization	+	+ + + +
ICT integration	0	+ + + +

Recently, major software companies such as Adobe and Microsoft have shown strong interest in the UNeDocs concept and contacted the UNECE. UNeDocs has now started joint research and development to integrate automated access to UNeDocs trade documents into the next generation of standard office software. This will provide traders from SMEs and transition economies with low cost software to participate in automated international supply chains. Traders will have access to UNECE trade standards and best business practice directly from their desktop. The integration is an example how standards combined with latest information and communication technologies can bridge the digital divide and integrate trade. The following chapters provide more detailed information on how this is done in practice.

The objective of the UNeDocs project is to provide technologies and solutions, which would contribute to trade growth, attract investment, and achieve better integration in the regional and world economy. A standard system of electronic documents will improve the flow of trade information across borders and towards customs and other government agencies. For this reason, UNeDocs has the potential of enhancing the global effort to improve the security of international trade.

DIGITAL PAPER FOR TRADE

UNeDocs: cooperation and status

The international nature of trade requires solutions that are accepted and used by traders from all nations. In developing the concept of UNeDocs the UNECE has therefore liaised with its working group for International Trade Procedures (ITPWG), with the UN regional social and economic commissions for Western Asia (ESCWA) and Asia and the Pacific (ESCAP), the United Nations Conference on Trade and Development (UNCTAD) and with private-sector enterprises. UNECE is cooperating on the UNeDocs project with an increasing number of public and private partners, including the Simpler Trade Procedures Board (SITPRO) in the United Kingdom; the Swiss State Secretariat for Economic Affairs (SECO); the United Nations Economic and Social Commission for Western Asia (ESCWA); the International Federation of Freight Forwarders (FIATA); Gesellschaft für Elektronischen Geschäftsverkehr mbH (GEFEG); EDIFOR; the Universal Postal Union (UPU); the OASIS Universal Business Language (UBL); the United Nations Centre for Trade Facilitation and Electronic Business (UN/CEFACT); Canada Post; and Swedish Post. For the further development of UNeDocs, the UNECE welcomes the participation of all interested organizations in the project.

Much has been written and said about the complexity of the contemporary supply chains, but one sometimes forgets that export capability is as strong as the weakest link in the chains, as this is where bottlenecks and blockages occur. The objective of UNeDocs is to strengthen international supply chains exactly in their weakest links, contributing both to the faster movement of goods and to security by improving the information flows. If, for example, the documents accompanying a certain consignment can be sent to all border crossings and customs offices along the route of transportation in a standard electronic form well in advance, instead of supplying them physically at the time of arrival, this will significantly raise the planning and risk assessment capabilities of official controls. UNeDocs thus has a potential to increase the efficiency of the system.

The issue is not that various countries cannot produce electronic documents or automate customs clearance on their own. The greatest advantage of UNeDocs is that it suggests a solution, developed in the United Nations, where the document will be recognized across the border, in neighbouring and far away countries. UNeDocs is going the major part of the road, starting from standards for paper documents, UNLK, UNTDED, best business practice, codes and standards for e-business. What remains to be done is to internalize the tool, transferring existing standards and best trade practices into a document data model according to each country's national documentary requirements, and extend this model into an electronic syntax.

Figure 5.1.2. UNeDocs: one single electronic document adapting to various information processing concepts

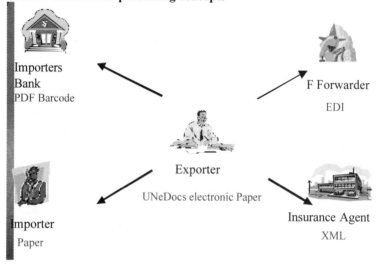

Figure 5.1.2 illustrates the idea of adapting one single UNeDocs electronic document to different information processing concepts. A UNeDocs document can be opened in PDF electronic format, which allows it to be printed out on paper in one and the same physical layout anywhere in the world, but one can also use barcode technology, which will allow for an easy migration path back from paper to an electronic format. The UNeDocs project opens an easy migration path to and from electronic data interchange messages (e.g. UN/EDIFACT), and it can also be processed in

an XML format in the Internet environment (Figure 5.1.3). The following chapters will go into some details of these processes, as well as the possibility to use UPU postmarks as the standard for cross-border recognition of electronic signatures in UNeDocs. The project thus complements paper with electronic documents and traders or administrative officers can choose the formats they want to use.

Figure 5.1.3. The negotiable FIATA multimodal transport bill of lading in XML format

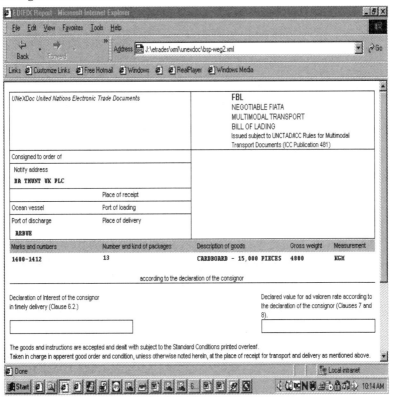

UNeDocs provides support for advanced security concepts at a time when advance exchange of data and automation of data entry are becoming a key element in the international trade infrastructure. This infrastructure relies on the standardization of documents and document data, the automation of data validation and risk assessment, access to relevant applications, and the use of new technologies, such as electronic signatures, mobile document access and barcodes.

Conclusion

The tools and the potential for automating customs clearance and international trade procedures exist, but a more complex problem remains – how to integrate customs and other administrative agencies in the supply chain in such a way that by using electronic means we can reach the "last mile". And by reaching the "last mile" we understand automating the exchange of information not only between customs and the top 10 or 20 per cent of companies which manage the best part of world trade but also integrating the smaller players – SMEs and developing countries. The objective of the UNeDocs project is to integrate everyone: big and small players, customs and other agencies active in international trade, in a solution that will automate the documentary procedures. The idea is not to create new standards or new procedures, but to create electronic solutions, connect the existing trade standards and international best practices to ubiquitous ICT platforms and automate these standards. By relying on standard software platforms, we are reaching out not only to the highly technologically enabled businesses but also to the small players. This is not only the vocation of the United Nations to reach out to the small people and help them integrate in the global society, but also a valuable tool in the new security environment, when it is important to include everyone in the exchange of information. By reaching the "last mile" UNeDocs will contribute to the creation of a safe and inclusive trading system in the future.

Chapter 5.2
Smart Client for On-Line and Off-Line Processing of XML Forms: Microsoft Supporting UNeDocs through Microsoft® Office InfoPath™

Zdenek Jiricek, Public Sector Manager, Microsoft Eastern Europe

The challenges to international trade today include the need to enter data into various client applications multiple times, the fact that there are different clients for different applications, resulting in unnecessary re-typing and data entry errors. Custom forms are hard to use, inflexible and costly to maintain. People still lack experience in editing and validation on filling in every field of the forms. The existing static forms have limited ability to provide the required information. It is difficult to modify these forms and adjust the underlying processes. The custom coding required for validation further complicates the task. The data across business processes is hard to reuse. For this reason, significant development work is necessary, in order to bring the standard electronic trade documents to the requirements of our time.

People say that there are opportunities in every problem. There are opportunities for third parties in this situation too. There are opportunities for ISV solution providers, for example, for those who deal with electronic customs declarations, the Single Window concept, or with enterprise trading applications (e.g. Acord, RosettaNet, HIPAA, or HL7). There are opportunities for value-adding web services, for example in the areas of: complex validation; digital signatures (e.g. UPU Electronic PostMark); document conversion to other standards; checking compliance with customs regulations; electronic duty payments; and customs submissions and registration.

How can InfoPath support UNeDocs

Figure 5.2.1 visualizes the concept of InfoPath, and an illustration of the use of InfoPath is given in figure 5.2.2 with the FIATA Forwarding Instruction.

Figure 5.2.1 InfoPath as a smart client for UNeDocs and web services

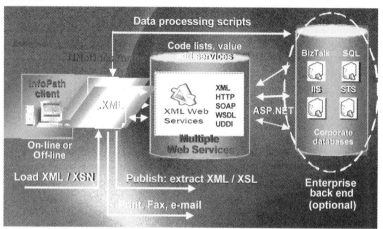

Figure 5.2.2 Filling in and validation of a UNeDocs document using MS InfoPath and web services

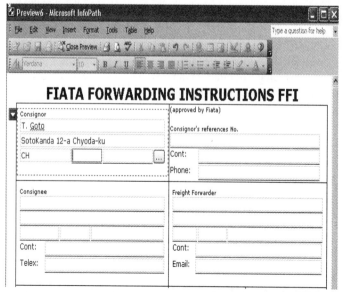

The UNeDocs version of a FIATA Forwarding Instruction can be opened with Microsoft InfoPath, and the form can be filled in (see Figure 5.2.2). A validation occurs in real time against a web service. If data corresponding to a code are entered in a certain field, one can proceed normally, if the code is correct. If the code is not correct, the field's border becomes coloured in red. A dictionary form opens to help the user to "pick from a list". On top of that, the web service can help the user navigate and search or filter the right value by intelligent zooming in as described further on.

Figure 5.2.3 illustrates the search for codes for country and location (city). In the location field one can filter from a list of 37,000 code entries, adopted by the UNECE. The drop down list is created and filled with data from web services, and gives the possibility for multiple choices to retrieve the correct Location Code. There is an option to use a reverse filter mode, i.e. if one fills in the location code name one can retrieve the corresponding city, state, or other location. There exists a possibility to look for a code by entering only part of the location name and searching through the %(joker) function. Every country, currency or unit of measurement in the form will be validated in the same way.

Figure 5.2.3 Entering location codes

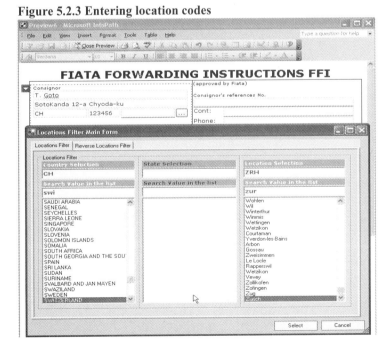

As a result, InfoPath provides several benefits for UNeDocs. Firstly, it provides a possibility to gather information more efficiently and accurately: validation through scripting or web services; using of conditional formatting capabilities; and easy to implement digital signatures (e.g. using a UPU web service). Secondly, information is managed in a more flexible manner on-line, off-line and using e-mail support. InfoPath allows for a visual creation and modification of forms. Forms thus become dynamic: one can lock them, create optional fields and do various other operations. Thirdly, one can take advantage of existing IT investment and knowledge, as one is offered a web-based solution, which supports any XML schema. People can also benefit from the familiar Microsoft Office user experience. Fourthly, the user can share information across business processes, connect to XML web services, and connect to multiple business processes on the back-end side via Microsoft BizTalk Server. Several back-end applications can thus be connected to a single InfoPath client form, while the business processes can be easily maintained and modified by means of Microsoft BizTalk Server.

Chapter 5.3
Empowering Trade Documents: Digital Paper for Secure and Efficient Business and Communication Chains

Alexandre Salzmann, Country Manager Switzerland, Adobe Systems Inc

As global trade transactions increasingly multiply in number and complexity, parties involved in trade are asked to juggle the diverse demands accordingly imposed on them. Although the list of such growing demands can be long, some of the persisting challenges to effective trade networks, two-way communication and the general efficiency of trade transactions have been the creation of international standards, accessibility, limited budgets, interoperability and often cumbersome dealings with local law authorities. Exacerbated by the recent acts of terrorism, heightened security and accurate intelligence are the most recent challenges for trade partners in maintaining efficient business and communication chains.

The IT sector has tried to contribute its share in developing ways to facilitate trade operations. One of its main focus areas has been to advance the concept of *digital paper*. More flexible than commonly perceived, automation and doing business on-line offers numerous ways through which all parties in a trade transaction can benefit. Among its advantages, *digital paper* allows for a client to fall on paper any time, it integrates well and is compatible with many IT programs, and it provides access to effective exchanges of information. In addition, it is ubiquitous as well as it offers security and protection to trade partners sharing information.

Adobe Systems Inc. is very much interested in establishing ways to empower the utility of trusted trade documents and in facilitating trade. In the past ten years, as a member of the Adobe Acrobat product family, Adobe PDF has established itself as a reliable and useful IT standard with proven lineage. One can print out a PDF file from different computers, and it will have the same layout, which is a major advantage in a world of harmonizing trade document standards. Adobe PDF offers secure solutions in the standardization process and the empowerment of digital communications chains in trade transactions. Whether files need to be shared across the office or around the globe, the Adobe Acrobat product family enables organizations to simplify document processes using Acrobat PDF. Acrobat PDF's reliability and effectiveness have been attested by its high demand and widespread usage. Over the past decade, the distribution of Adobe Reader Licenses has reached the 500 million mark. It has been mandated by governments, standards bodies and international organizations world wide, and it has been adopted by Fortune Global 1000 enterprises. Acrobat PDF is versatile in its application as it integrates well with XML, web services and backend systems. Moreover, it receives broad support from industries such as PDF/X, PDF/A, and PDF/is.

Figure 5.3.1 below shows an electronic UNeDocs Freight Forwarding Instructions document implemented as Adobe PDF form. The form itself contains international trade standards and best practice and code lists for trade information encoded in instructions that execute when users perform data entry. It may also contain business rules, which formulate consistency checks on the form data and helps screens that guide users in filling out the data correctly.

Usually the party that has interest in receiving quality data such as the Freight Forwarder has developed the form. The Freight Forwarder can provide the document for download on the Internet. There are no licence fees involved for the user of the document. The trader opens the PDF form with an Adobe Acrobat reader. The trader can then enter data in the boxes. For complex boxes special data entry screens open, guiding the user through the entry process (see Figure 5.3.2). The data entry screens also contain all required code lists as pull-down menus.

Figure 5.3.1 The FIATA forwarding instruction

FIATA FORWARDING INSTRUCTIONS FFI

Consignor Meyer AG BAUMACKERSTRASSE 24 Oerlikon CH 8050 Zurich	(approved by FIATA) Consignor's reference number:	
Consignee T. Goto SotoKanda 12-A Chyoda-ku JP 200/00 Tokyo Jackiecham S Telex: 0034121715454	Freight Forwarder FA. Bonm &CO Fracluth of West 30-40 CH 8058 KLOTEN AP Jean Chirac Electronic Mail: 00412291715454	
Notify party H.Ikeda Narita AP Building 333-1 JP 8058 Narita	Country of origin	Documentary credit MC986CH34 20020708
Goods ready for shipment Place Date 0	Conditions of Sale Free On Board Incoterms 2002 FOB Free On Board	
Mode of Transport ☐ Air ☐ Road ☐ Rail ☐ Sea	Transport Insurance ☐ Covered by us ☐ Covered by Consignee ☐ To be covered by you.	Insurance Conditions Currency and value insured 0,00

Place of destination CHZUR Zurich				
Marks & numbers Number & type of packages Description of goods	Commodity code	Gross weight		Cube
☐ ADILMA Trading Via 23 ☐ Cases ☐ Cylinder-Press Completely Assembled	1288	23 KGM	9	MTQ
☐ Infosys Trading Via 4 ☐ Parce.☐ Packaged and Sealed by GOV	1352	48 KGM	57	MTQ
		Net net weight	Value CHF 150☐ CHF 500☐	

The goods and instructions are accepted and dealt with subject to the Trading Conditions printed overleaf.

Handling instructions (dangerous goods etc.)

KEEP AWAY FROM FOOD STAFF

Dimensions/Measurement and weight of each package

Documents enclosed	Documents required	Orig. Copy	Terms of delivery
			Place and date of issue
			Authentication

Print

Figure 5.3.2 Entering data into the forms

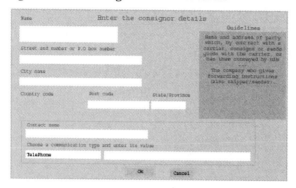

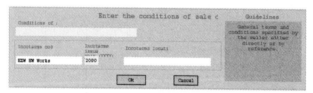

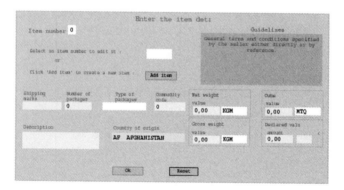

After finalizing the data entry the user has three options: print the form on paper and send it as a standard paper document, save the document as PDF document and send it to the Freight Forwarder by email or save the document as UNeDocs XML document for integration in electronic business. This example demonstrates that a standard office solution such as Adobe Acrobat can provide access to UNeDocs electronic document processing on a standard office PC. The Acrobat reader enables the user to transition between the paper and the electronic version of the document, depending on the business needs and the legal and regulatory requirements. The major advantage of PDF is that printouts look the same (have the same layout) no matter from what computer you print them. UNECE codes (location codes, codes for weight units, types of cargo, etc.) will be used whenever possible.

It is the aim of Adobe through its programs and applications such as Adobe PDF to empower trade documents by supporting dualism of paper and electronic document collaboration and presentation. This brings our objectives and the objectives of the UNeDocs very close together. We believe that it is through the exchange of trusted trade documents that further standardization, interoperability, increased efficiency, and facilitation of global trade transactions can be attained.

Chapter 5.4
Electronic PostMark (EPM): Security and Authentication for UNeDocs

Steve Gray, Program Manager, e-Business, UPU International Bureau

The Universal Postal Union (UPU) is a specialized agency of the United Nations based in Bern, Switzerland, and it has 189 member countries with 700,000 postal outlets. It is the primary forum for cooperation among postal services and helps to ensure a truly universal network of up-to-date products and services. UPU is an international standard setting body, it is the largest physical distribution network in the world, and it helps realize the fundamental right to communicate.

UPU coordinates the work on the Electronic Postmark (EPM) Standard Interface, working with technology companies (for example, Microsoft, Adobe, and Sun) on a non-exclusive basis. EPM is, fundamentally, a **non-repudiation service** supporting: digital signature verification; time-stamping of successfully verified signatures; encryption; storage and archival of all non-repudiation evidence data required to support subsequent challenges; and legislative protection (i.e. as for physical mail). EPM provides secure information on: what document was signed; when the document was signed; who signed the document; and why the document was signed. In e-signature legislation EPM corresponds to a compliant declaration of intent. This means that if I am signing this document I do it because (pick one):

- I **Agree** with the terms of the document
- I **Disagree** with the terms of the documents
- I am the **Author** of the documents
- I am a **Reviewer** of the document...

EPM adds value to electronic trade because it: reduces costs; speeds up the process; guarantees confidentiality; improves the security of the transaction; provides authentication; helps document management (storage & archiving); ensures document integrity and non-repudiation; and provides a trusted third party for the transaction. EPM is service oriented. It provides a valuable everyday service and transparency for trade in the digital domain. In the contemporary world of booming communications, it is essentially low-cost, evoked only in transactions on a case-by-case basis. There are prerequisites for the success of the Electronic Postmark concept, such as its in-person proofing, global policies (in the universal framework of the UPU), and PC software ubiquity, which means that one needs only standard and universally accessible software in order to use the Electronic Postmark system.

Figure 5.4.1 The "Authentication" window in a UNeDocs electronic document using Electronic Postmarks

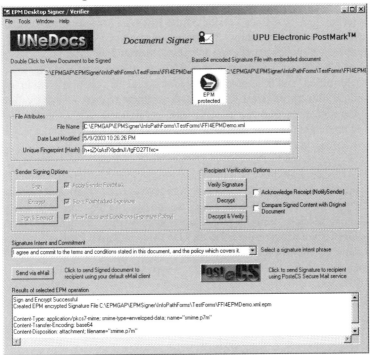

EPM provides support for developing countries, because it supports a hybrid processes for international trade (based on both electronic means and paper); it offers a solution that does not limit developing countries (by an indispensable requirement to get online); it is realized through a well-established postal network present in all countries (Universal Service Obligations); it is expected to bring technical infrastructure investments by developed countries, from which developing countries can benefit; it suggests various solution models (host, lease, factory, etc.); and it provides the bridge between online and offline communications, between electronic and paper environments. All this suits perfectly the objectives of the UNeDocs project.

In the familiar UNeDocs version of the FIATA Forwarding Instruction form (Figure 5.2.2 in one of the previous chapters) one can enter the "Authentication" box in the lower right corner, and the prompt in Figure 5.4.1 will show up. The user can then fill in the "File Name" slot, the "Date Last Modified" slot is automatically updated, and the system will fill in the "Unique Fingerprint (Hash)" slot. The programme will ask for verification of the signature, and the process will be finished. After closing the "Authentication" prompt the electronic signature will appear in the way it shows in Figure 5.4.2.

Posts are currently busy building the digital evidentiary services required by the Information Society, such as the Electronic Postmark and Identity Management. They are developing Standards and Policies with ISVs (Microsoft, Adobe, Sun) for global interoperability. It is for this reason that the UPU is investing resources in the UNeDocs initiative. Posts are willing to move to pilot projects with interested parties involved in international trade.

Figure 5.4.2 The electronic signature of a UNeDocs document

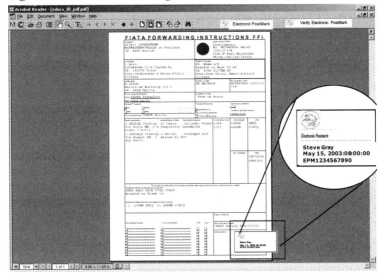

Chapter 5.5
Online Trust – Canada Post Context: A Case of Using the Electronic Postmark ^{TM} [69]

Introduction

While the Internet and the e-revolution present tremendous opportunities, they also pose challenges for businesses and consumers alike. Privacy and security concerns, which chisel away at consumer trust, have resulted in slower than expected adoption of e-commerce.

Trust is essential for building consumer confidence in the online environment and therefore requires a trusted third party that can assure that transactions occur in a secure, trusted environment. There must also be assurance that valuable transactions are conducted with legal validity and recourse for third parties in case of a court challenge. Unquestionably, Canada Post is a highly trusted agent whose ability to deliver messages and parcels securely goes back over a hundred years and is as relevant today as ever.

Canada Post has already built a reputation as a trusted, online service provider, providing e-commerce solutions for a number of years. From providing facsimile services before this technology was commonplace to the most current Internet technologies, Canada Post has evolved its business as the technology landscapes changed.

---

[69] This article was contributed as a "white paper" to the May 2003 International Forum on Trade Facilitation by the Universal Postal Union (UPU) and Canada Post Corporation. For more information on this article, please contact Elizabeth Myers, Director, eBusiness, Canada Post Corporation, tel. +1-613-7343387 (e-mail: elizabeth.myers@canadapost.ca) Electronic Postmark^{TM} (EPM ™) is a trade mark of Canada Post Corporation.

An essential element of Canada Post's Internet services is the Electronic Postmark™ (EPM™). Just as the postal stamp, indicia, cancellation mark, etc. have long since been accepted as the "trust marks" symbolizing the trustworthiness of the posts, Canada Post's EPM is the visible mark of trust in the electronic environment.

EPM service provides time and date of delivery and the assurance that the message has not been tampered with. This unique element ensures privacy, security and trust of electronic mail that is received and delivered using a Canada Post service. This paper presents the legal and legislative framework within which the Electronic Postmark was developed, and highlights the EPM service.

Background

Canada Post Corporation is mandated by the Government of Canada to provide mail service to all Canadians, businesses and organizations through the secure delivery of letters and parcels to all addresses in Canada and around the world.

In 1981, the Parliament established the Post Office as a Crown Corporation through the *Canada Post Corporation Act (the "Act")*. The Act sets out the current legislative basis for mail service in Canada. Within the Act is the continuation of a commitment to the sanctity of the mail that was founded in customary and historical practice as well as in legislation passed by Parliament throughout the years. Notably, the 1981 Act established a new mandate to expand its activities into electronic services:

"While maintaining basic customary postal service, the Corporation, in carrying out its objects, shall have regard to (a) the desirability of improving and extending its products and services in the light of developments in the field of communications;"

Consistent with this new mandate, Canada Post has provided electronic services to Canadians and businesses over the past 20 years. Further, Canada Post is mandated to ensure that the same privacy and security provided to physical mail is provided to electronic messages that it delivers.

Are electronic messages "Mail"?

Messages transmitted through or by means of Canada Post are "mail" under the Act. Specifically, the Act sets out the definition of "mail". The Act defines "mail" as any message sent or conveyed from one place to another by any physical, electronic or other means, through or by means of Canada Post Corporation.

Thus the Act provides a statutory framework for Canada Post's mandate to " improve and extend its products and services in light of developments in the field of communications" and includes the electronic transmission and conveyance of mail.

Value proposition of legislative protection

As e-commerce grows, so also do the concerns about its deployment. Canadians have concerns about the security of their electronic messages and transactions; they question whether the legal framework has kept pace with the rapid change; and finally, they want to ensure that they can trust the entities with which they choose to do business. The issues of technology, and the existence of tangible, appropriate laws and their enforcement have allowed for impressive gains in using these tools to ensure that Canadians are protected when engaging in e-commerce.

Trust, however, is a central theme and concern. Unquestionably, Canada Post is a highly trusted agent whose role in the Canadian society and economy goes back more than 150 years and is as relevant today as ever. The "sanctity of the mail" speaks both to how Canada Post must operate as well as how legislation protects and enforces the protection of the mail. The Canada Post Corporation Act states that a person commits an offence if they "knowingly open, secrete, delay or detain...any... mail..." In addition, the Act also prohibits the search and seizure of any item while in the possession of Canada Post ("in the course of post"). Finally, "mail" is protected under the Criminal Code. There are serious consequences for theft from mail or using the mail to defraud. Because electronic messages delivered by Canada Post are "mail", these messages are provided the same protection and security as those in the physical world.

Canadians trust Canada Post to deliver their physical mail in a secure and private manner. Canada Post is uniquely positioned to provide the same security and privacy to the electronic mail that it handles today and in the future. Legislation provides the same protection and enforcement as for physical mail.

The Electronic Postmark™

There are many examples of legislation and regulations that expressly require that mail be "postmarked" as evidence of the date of mailing. An example of this type of regulation is the Excise Tax Act, which defines that an Income Tax Return is considered "filed" on the day on which the return was mailed and the date of the postmark is evidence of that day.

The Canada Post Electronic Postmark service will date and time stamp messages when they are sent and will use hashing technology to provide assurance of message integrity. This process will prove that the original mail piece was not tampered with.

Because electronic messages are "mail" while being delivered by Canada Post, the Electronic Postmark can have the same status as a postmark imprinted on physical piece of mail. It can support existing legislation that requires the "postmark" as proof of mailing. Further, this "official" postmark is considered by Canadians, business and government as more objective than a purely proprietary or commercial date stamp. The Electronic Postmark™ is therefore a further manifestation of the goodwill and confidence associated with a Canada Post postmark and Canada Post's status as a trusted third party.

The Electronic Postmark™ - service context

EPM overview

The EPM is backed by the Canada Post Corporation Act and founded on the corporation's solid track record of reliability, trust, impartiality and legislative status. Canada Post has developed a number of electronic products that incorporate this visible mark of trust. Notable among these are *epost*^{TM} (secure bill presentment and payment service) and *PosteCS*^{TM} (secure document delivery and e-messaging solution), both of which are services based upon the secure transport of vital electronic information, given value by the Electronic Postmark (a testimonial seal) - an electronic equivalent to the stamp, indicia, cancellation mark, certified mail, etc.

Canada Post provides non-repudiation services as part of EPM to the Government Secure Channel initiative. The corporation is also working with other postal administrations and the Universal Postal Union (UPU) to develop a Global Electronic Postmark Service.

EPM specifics

Canada Post's EPM service is evidence that the business transaction was completed in the context of security, privacy, and non-repudiation with respect to:

- Who sent it?
- Who received it?
- When was it sent?
- When was it received?
- Was the content intact throughout transmission?
- Have both parties been notified of these significant events?

The EPM involves a number of key services to ensure end-to-end transaction confidentiality and integrity, as follows:

- Authentication services
- Digital signature services
- Time stamping services
- Persistent logging services (for all transactions, documents, messages, and events).

Canada Post's EPM will provide a number of graduated, customizable services to meet different client needs. The following service elements of the EPM can be combined and used by subscribers in any combination they deem appropriate, ranging from simple time stamping to more complex multi-party, multi-event business processes:

- Verify and PostMark signature at origin
- Issue induction receipts to service subscriber
- Capture and timestamp significant intermediate events
- Verify and PostMark epackage delivery or pick-up
- Timestamp business transaction completion event
- Issue transaction completion receipt to service subscriber
- Provide "light-weight" notarization service with built-in receipt support, appropriate for low-value transactions
- Support multiple parties, multiple time disconnected events, and a sign-for-pickup facility

The *non-repudiation* services of EPM will provide customers with audit trails, digital receipts and notarisation of online transactions and documents. It essentially allows customers to conduct secure irrefutable e-commerce. To support non-repudiation of business activities, all significant events in a business transaction's life-cycle will be logged. This service provides transacting parties the assurance that:

- Any future challenges surrounding the integrity and evidencing of the business transaction will be supported by the non-repudiation service.
- At challenge time, Canada Post's non-repudiation service can extract and reproduce (from its logging and/or archiving facilities) electronic evidence for use by all parties.
- Canada Post, being a Trusted Service Provider, will bring credibility to evidence used in court cases involving transaction challenges.

<u>Benefits of EPM services</u>
Canada Post's EPM services provide a number of benefits to parties transacting business, and assurance that:

- they are dealing with a reliable, trusted third party
- the parties they are doing business with can be trusted
- their privacy will be protected
- the transactions have integrity that cannot be repudiated
- there is the Canada Post legislated framework and mandate to support a court challenge

Summary

By virtue of the Canada Post Corporation Act electronic messages delivered by Canada Post are "mail" and have the same legislative protection as physical mail pieces. No other organization can provide this framework in the e-business world to Canadians.

Because the Electronic Postmark is applied to "mail" as defined by the Canada Post Act, it may be acceptable under other legislation and regulations as a legal "proof of mailing." Again, Canada Post is uniquely positioned to offer this assurance to Canadians.

Canada Post has moved assertively to offer Canadians, business and government a growing number of electronic services in support of its mandate as set out in the Canada Post Corporation Act. It has also ensured that the elements of trust, security and privacy have been carefully woven into the new e-business fabric. Backed by the Act, which defines what is "mail", and with the development of the Electronic Postmark and non-repudiation services, Canada Post will continue to be trusted by Canadians to receive and deliver mail - as it has for over 150 years.

Chapter 5.6
Electronic Documentation in Trade Transactions

Michèle Barker, Head of Electronic Business, SITPRO

One of the increasingly important market requirements for international traders is the ability to use electronic documentation and paper versions at any point in a trade transaction. Some leading tools in electronic documentation used currently in international trade are the Aligned Export Documentation (TOPFORM), the Electronic Transmission of Export Documentation (Electra), and the browser based completion and transmission of Export Documentation – WebElecTra.

Another useful and internationally recognized tool in electronic documentation has been developed through the UNeDocs project established by the United Nations Economic Commission for Europe (UNECE). UNeDocs offers users conducting trade transactions one single electronic document which has the capacity to adapt to different information processing concepts. Furthermore, it allows traders and administrations to automate documentary procedures and to reduce risks through the use of technology. For example, through UNeDocs an exporter has the ability to validate trade data by simultaneously accessing the Importers Bank through the *PDF Barcode*, monitoring information concerning the freight forwarder through the *EDI,* managing his insurance requirements through the *XML system* and communicate with the importer. UNeDocs trade documents fully integrate international recommendations and best business practice in using international codes for trade information. In addition, UNeDocs provide new and automated means to access and process the code lists directly from the PC of the user.

Businesses and exporters in the United Kingdom have significantly benefited from the national implementation of UNeDocs. It has proven to be a well-documented and easy-to-maintain solution for IT providers, and with time and expanded usage, the UNeDocs has become a standard solution for UK traders. With support from SECIPRO – the regional trade facilitation body of the countries in Southeastern Europe - and the commitment of their respective government and customs authorities, UNeDocs pilot projects in Turkey and at Bulgaria's Transport Corridor have great potential.

SITPRO is collaborating closely with UNECE to further develop and expand the usage of UNeDocs in international trade transactions. What we are currently working on is the UNeDocs Tool Kit, which will consist of a Reference Model of the Business Processes and the Documents/Data/ Message structures needed to enable Cross Border trade. These initiatives aim to improve and simplify trade transaction procedures for all involved in a trade transaction. We are very much aware that the deliverables must reflect the needs of small and medium-sized enterprises (SMEs), which are based on simple solutions. However, the successful implementation of UNeDocs on national and international levels equally requires the commitment and political will of individual governments.

In its attempt to facilitate trade through the usage of UNeDocs, the UNECE hopes to offer a potential "simple" solution to developing countries and transition economies in their conduct of imports and exports. In addition, it trusts that UNeDocs standards will be successfully implemented on national level in an increasing number of countries, and that the adoption of UNECE's Trade Facilitation Recommendation No.1 on aligned documentation in international trade will become widespread.

Part Six:

Intellectual Property Rights and Trade Facilitation: "Identifying Opportunities and Roadblocks"

The papers in this section were presented at the Workshop on Trade Facilitation and Intellectual Property Rights, whose objective was to identify opportunities and problems for trade facilitation related to IPR and patenting procedures. The themes cover the relationship between trade facilitation and IPR enforcement; IPR policy in trade facilitation standards in the UN environment; the role of patent rights; territorial aspects of IPR and patenting rights. The first article presents the summary of the discussion at the workshop, and was prepared by the Rapporteur.

Chapter 6.1
Workshop on Intellectual Property Rights and Trade Facilitation, UNECE in cooperation with The European Patent Office (EPO) and Service Management Group[70]
Eskil Ullberg, Service Management Group

This Workshop was created as a response to the fact that practically all products and services traded today have intellectual property rights (IPRs) attached to them. The focus was to identify "roadblocks" but also opportunities related to trade and IPR. It was also an attempt to begin to place the IPR issues on the Trade and Trade Facilitation agenda – without "duplicating" WTO's work on TRIPS. Four themes were covered:

1. The general role of IPR and patent rights in international trade flows (Mr. Schatz, EPO)
2. The territorial aspects of IP and patenting rights and the lack of cross-border recognition as possible roadblocks (Mr. Heath, Max Plank Institute Germany)
3. IPR in the development of international standards in trade facilitation and electronic business (Mr. Marsh, Dickinson Dees, United Kingdom)
4. The balance between IPR enforcement and international trade flows (Mr. Trainer, International AntiCounterfeiting Coalition Inc., United States)

Several roadblocks to trade, both policy and technical, were identified. A summary of the speeches is followed by text versions of each of the four articles. Powerpoint presentations were made available for themes 1, 2 and 3.

---

[70] This summary report was published in the PROGRES newsletter, June 2003. The Workshop on Intellectual Property Rights (IPR) and Trade Facilitation: Identifying Opportunities and Roadblocks was held in the framework of the International Forum on Trade Facilitation, 14-15 May 2003.

IPR and patenting on the "social agenda"

Only very recently, about 15 years ago, was IP related to trade. Prior to this, patenting had to do with technology and products but the trade aspects were not explicitly recognized. This resulted in the TRIPS agreement becoming the third pillar of WTO besides GATT (goods) and GATS (services).

Today, the social aspects of IP are at stake since IPRs in general are granted for certain territories and thereby create limitations to trade both in respect to the right and the products and services which fall under the scope of the protection of that right. This has a direct impact on the pricing of the products. Suppliers (who hold patents) then use the system for local pricing. This procedure does not go very well with global trade of goods and services. In the case of pharmaceuticals, the developing countries favor "global" exhaustion of rights, which would introduce some sort of global pricing different from today's "supplier pricing". It would also challenge manufacturing worldwide and parallel imports. It has lead to a de-facto change of the TRIPS agreement in the Doha Round of WTO negotiations. The success of the patenting and IPR system has therefore first to be based on a social success.

The **cost / benefit** "equation" then has to take into account the social aspects. This may challenge current mechanisms of, for example, pricing and the national exhaustion of patent rights for a global exhaustion within certain fields related to public health, etc.

Patent density

The patent density, i.e. the number of patents per capita, GDP, etc., has a highly uneven distribution among countries. A high patent density is needed for trade facilitation. It is necessary to have something to trade! This is true for trade between developed and developing countries.

This is due to:
- the territoriality of patents (they are geographically limited)
- the cost/benefit balance, which is negative for developing countries (at least initially),
- market access or "network access" (access to knowledge, finance, trade infrastructure in general), which is limited for developing countries

One way of solving this is to internationalize patent granting mechanisms. Here centralization is a good idea due to the fact that any system has to compare with the "prior art". To have skilled people in every field is an insurmountable obstacle for many countries. This would call for a central body or centrally managed database used for prior art searches. The views on patents and IPR are many. A more coherent global patenting system is welcome.

Maximum standards
The developed countries are here setting the standards according to their needs. During TRIPS these standards, as mentioned above, were set at European and US and Japanese levels. The "minimum standards" required by TRIPS therefore became, in reality, "maximum standards".

Complexity is expanding
In trade facilitation simplification is a key issue. However, in the area of patenting and IPR the complexity of the issues is expanding along with technology expansion. Contract law and other laws are affected by changes in IP policy. Free and fair trade needs IPR. A level of confidence in the national system is also important. This means that industry is part of the solution.

Bilateral versus multilateral
Trade policies are in practice much too single sided or "export oriented". This is true also when it comes to IPR. A central and critical issue here is the development of the multilateral trading system versus bilateral agreements. Bilateral standards represent great risks to trade since they (a) are inequitable and imposed by superior economic powers, and (b) disturb

equitable economic conditions for trade. Bilateral standards then de facto are raised above multilateral standards, imposing even a higher degree of challenges. This issue was also raised in the workshop due to the recent agreement between Singapore and the United States where Singapore promises not to infringe US IPR in exporting to the US. This is a very strategic issue and currently a top priority on the WTO agenda.

The validation system
The "validation system" was presented by EPO as being a successful solution for developing countries. Is provides free access to world-class patents provided you want it and is without any obligation. It is available to all Patent Cooperation Treaty (PCT) member states.

UNECE standards and IPR (UN/CEFACT)
Owing to technology development and that patents are more about "intangibles" (software, business process patents in the US) than "tangibles", the used patenting technology in goods and services challenges the United Nations in setting standards "free of charge". This challenges the legal environment. IPRs have to be carefully crafted in this more "competitive" environment for technical standards setting. A proposal is made for "royalty free licensing" of IPRs included in United Nations standards.

Recommendations

More work should be directed towards:
1. Better understanding of the cost/benefit equation for developing countries
2. Better understanding of global markets by IPR experts and of IPR issues by the international trading community
3. A coordinated approach to capacity building and technical assistance on IPR issues.

Chapter 6.2
Intellectual Property and UN Technical Standards: A Legal Perspective

David Marsh, Legal Rapporteur of the United Nations Centre for Trade Facilitation and Electronic Business (UN/CEFACT)[71]

Before attempting to analyse the legal problems I envisage, it would be wise to give my simplistic lawyer/layman/non-technical understanding of what XML actually is. The letters stand for Extensible Mark-up Language and the application of this language in the electronic business environment is what is called "ebXML". How and why is it new and different? The fundamental change is that it does something which the existing Internet standard, html (Hypertext Mark-up Language), does not do. The big difference is that when I look at a page received from the Internet in html form, as a human being I can read and understand what I am seeing. However, the computer that I am using cannot read the text and cannot, therefore, automatically acquire the data contained in the message. If the message is an order or an order confirmation there is no automatic interaction between the incoming html message and my stock control system (this is, of course, not the case in the closed world of EDI using the UN/EDIFACT standard). The benefits of avoiding re-keying are very significant and the interaction between incoming messages and the "back office" systems are capable of producing very significant business process advantages.

XML, and ebXML in particular, will enable all the data elements of a message received from the Internet to be recognized by the receiving system so that an incoming ebXML standard message will have all the functionality of a UN/EDIFACT "closed world" EDI message.

---

[71] David Marsh is the head of IT and electronic business law with the UK law firm of Dickinson Dees. In addition, he is the Legal Rapporteur of UN/CEFACT, which deals with the development of trade facilitation and electronic business technical standards within the United Nations system. In that role, Mr. Marsh has been closely involved in the legal aspects of the development of the ebXML standard.

However, there are a number of potential legal hurdles that need to be overcome before an ebXML standard can be safely available for use. These problems fall into two general categories. The first relates to how an ebXML standard would actually work. The second relates to the intellectual property rights associated with the standard.

As a comparison, if I wish to send a UN/EDIFACT standard message, then I will have to use a specific format that has been approved under the UN/EDIFACT standard. Of course, I can do that because UN/EDIFACT is the United Nations approved standard and it will (or certainly should) go without saying that if the United Nations approves and supports a standard then it must be an open and free standard available to any user without the need to pay a proprietary owner for a licence to do so. UN/EDIFACT is freely available to be used without paying any royalty or fee to anyone.

The development of electronic commerce over the past thirty years has resulted in a rather interesting change in the structure of technical standards. Originally a standard was a norm that identified the way in which a particular business process should be conducted. There was no perception that implementing a standard might, itself, involve the need to obtain consents in the form of licences or other types of intellectual property authority from owners of proprietary rights embedded in the standard process itself. All of that has changed because of the coming together of the technology within electronic business and the means of implementing that technology in a standard way coupled with the enormous growth, particularly in the United States, of business process patents. These are patents filed mainly by IT companies trying to obtain monopoly protection of parts of a standard system that they claim to have invented.

While the free and open use of new IT technical standards is a laudable and, arguably, an absolutely essential policy principle for the United Nations, its implementation in the real world is not free of uncertainties and commercial concerns. Like all standard-making bodies the United Nations has fundamental principles governing the basis for the contributions of potential participation in the development of standards. To put it relatively simply, if anyone wishes to contribute to the development of the United Nations based electronic business standard then they are only permitted to do so if they agree that if they bring new technology to the process, then they must do so on the basis that they freely and readily agree to grant to the United Nations, for the benefit of the potential user base of the standard, such intellectual property licence as is necessary to ensure the free and open use of the standard by all those who wish to do so.

As a general principle, the above analysis seems clear enough but it is vitally important that all those who do contribute to the creation of international standards must be aware of and must agree to this basis on which their contributions are made.

This is not a problem of general theory. It is a problem of real pressing practical concern simply because in the last twenty years there has been a significant development of business process patents. These are perfectly legitimate attempts by developers of electronic business in the world IT industry, particularly in the United States, to file applications for patent protection (and remember that this means an absolute monopoly right for twenty years) for electronic business processes. In many circumstances such patents may claim monopoly rights for aspects which may be an essential and, indeed, vital part of the development of the standard.

I describe such patents as "road block patents". If they stand in the way of the development of the standard they create a significant problem that can only be resolved by negotiations with the patent owners for a licensing regime in favour of the United Nations and the users of the standard. Such negotiations will permit the use of the ebXML standard without users being afraid that they could be at the wrong end of an action for infringement of a patent supported by a patent owner with significant resources and therefore able to afford expensive litigation to enforce the patent monopoly.

If that causes you some concern then you need to be aware that it is also quite important that the essence of the ebXML standard involves using messages that can be identified by the receiving computer because of the use of tags. The tags in question are invisible attachments recognizable by the computer receiving the message. It should immediately be apparent that the only way that these tags can be recognized is if they come from a standard, generally available database. In addition, because of the nature of ebXML and its operation in the real world, the database must be completely up-to-date and available online "24/7".

This, to a cynical lawyer like me, immediately prompts a number of questions. Who owns the intellectual property in the database? Who will pay for the database to be kept up-to-date? Who will be responsible if the database is in error? Who will pay – and, if so, how much – for the cost of accessing the database in order to use the standard and read the ebXML message? These are all major issues which need to be addressed as a matter of urgency before it is possible for the United Nations to endorse and approve a stable ebXML standard in a form which permits open use worldwide without cost to potential users. I cannot offer solutions to these problems yet but I can confirm that they are currently being addressed within the United Nations and, even though at present there are no clear solutions, there is a clear awareness of the nature of the problem.

The major commercial contributors to the development of the ebXML standards are also aware of these potential barriers to the development of an ebXML standard. However, there are competing interests involved and it is essential to strike a balance between the proprietary rights of the contributors, their willingness to support an open standard and their legitimate need to obtain a return upon their investment in the development of the technology.

Chapter 6.3
Trade Facilitation: Trends in Free Trade Agreements

Timothy P. Trainer, President, International AntiCounterfeiting Coalition, Inc. (IACC)

The United States has recently concluded free trade agreement negotiations with Chile and Singapore and is in negotiations with Australia, Morocco, a group of Central American countries and the western hemisphere. These negotiations cover a multitude of trade issues that will impact tariffs, national laws, movement of goods and enforcement of obligations.

Intellectual property (IP) is one area that will have its own chapter in these agreements. The IP provisions will obligate the government to implement practices that provide effective protection of intellectual property. Such protection includes enforcement mechanis ms in the domestic market and at the border. The provisions that affect the latter may have a direct impact on the flow of goods.

Trade Agreement provisions

There are developments between governments and within intergovernmental organizations that will have an impact on activities at the border that, in turn, may have an effect on trade facilitation. In February 2003, the World Customs Organization (WCO) issued a revised Model Legislation document regarding protection of IP at the border. In that document, it recommends enforcement against infringing goods and raises the recommended level of enforcement to include goods intended for export and moving in-transit.

Article 4

The procedures under Articles 1, 2 and 3 shall enable right holders to submit applications for imported goods, goods destined for exportation and goods in transit.[72]

Because WCO's Model Legislation is simply a model, no customs organization or government is obliged to incorporate these provisions into national law.

There are, however, new agreements that do oblige governments to take steps to implement mechanisms that will provide IP protection at the border to stop exports and goods in-transit. The United States concluded free trade agreements (FTAs) with Chile[73] and Singapore[74], which included heightened levels of border enforcement to expand the required border measures to exports and goods in transit. The U.S.-Chile FTA states that border measures:

[s]hall be used when there is reason to believe or suspect that goods being imported, destined for export or moving in transit are counterfeit or pirated.[75]

The parallel provision in the U.S.-Singapore FTA states that border measures:

[s]hall apply to shipments of pirated and counterfeit goods imported or exported out of their territories, including shipments consigned to a local party.[76]

---

[72] The full text of the Model Legislation may be viewed by clicking on "Model Legislation" at www.wcoipr.org

[73] The Office of the U.S. Trade Representative announced that a Free Trade Agreement was reached on December 11, 2002. See www.ustr.gov/releases

[74] The United States and Singapore concluded their negotiations on the Free Trade Agreement on January 15, 2003.

[75] U.S.-Chile Free Trade Agreement, Chapter 17, Article 11(20).

[76] U.S.-Singapore Free Trade Agreement, Chapter 16, Article 16.9(19). Comparing the U.S.-Singapore FTA to the Singapore FTAs with Australia and the European Free Trade Association (EFTA), the FTAs address these issues in a manner that reflects different objectives of governments during such negotiations. For example,

Thus, the imposition of border measures to check exports and in-transit shipments provide copyright and trademark owners, in some cases, with greater opportunities to engage customs and other designated enforcement officials.

Given these developments, it is possible that new procedures affecting exports may have the unintended effect of interrupting trade flows. This, however, should be limited to a near term period of time when authorities and the IP owners are adapting to new laws, regulations and procedures. Once new systems become familiar to those who must implement them and use them, there should be very limited problems regarding the facilitation of trade.

This trend in the free trade agreements should not come as any surprise. The fact is that under the current international standards the burden of IP enforcement at the border rests with the countries of import.[77] Thus, the countries around the world that are the major markets have the burden of checking imports while major exporters, i.e. the countries of export, have no similar obligation. As a result, it is only natural to see that the countries that are major importers insisting that exports and goods in-transit be subject to border measures to stop the cross-border trade in counterfeit and pirate products.

---

the Australia-Singapore Free Trade Agreement, concluded in November 2002, states that "Each Party, on receipt of information or complaints, shall take measures to prevent export of goods that infringe copyright or trade marks, in accordance with its laws, rules, regulations, directives or policies." Chapter 13, Article 4. Thus, the Singapore-Australia FTA appears to be permissive with regard to exports because of the "in accordance with" text that addresses the current state of the law. The Singapore-EFTA FTA, which went into effect on January 1, 2003, simply states that the enforcement of intellectual property should be at the levels provided for in TRIPS Articles 41-61. Singapore-EFTA FTA Annex XII, Article 8.
[77] Article 51 of the World Trade Organization's Agreement on Trade Related Aspects of Intellectual Property Rights requires that member states implement procedures for border measures to stop infringing imports.

Changes in national laws and the implementing regulations that will put these new obligations into practice can be less disruptive to trade if the various government agencies responsible work together and with foreign counterparts to learn how to screen shipments and target shipments that are most likely to contain infringing goods. There is no doubt that the negative effects of these new standards can be offset by adopting policies that seek to incorporate better techniques at targeting shipments and working closely with IP owners and their representatives, who are in the position of being able to assist the authorities in identifying those shipments that are likely to contain goods that infringe IP rights.

Conclusion

Recent global trade trends point to the desire of governments to increase cross-border trade. Moreover, this desire is accompanied by global efforts to streamline procedures at the border in order to move goods to their destination. Unfortunately, there are concerns that reduced vigilance at the border makes countries vulnerable to illegal activity. Those who trade in illicit goods are now likely to take the risks involved in order to profit from trade in illicit goods. Thus, a balance must be struck. Today, the global trade in counterfeit and pirate products is extremely high and unlikely to decrease in the foreseeable future. Therefore, efforts to get governments to be more active in the effort to stop the importation, exportation and movement in-transit of counterfeit and pirate products are increasing. It will take time to adopt effective procedures as authorities will now have to inspect exports and good in-transit. In view of the injury suffered by IP owners and threat to consumers, the expansion of enforcement at the border to cover exports and goods moving in-transit is not an unexpected development.

Chapter 6.4
The Role of IPR in the Global Knowledge Economy and Impact on International Trade Flows

Dr. Ulrich Schatz, former Principal Director for International Affairs and Patent Law, European Patent Office

This paper identifies a series of strategic issues in relation to the role of Intellectual Property Rights (IPR) in the emerging knowledge economy and their impact on international trade flows. IPR confer exclusive proprietary rights that impose limitations on free competition and trade. At the same time IPR are intangible assets that, as such, become tradable goods. The first section outlines the role that IPR, specifically patents, play as the key resource in the global economy. The second section explains the principle of territoriality and its impact on international trade. The third section describes the legal and procedural IPR infrastructure that has been put in place in response to the needs in the emerging global knowledge economy. Finally, the fourth section explores the possible ways towards **a world patent system** that complies with the strategic objective to promote free trade, innovation, equal conditions for competition and economic growth for both developed and developing economies. This paper cannot possibly treat in appropriate depth and detail the strategic issues it addresses. Its purpose is to encourage further discussion and research.

IPR as the key resource in the global knowledge economy

Figure 6.4.1 illustrates that centres of economic power over the previous four centuries have been based on a relative scarcity of valuable, economic resources. Where there is such a scarcity in a market economy, markets will emerge to enable trade. For these markets to function efficiently, certain networks are required. Without these networks, the markets will be inefficient and the economic wealth of the society will be negatively affected.

Consequently, societies that enable or create efficient markets in relatively scarce, valuable economic resources succeed globally (provided they have access to "trading networks").

Figure 6.4.1 The emergence of the global knowledge economy: networks throughout the ages

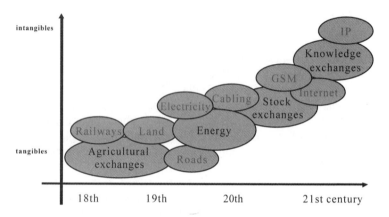

Source: "A market in ideas" (working paper), Ullberg, McGinley, et. al.

Prior to and during a large part of the industrial revolution, the centre of economic power lay with agricultural exchanges. Market towns, corn markets, spice markets, cattle markets and the weekly market places are all instances of these agricultural exchanges. These agricultural exchanges functioned with increasing efficiency thanks to a number of networks. These networks were mostly physical or "tangible". Road networks, shipping (e.g. the Dutch East India Company), railways and even networks of land (i.e. colonies) are all examples of how these agricultural exchanges were enabled to function efficiently. Those economies with the best networks, such as Great Britain, succeeded globally.

Towards the end of the 19th century, the industrial revolution had ensured that agricultural goods were no longer so scarce and had become commodities. The agricultural markets still exist, of course, and remain an essential part of the economy. Nevertheless the new industrial infrastructure needed energy. Initially this energy was available only locally and so steel mills and the like were frequently located near large deposits of coal. With the arrival of electricity networks, the industrial era could take a new leap forward since energy became networked and available anywhere. Energy networks – coal, gas, oil, nuclear – have remained at the basis of economic growth during the 20th century. With energy duly networked and readily available, the new scarce resource then became money or, more accurately, financing. And so a new centre of economic power emerged based on sources of finance – banks, stock exchanges, bond markets, and, more recently, foreign exchange markets. These financial exchanges also functioned with increasing efficiency thanks to a number of networks.

Today, what has emerged as the new scarce resource is knowledge. Most of that knowledge is easily accessible from all around the globe, through networks such as, in particular, the Internet and GSM (as well as air transportation). Some of that knowledge is available for free use but other parts of it are protected by IPRs. It is that "intellectual property" that provides their owners with a superior position in competition as well as with access to large financial resources. A few figures illustrate the growing importance of IPRs:

- By 1998, 85% of stock market value was related to intangible assets such as IPRs. Its share was 38% in 1985.
- Considering patents alone, licensing revenues have been worth 120 billion USD, or the equivalent of 11% of the accumulated earnings of the worlds quoted companies.
- Apart from licensing, the added market value of products that are sold with the benefit of patent protection is estimated at least five times higher than licensing revenues, thus at about $600 billion per year.

In brief, patent rights have become a key resource in the modern economy.

The principle of territoriality in the field of patents

The principle

The grant of patent is a sovereign **act** of **authority** of **state**, the effect of which is **limited to** the **territory of the state**. Existence and scope of protection will depend on:

- legal and administrative standards applied by individual patent offices/courts.
- the choice of applicants under cost/benefit aspects "Value for money"

Protection density

Protection density in different economies depends on a choice made by technology owners under the aspects of cost/benefit.

The **costs** include attorney's fees, translation costs, official procedural and maintenance fees. The **benefits** include, first, size and importance of target market (in terms of GNP or presence of competitors); second, commercial potential of invention; and third, risk of imitation/infringement (highest in the pharmaceutical, lowest in the aeronautic sector). The expected result is protection density up to 50 times higher in large developed economies (e.g. USA, Japan, Europe) than in smaller, less competitive markets in particular developing countries

Consequences for international trade

Patent rights as an object of trade
Patents make technology a tradable commodity through: licensing, direct investment, or national Research and Development investment building on imported technology. Actual transfer, however, depends on other factors in recipient countries (political, educational, local production facilities, salaries, etc.)

Protection density and market access
In the modern knowledge economy the majority of products incorporate technologies that are protected by patents in some or all of the large and high profit yielding markets. Examples can be cited from the car and textile

industries. There is little interest in low protection density in local markets since products infringe patents in high protection density economies that have no access to large high profit yielding markets.

In conclusion, in the global economy, the strategic issue is no longer "to protect or not to protect", but how to increase patent protection density in local markets through regional (or global) patent granting systems and international networking.

International networks supporting the integration of markets in the global knowledge economy

A global market for technical knowledge cannot be organized by liberal policies at the national level alone. It essentially will rely on international instruments that provide for:

- international minimum standards for patent protection
- harmonization of procedural und substantive patent law
- internationalization of patent filing procedures
- availability of search and examination capacities supporting national patent granting systems in countries with limited IPR resource.

Substantial progress has been made in all these respects.

1. The Patent Cooperation Treaty (PCT) of 1970 has created an international filing system, comprising 120 member states. International search and preliminary examination reports prepared by International Authorities facilitate the patenting process in designated States.

2. The "Agreement on trade related aspects of intellectual property" (TRIPs) has, in the field of patentability and enforcement, set standards that are substantially the same as those already prevailing in Europe and other highly developed economies. All states party to the WTO are bound by these standards, at the latest when certain transitional periods provided for developing countries will have expired.

3. Harmonization of formal and procedural patent law is provided for by the Patent Law Treaty of the year 2000 - yet to enter into force. "Deep harmonization" of substantive patent law is currently being negotiated in the framework of the World Intellectual Property Organization (WIPO).

Figure 6.4.2. The PCT system

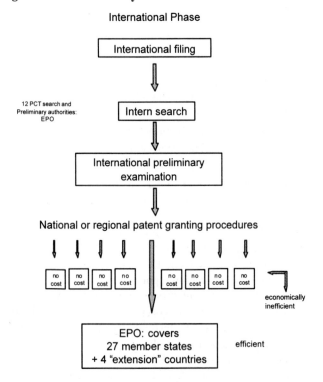

International Phase

International filing

12 PCT search and Preliminary authorities: EPO

Intern search

International preliminary examination

National or regional patent granting procedures

no cost | no cost | no cost | no cost | no cost | no cost | no cost | no cost

economically inefficient

EPO: covers 27 member states + 4 "extension" countries

efficient

While treaty making is in progress, de facto harmonization of patent law has taken place to an extent that has gone almost unnoticed. First, new legislation in both reform and developing countries has consistently taken European patent law as a model. Second, the European patent system in its entirety has been served as a model for other regional systems such as the Eurasian Patent Organization (EAPO), Organisation Africaine de la Propriété Intellectuelle (OAPI), and the African Regional Industrial Property Organization (ARIPO).

As a result, the European patent granting procedure has the potential of supporting patent granting in a large number of economies, which do not adhere to the European Patent Convention, and which lack adequate resources at the national level (developing countries and transition economies).

Towards a global system for the grant of patents

Shortcomings of current PCT system
Despite all progress that has been made at the international level, we are still far away from an integrated patent system that an equal flow of trade with patent rights and equal conditions for competition worldwide. The gaps to be closed are:

First, while the PCT has become a highway to extending protection to up to 120 countries, it ends up in multiple and costly national patent granting procedures that, taken together, are a large cost factor.

Figure 6.4.3 The International Searching Authority (ISA) and International Preliminary Examination Authority (IPEA) work share

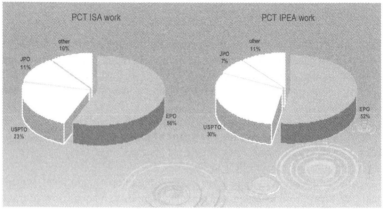

Second, there are 12 different PCT Search and Preliminary Examination Authorities, which do research and prepare preliminary examination reports. Most PCT Authorities are National Patent Offices that act exclusively or mainly for their national constituency.

Third, PCT Authorities cannot decide on an International Preliminary Examination Report (IPER), which is "non binding preliminary opinion" (Art. 33 PCT) and, as a consequence, applicants tend to amend, restrict or renounce claims only when entering the national patent granting procedures. Decision to grant / reject the application will be taken by national or regional patent offices.

Possible remedies to the shortcomings of the PCT system
There exist unofficial proposals in WIPO concerning this issue. A PCT "certificate of patentability" can be optional for designated offices. The major advantage is the key idea to supplement "preliminary" examination by "full" examination. The "certificate of patentability" is the equivalent of a national patent in each participating country. National patent-granting procedures become, thereby, redundant. The major disadvantage is that

most of the PCT-International Authorities are in fact national Patent Offices acting mainly or exclusively for their national constituencies. There are thus serious reservations concerning impartiality and quality conditions for competition in target countries. These conditions may be different depending on the country of origin of the application.

The European Patent Office (EPO) *validation* system
As a regional patent granting authority the EPO grants patents that are the equivalent of a national patent in 27 member countries: the 15 current EU members, plus 5 non-EU countries, and 7 new members (Bulgaria, Czech Republic, Estonia, Hungary, Romania, Slovenia, and Slovakia). These countries represent a market of over 450 million inhabitants, and they are national economies of various economic and innovative capacities. Five countries are likely to join soon as members: Israel, Latvia, Lithuania, Norway, and Poland. Six countries have adopted the "extended" validation system: Albania, Latvia, Lithuania, Romania, Slovenia, and the Former Yugoslav Republic of Macedonia since 1994, and this system has proven its efficiency to their full satisfaction. Romania and Slovenia became EPO members in 2002. Croatia and Serbia and Montenegro are likely to adopt the system soon. EPO has 5,500 staff and 3,400 examiners. 600,000 European patents were granted since 1980, and about 165,000 patent applications are expected in 2003.

Figure 6.4.4 The European patent system expanding

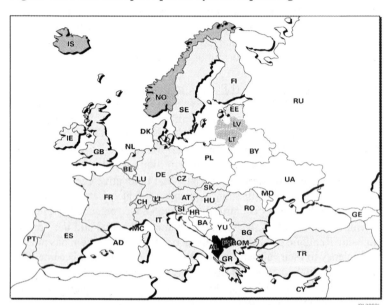

(01.2003)

The European patent system provides high-quality standards to the member states of the European Patent Office (EPO). In addition, thanks to bilateral cooperation agreements, European patents can also take effect in a series of non-member countries through the validation system. Since 1998 the validation system has been open to accession by non-European countries. The key idea of the validation system is to make available the benefits of the centralized European patent grant procedure to any PCT member country that wishes to do so.

The main benefits of the system are:
- high quality patents for the benefit of the national economy
- increase in the patent protection density in the participating country by a factor of 5 to 10, depending on the size and state of development of the national economy
- growth of income from national maintenance fees by the same factor
- increased attraction of foreign investment and technology transfer
- support of national systems in the field of technical information, automation and patent awareness through cooperation with the EPO
- strengthening the IPR infrastructure at the level of both official authorities and private patent practitioners
- patenting policy capabilities for developing countries.

Chairman's Conclusions: The Way Forward to Facilitate Trade[78]

Luzius Wasescha, Delegate of the Swiss Government for Trade Agreements

On 14/15 May 2003, the International Forum on Trade Facilitation provided the opportunity to address the following topics:
- How to achieve benefits for all from trade facilitation?
- Trade facilitation policy and new security initiatives
- The role of the business community: mechanisms of cooperation
- Open regionalism
- Intellectual property rights and trade facilitation
- Leading edge technical issues in trade facilitation

The Forum provided an opportunity to formulate a strong message towards trade liberalization in an economically challenging surrounding having in mind the variety of situations, especially in developing countries and countries in transition. Furthermore, the Forum confirmed the conviction of the trade facilitation community that trade facilitation is a winning runner for the ongoing WTO trade negotiations with potential benefits for all

---

[78] The Second International Forum on Trade Facilitation, which took place on 14 and 15 May 2003, gathered around 500 participants: policy makers and experts from Governments, international organizations, the business community, and civil society from nearly 80 countries. This was not an inter-governmental meeting, with formal decisions, but rather a broad platform for policy debate, involving governments, international organizations, the business community and NGOs. Everyone who participated in this event, including representatives of industrialized and developing countries, expressed their own vision of trade facilitation. The Chairman of the Forum, Ambassador Wasescha, Delegate of the Swiss Government for Trade Agreements, prepared his Conclusions on the basis of reports written by rapporteurs from the various sessions and his own observations. The Chairman's Conclusions thus represent the product of his effort and are his personal contribution to an overview of the Forum, a procedure agreed upon before the first Forum, in May 2002.

CHAIRMAN'S CONCLUSIONS

members. Trade facilitation covers a broad range of both private and public issues in goods and services, and therefore requires a close cooperation of all actors involved. The participants were aware that a large number of developing countries and countries in transition needed specific technical assistance and capacity building in addition to that provided by WTO, in order to benefit fully from the results of trade facilitation. There is a potential saving of billions of US dollars and improved market access conditions in the implementation of trade facilitation measures.

The Forum expresses its deep recognition to UNECE and the twelve other organizations which collaborated in the preparation of the event as well as to the sponsors for their contributions for the thorough conduct of such a useful and timely event. The Forum expresses its gratitude to the speakers and rapporteurs for their valuable contributions to the success of the meeting. Close to 500 participants represented governmental, intergovernmental and private sector interests. A very interactive discussion took place.

Session 1: How to achieve benefits for all from trade facilitation?

1. Trade Facilitation is a broad issue, which, if addressed fully, can generate benefits for society in general, trade, producers, distributors and consumers, private actors and Governments. The benefits could include:

    •   Promotion of trade and investment leading to a better distribution of wealth;

    •   Lower transactions costs;

    •   Improved revenue collection. Government resources could be used to support pro-poor or social improvements;

    •   Better allocation of resources;

    •   Benefits for small businesses by easier access to international trade and greater consistency and transparency;

    •   Lower administrative costs, especially for developing countries and economies in transition.

2. Greater political support and commitment is required to raise the awareness and importance of trade facilitation, including customs procedures, other procedural and compliance costs, and standards requirements, transport costs, especially in large markets. This would give an impetus to the development of concepts such as a single submission to a single window and coordinated controls. In this context a review of data requirements could be appropriate.

3. Participants focused on the work of the WTO on trade facilitation. Many favoured a multi-lateral approach towards binding rules and a strengthening of the work already carried out by countries and international organizations. However, certain skepticism still prevails about a WTO approach unless due account is taken of the concerns expressed by developing countries.

4. Participants emphasized the need for additional coordination of the work of organizations engaged in trade facilitation and the need to avoid duplication.

5. There is a need for better-focused capacity building and strengthened coordination efforts of the various capacity building programmes, including enhancing integrity. This requires the allocation of adequate resources. Benchmarking, transparency, and sharing of information and experiences could assist.

6. Trade facilitation and security requirements are compatible. Customs administrations were identified as the lead entities to make trade facilitation and security requirements mutually supportive.

Session 2: Trade facilitation policy and new security initiatives

1. For security measures there should be a move towards an internationally agreed supply chain security concept (with "end to end" or "origin to destination" controls) to secure and facilitate international trade on a global scale with a pivotal role for customs administrations.

CHAIRMAN'S CONCLUSIONS

An internationally agreed supply chain security concept should replace unilateral measures to achieve worldwide secure and facilitated trade to arrive at a win-win situation for all stakeholders involved. A coordinated move forward should be based on advance information and earlier controls based on risk analysis.

The WCO work in this area should be the basis for further efforts to realize maximum security and facilitation. Due account should be taken of suggestions for security applications, a holistic approach and recognition of UNECE standards and recommendations.

Customs remains the primary control and enforcement agency at the border in the international movement of goods. Close cooperation and interactivity with other enforcement agencies, private business and other customs administrations is essential to strengthening this pivotal role.

Further work should focus on:
- Data required, including unique consignment reference;
- Methods of certification of authorized operators/traders;
- Common approach to risk management/analysis;
- Cooperative agreements with private business;
- Mutual Administrative Assistance based on a clear legal basis, preferably on the new WCO multilateral agreement;
- Single window concept;
- Electronic, paperless customs based on international standards;
- Cooperation with other law enforcement agencies;
- Cooperative agreements with trade partners;
- Further efforts by traders and administrations to enhance integrity and fight corruption.

2. UN Security Council resolution 1373 (2001) is the basis for global action against terrorism to be complemented by regional and national efforts, which are required to get the political support needed on those levels to avoid becoming the weakest link in supply chain security.

WCO programmes for establishing Memoranda of Understanding between Customs and Trade have led to mutual confidence building. This cooperation needs to be taken several steps further to get into cooperative agreements between customs and its business partners to jointly improve supply chain security in open discussion and fully recognizing and respecting each other's interests.

Further work should include:
- Building on the Security Council resolution and work in the Counter Terrorism Committee;
- Further developments in UNECE Forums and meetings;
- Regional and national efforts to engage fully in supply chain security;
- Identify, assess and publicize benefits of supply chain security;
- Cooperative agreements;
- Reliance on information, intelligence and expertise available in business circles;
- Least possible interference with normal logistical processes.

3. On the issue of capacity building, there is a need for additional capacity building for all administrations (with particular attention to developing countries) to enable worldwide implementation of supply chain security. The modernization and reform of customs administrations should be based on proper diagnostic tools and not on "one size fits all" solutions. The Revised Kyoto Convention should be the point of reference.

CHAIRMAN'S CONCLUSIONS

Session 3: The role of the business community: mechanisms of cooperation

1. Trade Facilitation is alive and well – this is the good news. However, the business community is increasingly concerned about the lack of progress and coordination in the international organizations dealing with trade facilitation. Much preliminary groundwork has been done by business around the world on standards, certification, and risk management. Business will continue irrespective of any WTO agreements, but it strongly urges WTO members to address the Doha agenda with more flexibility and energy in the run-up to Cancún. The Fifth WTO Ministerial Meeting may well be the last chance to start formal negotiations on trade facilitation in the Doha Round. The Forum noted all very valuable efforts made in the field of trade facilitation. There was a widespread view that without a rules-based system with global applicability many the full potential of these initiatives will never be realized. We urge the Fifth WTO Ministerial Meeting in Cancún to enter into substantive negotiations on trade facilitation.

2. Business is strongly committed to trade facilitation, and should be encouraged to stimulate the implementation of governmental trade facilitation instruments and enhanced integrity within the business community. The ICC, the world's business voice, has launched a website www.BATF-Action.net to promote active support of trade facilitation in the run-up to Cancún. All participants at this UNECE event are encouraged to interact with this site. ICC members are active in the UNECE and WCO work on standards, security and trade facilitation and international supply chain improvements.

3. Widespread recognition that standards require genuine public/private partnerships involving business, governments and regulators. The postal services have a vital role to play as an enabler and trusted third party between business and regulators. Postal services offer opportunities to bridge the digital divide. Ongoing efforts of public/private partnership in Southeastern Europe demonstrate how trade facilitation can be applied in transition economies. Such

examples should stimulate interest elsewhere. Business is heavily involved in the UN/CEFACT processes and in work with UNCTAD.

4. The Forum welcomes the continuous effort of UNECE to develop tools for electronic trade documents, which comply with existing paper document procedures, in order to support national administrations and the trading community around the world. Working with Governments and other institutions, UNECE should ensure that these tools are made accessible to small and medium-sized enterprises (SMEs), transition economies and developing countries.

Session 4: Open regionalism

1. The pursuit of open regionalism finds its expression in the cooperation amongst the five UN regional commissions in developing and implementing global standards based on local input and experience. Trade facilitation at national and regional level through international standards and simplified, modern administrative and customs procedures is vital for reaping the economic benefits of trade liberalization achieved so far and for integrating developing countries into the world market and the multilateral trading system.

2. The participants in the Forum suggested a collaborative approach among relevant organizations for standards development, especially in the area of required standards for facilitating trade security.

3. The United Nations regional commissions place great importance on capacity building, public/private partnerships and the exchange and sharing of information and experience in their formulation and implementation of trade facilitation tools and projects at the regional, sub-regional and national levels. The Forum strongly supported the establishment of national trade facilitation bodies.

4. The participants in the Forum supported the objectives of the joint project of the five regional commissions agreed on at the first Trade Facilitation Forum, in 2002. Most developing and transition countries need extensive technical assistance to (a) enhance negotiating

capacity; (b) reduce transaction costs in both domestic and international trade; (c) strengthen competitiveness; (d) engage in trade promotion and diversification; (e) increase participation of SMEs in global supply networks; (f) design and implement trade facilitation policies at national and regional levels; and (g) increase the use of knowledge management and ICT in supply-chain management.

5. Support for the launching of negotiations on a multilateral framework on trade facilitation at Cancún during the Fifth WTO Ministerial Conference was not unanimous. While some countries felt overburdened by existing WTO obligations and hesitant to engage in new commitments in view of their development problems, others stressed the n eed for WTO rules on core standards and the elaboration of disciplines in the area of trade facilitation, albeit with graduated facilitation levels adapted to the implementation capacity of developing and least-developed countries, and the necessary capacity building and technical assistance to help their integration into the global trading system.

6. In sum, the UN regional commissions are instrumental in promoting trade facilitation. They provide essential guidance and support for developing and transitional economies to strengthen their transport networks, modernize ICTs and harmo nize and simplify border measures through the sharing and coordination of expertise gained locally and regionally, thereby allowing global standards to reflect diversity. In this context, an express wish was stated for more collaboration between the commissions and UN/CEFACT.

Workshop on intellectual property rights (IPRs) and trade facilitation

Participants in this workshop identified a certain number of issues that deserve to be addressed with IPR specialists, such as:

*   Advantages and burdens of IPR systems for developing countries;

- Improving the understanding of IPR experts of the functioning of the global market and the knowledge of the international community of the IPR system in a global world;
- Ensuring coordinated approach of capacity building and technical assistance on IPR issues.

Workshop on leading edge technical issues in trade facilitation

Participants stressed that it is necessary to:
- Provide advanced technologies to automatically track and assess shipping contents relative to manifest, and verify the integrity of the cargo;
- Develop and adopt a distributed, secure worldwide data exchange utility where public/private stakeholders are able to obtain highly secure information for any shipment;
- Deploy a standardized, dynamic open information systems architecture for integrating people, process and technology data into cargo management systems with supply chain security in mind;
- Make security a core part of the business process, so that it enhances operational efficiencies daily and provides efficient risk management when required.

CHAIRMAN'S CONCLUDING REMARKS

As Chairman of this second Forum on Trade Facilitation, I recognize three main areas where short-term progress should be possible on the road to full implementation of trade facilitation measures:

First, on the governmental level, all efforts should be made to ratify the WCO revised Kyoto Convention, and this with a sense of urgency.

Second, on the agenda setting for the 5th WTO ministerial meeting in Cancún (September 10-14, 2003), trade facilitation should have high priority and all efforts should be made to arrive at an explicit consensus that the WTO is enabled to play a constructive role in the substance, in capacity building and in technical assistance related to trade facilitation. Given the broader scope of trade facilitation than the one defined in the Doha Development Agenda, it is of paramount importance that the WTO and its members ensure coherence and avoid duplication of work in the area of trade facilitation.

Third, I note an extraordinary networking among trade facilitation specialists. Our two Forums have provided an opportunity to interlink policy and expert levels from governments, intergovernmental and private sectors. This should be further pursued. I suggest that reflections start after Cancún about the best way to pursue these efforts towards a better coherence among the numerous actors in trade facilitation.

I thank the 13 organizations that have contributed to this Forum. In order to ensure an adequate information exchange, I recommend to all of them to inform the UNECE secretariat about any follow-up action they decide on the basis of the work achieved in these two days in Geneva.

I thank the UNECE secretariat for the preparation and the services during the Forum. For any future event of that kind, as defined by the 13 coorganizers, it would be worthwhile to increase interactiveness between the panels and the participants. Almost all of them would be in a position to contribute with personal experiences giving additional practical relevance to our reflections.

I thank the interpreters for their essential assistance. I thank the chairpersons, the speakers and the rapporteurs, as well as all participants, for their highly appreciated contributions that brought us to this successful outcome.

****

Index

Sharing the Gains of Globalization in the New Security Environment: The Challenges to Trade Facilitation is the second volume coming out of the International Forums on Trade Facilitation, which have been organized by the UNECE in collaboration with other international organizations and the business community. This book is intended to make available to a wider audience papers of topical interest on how to share the benefits of trade facilitation in a fair way and on the link between facilitation and enhanced security in the international trade flows.

Comments and enquiries should be addressed to:

Mario Apostolov, Regional Adviser
Trade Development and Timber Division
United Nations Economic Commission for Europe
Palais des Nations
CH-1211 Geneva 10
e-mail: mario.apostolov@unece.org

To obtain copies of publications contact:

United Nations Publications
Sales and Marketing Section
Palais des Nations
CH-1211 Geneva 10
Switzerland
e-mail: unpubli@unog.ch

Printed at United Nations, Geneva
GE.04-30091–February 2004–4,610

ECE/TRADE/330

United Nations publication
Sales No. E.04.II.E.3

ISBN 92-1-116889-9